S0-BDL-799

Praise for previous editions of

Missouri
Off the Beaten Path®

"Missouri Off the Beaten Path can lead a reader to . . . the best place to watch eagles, go trout fishing, or find an honest-to-goodness 19th-century country school, one where the kids learned the 'three R's' and one of them wasn't 'reload.' "

—*Kansas City Star* (Mo.)

"Missouri Off the Beaten Path...suggests many interesting and sometimes unheard of destinations.... It can help plan some enjoyable weekends out in the fresh air."

—*Belleville Journal* (Ill.)

Help Us Keep This Guide Up to Date

Every effort has been made by the author and editors to make this guide as accurate and useful as possible. However, many things can change after a guide is published—establishments close, phone numbers change, facilities come under new management, etc.

We would love to hear from you concerning your experiences with this guide and how you feel it could be improved and kept up to date. While we may not be able to respond to all comments and suggestions, we'll take them to heart and we'll also make certain to share them with the author. Please send your comments and suggestions to the following address:

The Globe Pequot Press
Reader Response/Editorial Department
P.O. Box 480
Guilford, CT 06437

Or you may e-mail us at
editorial@globe-pequot.com

Thanks for your input, and happy travels!

OFF THE BEATEN PATH® SERIES

Missouri

SIXTH EDITION

by
Patti DeLano

Revised and updated by
Jeanie Ransom

The Globe Pequot Press

Guilford, Connecticut

Copyright © 1990, 1993, 1996, 1998, 2000 by Patti A. DeLano
Revised text copyright © 2002 The Globe Pequot Press

All rights reserved. No part of this book may be reproduced or transmitted in any form by any means, electronic or mechanical, including photocopying and recording, or by any information storage and retrieval system, except as may be expressly permitted by the 1976 Copyright Act or by the publisher. Requests for permission should be made in writing to The Globe Pequot Press, P.O. Box 480, Guilford, Connecticut 06437.

Off the Beaten Path is a registered trademark of The Globe Pequot Press.

Text design by Laura Augustine
Text illustrations by Cathy Johnson
Maps created by Equator Graphics © The Globe Pequot Press

ISBN 0-7627-2472-2
ISSN 1539-8129

Manufactured in the United States of America
Sixth Edition/First Printing

*To Tom Stapleton, who has made
traveling in the Heartland fun again,*

with love

—Patti

Acknowledgments

No book comes easily, but a sense of humor helps. It's especially true of a book of this sort, which requires so many hours of research and fine-tuning.

The Missouri Tourism Bureau and the Missouri departments of conservation and natural resources, not to mention all the visitors' bureaus and chambers of commerce I contacted in hundreds of little towns, made it easier. I want to offer special thanks to the hundreds of people around the state who sent me new information and helped make the sixth edition even more fun. Special thanks also to my friend Cathy Johnson for all her help and encouragement.

It's impossible to include all the wonderful, quirky places I discovered in the course of researching this book—it would weigh five pounds. Others I simply did not know about; still others have recently appeared or, sadly, have gone out of business. If you know of a special place, or a change in an existing listing, please write the publishers so that I can add this information when I next update the book. They would love to hear from you concerning your experiences with this guide and how you feel it could be improved and be kept up to date. Please send your comments and suggestions to the following address: The Globe Pequot Press, Reader Response/Editorial Department, P.O. Box 480, Guilford, CT 06437. Or e-mail them at: editorial@globe-pequot.com.

Contents

Missouri Information. x

Introduction xi

Southeast Missouri. 1

Southwest Missouri 57

Central Missouri. 101

Northwest Missouri 163

Northeast Missouri. 205

Indexes:

    General 245

    Bed-and-Breakfasts and Inns 253

About the Author and Editor. 255

Missouri Information

State flag: The field is made up of three horizontal bands—red, white, and blue—of equal width. The state coat of arms appears in the center. It is encircled by a band of blue bearing twenty-four white stars.

Capital: Jefferson City

Statehood: August 10, 1821, the twenty-fourth state

State bird: Bluebird

State tree: Flowering dogwood

State flower: Hawthorn

State insect: Honeybee

Origin of name: From Native American sounds meaning "owners of big canoes." First applied to the river, then to the land.

Nickname: The Show Me State

State song: "Missouri Waltz" by Jr. Shannon, music arranged by Frederick Logan from a melody by John Valentine Eppel.

State seal: A coat of arms appears on the seal. The shield in the center of the seal is divided into two parts. One half shows a bear and a crescent, representing Missouri. The other half shows the eagle of the United States. The two halves are bound together, or united, by a band ending in a belt buckle. The words in the band—"United we stand; divided we fall"—reflect the need for all the states to be united. Two bears support the shield and stand on a streamer on which the state motto is inscribed. A helmet appears above the shield; the twenty-four stars above the helmet indicate that Missouri was the twenty-fourth state. The date at the bottom in Roman numerals (1820) is the date of the Missouri Compromise.

Introduction

Think of Missouri and a hundred images tumble forward like candy from a piñata. The Pony Express. The Santa Fe Trail. Lewis and Clark. The Civil War. Frank and Jesse James. Mark Twain (who once said that he was born here because "Missouri was an unknown new state and needed attractions"; we certainly got one in Samuel Clemens).

But all of the images are not from the distant past, flickering like a silent movie through the veil of time. There's Branson, now threatening Nashville as the country music capital of the country, with countless entertainment palaces boasting big-name stars of everything from music to magic. There's even a rodeo restaurant! (I'll tell you how to beat the crowds and traffic and help you find a quiet B&B instead of a computer-located motel.) There's also the Plaza, the world's first shopping center. Kansas City steaks. Charlie Parker and jazz. General John J. Pershing. The Gateway Arch. Barbecue. Writers Calvin Trillin and Richard Rhodes. Actors Bradd Pitt, Kathleen Turner, Bob Cummings, John Goodman, and Don Johnson, as well as Walt Disney, all have ties to Missouri. And of course, our own Harry S Truman. Now you're on a roll.

What you may not think of immediately are the things I will show you in *Missouri: Off the Beaten Path*. Did you know that J.C. Penney got his start here? There's a museum to honor his modest beginnings in Hamilton. And Jacques Cousteau—when you think of the man, you imagine oceanic dives in faraway places, right? Not always. Cousteau filmed a "deep-earth dive" right here in Bonne Terre and explored his way up the Mississippi and Missouri Rivers as well. Then there's the Kingdom of Callaway, with its postwar ties to none other than Winston Churchill. There are wineries and breweries and distilleries, and there are elegant restaurants and comfort-food cafes that range from fine French to fire-breathing Cajun, with home-style cooking settled somewhere in between.

What we are not is flat farmland, empty prairie, or wall-to-wall cows (or cowboys and Indians, for that matter). There's a rich diversity of landscape here.

Missouri is covered with forests and rolling hills. It boasts more than 5,000 caves, and those are only the ones I know about. The rugged white bluffs along the rivers (the rocky remains of a prehistoric inland sea) and the volcanic formations and underground streams and caverns in the Lake of the Ozarks area are among the most beautiful in the country. The rivers that sculpted all this spectacular scenery are magnets for explo-ration; the Jacks Fork, Eleven Point, and Current Rivers are designated

National Scenic Riverways. Remnant prairies still beckon—patchwork bits and pieces left over from presettlement days, when the big bluestem and gayfeather were tall enough to hide a man on horseback, and the wind-driven waves imitated a sea of grass.

In 1673 Marquette and Joliet came down the Mississippi River and saw the land that is now called Missouri. The Mississippi River, which forms the eastern boundary of the state, is still one of the busiest shipping lanes in the world and has been flowing here since before the dawn of time. The upstart Missouri River, on the other hand, was the gift of a departing glacier a short half million years ago; it simply wasn't there before that time. The division between the glaciated plains to the north (rolling and covered with a generous layer of topsoil, also a legacy of the wall of ice, which stole the soil from points north) and the bony Ozark region to the south (rough and hilly with valleys cut deep into rock) is the river that bisects the state from Kansas City to St. Louis. Missouri is where old prairie runs up against the oldest mountain range in the country—a fitting symbol for one of the most historically divided states in the Union.

It was in Missouri that the Civil War was most brutal, issuing as it did from tension that had been building for decades. This pre–Civil War strife between free-state Kansas and the Southern-leaning Missouri was bloody, especially because many Missourians believed that slavery was wrong and worked with the Underground Railroad to help slaves to freedom.

After the Civil War Quantrill's Raiders and such legendary outlaws as Cole Younger and the James brothers continued the bloodshed. The state bears the reminders to this day. Civil War battlefields and tiny cemeteries, with their solemn testimony of the losses of the war, embody the lingering dichotomy between Northern and Southern sensibilities.

Before the Civil War and for some years afterward, the two rivers—the Missouri and the Mississippi—were main arteries of commerce. All of Missouri's large cities began as river ports, with a lively competition between them for business and settlers. Kansas City and its popular hot spot, Westport (formerly Westport Landing); St. Joseph, Lexington, Boonville, and Jefferson City, the capital; and Hermann, Washington, and St. Charles, the first capital, all began as ports on the Missouri. Hannibal, St. Louis, Ste. Genevieve, Cape Girardeau, and New Madrid were ports of call on the Mississippi.

Today the big rivers and their connecting waterway system make a 22,000-mile navigable network. Almost all year the tugs and barges can be seen wherever public and private docks allow commodities to be moved inexpensively by water. Only winter's ice jams stop the flow of traffic.

Kansas City, Missouri's second-largest city (now outgrowing St. Louis, much to the pride of the western part of the state), had its beginnings as a shipping point on the Kansas (called the Kaw) River bend of the Muddy Mo, where the river turns sharply east on its trek across the state's midriff. The region known by early explorers as the Big Blue Country was occupied by the Kanza (Kansas) Indians, whose name means "people of the south wind." The peaceful Kanza engaged in farming, fishing, and trapping; they were quickly displaced when settlers began to move in.

Missouri was once as far off the beaten path as one could get, the jumping-off point to the trackless West; beyond was the great unknown. You can still see the tracks of the wagon wheels etched deeply into our soil on the Santa Fe, California, and Oregon trails.

Now everything's up to date in Kansas City, as the lyrics to a song once told us. A beautifully modern metropolis, Kansas City has more fountains than any city except Rome and more miles of tree-lined boulevards than any other American city. The Nelson-Atkins Museum of Art owns one of the finest collections of Oriental art in the country.

St. Louis, on the other side of the state, has a world-class botanical garden and a rich cultural heritage that rivals any big city in the East. Not surprisingly, St. Louis is proud of its French legacy, a gift of the early explorers.

The KATY Trail (its name is derived from MKT, the Missouri-Kansas-Texas Railroad) begins nearby in Machens just north of St. Louis. This bicycle and hiking trail follows the old MKT railroad route to Sedalia, 90 miles east of Kansas City. It will soon cover 200 miles of river bluffs, forests, and farmlands with cafes and shops along its route to cater to trail buffs.

The word *Missouri* first appeared on maps made by French explorers in the 1600s. It was the name of a group of Indians living near the mouth of a large river. Pekketanoui, roughly its Indian name, means "river of the big canoes," and the Missouri would have required them—it was big, swift, and tricky to navigate before the locks and dams of the U.S. Army Corps of Engineers tamed it, or attempted to.

We don't know how the Native Americans pronounced *Missouri,* and it is about a fifty-fifty split between the state's current residents. In a recent survey a little more than half the population, most in western Missouri, pronounced the name "Missour-uh." The eastern half of the state favored "Missour-ee."

The "Show Me State" carries its nickname proudly. We have a reputation as stubborn individualists, as hardheaded as our own Missouri mules—or so they say—and we won't believe something until you show us. It's not such a bad way to be. Our people, like our agrarian ancestors, want concrete proof—we'll change, all right, but only when we're fully convinced that change is synonymous with progress and that progress is indeed an improvement. The past is definitely worth preserving when it is as colorful as ours.

So I will show you parts of the Show Me State that are tucked away off the beaten path. Some are in the middle of farmland, some are in national forests, and some are in our largest cities. There will be no "Worlds of Fun" or "Six Flags Over Mid-America" or Royals' Stadium plugs in this book; such places are definitely on the path, and you can find them on your own. What this book does have is something for everyone, as out of the way—and "far from the madding crowd"—as you could wish.

No matter where you're from, whether you love a fine Bordeaux or a fine bourbon, whether you like to go in a sports car dressed to the nines or in a pickup truck wearing an old pair of jeans, you will feel at home in Missouri.

The prices and rates listed in this guidebook were confirmed at press time. We recommend, however, that you call establishments before traveling to obtain current information.

Southeast Missouri

To call southeast Missouri the most beautiful part of the state wouldn't be fair; beauty is a mysterious commodity based on personal definition, as intangible as smoke. But it has plenty to offer. There is natural beauty—dappled shade of the national forests, cascades of clear blue springs and rivers, and white river bluffs and volcanic rock formations of the Johnson Shut-ins—that meets everyone's definition of beauty. Antebellum and Victorian homes on wide boulevards grace the oldest cities west of the Mississippi. Both beautiful and historic, southeast Missouri will appeal to all your senses with its food, wine, scenery, and rich and varied past.

When the river was the frontier to the American West, thousands crossed it in search of land, freedom, and a new life. Trappers, traders, explorers, and settlers joined Native Americans in the fertile river valleys and rich prairies.

Enter the state from the east, and you will encounter the St. Louis area, the big city/small town that spreads west on Interstate 70 and south on Interstate 55. Sneak off of these two freeways, and the many small highways branching off from them, to find some of the most charming towns in the state, towns that date back to the beginning of the westward expansion of the country.

Here you have a choice of crowded festivals and busy public campgrounds or the isolation and peace deep in the national forests and wildlife preserves. Missouri in winter is quietly beautiful and secluded; in summer, it is lively and fun. Adventures here range from scuba diving (yes! deep-earth diving in Missouri!) and whitewater canoeing to wine tasting and genealogical searches in the oldest records in the American West. Whether you want to party or to get away from it all, you can wander off the beaten path into southeast Missouri.

Graduate Education

The oldest university west of the Mississippi River is St. Louis University, which began as an academy in 1818.

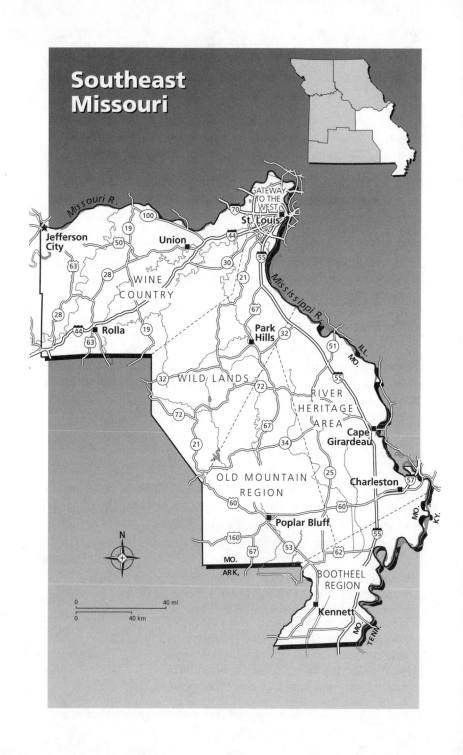

Gateway to the West

Author's Top Ten Favorites in Southeast Missouri

Washington

Bias Vineyards

rock eddy bluff farm

Kimmswick

Blue Owl Restaurant and Bakery

Bonne Terre Mines

Whistle Stop Cafe

Ste. Genevieve

Southern Hotel

Broussard's Cajun Restaurant

The bustling **St. Louis** area is still the best place to begin westward exploration. Located on a shelf of riverfront under a bluff, the original city spread to the prairies surrounding it. It was the starting point for the Meriwether Lewis and William Clark expedition in 1804. The history of western expansion begins here where the Missouri and the Mississippi Rivers meet.

St. Louis, founded in 1764, boasts the oldest park west of the Mississippi (Lafayette Park), the second-oldest symphony orchestra in the nation, the world's largest collection of mosaic art at the Cathedral of St. Louis, and one of the finest botanical gardens in the world. The graceful Italianate mansion, **Tower Grove House** at the Missouri Botanical Garden, blooms with color each Christmas season. Local garden clubs, the Herb Society of St. Louis, and others bathe the house in wreaths, seasonal flowers, and greens. Candlelight tours and teas and holiday luncheons are the special events. The home and seventy-nine-acre garden are open for tours every day from 9:45 A.M. to 4:00 P.M. (The house is closed in January.) Admission to the house is $2.00 for adults and 50 cents for children six to twelve, free for those under six. Write Missouri Botanical Garden, P.O. Box 299, St. Louis 63166-0299 (800–642–8842 or 314–577–5150) for more information.

Also in St. Louis are the futuristic Climatron, and the country's tallest manmade monument, the **Gateway Arch,** which is also the world's third most popular tourist attraction (but we're talking beaten path here, aren't we?).

It's also a city of firsts. The first Olympiad in the United States was held here in 1904; the first hot dog, ice-cream cone, and iced tea were all introduced at the 1904 World's Fair. Remember "Meet me in St. Louie, Louie, meet me at the fair?" For more information about the city, look for the St. Louis Web site at stlouis.missouri.org/.

The Gateway to the West (or to the East if you are traveling the other way) was fed by train travel beginning in the early 1800s. More than 100,000 passengers passed through the one-hundred-year-old **Union Station** each day. (Actually, it sounds more like a revolving door than a gateway.)

Elementary Education

The first public kindergarten in the country was opened in St. Louis in 1873.

This is a 2-block-long gray limestone fortress with a red-tiled roof that features a clock tower that looms 230 feet in the air. When the last train left the station in 1978, the city had a white elephant of gargantuan proportions on its hands. Union Station was too historic to tear down, too expensive to keep up. So, it received a new identity: It is a retail, restaurant, and entertainment complex whose one hundred shops, cinema, restaurants, and nightclubs are drawing tourists downtown again and sparking a revival of the area. There's even a virtual-reality mini-arcade, called Virtuality, where you can slip on a helmet and join the cyberworld of Zone Hunter.

The Grand Hall, once the waiting room, is now the lobby of the 546-room Hyatt Regency Hotel. Look up at the 65-foot barrel-vaulted ceilings and finely decorated walls. Arches and columns abound. The famous "whispering arch" allows you to whisper to a friend 40 feet away. Sculpted maidens holding gilded torches, floral flourishes, and scrollwork entice the eye. Most impressive is the glowing stained-glass window depicting three women representing New York, San Francisco—and the one in the middle—St. Louis, the crossroads of America.

Downstairs is the Midway and cavernous Train Shed. More than 130 shops, cafes, and restaurants surrounded by walkways, bridges, fountains, and flowers fill the space. On most weekends strolling mimes and jugglers entertain shoppers. Boats cruise on a man-made lake next to an open-air *biergarten.* And although the trains don't stop here anymore, you can grab the MetroLink public rail system right outside for a ride to the Gateway Arch or Busch Stadium. The station can be reached from the airport, so if you are stuck at Lambert Field, you can get on the train and spend a couple of hours enjoying a good meal or just doodling around at Union Station. Stop at the sculpture fountain across the street from the station. It's called "Meeting of the Waters" and it symbolizes the confluence of the Missouri and Mississippi Rivers.

First, though, get a map of St. Louis. Although its many interesting little neighborhoods make the city charming, it also makes it difficult for visitors.

The Gateway Arch may not be exactly off the beaten path—after all, it's one of the most-visited tourist destinations in the country—but did you know there's a wonderful museum tucked away underground beneath the Arch in the Jefferson National Expansion Memorial? It's the **Museum of Westward Expansion,** which documents our irrepressible urge to explore and settle lands ever farther westward. We didn't stop

Bowling, Anyone?

until we reached the Pacific Ocean; the museum makes you feel you were along for the trip. You'll see artifacts and displays that relate to the Lewis and Clark expedition, which was intended not only to find a trade route to the West but to discover the natural history of this new land encompassed by the Louisiana Purchase. You'll find Native American and pioneer artifacts as well, and when you come back out blinking into the sunshine, you'll experience a moment of disorientation as you reenter the twenty first century.

The museum has a $2.00 National Park fee, and it's more than worth the cost (tram fee to the top of the Arch is a bit higher). Also under the Arch are a fine bookstore and gift shop run by the National Park Service; be prepared to take a bit of history home with you.

Just south of the Arch the *Tom Sawyer* and *Becky Thatcher* riverboats provide one-hour cruises of St. Louis Harbor. Call **Gateway Riverboat Cruises** (800–878–7411) for times and prices. Gateway descends from Streckfus Steamers, which was established in 1884. Captain John Streckfus ran steamboats from New Orleans to St. Paul, Minnesota, and stopped in towns along the way. There was live music aboard and Streckfus would comb the clubs in New Orleans looking for good musicians. One day in 1918 he found a musician who was fresh out of reform school. His name was Louis Armstrong and he would work the riverboats *Sidney* and *Capital* until 1922. Legend has it, believe this or not, that the musicians called the new kind of music they played on the Streckfus riverboats "J.S." (for John Streckfus) and that eventually became the word "jazz."

The history of bowling goes back to the ancient Egyptians and Vikings and, according to the **International Bowling Museum and St. Louis Cardinals Hall of Fame** *(111 Stadium Plaza Drive, next to Busch Stadium, in St. Louis 63102) maybe even Fred Flintsone. The 5,000-year history of this game is only part of the fun. Your admission includes four free frames of bowling on old-time or modern lanes and two movies. Admission is $6.00 for adults, $4.00 for children six to twelve, and free for children under five. The museum is open daily from 9:00 A.M. to 5:00 P.M. and until 6:30 P.M. on Cardinals' home game nights. Stadium/museum combo tickets are $9.50 for adults, $7.50 for children. Stadium tours are offered from 9:00 A.M. to 2:00 P.M. daily. Call (314) 231–6340 or (800) 966–BOWL for information.*

While you history-minded folk are in the neighborhood of the Arch, don't miss the **Old Cathedral Museum,** visible just to the west and still in the Gateway Arch park. Here you'll find some of the finest (and oldest) ecclesiastical art in the country, with works by the Old Masters not uncommon. Documents dating back to the beginning of the cathedral as well as photographs on the building of the Arch are all part of the museum. If it's Sunday evening, you can attend Mass at the cathedral at 5:00 P.M.

The Old Cathedral Museum (314–231–3250) at 209 Walnut in St. Louis 63102, is open daily from 10:00 A.M. to 4:30 P.M.; there is a 25-cent admission charge.

Author's Favorite Annual Events in Southeast Missouri

July

St. Louis—Soulard Bastille Day Celebration, (314) 773–6767

Cape Girardeau—Balloons & Arts, a festival of hot air balloons, (573) 334–9233

August

St. Louis—Strassenfest, a German street festival, with bands and dancing. Downtown, (314) 849–6322

Sikeston—Annual Jaycee Bootheel Rodeo and Redneck Barbecue Cook-off, a world championship event with top Nashville recording artists performing nightly, (573) 471–2498

Ste. Genevieve—Jour De Fete, a large craft fair, (573) 883–7097

Vienna—Maries County Fair, with rides, music, demolition derby, and tractor pull. City Park, (573) 422–3061

September

St. Charles—Civil War Reenactment; authentic encampments, battle reenactments, cannons, horses, (636) 946–7776

St. James—Annual Grape and Fall Festival, (573) 265-3899

Sikeston—American Legion Cotton Carnival, (573) 471–9956

St. Charles—MOSAICS, an upscale yet affordable showcase of fine artisans from across the state,. (636) 946–7776.

Hermann—Wine Country Harvest Antique show, (573) 676–3014

October

St. Charles—Annual Missouri State Square and Round Dance; a weekend of line dancing, square dancing, round dancing, (636) 723–4493 or (636) 947–2497

Hermann—Oktoberfest; citywide. Every weekend in October, (573) 486–2744

Cape Girardeau—Octoberfest, second full weekend in October, with craftspeople in traditional dress, bluegrass music. Black Forest Village, (an 1870s replica village), (573) 335–0899

December

Kimmswick—Kimmswick Historical Society's Annual Christmas Tour of historic homes, each with a different theme, (636) 464–8687

St. Charles—Las Posadas, a lighted Christmas walk with Mary and Joseph, takes place on the first Saturday night in December, (636) 946–7776

If you visit the new **St. Louis Cathedral** on Lindell in the Central West End, look up to the heavens, or the ceiling in this case, and you will see the largest collection of mosaic art in the world.

Still in the downtown area (and the air of the past) is the **St. Louis Mercantile Library Association** at 510 Locust. If you admire the works of Missouri artist George Caleb Bingham, who captured our history on canvas; if you're awed by the accomplishments of George Catlin as he traveled among the tribes of Native Americans and painted them one by one; if you've wished you could see a painting by one of the famous Peale family of nineteenth-century artists (portrait painter Sarah Peale, in this case, who supported herself for many years here in the past century); you won't want to miss this place. Admission is free.

This is the oldest circulating library west of the Mississippi, and in addition to art, you can find rare books: Americana, westward expansion, river transportation, and so on.

The name doesn't tell you the reason for searching out this place, but once you know, you will be a regular at the **Crown Candy Kitchen** just 1¼ miles north of the Arch at 1401 St. Louis Avenue, St. Louis 63106, where wonderful chocolate candy has been made since 1913. The main attraction here, however, is the city's oldest soda fountain. Owners Andy, Tom, and Mike Karandzieff grew up here, and the place has been in the family since their grandfather opened it more than eighty-five years ago. Nothing much has changed in their world-class milk shakes: homemade ice cream, milk, and your choice of syrups. If you want a "malted," you can have that, too. Of course, what is a milk shake without a chili dog? Andy and Mike can fix that up for you, no problem. The malted has 1,100 calories in it, so what difference will a little chili dog make in the big scheme of things, right? Oh yes, they still make fresh chocolate candy in the winter. Summer hours are Monday through Saturday from 10:30 A.M. to 10:00 P.M. and on Sunday from noon to 10:00 P.M. In the winter they close at 9:00 P.M. Call (314) 621–9650 for more information.

As long as we are talking about ice cream it's only fair to tell you about another favorite. This is the old 1950s walk-up kind of place with a packed parking lot. See a lot of people in bright yellow T-shirts? Lucky you; you have found **Ted Drewes Frozen Custard** at 6726 Chippewa Street, St. Louis 63109. This place has been a St. Louis favorite since 1929 when Ted's father started the business. Drewes is known for the thickest shake anywhere (you can hold it upside down and the spoon and straw stay put), so thick ("how thick is it?") he calls it a "concrete," because it just won't shake. So thick the server wears a hard hat. These thick—very thick—shakes have mysterious names such as the "Cardinal Sin," named for the baseball team (fudge sauce and red cherries), or the "All Shook Up" (Elvis's favorite snack; peanut-butter cookies and banana). But the strawberry shortcake is the best thing on the menu. Hours are from 11:00 A.M. until a little after midnight seven days a week. For information call (314) 481–2652. There's a second location at 4224 South Grand, St. Louis 63111 (314–352–7376), if one wasn't enough. This time order the "Abaco Mocha," a tropical treat, or a "Foxtreat" with fudge sauce, raspberries, and macadamia nuts.

The *Admiral* was a rusty old riverboat that had been moored in the city since 1940. When riverboat gambling was legalized in Missouri a few years ago, the *Admiral* was born again. She underwent a $40 million renovation and became **The President Casino on the Admiral.** Her art deco splendor and 1,500 slots and gaming tables are something to behold. You can get off the beaten path (Leonore Sullivan Boulevard on the north lake of the Arch) and onto the river aboard this dockside casino for a $2.00 entry fee. There is a food court on the A deck for sandwiches and the St. Louie Restaurant, with lunch (brunch on Sunday) and a prime rib dinner buffet for only $12.95. Call (800) 772–3647 or check out the Web site at www. PresidentCasino. com for reservations.

St. Louis is the hometown of Chuck Berry, so you might be in the mood for some golden oldies. It seems only right that you should find your thrill on **Blueberry Hill.** This place will bring back a lot of memories if you are of a certain age. A real 45-rpm juke box with hundreds of rock 'n' roll and rhythm-and-blues titles dating from 1950 waits for your coins. All 2,000 selections are cross-indexed in a large notebook, and the dates are handwritten on the selection buttons to settle the arguments over who and when. Rock and Roll Beer, fabulous hamburgers, and the best rest room graffiti in the state add to the feeling. There's an Elvis room and lots of Howdy Doodys. Drinks are served from the 106-year-old mahogany bar from 11:00 to 1:30 A.M. six days a week (until midnight on Sunday). Oh, and look closely at the window display done by Linda Edwards. Sometimes the display pieces are alive. Owner Joe Edwards says he is a friend of Chuck Berry's, but the place is actually named after a Fats Domino song. Take the University City loop on the western edge of the city to 6504 Delmar Boulevard, St. Louis 63130. Be sure to see the St. Louis Walk of Fame, where stars and plaques honoring famous St. Louisians are embedded in the sidewalks of the University City Loop. Call (314) 727–0880 for more information.

If hotels and motels are not to your taste, call Lori and Dean Murray to join them in their home at 703 North Kirkwood Road, St. Louis 63122. *The Eastlake Inn Bed and Breakfast* is a 1920s colonial inn comfortably set on a wide green lawn surrounded by flowering catalpa, magnolia, and dogwood trees. As the name suggests, the home is filled with original Eastlake furnishings. After a full breakfast you can walk to antiques shops and restaurants for dinner. You'll feel like a St. Louis native. Rooms are $70 to $200. Call (314) 965–0066 for reservations; 703 North Kirkwood Road, St. Louis 63122-2719; www.eastlakeinn.com.

The Laumeier Sculpture Park is located about 12 miles southwest of downtown St. Louis. The artwork here is grand and huge. Artist Alexander Liberman's *The Way* is made of steel cylinders intended for use as underground storage tanks. He arranged them in bent piles and welded them together. The whole thing was painted bright red. In June and July sculptors work for weeks on detailed sand castles; in winter a

The Mother Road

*G*etting your kicks on Route 66 is still possible in Missouri. As the famous highway winds from Chicago to L.A. "you go from St. Louie and Joplin, Missouri . . ." along the Mother Road. In St. Louis, Drewes Frozen Custard has been a stopping place on old Route 66 since 1929. Farther on you can still see the distinctive Art Deco tile–front from the Coral Court Motel at the Museum of Transportation. Next is Route 66 State Park, where the state is creating a museum devoted to roadside Americana. You can walk among Missouri's wildflowers at the Shaw Arboretum of the Missouri Botanical Garden at Gray Summit and visit Meramec Caverns at Stanton as people have been doing since 1933. Spend the night at the circa 1930 Wagon Wheel Motel, which still stands in Cuba.

Perhaps the most beautiful spot on

Missouri's portion of Route 66 is Devil's Elbow along the bluffs over the Big Piney River. The 1940s Munger-Moss Motel is in Lebanon, where you can rest up for the drive through Springfield. Be sure to watch for the Shrine Mosque, an Arabian Nights–style edifice that has hosted concerts since the 1950s. On to Carthage's magnificent Victorian homes and the Route 66 Drive-In Theatre. The new highway created some havoc. Spencer is a ghost town now but some of the original roadway still remains from when the town was bypassed.

Joplin, the western end of Route 66 in Missouri, is one of the dozen towns named in the famous song immortalizing the more than a 1,000 mile route that winds from Chicago to Los Angeles through the heart of Missouri.

fire-and-ice sculpture made of giant ice blocks glows amid roaring bonfires. The ninety-six-acre park has more than sixty pieces. The wooded path hides human-size sheet metal figures by Ernest Trova. Special events—symphony, dance, ballet, and theater productions—and a gallery full of indoor art are there, too. A cafe and museum shop are inside, but outdoors is more fun. Take Interstate 44 to Lindbergh Boulevard, go south ½ mile, and turn right on Rott Road; the park entrance is ½ mile on the left. It is open daily from 8:00 A.M. until a half hour after sunset. Gallery hours are 10:00 A.M. to 5:00 P.M. Tuesday through Saturday; noon to 5:00 P.M. on Sunday. Admission is free. 12580 Rott Road, St. Louis 63127; (314) 821–1209; www.laumeir.com.

Webster Groves is home to an unlikely looking restaurant in an old gas station painted lavender. But venture into **Zinnia,** 7491 Big Bend Boulevard (314–962–0572), at lunchtime and have an eating experience that has created a word-of-mouth popularity for this place that fills it up daily. The food is pleasantly different with entrees such as tandoori-flavored chicken grilled and served with a rich Asian broth, vegetables and noodles, or a smoked trout filet. Desserts demand attention, too. The warm toffee pudding or crème anglaise and caramel sauce are great choices.

You should not go to St. Louis without visiting The Hill, southwest of the city, an Italian neighborhood famous for its restaurants. There is no favorite, because it depends on the type of ambience you seek. The best bargain is probably **Cunetto's House of Pasta** at 5453 Magnolia Avenue, St. Louis 63139. It's a good place to take the family, prices are moderate, and the atmosphere is Continental—tablecloths, wine, no bright lights, and a full-service bar. Owner Frank Cunetto calls it gourmet Italian with good prices. His dad and uncle opened the doors more than twenty-three years ago, and it has been a popular spot ever since. Hours for lunch are Monday through Friday from 11:00 A.M. to 2:00 P.M. Dinner is served Monday through Thursday from 5:00 to 10:30 P.M. and on Friday and Saturday until 11:30 P.M. Call (314) 781– 1135 or visit their Web site at www.cunetto.com for information.

But more interesting is **Charlie Gitto's** at 5226 Shaw Avenue, St. Louis 63139, because this is where one of the best-loved Italian dishes—toasted ravioli—was invented in 1947. It was a lucky accident that Charlie's father was the maitre d' at this very spot when it was called Angelo's. He and Angelo were messing around with different ravioli recipes and dropped the little stuffed pillows into oil instead of water. Now they are dusted with fresh Parmesan and served with marinara sauce for the perfect appetizer ($6.95). If you can't decide what to order, ask for the trio of the day, smaller portions of three menu items selected by the chef.

OTHER ATTRACTIONS WORTH SEEING IN SOUTHEAST MISSOURI

The Gateway Arch,
St. Louis

Magic House,
516 Kirkwood Road,
St. Louis

City Museum,
701 North 15th Street,
downtown St. Louis

Dessert must be tiramisu, Charlie's mama's family recipe made with cocoa, Marscapone cheese, and homemade cookies soaked in sambuca and espresso. Call (314) 772–8898 for reservations.

There are about twenty Italian eateries on The Hill, but if you want to take something home, run in to **Mama Toscano's** at 2201 Macklind, St. Louis 63139 and carry out homemade ravioli ($5.79 a pound), cannelloni, meatballs, and sauce to go. Nick and Virginia Toscano make thousands of ravioli by hand, rolling out the pasta with a rolling pin. This will be much more appreciated than a T-shirt when you get home. Call (314) 776–2926 for more information.

Be sure and take the time to visit **St. Ambrose Church,** the Hill's center-piece about 4 blocks from Cunetto's. It's Lombardy Romanesque and was the first acoustical plaster church in St. Louis. The columns of scagliola plaster look like marble. It is a lost art using plaster, ground gypsum, sponges, and polishing. The statues were donated by groups from different villages in Italy. Across the street is **Milo's Bocce Garden,** where locals gather. When you settle in with one of the restaurant's Italian sausage sandwiches or anchovy pizzas to watch the bocce leagues play, it sounds—and feels—as though you have crossed the Atlantic.

If you prefer to head south instead, you'll find St. Louis's own French Quarter in historic **Soulard,** 2 miles south of the Arch on Broadway. There's a dandy mix of period architecture and pubs, cafes, and shops for you to browse in. You can buy everything from turnips to live chickens on Saturday mornings in the busy farmers' market in this French/Irish neighborhood, and finish up at a well-stocked spice shop. Soulard is an old brewery neighborhood where rehabilitated row houses line the streets. The Anheuser-Busch brewery is nearby, and when the wind is right you can smell hops and barley cooking. Soulard also has a large collection of jazz and blues clubs.

For information on many bed-and-breakfasts in the state, you can call **Ozark Mountain Country Reservation Service,** P.O. Box 295 Branson 65615; (800) 695–1546, (417) 334–4720, or e-mail them at mgcameron@aol.com. (Kay Cameron is especially helpful if you are touring the Ozarks and headed for Branson.)

Antiques stores line both sides of Cherokee Street for 4 blocks in the funky antiques district south of downtown. Prices here are very affordable, and there are dusty treasures in dark corners and beautifully

Trivia

People streaking along Highway 40 near the Oakland Avenue exit are likely to hit the brakes when they see massive turtles sunning themselves on the banks of the road. These huge terrapins are not waiting to cross the road but are the creations of sculptor Robert Cassilly. If you look closely, the 40-foot-long snapping turtle, slick-shelled stinkpot, red-eared slider, Mississippi map, and soft-shelled turtle have children crawling inside their cave-like mouths, swinging from their necks, and grasping their eyeballs to climb up top their heads. A path leads to a sunken playground full of turtle eggs, some with freshly hatched crawlers emerging from the shells. Stop and visit the Turtles at Forest Park, Oakland Avenue, just off Highway 40 East anytime from sunrise to sunset.

restored pieces as well. You will find rare books, antique linens and lace, and glassware; and shop owners will still haggle on the price of more expensive items.

If you want to stay in the St. Louis area, but not in the city itself, there is a cluster of suburban cities nearby. Many of them have bed-and-breakfast inns available. Check out the charming cobble-stoned street of downtown St. Charles, once Missouri's state capital and now home to specialty shops and restaurants housed in historic buildings. There are seven B&Bs in St. Charles, located off Highway 70 west of St. Louis. Call (636) 946–7776 for more information.

Now Kansas City isn't the only Missouri city with a dollhouse museum. *The Miniature Museum of Greater St. Louis,* located at 4746 Gravois, St. Louis 63116, has a fine collection of dollhouses and miniatures, many of them painstakingly hand-crafted and donated by local miniaturists. The museum is a bit off the beaten path, but well worth the visit. Hours are Wednesday through Saturday 11:00 A.M. until 4:00 P.M., and Sunday 1:00 until 4:00 P.M. Admission is $5.00 for adults, $4.00 for seniors, students, and children ages thirteen through eighteen, $2.00 for kids two through twelve. Phone (314) 832–7790.

Okay, it's easy to make jokes about a dog museum, and everyone who writes for a living has given it a doggone good try. But man's best friend deserves to be celebrated, and this canine tribute, the *American Kennel Club Museum of the Dog,* located in the 1853 Greek Revival Jarville House in St. Louis County's Queeny Park, about 18 miles west of the St. Louis riverfront, is worth a visit if you are seeking the best art of dogdom. Begin with the oil-on-mahogany portrait of the ex-Presidential pet Millie, the English springer spaniel who called the White House home for four years. See a sculpted bronze whippet, a massive wooden mastiff (once part of a carousel ride), and many works of art commissioned by breeders of show-winning dogs. Coonhounds, retrievers, and herders join Dalmatians, bloodhounds, and Afghans. Pekingese, wolfhounds, and dogs of every variety, including those of more mixed heritage, are celebrated in paintings, woodcarvings, ceramic figurines, and photographs that show them doing what dogs do—sniffing, running, licking, sleeping, or just being. The gift shop will give you "paws" for thought with posters, stationery, and dozens of trinkets bearing likenesses of dogs and dog accessories (tie clasps made of tiny dog biscuits, for example).

On Sunday afternoons the popular "Dog of the Week" program features a guest breeder, trainer, or veterinarian and a dog for demonstration. A book-and-videotape library allows potential dog owners to judge the merits of various breeds. In the past well-mannered dogs were welcome to tour the gallery with their owners, but because of too many "accidents" that was stopped. The museum is at 1721 South Mason Road, St. Louis 63131 and is open from 9:00 A.M. until 5:00 P.M. Tuesday through Saturday and from noon to 5:00 P.M. on Sunday. Take Interstate 64/Highway 40 west past the Interstate 270 loop, exit on Mason Road and drive south. Watch for the signs. Admission is $3.00 for adults; $1.50 for ages sixty and up; and $1.00 for children ages five to fourteen. The program begins around 2:00 P.M. Call (314) 821–DOGS for more information.

To surf St. Louis go to www.explorestlouis.com.

The *Wild Canid Survival and Research Center* at Washington University's Tyson Research Center is a fifty-acre breeding area for red wolves and Mexican gray wolves. The goal is the eventual reintroduction of these beautiful doglike creatures, which are near extinction. The keepers here avoid touching them except for veterinary visits because it is essential to their survival to fear humans. But they do give them names: Anna and Rocky are two of fewer than one hundred Mexican grays left in the world. Sheila and Francisco are a breeding pair. They are big and strong and watch their puppies closely. Another pair, Alano and Frijole, prance with tails held high to show that this is, indeed, their territory. These canids are the species' last hope for survival. They are kept in fenced enclosures and can be seen from 9:00 A.M. to 5:00 P.M. daily. (Call in advance, because walk-ins are not permitted. Tours are by appointment only.) In May the center is closed for breeding. For more information: P.O. Box 760, Eureka 63025; (636) 938–5900; www.wolfsanctuary.org.

Florissant, just north of downtown St. Louis, is so called because the first inhabitants found it a beautiful, flowering valley. It still is—but that's not all the town has to offer. Jesuit father Pierre Jean DeSmet, champion of the Indian nations, founded the *Old St. Ferdinand's Shrine.* It's now open to the public at 1 Rue St. Francois, Florissant 63031; 314-837-2110. The picturesque St. Stanislaus Jesuit Museum, once a self-sufficient monastery, complements the shrine; it also boasts a surprising collection of rare Greek and Latin tomes dating from 1521. The address is 700 Howdershell Road, just north of Interstate 270. The shrine is open from 1:00 to 4:00 P.M. on Sunday from mid-March to early December, except for Easter and Mother's Day. Call (314) 837–3525 for more information.

If you just want to get out of St. Louis for a bit, here's a day trip an hour southwest of the city that you might enjoy. Take I–44 and get off on Highway 50 near *Union.* Stop for your morning sweet roll and coffee at *Schulte's Bakery, Deli and Coffee Shoppe* at 410 Highway 50, Union 63084; (314) 583–2277. The Schultes have been baking here since 1932. A mile or so up the road is the *Union Italian Market,* 317 Highway 50, Union 63084 (636–583–3252), brimming with such goodies as homemade pastas, imported groceries, and bulk spices. Owner Mary Kellerman will enjoy meeting you. Next is *Rosebud* and a batch of antiques shops on either side of the highway. *Log Cabin Pottery* at 2456 Bluehouse Road off Highway T in Rosebud 63091; (573) 764– 2049 isn't easy to find, so call Vivian Detert, tell her you're coming, and get good directions. She will welcome you and show you her three decades of work with clay. Then get on Highway 28 and aim for *Owensville,* where you can settle in with your maps and have some tea, coffee, and nibbles courtesy of Bob and Marsha Adams at *Peter Street Leaf and Bean,* 104 East Peters Avenue, Owensville 65066. If you decide to spend the night, call Nancy and David Caverly at *Caverly Farm Orchard Bed and Breakfast* at 100 Cedar Ridge Road near Bland 64062 (573–646–3732, e-mail: caverlydn@socket.net). Large and simple rooms are $50 to $75 in this countryside hideaway.

Wine Country

Towns cluster along the riverbanks like hardy grapes on vines. The towns of Defiance, Augusta, Washington, Dutzow, Marthasville, New Haven, Berger, and Hermann all have wineries and produce a variety of wines, both dry and sweet. The Seyval makes a crisp medium-bodied wine similar to a Chenin Blanc. The Vidal, a full-bodied wine with fruity characteristics, is somewhat like an Italian dry white wine. The Vignole is more versatile and can range from the style of a German Riesling to a sweet, late-harvest dessert wine. The Norton (Cynthiana) grape produces rich, full-bodied red wines, the Chambourcin a medium-bodied red with a fruity aroma. The Concord and Catawba produce sweet wines.

Outside St. Louis on Interstate 44 west is the town of *Eureka,* home to more than sixty antiques and craft shops. Pick up a complete list of shops at the first one you spot as you come off the interstate. This town could be a one-stop, shop-till-you-drop experience, but that would be crazy, because you are now heading into an antiques-hunter's heaven.

First, you will find two places named for their former lives. The *Ice House Antiques* at 19 Dreyer in Eureka 63025 (636–938–6355) is as interesting as the furniture, tools, and collectibles inside. So, too, is the *Firehouse Gallery and Antiques* at 131 South Central Avenue, Eureka 63025; (636) 938–3303. It is filled with fire-fighting memorabilia as well as crafts by local talents. Next is the *Eureka Antique Mall* at 107 East Fifth Street, North Outer Road, West Eureka 63025 (636–938–5600) followed by *Wallach House Antiques* at 510 North West Avenue in Eureka 63025 (636–938–6633) filled with old and new finds.

If all the bargain hunting makes you hungry, take a break at Hanephin's Restaurant. But ask before you sit in just any chair—the locals have their favorites! Be sure to try the homemade pie. Open Monday through Saturday from 6:00 A.M. to 2:00 P.M. Hanephin's is on 122 South Central Avenue, Eureka 63025. Call (636) 587–2321.

Between Eureka and the town of Pacific is a place to slow down, be quiet, and meditate. The *Black Madonna of Czestochowa Shrine and Grottos,* operated by the Franciscan Missionary Brothers, is located there. Whether your interest is historical or spiritual, don't miss this one. Take a tour or just have lunch in the large picnic pavilion. Call (636) 938–5361 for information.

Midwesterners seem to have a deeply rooted preference for all things smoked, probably from all those nights our ancestors spent around a campfire. Who can resist a terrific country ham, hickory-smoked bacon, or a tender slab of ribs? You won't have to if you pay a visit to the *Smoke House Market* at 16806 Chesterfield Airport Road in Chesterfield 63005; (636) 532–3314. Everything is smoked the natural way, with no preservatives and real hickory smoke. Smoked pork chops, lamb chops, Cajun sausage, along with the ribs and bacon, are available in the shop. Owners Thom and Jane Sehnert planned it that way, and Jane's got the background for it; her folks had owned the business since 1952. Hours are Tuesday through Sunday 9:00 A.M. to 8:00 P.M.

The Sehnerts branched out and opened *Annie Gunn's* next door, a grill with an Irish theme, complete with Irish potato soup and a menu of unusual sandwiches and meat from the smokehouse. The most popular is the Boursin burger, which is covered with highly spiced garlic and herb cheese. And there is the Braunschweiger sandwich, the Cajun sausage sandwich, fabulous smoked lamb chops, ribs, Reubens, French dips . . . and the list goes on.

To find the smokehouse, follow your nose, or if your sniffer isn't highly trained, follow Highway 40 to the Airport Road exit and double back; it's about 30 miles west of St. Louis. Put your name on the restaurant waiting list before you shop at the smokehouse. Annie Gunn's is a popular place for locals and visitors alike.

Highway 100 along the Missouri River is a beautiful drive any time of year, because of the white sycamores marking the river's course; in autumn it's spectacular. The Missouri River Valley deserves plenty of time; there's a lot to see and experience.

St. Albans is an anachronism, a tiny, planned community founded in the 1930s by the Johnson Shoe Company family. Five thousand acres of gorgeous rolling hills and meadows reminded Mr. Johnson of an area in England known as St. Albans, and he made it into a working farm. It is some 30 miles west of the city limits of St. Louis on Highway 100, an easy day trip and a destination not to be missed.

Aficionados of French cuisine may remember Le Bistro in the town of Chesterfield. Restaurateurs Gilbert and Simone Andujar closed that place when highway work made it difficult to reach, but take heart. Simone spotted the lovely gardens of St. Albans and chose the location for **Malmaison,** St. Albans 63073 (636–458–0131). (Those whose French is a bit tenuous may wonder if the name means "bad house," and it would if it were two words. Native Frenchwoman Simone says that the lovely flowers reminded her of the garden where Josephine met Napoleon in her homeland, a garden named Malmaison.) The dining experience here is superb, as is the food; it's a favorite retreat for St. Louisians. Hours are Wednesday through Saturday, 5:00 to 9:30 P.M. (10:00 P.M. on Saturday), Sunday 4:00 to 9:30 P.M.

Hard-core bicyclists love the St. Albans region. It is full of challenging hills near the Missouri River and great views.

The **Staats Waterford Estate Bed and Breakfast** at 4550 Boles Road, Labadie 63055, was built in 1850 by Civil War surgeons. Hosts Lucille and Charles Staats greet guests with a welcome tray when they arrive and wake them up with fresh coffee at the door and a full breakfast. The rooms have a private entrance and a New Orleans–style courtyard. Rates are from $85. Call (636) 451–5560 for more information.

This is Missouri's Rhineland, the wine-growing region. Both oenophiles

Attractions in Washington and Hermann

(wine connoisseurs) and devotees of wine coolers will enjoy tasting what the state has to offer. There are two schools of thought about Missouri wines: Some say that because a majority of the grapes grown here are European vines on wild grape or Concord root stock (and some self-rooted French hybrids), the wines will be different from California or French wines. Others, purists to be sure (and the Mt. Pleasant Winery falls into this category), say that they will hold Missouri's best wines against California wines in a blind tasting any day and challenge connoisseurs to single them out. They have done so for *Les Amis du Vin,* or Friends of Wine, a wine tasting club. Whether you are a member of *Les Amis du Vin* or just a wine lover, you will notice that the wines of Missouri are as varied as the vintners who make them, so don't judge Missouri wines by the first place you stop.

The Frene Creek white wines rival those of the Rhine River Valley. Pop wine drinkers will love Missouri's blends of fruit wines. The peach wine made by Stone Hill and the cherry wine by Hermannhoff are a treat over ice in the hot summer months.

Washington Landing was first settled in the early 1800s. Lewis and Clark passed through the site of the future town of **Washington** in search of the Northwest Passage, and pronounced it promising because of its excellent boat-landing site. Located in the curve where the great river reaches the most southern point in its course, Washington is still a good place to stop when headed west. Visit the Web site at www.washmo.org or call (888) 7–WASHMO for information.

Don't miss the **Gary R. Lucy Gallery** at Main and Elm Streets, Washington 63090. You may recognize Gary's work if you've picked up a Southwestern Bell telephone book from recent years; his work has graced the cover.

Gary is an extremely thorough young man. To get just the right feeling in his series of Missouri River paintings, the artist took his boat as far upriver as was navigable, to Ft. Benton, Montana, and explored interesting areas from there back to Washington. No wonder his paintings ring true. Gary's paintings are like those of other famous Missouri artists such as George Caleb Bingham and Thomas Hart Benton. He paints river scenes seen only in his mind's eye. Gary mixes research and what he sees from the window of his studio to obtain historical realism. River scenes are shown with side-wheelers and keelboats, ironclads running Confederate guns, or a card game on a flatboat. The price of an original is approximately $34,000, and his early works have quadrupled in price. Prints of his oils are for sale in his studio. Call (636) 239–6337 for information.

Linen & Lace, at 106 Elm Street, Washington 63090, is a shop full of lovely European-style lace curtains, bedcovers, and tablecloths, occupying a Federal-style building beside the river. Owner Sunny Drewell's business has done so well that she closed the Zechariah Foss Bed and Breakfast upstairs and moved Linen & Lace into the entire building. The mail-order catalog is a charmer, photographed right here in the house. If you can't make it to Washington (much less to Europe) in person, call (800) 332–LACE to get the Linen & Lace catalog or call (636) 239–5634, or visit the Web site at www.linen.lace.com. Hours are Monday through Friday 8:30 A.M. to 5:00 P.M.

Right across the street you can spend a night steeped in history. The 1837 *Washington House Inn* at 100 West Front Street, Washington 63090, first served as an inn. It has since put in its time as a general store, riverboat captain's house, fish market, speakeasy, restaurant, and apartment house. Now it has come full circle, offering nineteenth-century lodging combined with contemporary comforts. Both rooms feature views of the Missouri River, queen-size canopy beds, private baths, and a fine breakfast. Stenciled walls and period furniture, mostly from the Missouri Valley area, add to the ambience. Take time to unwind and watch the river traffic and trains from the balcony or terrace. (If you find the sound of night trains romantic, the tracks are just across the street.) Hosts are Susan and Terry Black. For reservations call Susan's pager at (888) 229–8341. Smoking is prohibited due to the historic nature of the building and its furnishings. Downstairs, Susan runs *Attic Treasures,* featuring everything from old to new. Antiques are blended with new gift items; flower arrangements are available. The shop carries a line of candles, too. Hours are Tuesday through Sunday from noon to 5:00 P.M. (and catch as catch can on Mondays). Call (636) 390–0200. Carolyn McGettigan offers a wonderful selection of coffees, herbs, teas, and dried bouquets at *Not Just Cut and Dried,* which has moved to 227 Elm, Washington 63090. Sit down and have a steaming cup of cinnamon coffee with Carolyn, and she will make scouting Washington easier. Go ahead and have a tasty dessert, too. Hours are 10:00 A.M. to 5:30 P.M. weekdays, 10:00 A.M. to 5:00 P.M. Saturday, and noon to 4:00 P.M. Sundays; (636) 239–9084.

Char's on the Riverfront, 116 West Front Street, Washington 63090, offers certified Angus beef, fresh fish, seafood, chicken, veal, and Italian specialties. Seasoned outdoor patio dining affords a nice view of the Missouri river, as does the big bay window inside the restaurant. Char's has an extensive wine list featuring Missouri wines as well as the usual California choices. There is a full bar. This is the place for fine dining in a casual atmosphere. Call (636) 239–2111 for information. Hours are Tuesday through Thursday 4:00 to 9:00 P.M., Friday 11:00 A.M. to 2:00 P.M. and 4:00 to 10:00 P.M., and Saturday 4:00 to 10:00 P.M. The restaurant is also open on Sunday for brunch 11:00 A.M. to 2:00 P.M. and then for dinner 4:00 to 8:00 P.M.

Elijah McLean's Restaurant, Washington 63090, is in a beautiful white mansion built in 1839 overlooking the mighty river. This is a romantic spot for dinner and is worth seeing for the structure alone, but the food is so good you might as well enjoy the view while eating one of the German specialities that chef Taylor Stecker prepares. He and his wife, Kiki, want to share the beauty and history of the house with you. The mansion was altered to become a restaurant in the early 1960s. The grand dining room was extended, and the floor above the parlor was removed to allow construction of the 24-foot-high barrel-vaulted ceiling. The chandeliers, cast in bronze and adorned with imported crystal, are from a museum in England.

Elijah McLean's is open for lunch Monday through Friday from 11:00 A.M. to 2:00 P.M. Monday through Thursday dinner is served from 5:00 to 8:00 P.M. and until 9:00 P.M. on Friday and Saturday. The restaurant is open on Sundays from 11:00 A.M. to 8:00 P.M. The menu is diverse, but the specialities of the house are German dishes such as Chicken Knisten and Jaegerschnitzel. Prices are moderate, ranging from about $8.00 to $17.00 for dinner. There is a full bar and a wine list. Call (636) 239–9463.

Only fifty years or so after Meriwether Lewis, his dog Scannon, and his partner William Clark passed by this likely town site, Bernard Weise built his home and tobacco store here on Front Street.

Now that location holds the ***American Bounty Restaurant,*** and although the magnificent view is still one of soft moonlight reflecting on the river flowing outside, inside white tablecloths await lovers of fine food and wine. Owner Dan Hacker and chef Brian Manhardt have restored this 104-year-old building at 430 West Front Street, Washington 63090, to its original splendor. The food is what they call "New Age American," or American food with a flair. Examples include encrusted chicken rolled in hash-browned potatoes, nine-way pasta, and red baby-clam sauce. The green-apple cobbler is a specialty, but it takes a half hour to prepare so order it with dinner to ensure it arrives hot when you are ready for it. Lunch is served from 11:00 A.M. to 2:00 P.M. on Friday and Saturday and 11:00 A.M. to 3:00 P.M. on Sunday, and you can eat on the patio when the weather is nice. Dinner is served from 5:00 to 9:00 P.M. Wednesday through Sunday. Seating outside in the wine garden creates a romantic mood, and the wine list features both California and Missouri wines. Call (636) 390–2150 for reservations.

The *Schwegmann House* is a bed-and-breakfast inn at 438 West Front Street, Washington 63090. The original Schwegmann was a native of Hanover, Germany, and became a successful miller on the riverfront. The stately residence he built nearby now belongs to Cathy and Bill Nagel. They offer hospitality in nine elegant, air-conditioned bedrooms with private baths, telephones, antiques, and handmade quilts. Guest rooms have queen-size beds or two double beds. The double parlors invite guests to relax, and refreshments are served there each evening by the fireside. A generous breakfast is served at your leisure. Rooms are $95 Sunday through Thursday. The suite is $140. Friday and Saturday the suite is $150 and regular rooms are $110, and it has an entrance from the private sitting porch. A chilled bottle of Missouri wine awaits you when you come in. Breakfast is served on the porch in good weather, or delivered to your room. Call (800) 949–ABNA or (636) 239–5025.

The town of *New Haven* sits quietly on the river, and there are a number of places worth looking for downtown. One of them is Carol Hebbler's shop at 125 Front Street, New Haven 63068, called *Collections Old and New.* It is a shop filled with silk flowers, antiques, crafts, gifts, and collectibles of all sorts. Hours are from 10:00 A.M. until 5:00 P.M. Wednesday through Saturday. Call (573) 237–3534.

You are deep into wine country here, and there is no shortage of wineries along the valley. Most offer tastings; you can choose the ones most convenient for your schedule and location. Some offer unusual wines and are well worth the effort to search out.

Bias Vineyards & Winery, 3166 Highway B, is in picture-postcard *Berger* (pronounced BER-jer, population 214) just off Highway 100. The setting sun at Berger reflects on the river and rugged limestone bluffs; it throws long shadows across the tilled bottomland along the river. Follow the signs to a wooded hillside. As you start up the hill, there is a railroad crossing at the foot of the rise to the vineyards. (It could be dangerous when you leave; a mirror hangs in a tree to give drivers a view of the tracks, so proceed slowly.)

Owner Jim Bias is a TWA captain based in St. Louis. He and his late wife, Norma, bought the land more than fifteen years ago when they were looking for a country spot within commuting distance to St. Louis's Lambert Field. It came with seven acres of vines. They invested in a roomful of stainless-steel tanks and went into the wine business. One thing led to another, and soon a banquet business followed.

Saturday night buffet dinners are scheduled on the vineyard grounds from March to December; reservations are a must. Gourmet meals are served along with Bias's wines. Winter is less hectic and cross-country skiing is allowed on the property when the snow comes. Bias offers vine cuttings during the January pruning season for creating wreaths or smoking meats. Call (573) 834–5475 or (800) 905–2427 for more information. Winery hours are 10:00 A.M. to 5:00 P.M., Monday through Saturday, and from 11:00 A.M. until 5:00 P.M. on Sunday.

Bias now has a microbrewery at the vineyard. *Gruhlkes,* the brewery, makes many types of beer—wheat beer, porter, stout, amber, and pale ale. It is one of the only wineries to have a microbrewery. Visit the Web site at www.bias.com for more information about Bias.

Next on the road is *Hermann.* To orient yourself, begin at the *Hermann Visitors' Information Center* at 306 Market Street, Hermann 65041. Jack Haney, the guy with the moustache and Bavarian hat, also runs Whiskey Jack's Museum of Prohibition-era memorabilia. He will tell you all about Hermann. Founded in 1836 by members of the German Settlement Society of Philadelphia, it was intended as a self-supporting refuge for German heritage and traditions, a sort of "second fatherland."

George Bayer, who had immigrated in 1830, selected a site in Missouri that resembled his home in the Rhine Valley in terms of climate, soil, and richness of wild grapevines. Bayer and the other German immigrants dreamed of building one of the largest cities in the United States in the Frene Creek Valley.

The dream quickly attracted a variety of professionals, artisans, and laborers who began the task of building the city of their dreams. It never did become that giant metropolis of the immigrants' dreams; now it is a city of festivals. There is Maifest, Wurstfest, and Octoberfest, each drawing thousands of folks from all over. Amtrak helps to alleviate traffic on festival weekends.

In winter and on non-festival weekends, Hermann is just what it looks like—a quaint German town, quiet, and filled with B&Bs, from the huge White House Hotel to the tiny Seven Sisters Bed and Breakfast Cottage. You'll find galleries, shops, and brick homes snugged right up to the street, European-style. During the festivals, though, it becomes crowded and noisy, as busy as Bayer's dream city. Portable toilets appear on street corners, and the revelry spills from wineries downtown. If you want to be off the beaten path around here, you should aim at a weekday in the off-season. Then a traveler has this sleepy hamlet all to himself. Visit the Web site at www.hermannmo.com.

The **Stone Hill Winery** on Stone Hill Highway just off Twelfth Street, Hermann 65041 (800–909–WINE), is owned by Jim and Betty Held. The world-renowned cellars are carved into the hillside and are reputed to be the country's largest underground vaulted cellars, and there's a breathtaking view of the town. **Vintage 1847 Restaurant** shares the picturesque hilltop location; a huge window at one end of the restored carriage house looks out on Missouri's blue hills. Visit the restaurant's wine cellar to choose the evening's libation, and do scrutinize the menu carefully—there's a cheesecake to die for. (Take home the *Vintage 1847 Cookbook;* it's a great gift idea.) Visit the winery's Web site at www.wine-mo.com/stonehill.html.

Once in town be sure to see the **Hermannhoff Winery Festhalle,** 330 East First Street, Hermann 65041, the world's largest wine hall, where you can dance to live German bands every Saturday and Sunday, starting at noon. There is no entrance fee. Enjoy a festival German dinner or a *brat mit krauts* on a bun. Contact the winery at (573) 486–5959.

There are so many great little antiques and craft shops that it would be impossible to list them all and, of course, there are many B&Bs in Hermann. Among them is **Birk's Gasthaus,** Rick and Dianne Pankau's place at 700 Goethe Street (573–486–2911). This Victorian mansion was built by the owner of the third-largest winery in the world and is furnished in period antiques, including some 6-foot-long tubs with gold eagle-claw feet, brass beds, and 10-foot-tall doors with transoms. Rooms are $97 for a king, $87 for a queen, and $65 for a room with a shared bath, tax included. On weekends, rooms are $75 weekdays. Visit the Web site at www.gasthaus.com. Another B&B, **Montagues,** located in the heart of Hermann's hispanic district, 301 Schiler Street, Hermann 65041, also has a coffee shop for latte lovers; (866) 237–2043 or (573) 486–2035.

Goody's General Store, 201 Schiller Street, Hermann 65041 (573–486–5507) is a real find for baby boomers or for those looking for fun, inexpensive items to bring home to the kids or grandkids. Proprietor Michael Romick has a knack for nostalgia, stocking toys and treats favored by children growing up in the 1950s and 1960s. If Michael doesn't have it, he'll try to find it, or suggest an alternative. Visit Goody's and other Hermann establishments on the Internet at www.hermannmo.com.

River's Edge Restaurant is right there, too, at 1720 Ferry Road, Fredericksburg 65061. Steve and Linda Simon serve Cajun food at the riverbank location Wednesday through Sunday. Open at noon each day, the restaurant closes at 8:30 P.M. Monday through Thursday, 10:00 P.M. on Friday and Saturday, and 8:00 P.M. on Sunday. Call (573) 294–7207 for more information. (Note: You can take the road or the ferry—off Highway J—to get to River's Edge. Ask Steve or Linda for directions.)

Take Highway 50 to Loose Creek. Turn on Highway A and go north 6 miles to *Bonnotts Mill.* This tiny town is so picturesque that the Jefferson City Active Sketch Club has come here to work many times. The views of the autumn foliage and the silvery river are glorious. On Iris Avenue, nestled in a valley between two bluffs, the *Dauphine Hotel,* Iris Avenue, Bonnotts Mill 65016, has found a new life. The hotel has been part of Bonnots Mill since 1875, but until Sandra and Scott Holder left Washington D.C., to visit cousins here, it was just another old, two-story hotel with a for sale sign hanging on it. Now it's a bed-and-breakfast inn with six guest rooms. In the old days the hotel had one (yes, one) bathroom for all of its guests. "We had to add a lot of bathrooms," Sandra says, "and central heat and air conditioning. But we are where we want to be, doing what we want to do now." A big breakfast is served in the eat-in kitchen or the dining room from 7:30 until 9:30 A.M. every day. The rooms have the original bead-board ceilings and wood floors and are filled with charming antiques—many of them dating back with the hotel—and handmade quilts. After breakfast guests can lounge on the double-decker front porch or stroll down the 2 blocks of Main Street and wander up Church Hill Street (which was not named after anyone but does go up to the only church in town.) The whole town, which was originally named Dauphine, is on the National Register of Historic Places. In 1993 most of Bonnotts Mill was under 4 feet of water, when a flood swept through the town, which is situated where the Osage and Missouri Rivers come together. Rooms are $60 with a private bath, or $50 with a shared bath. Call (573) 897–4144 or visit www.dauphinehotel.com.

The small village of *Westphalia,* south on Highway 63, perches like a lighthouse on the hill. There is only one street, with homes built right up to the sidewalk as they are in Hermann. Everything is spic-and-span and a pleasure to the eye—*das ist gut.*

Huber's Ferry Bed & Breakfast, 4 miles north of Westphalia on Highway 63, at County Road 501 in Westphalia 65085, has a magnificent view of two rivers. It sits high on a bluff overlooking both the Osage River and the Maries River. David and Barbara Plummer are the hosts in this 1881 Missouri German-style three-story, red-brick home. The house is near the intersection of Highways 50 and 63, is surrounded by four acres, and boasts the original barn, built in 1894, the oldest in the county. There are four rooms, each with a private bath. Barbara's breakfasts begin with the aroma of homemade bread baking, then there is fresh fruit, eggs, the whole nine yards. Rooms are $70 to $90. Call (573) 455–2979 for reservations and directions.

Barbara recommends the *Westphalia Inn* (573–455–9991) at 106 East Main, Westphalia 65085. The inn offers family-style meals—mashed potatoes and gravy, green beans, and an unbeatable fried chicken dinner. It is nothing fancy, just good old "comfort food" at reasonable rates. Tom and Melody Buersmeyer feed folks from 5:00 to 8:00 P.M. Friday and Saturday and Sunday from noon until 8:00 P.M. The inn is closed in January and February.

On the east side of Highway 63 at *Vienna,* the *Americana Antique, Art and Curio Shop* is a house and garage and several outbuildings (including a huge barn), all filled to the ceiling with what owner John Viessman calls "stuff." Everything you can imagine, from old army uniforms to a disassembled log cabin he is rebuilding—to hold some more stuff. Stuff like time-card racks out of an old factory, pictures, ancient trunks, and dolls. Not just little stuff, but big stuff, like a walnut wardrobe that measures 6 feet wide and 9 feet tall. But his real passion is books, especially books about Missouri history, and there are over 30,000 books in the house, two deep in floor-to-ceiling shelves running through what was once the living room. Volumes on the Civil War, Jewish folklore, and the black experience in America are crammed together in some kind of order ("it's a constant struggle," he says) along with old Dick and Jane books and *McGuffey Readers* and an 1824 textbook. Books are everywhere among the other stuff, too. There is a whole wall of *Life* magazines set up by year so that people can find their birthday issue. John still goes to auctions and sales and carts more stuff home, and he has been doing this for more than twenty years. He and his wife Kelley McCall have a studio there, too—Kelley is a photographer, and John paints. John seems to know everyone for miles around Vienna. John is around most weekends, when he isn't at a sale, and the shop is

Just a Pickin' and a Grinnin'

I fell in love with a man who plays a 1932 gold-plated five-string Gibson Mastertone banjo. I took some acoustic guitar lessons at one point in my life, but . . . bluegrass music? I knew nothing about it. I was more into classical guitar and '60s folk music. That is, until he took me to a bluegrass festival near Dixon.

The festival usually begins on a Thursday, but people start showing up a week and a half before that. Usually as soon as there are three people at the site, the music begins. People show up in campers, RVs, and pickup trucks. Tents go up, instruments come out, and the music is nonstop until the last three people leave on Sunday or Monday night.

The actual festival consists of about ten well-known musicians and groups that perform on a stage throughout the day and evening, but most of the really good music can be heard at the campsites in the woods—and goes on twenty-four hours a day. Don't plan to sleep much.

Although you do not have to play to enjoy the music, about 70 percent of the people do play. That's what makes it so much fun. All instruments are acoustic. People play banjos, steel guitars, and mandolins. People more oriented toward folk music play dobros, hammer dulcimers, and dulcimers and sing the lilting melodies of bygone days. Fiddle players compete with one another. Music is accompanied by both stand-up bass and washtub bass, and even spoons—all instruments early settlers might have made and played.

While there are hundreds of festivals all over the country celebrating bluegrass music, Bill Jones made Dixon the bluegrass capital of the Midwest when he built Dixon Park. This place has a kitchen, guarded toilets and showers, parking for a thousand cars, electricity for 400 RVs, and music, music, music.

A bluegrass festival is a family affair. According to Jones, there's "no alcohol, no drugs, no way!" allowed in the parks. You can literally bring your children to these festivals, have a check-in spot where you meet several times a day, and let them follow their own musical wanderings. It is always a pleasure to see a young-ster working with his dad or grandpa. I saw a family with a nine-year-old girl who played the stand-up bass. They dug a hole in the ground for the bass and she stood on two wooden Coke cases to play, but play she did. In that same family, three daughters sang everything the Andrew Sisters ever knew. There were eight people in this family, including grandma and grandpa and a boyfriend, and they all slept in one tent and cooked meals over a fire.

An amateur can join with a group a little above his or her ability at a campsite when they play a familiar melody. You simply turn your back to the group and play softly until you can keep up. When you get the courage to turn around and play with the group, they welcome you and you have moved up a step in your skill level.

There is an admission charge, but it's the best money you will ever spend. Maybe next year I'll take my guitar. Call Bill Jones at (573) 759–7716 or his daughter Carol Pitts at (573) 759–6041 for more information about the festival.

open by chance or by appointment. There's a large sign in the front yard announcing OPEN or CLOSED so you can just drive by and check it out (573–422–3505).

Vienna has only about 600 residents, but what an interesting bunch of folks they are! There's even a recording studio in town that people from Nashville come to use. The Old Jail Museum is 3 blocks east on Highway 42, and you can visit it from 2:00 until 4:00 P.M. on Sunday, June through October (skip July and August, it's too hot). The circa 1855 Latham Log House has been restored (with a fireplace, too); it is near the Old Jail Museum.

Kathy and Tom Corey returned home to Maries County after thirty years and built their dream home in the rock-strewn hills above the Gasconade River near Dixon. They decided to share it and a country inn was born. The name, **Rock Eddy Bluff Farm,** comes from the location of the inn. It sits atop a rugged limestone bluff overlooking the river. Here the water curves and quickens over a shoal, then calms into a deeper pool set against the bluffs. A series of large boulders rises above the water (Thox rock is the largest), which gave this section of the river the name rock eddy. The inn offers private access to the Gasconade River, and canoes are available. You can see 10 miles across the river valley between Vienna and Dixon from here. It is more a country retreat than a B&B. There's hiking and a horse-drawn Amish spring wagon. Scenic Clifty Creek has worn a natural arch through the bluff. The inn's upper story boasts a pretty view of the river; it offers an upstairs suite that gives the sensation of being snuggled into the treetops, hence the name "The Treehouse Suite." The cost per night for one or two people is $120.

The handmade quilts and ceiling fans in this suite create a restful atmosphere. You can relax on the deck and eat breakfast or watch the sun set while soaking in the hot tub dubbed "The Think Tank." The price at the inn is $95.

Turkey Ridge Cottage is away from The Bluff House and has three bedrooms and a fireplace. It is romantic and quiet. The breakfast room has a stocked fridge or you can dine nearby. One guest left a note saying, "I am convinced that time spent at Turkey Ridge does not count against life's allotted length." The other, equally fine cottage is the Indian House Bluff Cottage. Cottages are $120 and $130 nightly or $600 and $650 per week.

The Line Camp Cabin is a new addition to the place. It was inspired by a herding cabin in Wyoming. Everything here is just like it was in the 1880s: heat from a wood stove, ice box (with ice), water from a pitcher pump, and light from kerosene lamps. Here you cook, sit in the porch swing, walk to the river, and relive the past. There's even a corral for your horse if you want to bring one along. The cabin is $75 a night ($10 for additional guests) or $375 per week. This is not for everyone, but if you like roughing it a bit, you will love it. It's worth every penny. You will see bald eagles that have been nesting there for years and a great blue heron rookery with about fifty nests in the clutch of trees.

Rock eddy bluff farm is on-line now. You can e-mail the inn at welcome@rockeddy.com or visit the Web site at rockeddy.com and see photos of the area. To find rock eddy bluff farm on the map, look for a small (nonexistent) town called Hayden off Highway 63, between Rolla and Jefferson City 10245, Maries Road 511, Dixon 65459. Call (573) 759–6081.

John Viessman and the Coreys at rock eddy bluff farm recommend other places in the area that are worth the trouble to find. The *Vienna Flea Market* is on First Street in Vienna 65582, and it is open on Thursday, Friday, and Saturday. There is an auction every other Saturday. Call (573) 422–3106 for a schedule. If you have never attended an antiques auction, you owe yourself a try at it. (Just remember: Don't make eye contact with the auctioneer or scratch your head unless you want to buy something.)

The *Rainey House* at 405 South Main Street, Vienna 65582, is a historic home where you can buy gifts. Hours are Monday through Friday from 9:00 A.M. until 4:00 P.M. and Saturday from 9:00 A.M. until 2:00 P.M. Call (573) 422–6216 or 422–3331.

Carroll's Antiques is at 1707 Highway 63 South, Vienna 65582 (573–422–3298), specializing in tools as well as general collectibles.

Vienna hosts a Bluegrass Festival in March with four or five good bands playing for your enjoyment.

Five miles west of Vienna, on Ball Park Road, you can cross over a swinging bridge, one of only nine left in the state. Then you will find *Maries Hollow Herb Farm & Antiques,* where Sandy Shelton specializes in garden items and herbs as well as antiques. She has some eighteenth-century paintings and lots of hat boxes. Call (573) 422–3906 in the spring to find out when the herb farm and store are open.

Berry Moreland has the *Barn Swallow* near *Vichy,* 2 miles south on Highway 63, then 3 miles east on P Highway. This 115-year-old "barn with a face lift" has four levels of antiques, featuring both German and British furniture. Hours are from 9:00 A.M. to 5:00 P.M. six days a week, (573) 699–4443 or 699–4498.

A favorite local place is the **Vichy Wye Restaurant** at the intersection of Highways 63 and 28 (573–299–4720). Tim and Vikki Moeslein offer a smorgasbord on weekends that brings crowds from other towns around here. Diners will find chicken, fish, and ribs, bounteous vegetables, and salads. The menu offers catfish dinners and steaks. The homemade pies are well known around here, too. It's a lovely, scenic drive along Highway 63, so travel while it is still light and enjoy the view.

It's only 9 miles from Vichy to **Rolla** on Highway 63. Here the famous Rolla School of Mines is located. If you are interested in mines or minerals, it's worth your while to see the museum. Be sure to take the time to see **Missouri's Stonehenge,** a half-scale version of the English one built 4,000 years ago. Missouri's version was built by the school's specialists in the fields of mining engineering, rock mechanics, explosives research, civil engineering, and computer science. It was built to honor the techno-nerds of long ago who built theirs to pinpoint the solstices and changing seasons with moonlight and sunlight falling through precisely positioned stones. The new Stonehenge, however, was built of 160 tons of granite, shaped by cutting torches and high-pressure water jets and aligned by computer. It also includes an "analemma" solar calendar used by the Anasazi Indians in the American Southwest more than 1,000 years ago and a Polaris window for sighting the North Star. It was dedicated in 1984 on the summer solstice. A member of the Society of Druids offered ancient incantations over this blend of the ancient and ultramodern.

Where did a name like **Temerity Woods** come from? Strange name for a B&B, isn't it? Sandy Palmberg explains that her husband, Bruce, knew that the land where the Air Force Academy in Colorado was built was Temerity Ranch and he just liked the name. Couldn't call it a ranch, though, because it sits on forty acres of woods. Hence the name. This is more than just another bed and breakfast. Four cabins are scattered throughout the woods with hiking trails and primitive campsites available. Guests have use of the kitchen in the main lodge, where nighttime bonfires and marshmallow roasts occur. The cottages have two bedrooms, some with bunk beds, all with showers and air conditioning. This is a very popular place for family reunions, business meetings, and retreats. The cabins are $75, the campsites $10. The acreage is halfway between Salem and Rolla on Highway 72 near a little hamlet named **Lake Springs.** Write to Temerity Woods, 13925 County Road 5480, Lake Springs 65532, or e-mail at temerity1@aol.com.

If you are an alumnus of University of Missouri Rolla, then the name of this B&B makes perfectly good sense to you. At least that's what Ron Kohser thought when his wife, Barbara, voiced some doubts about it.

Looking for Silver, They Found . . . Lead

Miner Indulgence Bed and Breakfast at 13750 Martin Spring Drive in Rolla 65402 celebrates the Miners—Ron is on the faculty—and has plenty of alumni and parents as guests as well. It could be the peach French toast that is often part of the full country breakfast, or the hot cup of coffee on the porch before breakfast, or the swimming pool and hot tub outside the two-story red-brick colonial home that brings people back. Whatever it is you can surf on over on the Web and make up your own mind at www.bbonline.com/mo/miner/ or see it in person: Take exit 184 from I–44 and turn onto the south outer road (which is Martin Spring) and go 1½ miles west. Rates are $65 a night. Call (573) 364–0680 or e-mail the Kohsers at bestrest@rollanet.org .

The early French miners came looking for silver that was rumored to lie along the Meramec River but found instead one of the greatest lead fields in the world. The viburnum trend in the St. Francois Mountains now supplies more than 90 percent of the lead produced in this country, and a high-grade zinc is smelted from the slag left from the lead refining process.

After that have a major indulgence at a *Slice of Pie* at 601 Kingshighway, Rolla 65401, which was begun by a teacher and now serves the best pie you could ever want. Call (573) 364–6203. Or, if you've eaten enough, you can visit the *Museum at the Old Courthouse* at 305 West Third Street, Rolla 65401, which dates back to the Civil War. It has an art museum and a batch of little shops inside. Call (573) 364–5977. Learn more about the city of Rolla at its Web site, www.rollanet.org/~city.

There's a lot happening in *St. James* on Highway 68 east of Rolla, if you are an oenophile (that's a wine lover, remember?). Stop by *St. James Winery,* at 540 Sidney Street, St. James 65559 (573–265–7912). Jim and Pat Hofherr came here in 1970 with their three children and invested everything they had to begin the winery. After Jim's death in 1994, Pat and her three sons, Andrew, John, and Peter, ran the winery, which won more than seventy-five awards in local, national, and international wine competitions in 1995. In fact, *Bon Appetit* magazine named St. James's 1993 Seyval one of the top fifty wines in the world. Hours are Monday through Saturday from 8:00 A.M. to 7:00 P.M., Sunday from 11:00 A.M. to 7:00 P.M. Winter closing at 6:00 P.M. Call (800) 280–WINE for more information.

Heinrichshaus Vineyards and Winery is a family-owned winery specializing in dry wines, including Vidal Blanc and Chambourcin, located at 18500 Route U, St. James 65559. Heinrich and Lois Grohe are the owners and wine masters. Heinrich is from southern Germany, and their daughter, Peggy, went to school in Switzerland, where she studied wine making. The winery offers fresh grapes in season, Missouri cheeses and sausages, hand-thrown pottery, and original watercolors and prints by Missouri artists. Now this is a full-service winery—wine and cheese, a clay carafe, and original art to enjoy while you picnic on the winery grounds. Spring and fall bring festivals and bike tours to the winery. Call (573) 265–5000 for a calendar of events and directions, or watch for signs; this is on a rural route. A loaf of bread, a jug of wine, and a picnic! Hours are 9:00 A.M. to 6:00 P.M. every day but Wednesday and holidays.

Ferrigno's Winery and B&B, 17301 Route B, St. James 65559, is an interesting place to spend some time in the St. James area. Winemakers Dick and Susan Ferrigno grow seven varieties of French hybrid grapes such as the Chambourcin, a red grape, and the Seyval white grape. They now have fourteen acres in vines and make nine wines ranging from very dry to semisweet. Dick's favorite wines are made from the Cynthiana, which is a red grape, and Seyval grapes. Recent DNA testing proved what many wine makers had suspected for some years—that the Cynthiana and the Norton are the same grape. These wines are dry with a definite oak flavor. You may peer through glass to watch the wine-making process at the winery or wander in the surrounding vineyards. Susan serves dinner in the wine pavilion to private groups, and there is always wine, sausage, and other items available for picnics on the grounds. Winery hours are Monday through Saturday from 10:00 A.M. to 6:00 P.M. and Sunday from noon to 6:00 P.M. Call (573) 265–7742 for reservations.

Deep underground in the unchanging atmosphere beloved by spelunkers, a long underground river flows silently through *Onondaga Cave* in the *Daniel Boone State Park,* near *Leasburg* on Interstate 44 east of St. James. This is a place of superlatives: Massive stalagmites rise like peaks from the floor of the Big Room, said to be the largest cave living room in the world. In Daniel Boone's Room the abundance of cave formations is enough to make you shake your head in amazement. Old Dan himself discovered the place in 1798—or rather, he was the first white man to do so. Native Americans had used the area as a hunting sanctuary in earlier times.

Organizers of the St. Louis World's Fair in 1904 encouraged the cave's owners to open it to the public—it was a great hit, as visitors came first by railroad and then by surrey and wagon to explore the wonders.

Bourbon, off Interstate 44, was once a whiskey stop on the railroad—could you tell from the name? Now it's the home of *Meramec Farm Cabins and Trail Riding Vacations.* In the same family since 1811, and now into its seventh generation, this family farm has earned the Missouri

Century Farm sign awarded by the University of Missouri to farms that have been in the same family for at least one hundred years.

This is a real working cattle ranch, with critters and all—kids who don't have a grandma in the country will enjoy petting the horses, feeding the ducks, or playing in a real old-fashioned hayloft.

It's great for adults, too. If you want to help out around the farm, you may. If not, just enjoy the 10-mile trail (1½ miles follow the river's edge) that adjoins the highest bluffs on the Meramec River. Take a dip in a swimming hole, picnic on a gravel bar, or enjoy canoeing on a section of the Meramec that doesn't require a class-five rapids expert.

Prices are $75 per couple per cabin ($10 for each additional person). The 470-acre farm is just an hour's drive from St. Louis. It lies on a bend in the Meramec River near the Vilander Bluffs. A conveniently located five-acre gravel bar is there for people who want to fish and swim. Tubing and canoeing are some of the favorite activities, as are hiking and horseback riding. Ask about the many special packages that let you ride the horse that is native to the area, the Missouri Fox Trotter. According to Carol, These horses really "smooth out the rugged hills."

You also can bring your horse with you and Meramec Farms will provide a corral for that member of your family, too.

Carol Springer asks that you call ahead for reservations and directions. It is a working farm, and drop-ins tend to arrive at just the wrong time; but Carol and her husband, David Curtis, have been juggling it all for twenty years now, so they must be doing something right. For reservations call or write Carol Springer, 208 Thickety Ford Road, Bourbon 65441. You can also e-mail mfarmbnb@fidnet.com or visit the Web site at www.meramacfarm.com.

Wild Flower Inn, 2739 Highway D, ***Sullivan*** 65441 (573–468–7975 or fax 573–860–5712), is owned by Mary Lou and Jerry Hubble. The lovely country inn on forty-two acres is just 2 miles off Interstate 44. The four guest rooms all have private baths and televisions. There is a gathering room, and in the summer, guests can eat outside on the big front porch. Guests have access to the kitchen to make coffee any time, and a big country breakfast is served at the hour of your choice. What a choice, too: Belgian waffles, soufflés, quiches—this couple loves to cook— blueberry pancakes fresh in season, and they will custom cook for people with dietary needs. Everything is homemade and "you don't go away hungry," Jerry says. It could be a private getaway during the week, because most guests come on weekends. You even have your own key.

Strange As It Sounds

In the Mark Twain National Forest you will see what are called "Blossom Rocks," moss and lichen-speckled sandstone rocks that appear to have just "blossomed" from the ground. The massive rocks jut surprisingly from the gentle slope of a wooded hillside, surprising because no other rocks are present. One blossom rock—125 feet in diameter and 50 feet high—is covered with flowers in early spring.

The inn was built for a B&B; it's all new but looks like an old mill. Rooms upstairs cost from $80 to $85 plus tax. The honeymoon suite has queen-size beds and a large European-style bath, so you can feel like a country gentleman/woman. It's a quiet adult getaway place. Contact them at their Web site at www.ne3.com/flowers/.

There's an antiques mall in Sullivan; Mary Lou will direct you there. The town has a lot of mom-and-pop restaurants. It's lovely in the fall. Meramec River is nearby for floaters.

Meramec State Park Lodge at Sullivan, east on Interstate 44, is an excellent spot for canoeing and exploring, though it is often crowded on summer weekends. Meramec State Park on the scenic Meramec River winds through the rough, timbered hills just east of Little Bourbon.

Missouri is known as the cave state, with more known caves than any other state—5,200 counted so far. There are some twenty-two within the park. One, Fisher Cave, is open for guided tours; others are protected as habitat for an endangered bat species. (You didn't really want to go in that badly, did you?)

The folks at **Stanton,** farther east on Interstate 44, argue with the people of St. Joseph, who say Jesse James died there. Stanton proponents believe that the murder of Thomas Howard on April 3, 1882, was a clever plot to deceive investigators and authorities—with the backing of then Governor of Missouri, Thomas T. Crittendon! The ***Jesse James Wax Museum*** (573–927–5233) tells the story of James's life in 1882, the mechanics of his incredible escape from justice, and the look-alike outlaw killed by Robert Ford.

Skeptical? Well, that's the true Show Me attitude. Take your pick. Believe that Jesse died in 1951, just three weeks shy of his 104th birthday, or that he was gunned down by his cousin more than a hundred years ago. Of course, DNA testing on the body buried in Kearney proves them wrong, but old legends die hard. Admission to the museum is $4.00 for adults; seniors, military, and children are discounted. The museum is closed in winter.

Jesse was a member of Quantrill's Raiders, who captured a gunpowder mill and used the caverns as hideouts; beneath Stanton's rolling hills lies a complex of caves and finely colored mineral formations, as rare as they are beautiful. The nearby Meramec Caverns has guided tours, restaurants, and lodging. See more of Wine Country at the following Web site: www.wine-mo.com.

Wild Lands

South from St. Louis you have the choice of Interstate 55 or old Highway 61. (You can also take Interstate 270 if you want to bypass the city entirely.) However you get there, don't miss the museum and displays at *Mastodon State Park* near Imperial; the kids will love it and so will you.

The museum features life-size dioramas, reconstructed mastodon skeletons, Ice Age fossils, and artifacts more than 10,000 years old. Ancient Indians hunted mastodons with stone-tipped spears. This was the first place that archaeologists found definite evidence of them and it was an important discovery to say the least. Admission $2.00 for adults, children free. Hours are 9:00 A.M. to 4:30 P.M. Monday through Saturday and noon to 4:30 P.M. on Sunday. (Winter hours are in effect January 1 through Febrary 28. The hours are 11:00 A.M. through 4:00 P.M. Monday, Thursday, Friday, and Saturday, and noon until 4:00 P.M. Sunday. The museum is closed Tuesday and Wednesday.)

This area contained mineral springs, which made for swampy conditions perfect for preservation. Large mammals became trapped in the mineral-rich mud, which preserved their remains perfectly as the mud hardened to stone. You can still see the *Kimmswick Bone Bed,* which is one of the most extensive Pleistocene beds in the country and of worldwide interest to archaeologists and paleontologists. Explore the Visitors' Center, too. It offers a life-size replica of a mastodon skeleton, Clovis points, and other remnants of early human occupation. Mastodon State Park (636–464–2976) is south on Highway 55 at 1551 Seckman Road, Imperial.

Now aim just south for the town of *Kimmswick,* laid out in 1859 by a German named Theodore Kimm.

In the early 1880s, Kimmswick's beautiful Montesano Park attracted people from St. Louis by excursion boat. Riverboats and railroads stopped here. But the horseless carriage changed the destiny of Kimmswick; the new highway system bypassed the town and left it to become a sleepy little backwater. Even the trains and boats no longer stopped to trade. But that isn't true any more. Now the *Huck Finn* river-boat paddles down from St. Louis on the second and fourth Wednesday of each month from May through October and docks in Kimmswick; the train may even return soon, but the town no longer worries about being overpowered by St. Louis. Its shops and restaurants are some of the best along the riverfront. One little shop—*It's a Small World Christmas Haus* at Fourth and Elm, Kimmswick 63053—alone is worth diverting from the interstate to see. It is a year-round wonder-land guaranteed to put you in the Christmas spirit even during July sunshine. Shopkeeper Ann Thuston and her daughters, Peggy Biene-feld and Lynn Murphy, keep the shop stocked with European Christ-mas miniatures. Call at (636) 464–0779.

Mary Hostetter, owner of the *Blue Owl Restaurant and Bakery* at Second and Mill Streets, Kimmswick 63053, says that Kimmswick refuses to be "gobbled up by St. Louis" and works to maintain its indi-viduality as the "town that time forgot." Mary invites you to sit in front of a cheery fireplace and try a few of her specialties.

The building was erected in 1900 and called Ma Green's Tavern until the 1950s. It was restored in the 1970s and now has warm wood floors that are charmingly out of level and lace curtains in the windows. Railroad car siding covers the walls, and waitresses dressed in long pinafores serve lunch on delicate blue-and-white china. Mary recently added Miss Mary's Veranda, a Victorian veranda, for outdoor dining. A new dining room just opened, too, so now there are five dining rooms. There is live German music with Austrian Paul Knopf on the accordion. Park-ing is available in the restaurant's lot.

The Blue Owl (314–464–3128) is open year-round Tuesday through Friday from 10:00 A.M. to 3:00 P.M. and Saturday and Sunday from 10:00 A.M. to 5:00 P.M. From country breakfasts and homemade soups (the Canadian cheese soup is marvelous) on weekdays to the wonderful Sunday special of homemade chicken and dumplings, Mary will try to fill you up. If you happen to see the pastry case as you come in the door, you won't allow that to happen until coffee and dessert. Take a good look at the temple of temptation: Lemon dobosh has eight layers of lemon cake with filling between each and whipped cream on top. There's an Italian cream cake, Irish apple cake, red velvet cake, and the favorite, Death by Chocolate. The Levee High Apple Pie was created to celebrate the great flood of '93, when the river crested at 39.9 feet against the 40-foot levee. There is outdoor dining May through October.

Walk around Kimmswick; there is a lot to see here, from historic

Trivia

Built in 1927, the Old Chain of Rocks Bridge was the first bridge to span the Mississippi connecting Missouri and Illinois. The world's longest pedestrian and bicycle bridge, it is 24 feet wide and 5,353 feet long. It was once part of Route 66 and is located 12 miles north of the Arch.

homes and businesses to some fine little restaurants and shops. But keep in mind that everything is closed on Mondays. For a look at a local artist in action, visit **Kimmswick Pottery,** 6109 Front Street, Kimmswick 63053. Chris Ferbet creates hand-thrown pieces, some made from native red clay, which she digs herself. She also carries an international assortment of handcrafted art. You can watch her working at the pottery wheel or browse around the shop. Call (636) 464–3041 for more details.

The **Old House,** built in 1770, now stands at Second and Elm Streets, Kimmswick 63053. The second story and wing were added in 1831. When you see the size of the house, it's hard to believe that it was moved from the town of Beck in 1973 to save it from demolition. Inside are several rooms, two of which have massive brick fireplaces to warm the traveler, and food perfect for the atmosphere. Try the house specialty, fried chicken. Call (636) 466–0378.

Kimmswick Korner Gift Shoppe at 6101 Front Street, Kimmswick 63053, features not only body lotions, watches, and other such neat items, but also a collection of "Lunch at the Ritz" jewelry and Rubel angels. Alongside the gift shop is **Lillie's Cupboard,** featuring a world of chocolate and fudge, coffee, and teas. Hours for both places are 10:30 A.M. until 4:00 P.M. Tuesday through Friday and until 5:00 P.M. on Saturday and Sunday, and both can be reached at (636) 464–2028.

The **Wenom Drake House Bed and Breakfast** at 6055 Fourth Street, Kimmswick 63053, is a two-story 1877 house with a tin roof, gingerbread, and a solar greenhouse. Hosts Kenneth and Abby Peck offer three lovely rooms that are simply and comfortably furnished. One has a private bath and one a shared bath. A full breakfast is served each morning to get you on your way. Rooms are $60 to $80. Call (314) 464–1983 for more information.

Swing southwest on Highway 67 at Crystal City to the city of **Bonne Terre,** a year-round resort, as interesting in December in the middle of a blizzard as it is in the heat of a 100° summer day. There isn't all that much to see—above ground, that is. But if you choose **Mansion Hill** as your first stop and meet owners Doug and Cathy Georgan, the town will come alive for you. In this setting it would have to; the mansion occupies the highest point in Bonne Terre, on 132 acres of timber in the Ozark foothills. Each room has its own view of the estate (which

has a 45-mile view of the surrounding area).
Four huge fireplaces warm the great rooms.

The 1909 mansion was built by the lead-mining
baron responsible for **Bonne Terre Mines** (the
world's largest man-made caverns), which hon-
eycomb the earth under the city. Hand-dug with pick and shovel, the
mines are now flooded. They are the pride of the Georgans, who also
own West End Diving in St. Louis. The mines can be explored two ways
in any weather: by scuba diving, as do hundreds of divers who make
the trek to Bonne Terre winter and summer, or by walking along the
above-water trails.

Your first view of the mine is breathtaking; under the crystal-clear water,
illuminated from above by electric lights, divers can see all the remnants
of the mining days, including ore carts, elevator shafts, buildings—even
tools and drills left when the mine was abandoned in 1961. No less a
personage than Jacques Cousteau was a guest at the mansion and filmed
a dive here. Rooms at the mansion are worth every penny—$275 a
night—the place is gorgeous.

From the entrance to the mines, turn right on Park Street and go to
Allen Street. Follow it until you see the old St. Joe Lead Company Headquarters on the right and the 1909 depot on the left. **The Depot** is built
in the Queen Anne and Stick architectural styles and is on the National
Historic Register. The English-style phone booth outside, a caboose,
box cars, and rail lamps and posts give it a nineteenth-century flair.
Inside the depot, the Whistle Stop Saloon is filled with train memorabilia and open for banquets only. The second and third floors are part
of a turn-of-the-century bed-and-breakfast. Call (573) 358–5311 for
information. Rooms are $100 to $120 a night. The mansion and depot
are filled almost every weekend, year-round, by clubs who travel here to
scuba dive. All rooms have twin beds to accommodate the divers. Visit
the Web site at www.2dive.com for an exciting tour of everything.

Also in Bonne Terre is the **Victorian Veranda Bed and Breakfast** at 207
East School Street, Bonne Terre 63628. Hosts Galen and Karen Forney have
opened the doors of their elegant old home. Behind the wraparound
veranda lies a parlor and gathering room for your relaxation. A full country
breakfast is served in the dining room in the morning. Rooms are $70 to
$110. Call (573) 358–1134 or (800) 343–1134. You can e-mail them at vic-
toriaveranda@ldd.net or visit their Web site at bbim. org/vicveranda.html.

Located in an area of the Eastern Ozarks known as the Old Lead Belt,
Missouri Mines State Historic Site showcases the mining industry in a

19,000-square-foot former mine-mill powerhouse. In 1975, the St. Joseph Lead Company donated twenty-five buildings and the surrounding land to the Missouri Department of Natural Resources. There is also an excellent mineral collection at the museum, as well as a gift shop that sells very reasonably priced specimens. The Missouri Mines State Historic Site is open Monday through Saturday 10:00 A.M. until 4:00 P.M., and Sundays noon until 5:00 P.M. Summer Sunday hours are extended until 6:00 P.M. The museum is located on Highway 32 just outside Park Hills 63601. (The P.O. box is 492). Phone is (573) 431–6226.

History buffs shouldn't miss the Civil War battlefield at **Fort Davidson State Historic Site** at **Pilot Knob.** You can still see the outlines of the hexagonal fort built in 1863 by Union forces. Flanked on three sides by high hills, the fort was vulnerable to attack from above, which must have been apparent to General Thomas Ewing. After losing seventy-five men in the Battle of Pilot Knob, he had his soldiers muffle their horses' hooves with burlap and evacuate during the night.

If you happen to be on Highway 32 headed westbound for Dillard Mill, canoeing in Salem, or hiking in the Indian Trail State Forest, you might enjoy shopping in **Bixby** at the **Good Ole Days Country Store** on Highway 32, Bixby 65439. You will notice the bright red 1946 Missouri Pacific caboose tucked against one side of the store. Owners George and Charlene Civey have modern gas pumps and Model-A vintage pumps (also painted bright red) out front, and inside is the same blend of old and new. Twenty-five cents buys a cup of coffee (on the honor system) while above your head three O-scale model trains run on a track suspended from the ceiling, complete with flashing lights and whistles. There's more to see. Antiques fill almost every available inch of space on the hardwood floors. Out back is an old log cabin turned antiques store, which also houses a collection of minerals from surrounding hills.

Bixby's general store has never closed since it was first opened in 1906 when the railroad put a siding right next to the store. The store sold everything from casket materials to plows to groceries; locals didn't have to go anywhere else (not that there was anyplace else to go anyway). The store still has a lot of convenience items and a good deli for lunch and ice cream (get a real malt to eat in the caboose). Hours are 4:30 A.M. to 7:00 P.M. Monday through Saturday and 12:30 to 6:00 P.M. Sunday (except in winter, when it's closed.) For more information call (573) 626–4868.

One of Missouri's best kept secrets is the **Arcadia Valley**—and its villages of Arcadia, Pilot Knob, and Ironton—where there are quite a few antiques shops.

Lesterville may be on the map (and it is, south of Arcadia and west of Hogan on Highway 49), but it's really not a town anymore. This unincorporated village is a quiet little place nestled in wooded country that is dotted with old farms and barns. But just down the road is the *Yellow Valley Forge,* on Peola Road, Lesterville 63654, a combination blacksmith shop and pottery that looks more like a contemporary gallery from downtown St. Louis.

Doug Hendrickson makes elegant ironware and, in fact, does a brisk wholesale business in several states. He welcomes visitors—and spectators!—and will accept a commission if you've something special in mind.

Doug shares the shop with partner Lee Ferber, a talented potter whose *Peola Valley Pottery* is among the state's best. In addition to the *de rigueur* mugs and crocks, there are some terrific birdfeeders to add pizzazz to winter days. Take the old Peola Road at the north end of town (it's the only way you can go) for 3 miles. Watch for circular red, green, and yellow signs. When you cross Yellow Valley Creek, you've found Doug and Lee's place. For details call (573) 637–2507, or visit the Web site at www.peolavalley.com. Shop hours are 9:00 A.M. to 4:00 P.M. daily (except Sunday and Monday). Winter hours are "sporadic," according to Doug.

Just up the road from the forge is *Wilderness Lodge,* also on Peola Road, Lesterville 63654 (573–637–2295), a great old-fashioned Ozarks experience that includes Black River canoe and inner tube floats and hayrides in its package. The lodge is made of logs, and the cottages are quintessential rounded Ozark-river stone, each with a fireplace. Note: The lodge is closed during the winter.

Highway 49 leads to the town of *Annapolis* and a turn-of-the-century home near several rivers and lakes. Innkeepers Sharon, Joe, and Rachel Cluck invite guests of *Rachel's Bed and Breakfast,* 202 Second Street, Annapolis 63620, to share the large common room and the deck or veranda overlooking the attractively landscaped grounds. Rooms are $55 to $125. Call (573) 598–4656 or (888) 245–7771. Their Web site is at www.rachelsbb.com.

The nearby *Johnson Shut-ins* (north of Lesterville on Highway N) will surprise you with their rugged beauty, which is like terrain you'd expect to find in Maine or Colorado. These worn and convoluted forms have a story behind them; would you believe Missouri once had its own Mt. St. Helens? Prehistoric volcanic eruptions spewed tons of magma, towering clouds of ash, and acid debris, flattening vegetation and covering whole areas with newly formed igneous rock. Some 250 million years passed, and shallow inland seas encroached, covering the already ancient volcanic mountains with layers of sedimentary rock. These layers built up until they were hundreds of feet thick over the course of many millions of years.

There were more violent uplifts across the Ozarks; the seas retreated; and rain, wind, and moving water eroded the softer sedimentary rock layers, cutting the river valley ever deeper. Swirling over and between the buried igneous hills, the river scoured and carved potholes, chutes, and spectacular gorges. It is amazing that something as penetrable as water can cut the hardest stone—here's proof.

The Johnson Shut-ins are pocketed away in the scenic St. Francois Mountains; when you see them, you will understand the name. You feel isolated, hidden, shut in—but without a trace of claustrophobia. The Black River flows through the park and winds past some of the oldest exposed rock in the country. There are little waterfalls and swirling water everywhere. Adding to the unique nature of the area are the drought-adapted plants commonly found in the deserts of the Southwest. Scorpions and the rare eastern collared lizard (which rises to an upright position to run on its hind legs and is a treat to see) also find a home in the glades. (Never put on your boots in the morning without first shaking them out—scorpions love hiding places.) Call (573) 546-2450.

East of the park, the Taum Sauk section of the Ozark Trail leads to **Mina Sauk Falls** (the highest falls in Missouri) and Taum Sauk Mountain, the highest point in the state at 1,772 feet above sea level. (Okay, no snickering, this is not Colorado.)

According to Indian legend, the mountain's rugged face shows the grief of Mina Sauk, daughter of Taum Sauk, chief of the Piankishaws. Because of her improper marriage, her new husband of the Osage tribe was thrown off the mountain. In her despair, she leapt from the peak. The spot where she landed is considered the origin of Mina Sauk Falls, which cascade 200 feet over the granite ledges.

The **Ozark Trail** winds through the heart of Missouri. Miles and miles of rocky terrain ramble from Steelville and West Plains along glades, forests, and prairies. Here you can hear the wind and feel a snowflake on your face. The more-than-300 miles of pathways are serene and quiet, with scarcely another person along the trail. The solitude can be overwhelming and the views breathtaking. Some of the best views in the Ozarks can be found at Onondaga, Taum Sauk, and Johnson Shut-ins. (There are plans to extend the trail to 500 miles of Missouri wilderness and continue it into Arkansas for an additional 500 miles on the Ozark Highlands Trail.) The northernmost part of the trail—the Courtois Creek Section near Steelville—offers a blend of bottomland and hardwood trees. The area of the **Mark Twain National Forest** boasts some of the Ozarks tallest standing pines, and, of course, there are creeks, bluffs, and small waterfalls. The Berryman Trail for mountain bikers has a trailhead 17 miles east of Steelville and intersects the Ozark Trail at Harmon Springs. A fine spot to camp waits here with a spring and small pond. Many of these trails teemed with deer, elk, and herds of bison when they were traveled by Native Americans in the 1800s. The red wolf lived here, although none has been seen in years. Guides say black bears and wild horses may be seen. The trail offers views of the Current River valley, old graveyards, caves, and bluffs. Also rigorous hiking as well as more moderate hiking spots near the state parks are here. Primitive camping (at least 100 feet from the trail, water, and scenic areas) is allowed along most sections of the trail. Some areas are open to horses and mountain bikes. Although the trail is open year-round, the best times to visit are in the spring when the dogwoods bloom or in the fall under a canopy of russet leaves. The winters are mild in the Ozarks, though, and winter hiking can be fun. Summers in Missouri are not the best for hiking—they tend to be humid and buggy. But whatever the season, be prepared. Have a map, appropriate rainwear gear, and water—and let somebody know where you are going. For Ozark Trail Section Maps and other information, contact the Ozark Trail Coordinator, Missouri Department of Natural Resources, P.O. Box 176, Jefferson City, 65102, (573) 751–2479 or (800) 334–6946.

North of the Shut-ins, through some of the prettiest hills this side of the Great Smoky Mountains, is **Dillard** and the **Dillard Mill State Historic Site.** Like a Currier & Ives scene beside its mill run, it is one of the state's best-preserved water-powered gristmills. This picturesque red building sits squarely at the juncture of two of the clearest-flowing Ozark streams, Huzzah and Indian Creeks. The original mill machinery is still in operation, grinding away.

When you've finished with industrial history, check out the natural history. Dillard has a 1½-mile hiking trail through oak and hickory forests that ends at a pine-topped plateau.

Backtrack a bit on Highway 49 and turn east on Highway 32 to **Elephant Rocks State Park** near **Graniteville.** It is the first park in the state to have a trail designed especially for the visually and physically handicapped. Signs along the trail, written in braille and in regular text, describe the

Vive Bastille Day!

In Ste. Genevieve, the annual Bastille Day celebration on July 14th, which celebrates the town's proud French heritage, rivals our own Independence Day.

origin of the elephant rocks and guide visitors along a paved 1-mile path.

Elephant Rocks is one of the oddest geological formations—more than a billion years old—you're likely to find in Missouri. Here monolithic boulders stand end-to-end like a train of circus elephants, dwarfing mere mortals who stand beside them. Made of billion-year-old granite, the rocks were formed during the Precambrian era when molten rock forced its way to the surface, pushing the earth's crust aside. The magma cooled and hardened slowly as this area became less volcanically active; it broke in vertical cracks, which weathered and rounded to form the huge "elephants." This weathering eventually breaks even the largest rocks down into pebbles and gravel, but not to worry: More stone elephants are in the making all the time. The pink patriarch of the pachyderm herd is Dumbo, at 27 feet tall and 35 feet long and weighing in at a sylphlike 680 tons. Winding trails, colorful lichen and wildflowers, cool, oak-shaded grottos, and a picnic area in the shadow of the rocks add to the attractions here. Call (573) 546–3454.

River Heritage Area

I f you didn't head off into the wilderness back on Highway 67 at Crystal City but stayed on Interstate 55 or Highway 61, you will now enter the River Heritage area. From river bluffs and hills to lowlands, from historic towns to waterways, the River Heritage region boasts enough destinations for several vacations. The French influence is visible everywhere you look in *Ste. Genevieve,* from the name itself to the many buildings *à la française.* The earliest records of the Missouri Territory invariably mention Ste. Genevieve and its ball-loving inhabitants!

Ste. Genevieve has been clinging to the riverbank here since the 1730s, when French trappers sought valuable beaver pelts. The 5,000 people who call Sainte Gen home still celebrate Bastille Day and are justifiably proud of their French Creole–style buildings. The "Great Flood of '93" threatened the town, but it managed to stay dry with a lot of sandbagging by citizens and history-minded volunteers from all over the nation.

Many visitors to Ste. Genevieve are research scholars and genealogists from around the world. The records at the library, courthouse, and churches are the oldest in the West. St. Genevieve calls itself the oldest town west of the Mississippi (more than one Missouri town makes this claim, though) and says "all history of the West begins here."

Stop by the information center on Third Street. Many of the town's homes date to the 1700s and are preserved as historic sites and open for tours. Start with the *Ste. Genevieve Museum,* which houses one of the first bird mounts by John James Audubon himself, who did business—albeit briefly—here in the early 1800s. You'll see French-style *sabots* (wooden shoes), early songbooks, a flute belonging to Audubon's partner Rozier, and much more.

The *Bolduc House Museum,* 125 South Main Street, Ste. Genevieve 63670, was built circa 1770 and moved to its current site in 1785. The two-room French colonial is one of the best examples of its type of architecture along the Mississippi. Tour guides in period costume lead visitors through the building where the yellow glow of tallow lamps dimly light the flintlock rifles above the mantel and the bison rug on the floor. Outside an herb garden, a well, and an orchard are inside a typical French-style palisade enclosure.

Then choose among the homes, churches, shops, and country inns dotting the town. Search out places for little treats such as Sara Menard's *Sara's Ice Cream and Antiques,* at 260 Merchant Street, Ste. Genevieve 63670 (573–883–5890) or the *Kmetz Home Bakery* at 124 Merchant Street, Ste. Genevieve 63670 (573–883–3533) and try one of their famous cream-filled crumbcakes.

You can't help but notice the *Old Brick House,* built in 1780, which faces the courthouse square, at Third and Market Streets, Ste. Genevieve 63670. It's owned by sisters Rosie and Judy Schwartz. Judy says the favorite entree is liver knaefly, a liver dumpling. Before you liver-haters turn up your noses, this German cook urges you to try the dish. It wouldn't be a regularly scheduled favorite if it weren't great, right? Okay, you want something you know, how about a sizzling steak or secret-recipe fried chicken? Whatever you eat, enjoy the surroundings while waiting. They say that the bricks that built this wealthy merchant's home in 1785 arrived as ballast on French ships, and it is thought to be the first brick building west of the Mississippi. The building spent years as a courthouse, a school, and a tavern. In 1816 a duel was fought on its steps and a man was killed. Today the polished wood floors and lace curtains offer a more peaceful environment and the most dangerous thing here is the coconut cream pie. Hours are 8:00 A.M. until 9:00 P.M. weekdays, 11:00 A.M. until 10:00 P.M. Saturday, and 11:00 A.M. until 7:00 P.M. Sunday. Call (573) 883–2724 for information.

Just a couple of doors down the street from the Old Brick House is

The Anvil, at 46 South Third Street, Ste. Genevieve 63670, a bar and restaurant that serves great fried chicken and other real down-home food. Call (573) 883–7323 to find out more about it. Weekday hours are 11:00 A.M. to 8:00 P.M. and until 9:30 P.M. on weekends.

Creole House Bed & Breakfast is at 339 St. Mary's Road, Ste. Genevieve 63670, This French Creole–style house is on a quiet 2½ acres in the city's Historic District. Innkeepers Margaret and Royce Wilhauk offer guests wine and appetizers in the evening. All of the spacious rooms have private baths, and some have fireplaces and sitting rooms. A luscious breakfast will be waiting for you in the morning. There are two bedrooms and two suites. One is on the first floor with a private entrance and wraparound porch. Several have Jacuzzi tubs. Call (573) 883–7171 or (800) 275–6041 for more information. To obtain room rates and reservations or to see the room, visit their Web site at www.creole housebb.com.

Down the block at 146 South Third Street, Ste. Genevieve 63670, is the circa-1790 *Southern Hotel* (573–883–3493 or 800–275–1412). Barbara and Mike Hankins saw the old wreck, which had been abandoned since 1980, and fell in love with the red-brick, Federal-style three-story hotel. "It was such a mess," Barbara says just a bit wearily, "that finally everything quit working. We stripped it back to the walls and put in state-of-the-art electrical, plumbing, and furnace fixtures." Barbara

Back garden at Bolduc House Museum

insists they made it into a bed-and-breakfast to justify owning it! It is believed to be the oldest operating hotel west of the Mississippi River. The hotel is full of antiques and claw-foot tubs. Meals feature fresh herbs from the garden behind the hotel and flowers from the garden fill the rooms. The garden itself is magical. An arbor leads to a wide cedar swing at the center; Mike has wired the whole area with thousands of tiny white lights. When he hits the switch at dusk the garden is a romantic fairyland. Tucked away in a corner of the garden is a great little shop with dried flowers, herbal soaps, and hand-painted goodies—don't miss it! You can buy the *Pepper and Rose Cookbook* or enroll in the "Cooking Experience" class.

It has been open since 1987 with eight guest rooms, each with its own bath. Rooms cost from $83 to $128 and include such wondrous French breakfast items as strawberry soup, artichoke heart strata (a layered egg-and-bread dish), croissants, homemade lemon bread, juice, and coffee. The e-mail address is: mike@southernhotelbb.com, and the hotel's Web site is: www.southernhotelbb.com.

Inn St. Gemme Beauvais at 78 North Main Street, Ste. Genevieve 63670, is the state's oldest continually operated B&B. This lovely old Victorian will spoil you. All the rooms are suites, with big easy chairs in the sitting room and canopy beds and rockers in the bedrooms. Tea time is every day at two o'clock, and wine and hors d'oeuvres are offered every day at four o'clock. A full gourmet breakfast, of course, is served in the morning at eight and coffee is ready even earlier in the second-floor lounge for you early birds.

There is also a restaurant that can seat up to fifty people. Lunch is served there daily from 11:30 A.M. until 4:00 P.M. The cuisine is French, featuring soups, salads, quiches, and homemade desserts. Dinner banquets can also be arranged any time. Outside is a lovely herb and flower garden to enjoy. The hotel is on Main Street, and so it is within walking distance to everything. Suites range from $89 (for two) to $179. Visit their Web site at www.bbhost.com/inns+gemme/ or call innkeeper Janet Joggerst at (573) 883–5744 or (800) 818– 5744, or fax (573) 583–3899.

The *Steiger Haus Bed and Breakfast* is at 1021 Market Street, Ste. Genevieve 63670 (573–883–5881 or 800–814–5881). Rob Beckerman, who is an owner and the manager, cooks and serves a full breakfast ("I do almost everything," he says), and apple crepes and cheese omelettes are his specialty. This two-story house has an indoor pool, and, if you enjoy mysteries, special packages are available. Rates are $86 a night, more for the mystery packages.

Trivia

The longest cave in the state is Perry County's Crevice Cave, which has 28 miles of surveyed passages.

Steiger Haus Downtown at 242 Merchant Street, Ste. Genevieve 63670 (573– 883–3600) is a three-story brick home built in 1910. The summer kitchen attached to the house was built in 1811. There are four suites on the main floor, a dining room and parlor for the use of guests, and a gift shop. Guests are invited to use the indoor swimming pool at the other Steiger Haus. Breakfast is served in the dining room for both guests here and at the two cottages in town. Suites range are $91. The ***Hael Cottage*** on Main Street has a queen-size bed on the main floor and two twins in the attic. A queen-size sleeper sofa in the sitting room makes space for a family since the whole cottage is rented for $86. Breakfast is served at Steiger Haus Downtown.

The information presented here only begins to touch on what is available in Ste. Gen; there's the ***Sainte Genevieve Winery*** at 245 Merchant Street, Ste. Genevieve 63670 (573–883–2800), the ***Sweet Things*** confection shop at 242 Market Street, Ste. Genevieve 63670 (573–883–7990), all manner of antiques shops and restaurants, and a whole list of B&Bs.

At ***Perryville,*** off Highway 61, is the ***St. Mary of the Barrens Church,*** dating to 1827. The grounds are open to walk through; be sure to visit the church's museums. This is also the National Shrine of Our Lady of the Miraculous Medal. Perryville has a Web site at www.perryville.com.

For more history (and fun), detour east a bit on the Great River Road and watch for Tower Rock jutting up 85 feet out of the Mississippi. Don't miss the little German towns of Altenberg, Whittenberg, and Frohna. If you're ready to eat, ***Tric's Family Restaurant*** in ***Altenberg*** turns out a plentiful supply of German-style home cooking and wonderful buffets at 5:00 P.M. five nights a week. Most nights offer changing menus, but Saturday it's sauerbraten or bratwurst, and on Sunday there is a noon buffet. Homemade pies (of which coconut cream is the favorite) are plentiful, and there are always fresh fruit pies such as strawberry-rhubarb or peach. "We never, ever, use canned fruit," says Rose. Hours are Thursday through Saturday 8:30 A.M. to 8:00 P.M., Wednesday and Sunday 10:30 A.M. to 2:00 P.M. (winter hours may vary).

Tric's (573–824–5387) is on Highway C in Altenberg 63732, and is owned by Harlin and Rose Oberndorfer. Rose can direct you to other special spots in Altenburg and Frohna, including Lutheran monuments and Missouri's first Lutheran college.

Stay on Highway 61, and the next stop is ***Jackson;*** all aboard the old Iron Mountain Railroad. The oldest Protestant church west of the Mississippi,

Trivia

The Mississippi River is the reason St. Louis exists. It was the original highway for every civilization that thrived in the middle of the country. But it is also the most diverse inland river in the world. More than 500 species of wildlife use the river and its flood plains.

the Old McKendree Chapel (circa 1819), a national Methodist shrine, is here, and so is **Trisha's Bed and Breakfast and Tea Room and Craft Shop** at 203 Bellevue Street, Jackson 63755. It is the family home of Trisha and Gus Wischmann, and it is known here as "The Mueller Haus." There's a relaxed, congenial atmosphere (with respect for your privacy) and a home-cooked breakfast. It's a delightful resting spot. Rooms are from $65 to $80 on weekends, $55 during the week or for extended stays. The Victorian Rendezvous includes two nights in a romantic suite, dinner for two elegantly served by your hosts, and a vintage car to carry you away to a park where you can enjoy a delightful picnic basket packed with lunch for two. The second evening is dinner at a fine restaurant. A Golf Weekend includes greens fees and a golf cart at Bent Creek Golf Course, which is only a half-mile away. The Relaxation Getaway includes an hour of massage by a licensed therapist and a visit to the local fitness center. Hours are 11:00 A.M. to 4:00 P.M. Wednesday, Thursday, and Friday. Call (573) 243–7427, (800) 651–0408, or fax (573) 243–2787; e-mail trisha@igateway.net for more information.

The best attraction for you railroad fans is the **Iron Mountain Railway,** 505 Benton Road, Jackson 63755. It's the only steam-powered tourist railroad line in the region. Sights and sounds will carry you back to the late 1800s and early 1900s, when this was the preferred method of travel.

The "mother line" of nearly all the smaller rail lines that eventually became the historic Missouri Pacific, the Iron Mountain Railway is part of the St. Louis, Iron Mountain, and Southern Railway Company. Darren the Magician roams the train to entertain the child in you. There's the Dinner Train, or you might relive the 1880s train robbery by the James Gang, or experience the intrigue of murder on a Murder Mystery Train. You can send for a schedule or check them out on the Web at www.rosecity. net.trains. Take I–55 to exit 99 and go 4 miles west on Highway 61 to the intersection of Highways 61 and 25. Call (573) 243–1688 or (800) 455–RAIL for schedule and prices. The **Whistle Stop Cafe** is inside the train station. It's open Tuesday through Sunday. Call (573) 243–0020.

If you want to experience the elegance of the 1800s, stop by the **Oliver House,** 224 East Adams Street, Jackson 63755. The lady of the house is known as Missouri's Betsy Ross. Marie Oliver and a friend designed and made the first and only official state flag. The house is decorated with authentic furniture of the period and music plays on the Edison Victrola. Visiting hours are on the first Sunday of the month from 1:00 to 4:30 P.M. May through December. For more information call (573) 243–0533.

While you're near Jackson, take a side trip to **Burfordville** on Highway 34 east. The **Bollinger Mill** has been in continuous operation for more than 180 years—these people really kept their noses to the grindstone, didn't they? Located on the Whitewater River, the four-story, stone-and-brick structure shares the setting with the Burfordville Covered Bridge, one of five covered bridges remaining in the state.

Bridge building was begun in 1858 and, like much of Missouri's everyday life, was put on hold by the Civil War. The Burfordville Bridge was completed in 1868. It is a 140-foot span of incredibly long yellow poplar timbers, which grow near the river. It's another excellent setting for artists and photographers, not to mention history and nostalgia buffs.

You're deep in southern Missouri now, and headed for "Cape." On Interstate 55, **Cape Girardeau** is the biggest city in the area, with a population of almost 35,000. But Cape Girardeau has also preserved its heritage carefully, and it's a beautiful city in spite of—and in the midst of—phenomenal growth. Visit the Cape's Web site at showme.net/ capecity.

Cape Girardeau is radio-and-television talk-show host Rush Limbaugh's hometown, and the city offers a self-directed (very conservative) tour (with nothing but right turns?) past the hospital where he was born, his boyhood home, high school, and the barbershop where he got his first job. Then you can have lunch at his favorite hamburger joint, Wimpy's. Pick up a brochure at the Visitors' Bureau at 1707 Mount Auburn Road (800–777–0068), or visit his Web page at rosecity.net/rush/ rushtour.html.

Drive through the city and note the many nineteenth-century buildings. The beautiful Glenn House, circa 1880, is a good example. The old Court of Common Pleas has a lovely hilltop setting, and Cape Rock Park is a reminder of the early trading post that predated the city itself. Civil War fortifications still remain in the area. The convention and tourism bureau is at 601 North Kingshighway; if you plan to spend some time here, it may pay to stop.

Gothic Splendor

*An outstanding example of Renaissance architecture in the Gothic style is the **Old St. Vincent's Church** in Cape Girardeau. It was built in 1853 and contains more than 100 medieval-design plaster masks and intricate interior work. It is listed on the National Register of Historic Places.*

Although Cape is modern and expanding too fast, all is not lost. Proceed directly down to Water Street, which, as you may have guessed by the name, is along the mighty Mississippi. Unfortunately, a rather tall, ugly wall has been built to protect the area from flood, so the view lacks something—water, to be exact. There is an opening and a deck you can drive onto to enjoy the sights, though, if you are fond of rivers—and who isn't? There's just something about the power of that big river.

Get a feel for the history of the area with Cape's unique Great Murals Tour. It all began at the *Southeast Missourian* newspaper building where "The Art of Printing" and "The Art of Making a Newspaper" were done in 1947. Tourists enjoyed finding famous faces in the ceramic murals, which were the first of their kind in the country.

They were joined by the "Jake Wells Mural," representing the people whose dreams carved the region's progress. This is one of the largest murals in the state. In the city's downtown area five more murals celebrate the Mississippi River (in Waterfront Park), the Riverfest, The Riverfront, the Bicentennial, and the Silver Coronet Band Mural about Cape's musical legacy. The "Missouri Wall of Fame Mural" is in progress and will encompass twenty-five panels featuring famous Missourians.

If you love trains, especially Lionel Electric Trains, hunt up **Sneathen Enterprises** at 2526 Boutin Drive, Cape Girardeau 63701, where Bill Sneathen will sell, buy, or trade with you. Hours are variable, call (573) 335–8091.

The **Glenn House** is a circa 1883 two-story Victorian at 325 South Spanish Street, Cape Girardeau 63703. It is open for tours and contains period furnishing, 12-foot stenciled ceilings, and some good displays devoted to the steamboat era on the Mississippi. It is open from May through October on Saturdays and Sundays from 1:00 to 4:00 P.M. or by appointment. The house is also open Saturdays and Sundays from 1:00 to 4:00 P.M. in December. Call (573) 334–1177 for more information, or visit the Web site at rosecity.net/ glenn.html.

About a block away is what will probably be your favorite place if you have any Cajun instincts at all. **Broussard's Cajun Restaurant,** 120 North Main Street, Cape Girardeau 63701, even has a test on the back of the menu to see if there is a trace of Cajun blood in your veins. The "How to tell a full-blooded, dipped-in-the-bayou Cajun from someone who just wishes he was" test begins with the question "Did your grandmother regularly eat *couche* for breakfast?" and ends with "If someone stepped on your toe would you yell '*ho yii*' instead of 'ouch'?"

Trivia

Cape Girardeau was named after Jean Baptiste Girardot, who established a trading post here in 1733. When Spain offered inexpensive, tax-exempt land, Spanish immigrants were drawn to the area. Cape Rock (2 miles northeast via Highway 177 and East Rock Drive) is the site of Jean Baptiste Girardot's trading post. Although nothing remains of the original settlement, views of the Mississippi River are wonderful from the bluff. Good spot for a picnic.

If any of you good ol' boys are missing home, this is the place for you. Call (573) 334–7235.

The food here is authentic, fire-breathing Cajun. The menu has a glossary of terms and a key to spicy foods for those of you who don't like surprises. It is an inexpensive, casual place, but take enough money to try a Cajun Combo from $11.99, which includes a little bit of everything. Also, if you have room, the special includes a salad and French bread. Other entrees range from the $5.99 all-you-can-eat red beans and rice with sausage to the fried crawfish tails for $13.99. Polish it off with the "bottomless" draft for $5.00 on Thursday nights.

The **Blue Bayou** is Broussard's club next door. It features a live band playing blues and dance music Fridays and Saturdays from 8:00 P.M. until closing time. Broussard's motto is *"Laissez Les Bons Temps Rouler!"*— Let the Good Times Roll.

For a lovely bed-and-breakfast try the **Bellevue Bed and Breakfast,** 312 Bellevue, Cape Girardeau 63701. This 1891 Queen Anne Victorian has been faithfully restored—right up to the stenciled ceilings—and filled with period furniture. The parlor has a coal-burning fireplace. The music room houses a baby grand piano. But queen-size beds and private baths make this a very comfortable place to stay. Innkeepers Marsha Toll and her two beagles draw guests into the dining room for breakfast with the aroma of baking bread. The home is within walking distance of the Riverfront and the many nearby shops. Rooms are from $75 to $105, and all have private baths. Call (573) 335–3302 or (800) 768–6822 for reservations. You can call up their Web page at www. bbonline.com/ mo/bellevue/index.html,or e-mail at bellevuebb@ COM PUSERVE.com.

Fred recommends some of his favorite restaurants. **Molly's** at 11 South Spanish Street, Cape Girardeau 63703 (573–339–1661) serves "innovative pasta," he says, and the specialty at **Jeremiah's**—127 North Water Street, Cape Girardeau 63703—is cooking on the big grill in the center of the room. Frog legs keep this place from being just another grill. Call (573) 334–0508.

River Ridge Winery, County Road 321, Commerce 63742, is in a century-old farmhouse nestled in the hills where Crowley's Ridge meets

The Evil That Men Do . . .

During the forced removal in 1838, twelve detachments of Cherokee were ordered by General Winfield Scott to move to Oklahoma. All entered Missouri in Cape Girardeau County. Rain, snow, freezing cold, hunger, and disease took their toll on the emigrants as the ice prevented both boat and horse from moving. More than 4,000 Cherokee—nearly one-fifth of the Cherokee population—died in camps by the river waiting for the journey to resume. To learn more about this march, you can visit the office of the Northern Cherokee Nation of the Old Louisiana Territory on Independence Street (Tuesday through Saturday). You can also visit Trail of Tears State Park, located approximately 10 miles north of Cape Girardeau on Highway 177.

the Mississippi River, 2 miles north of **Commerce,** south of Cape on Highway N. The hand-tended French hybrid grapes are grown on the hills behind the winery. You may sample the fine dry and semidry table wines crafted by winemaker Jerry Smith. He and his wife, Joannie, also have a showroom of unique wine-related items. You can picnic by the river or in the vineyards, or relax by a warm fire at the house and enjoy Esicar's wurst and bread. Call (573) 264–3712.

Near Cape Girardeau grits begin to sneak onto the breakfast menu, and the accent begins to sound slightly more Southern than Midwestern.

On Highway 61 South watch the signs for **Lambert's Cafe** in **Sikeston,** home of "throwed rolls." Lambert's, at 2515 East Malone, Sikeston 63801 (573–471–4261), is a most unusual place. Yes, they do throw rolls at Lambert's.

It all began on a busy day in May 1976 when passing rolls real nice-like got too slow and a customer hollered, "Just throw me the *x*#! thing!" Before you could say "thank you kindly," others cried out for service, and they have been throwing rolls at Lambert's ever since.

The folks here take control of your dinner needs—and control is the right word (got to have it when you're lobbing a long one). Want another roll? Sing out and look alive, because one will come whizzing by. To complement the rolls thrown your way, another ladleful of sorghum (Missouri's answer to Vermont maple syrup) will be slopped onto your roll, which is already dripping butter. This will require a trip to the restroom to unstick your fingers. Lambert's is fun—if you like noise, confusion, and a lot of food and attention from the waiters.

If your plate begins to look empty, someone comes by with a ladle of beans, fried okra, or applesauce and plops it in the middle of your plate; when you finish dinner, you will be full. Very, very full. Then you will discover that they are famous for the size of their slices of homemade pie and cobbler. The drinks are served in gallon Mason jars and the atmosphere is a madhouse on a good day, but it's a spot you can talk about for years. Hours are 10:30 A.M. until 9:00 P.M. seven days a week.

Ken and Vicki Rubenacker also know their way around the area. A night at **Klein House,** a turn-of-the-century Victorian at 427 South Kings Highway in Sikeston 63801 will get you on your way around the area. This Victorian-style home offers a queen-size bed and private bath. And in true Southern style, you can relax in the porch swing in the shade of one of the town's oldest magnolia trees. Call (573) 471–2501, (800) 884–2112, or fax (573) 471–7264; e-mail kleinbb@ldd.net for reservations. Visit the Web site at rosecity.net/sikeston/kleinhouse bb/index.html.

The city has a Web page at sikestonmo.net/chamber.html.

Old Mountain Region

Now you have a choice—go south to the Bootheel region or loop back up toward St. Louie. West on Highway 60 toward Dexter, the flat, Kansaslike real estate will begin to curve again in the distance.

Maybe you saw geese in the air and heard their wild cries as you ate your frog's legs. A short trip will take you through **Puxico** to **Mingo National Wildlife Refuge,** a vital 21,676-acre link in the chain of refuges along the Mississippi flyway.

The hills flatten into wetlands and plant varieties change visibly. Mingo Swamp was formed some 18,000 years ago when the Mississippi abandoned its bed, leaving an oxbow that filled in with dense swamp species. Abundant artifacts point to the area's use by Native Americans, drawn here by swamp-loving wildlife. (No artifacts can be removed from Mingo, however, so arrowhead hunters, take note.)

The area offers boardwalk nature trails and a chance to see wildlife in its natural habitat. There is a resident waterfowl flock as well as thousands of seasonal migrants, and two active bald eagle nests are located on the refuge. Be sure to stop by the refuge visitors' center before heading into the swamp (especially during the winter months), not only to let someone know where you are going, but to enjoy the interpretive displays.

Together with the adjacent Duck Creek Wildlife Area, a state wildlife management area, this is the largest hardwood swamp remaining in the state. Lake Wappapello is also nearby; watch for signs.

If you didn't expect to find a museum of fine art in the Ozarks, you're in for a surprise. The **Margaret Harwell Art Museum** in **Poplar Bluff** boasts a growing collection of works by contemporary Missouri artists.

Housed in a beautiful 1883 home, the museum has mounted one-man shows by important artists such as sculptor Ernest Trova, Swedish artist Anders Zorn, and Missourian Thomas Hart Benton. There is no charge to view the two exhibits. The museum focuses on themes ranging from contemporary photography to fiber art and recognizes the importance of the native arts of the Ozark region. It has held exhibits of folk art, including quilting and basket making. It is the only art center within a 90-mile radius and the only art museum within 150 miles of Poplar Bluff. Docents conduct regular tours of the exhibit. The museum, at 427 North Main Street, Poplar Bluff 63901, is closed Monday and Tuesday. Call (573) 686–8002 for information. Hours are 1:00 to 4:00 P.M. Tours are by appointment only.

Bootheel Region

ou are in Missouri's Bootheel now, not really the Midwest anymore, more like the South. You can get all kinds of Bootheel travel help on line by e-mail at bootrpc@sheltonbbs.com.

Southeast of Sikeston you'll find hills that really roll. **Big Oak Tree State Park** tells the story of the 1811 New Madrid earthquake, which altered the topography of the southeast lowlands. All the land from Cape Girardeau south to Helena, Arkansas, sank from 10 to 50 feet, flooding most of what is now New Madrid, Pemiscot, and Dunklin Counties. Rich Bootheel forests were converted to swampland, providing temporary protection for the giant tree. You may see trees 120 to 130 feet tall. Enjoy a bayou setting for picnics or fishing. Big Oak Tree is east off Highway 102.

Nearby **Towosahgy State Historic Site** (off Highway 77) is sixty-four acres of prehistory. Archaeologists believe the site was inhabited between A.D. 1000 and A.D. 1400. Although other groups had lived in this area before that time, their societies did not reach such a highly organized level as that of the Indians at Towosahgy. Experts believe their use of the Mississippi for trade and transportation contributed to this advancement. The river was the link between Towosahgy and the ceremonial center near the present site of Cahokia, Illinois.

Cotton fields join wheat fields as you approach **New Madrid** (that's pronounced *MAD-rid*, much more Midwestern than Spanish) on Interstate 55. The Mississippi River Observation Deck offers a panoramic view of the New Madrid oxbow; 8 miles of river are visible from the top of the most perfect oxbow on the Mississippi.

SOUTHEAST MISSOURI

The oldest city west of the Mississippi (see, there's that claim again) has something for everyone. Begin at 1 Main Street. This building, on the banks of the Mississippi near the new observation deck, was once the First and Last Chance Saloon. There were no roads to New Madrid; all the traffic came off the mighty river. Here was the first—and last—chance to get a drink back in 1783. It is now the *New Madrid Historical Museum.*

New Madrid looks sleepy, dreaming away beside the river. It looks safe. It looks as if nothing much could happen here—indeed, as if nothing much ever had. If that's what you think when you see the place, you're wrong.

It balances precariously on one of the most active earthquake faults on the continent. In 1811, the balance shifted. The earth shrugged. The mighty Mississippi was suddenly dammed and ran backward, boats broke up and sank at their moorings, homes disintegrated before their owners' horrified eyes. John James Audubon recounted a hilarious—if frightening—tale of a wedding party broken up by the quake, and the naturalist John Bradbury described it in harrowing scientific detail as he calmly watched the earth come apart. The quake was so violent that it rang church bells in Boston.

In Missouri's early days, the lowlands around the Bootheel were known as "The Big Swamp" because they were covered with stagnant waters of marshes, swamps, and bayous. There were mosquitos everywhere that were the deadly enemies of settlers. A series of earthquakes in 1811 and 1812 further discouraged settlers. Today "Swamp-east Missouri" has been changed—through drainage projects—to some of the most productive land in the state.

All is not peace and quiet, even now. There is a measurable tremor on the seismographs almost every day that can be felt by local folks. The Center for Earthquake Studies at Southeast Missouri State University informs us that a major quake is not just possible, but inevitable; stresses within the earth slowly mount until something has to give. When it does, there will be damage over an area more than twenty times that affected by a California quake because of the underlying geologic conditions—the ground will literally liquefy.

Residents have developed a wonderful gallows humor—you'd have to! T-shirts read, with a certain quirky pride, "It's Our Fault" and "Visit New Madrid—while it's still here." So, you want real excitement? Head for New Madrid. (Of course, the author files a disclaimer here. If there's a quake while you're in town, it's "not my fault.")

While in New Madrid, visit the *Hunter-Dawson Home and Historic Site.* Built in 1859 by William Washington Hunter, this crisp white house with its ornate trim and contrasting shutters recalls a more genteel era.

Hunter-Dawson Home, New Madrid

The costumed guides who answer all your questions treat you with that special Southern charm and add to the atmosphere. A small admission fee is charged.

As you continue south from Sikeston and New Madrid, the land becomes flat bottomland. Southern-style cotton, soybeans, and peaches are the important crops here. From Kennett and Malden on the west to Hayti and Caruthersville on the east, hospitality is just what you would expect in this area of Southern heritage, and Missouri begins to feel like Dixie. Welcome, y'all.

**PLACES TO STAY IN
SOUTHEAST MISSOURI**

ST. LOUIS
Red Roof Inn,
11837 Lackland Road,
Westport 63146;
(314) 991–4900 or
(800) 843–7663

St. Union Station Drury,
201 South 20th St. Inn,
63103; (314) 231–3900

CUBA
Super 8 Motel, 65453;
(573) 885–2067

EUREKA
Ramada Inn at Six Flags,
Interstate 44 and
Allentown Road, 63025;
(800) 782–8108

LINN
Linn Motel,
1221 E. Main, 65051;
(314) 897–2999

ROLLA
Days Inn,
1207 Kingshighway, 65401;
(314) 341–3700

Zeno's,
1621 Martin Spring
Drive, 65401;
(573) 364–1301

*Best Western,
1403 Martin Spring
Drive, 65401;
(314) 341–2511 or
(800) 828–1234

SULLIVAN
Best Western Penberthy Inn,
307 North Service
Road, 63080;
(573) 468–3136

*Ramada Inn, Interstate 44
exit 225, 63080;
(573) 468–4172

VIENNA
Scenic 63 RV Park and
Motel, Highway
63 South, 65582;
(573) 422–3907

WASHINGTON
Super 8 Motel, Highway
47/100, 63090;
(314) 390–0088

FARMINGTON
*Best Western
Tradition Inn,
1625 W. Columbia, 63640;
(573) 756–8031 (only full
service motel in area)

*Days Inn,
1400 Liberty Street, 63640;
(314) 756–8951 or
(800) DAYS INN

*has restaurant

LESTERVILLE
Black River Family
Restaurant & Motel,
Highway 21, 63654;
(573) 637–2600

PERRYVILLE
Best Western Colonial Inn,
1500 Liberty Street, 63775;
(800) 528–1234 or
(573) 547–1091

CAPE GIRARDEAU
Drury Lodge,
104 S. Vantage Drive,
63866; (573) 334–7151
(free hot breakfast buffet)

Sands Motel,
1448 North
Kingshighway, 63701;
(573) 334–4491

Holiday Inn,
3257 William Street, 63703;
(573) 334–4441

STE. GENEVIEVE
Hotel Ste. Genevieve,
Main and Merchant, 63670;
(573) 883–3562

JACKSON
Drury Inn, 225 Drury
Lane, 63755;
(573) 243–9200
(quickstart breakfast, free
evening cocktails, cable)

POPLAR BLUFF
*Holiday Inn,
2115 North Westwood
Boulevard, 63901;
(573) 785–7711;

Super 8 Motel,
2831 North Westwood
Boulevard, 63901;
(573) 785–0176

SIKESTON
Holiday Inn Express,
2602 Rear East
Malone Street, 63801;
(573) 471–8660

Super 8 Motel, 2609 East
Malone Street, 63801;
(573) 471–7944

Best Western Coach
House Inn & Suites,
220 South Interstate
Drive, I–55 and
Highway 60, 63801;
(573) 471–9700

NEW MADRID
Super 8 Motel, Interstate
55, exit 40 Marston, 63866;
(573) 643–9888

PLACES TO EAT IN
SOUTHEAST MISSOURI

ST. LOUIS
LoRusso's Cucina,
3121 Watson (on the hill),
63139; (314) 647–6222;
www.the-hill.com/lorussos

Norton's Cafe,
808 Geyer (Soulard), 63104;
(314) 436–0828;

Selected Chambers of Commerce

Lebanon, (417) 588–3256
New Madrid, (314) 748–5300
St. Louis, (800) 916–0092

Casa Gallardo Mexican Restaurant & Bar, St. Louis Union Station, 63103; (314) 421–6766;

WASHINGTON

Cowans Restaurant, 114 Elm Street, 63090; (636) 239–3213

NEAR DIXON

The Point, Route 28, 65459; (573) 759–6100

RICH FOUNTAIN
White Stone Inn, Highway 63 East on State Road, 65035; (573) 744–5827

SOUTH OF VIENNA
Moreland's Restaurant, Highway 63, 65035; (573) 422–9918

FARMINGTON
Spokes Pub & Grill, Highways 67 & W at B Traditions Inn, 63640; (573) 756–8031

CAPE GIRARDEAU
Cedar Street Restaurant & Bar, Interstate 55 and Route K, 63701; (573) 332–7427

Port Cape, 19 North Water, 63701; (573) 334–0954

New Orleans, 300 Broadway, 63701; (573) 335–8191

NEW MADRID
Rosie's Colonial Restaurant & Tavern, Highway 61, 63869; (573) 748–7665

Tom's Grill, 457 Main, 63869; (573) 748–2049

ROLLA
Alex's Pizza, 122 W 8th Street, 65401; (573) 364–2669;

Johnny's Smokestack BBQ, 201 W. Highway 72, 65401; (573) 364–4838;

Gordoz, 1212 Highway 72, 65401; (573) 364–2780

HELPFUL WEB SITE FOR THE BOOTHEEL REGION

E-mail at www.bootrpc @sheltonbbs.com

Southwest Missouri

Mark Twain National Forest covers thousands of acres of southwest Missouri. Hundreds of miles of hiking and horseback trails free you from even the small, state-maintained highways. If you wander too far off the beaten path here, you will find yourself lost in the woods (and Missouri's bright bluebirds and crimson cardinals will clean up your trail of breadcrumbs).

Many of the lovely, quick-running streams are designated National Scenic Riverways, and the "tri-lakes" area has water, water everywhere. Resort towns are crowded in the summer and deserted in winter. Spring and fall (while school's in session) are just right for exploration. Campgrounds and canoe rentals are everywhere, and there are both gentle rivers for floating and white water for adventure.

If caves are fascinating to you, if you like spectacular rock formations, or if you collect rocks or minerals, southwest Missouri will keep you busy. Truitt's Cave at Lanagan, Ozark Wonder Cave at Noel, the Tiff Mines near Seneca, and the Carthage Marble Quarry at Carthage are a few spots you'll want to check. Fantastic Caverns at 4872 North Farm Road 125, Springfield 65803, has its own Web site, www.fantastic-caverns.com, which you can explore from home before paying the $14 admission fee.

Bed-and-breakfast fans can write Kay Cameron at Ozark Mountain Country Bed and Breakfast Service, Box 295, Branson 65616. You can call her, too, at (417) 334–4720 or (800) 321–8594 for a list of B&Bs in the area. She loves matchmaking and finding just exactly the right place for you.

Queen of the Ozarks

The hub of southwest Missouri is **Springfield** on Interstate 44, the state's third-largest city. Its location on the spacious, grassy uplands of Grand Prairie and Kickapoo Prairie, the rural landscape of the Springfield Plain, is one of the most beautiful in Missouri.

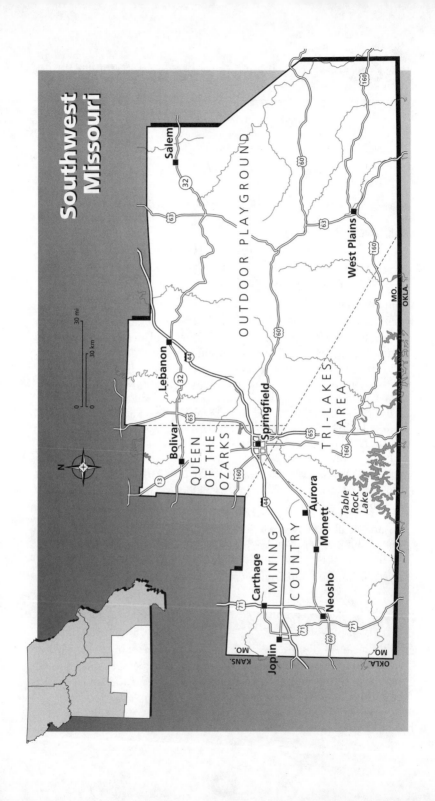

SOUTHWEST MISSOURI

AUTHOR'S TOP TEN FAVORITES IN SOUTHWEST MISSOURI

Bass Pro Shops Outdoor World

Japanese Stroll Garden

Caveman BBQ

Ozark National Scenic Riverways

Jackie's Country Store

Coldwater Ranch

Jolly Mill

Omega Pottery Shop

Candlestick Inn

Cathedral Church of the Prince of Peace

Here's a happy combination of forests, running water, and magnificent rock outcrops dotting a farmland that resembles the bluegrass area of Kentucky. Herefords, Black Angus, Charolais, and Simmental graze in the cleared uplands. Lespedezas, orchard grass, and fescue glaze the gently rolling pastures with green. The city Web site is springfieldmissouri.org.

At the east edge of Springfield's Commercial Street Historic District, a small brick building houses the *Frisco Railroad Museum* at 543 East Commercial Street, Springfield 65803. Its founder, Alan Schmitt, has a passion for the railroad system that employed his grandfather and most of the men in his wife's family. Alan grew up with the sound of the locomotives and clashing of couplers lulling him to sleep at night. By the 1970s, he had acquired enough Frisco memorabilia to build a train station in his basement. His hobby was fast becoming too big for his home, and his dream became a museum. He gathered others into his dream by forming a committee of former Frisco employees, model railroaders, and collectors. Driven by his enthusiasm in 1986, five years after Burlington Northern and Frisco merged, killing the Frisco line—the Frisco was brought back to life. The first museum opened in a detached garage next to Schmitt's house, the committee became a board of directors, and an organization called Frisco Folks with a newsletter fashioned after the old Frisco employee magazine *All Aboard* was launched. Soon photos and memorabilia began to flow in from all over the country. In six months more than 1,000 items had arrived, and the museum had outgrown the garage. Soon the railroad closed its last shop in Springfield and donated all the files filled with information and specifications on everything from locomotive design to depot architecture. Schmitt and the board began the search for the perfect building.

With the help of a successful fund-raiser, the Frisco's old centralized traffic control command center reopened as the Frisco Museum. But there is even more to this happy ending for railroad buffs. A new 9,000-square-foot building adjacent to the current museum has been constructed. It is filled with fifty life-size dioramas fashioned after the Smithsonian's Museum of American History. It includes a mock-up of an old brick engine house. On its mezzanine level, a 2,000-square-foot model railroad layout operates. An observation deck overlooks Burlington Northern's tracks just below. Oh, and the little newsletter is now a slick twenty-page magazine. It reminds you of *The Little Engine That Could*. Museum hours are from 10:00 A.M. until 5:00 P.M., Tuesday through Saturday. Call (417) 866–7573 for more information.

If you are an antiques hunter, Commercial Street Historic District is a good place to wander around after visiting the museum. South Campbell Street and Boonville Avenue shops just north of Park Central Square, and the stores just below the square on South Street, are all filled with antiques shops, too.

The **Victorian Garden Tea Room** is at 1838 South Campbell Avenue, Springfield 65807 (417–832–8588) whenever you are ready to sit a spell and have a spot of tea. Owner Linda Baird suggests you taste the Sampler; it contains some of their best stuff: a quiche and soup du jour with chicken salad, ambrosia, and a muffin all for $7.50. Hours are from 11:00 A.M. until 3:00 P.M. Monday through Saturday.

Okay, **Bass Pro Shops Outdoor World** at 1935 South Campbell, Springfield 65807—a major intersection in Springfield—is rather on the track. It bills itself as the world's greatest sporting-goods store, then lives up to that boast. How many sports shops have a two-story log cabin right in the store? Or a sumptuous restaurant like Hemingway's, serving lobster dinner and a glass of fine wine in front of a room-size aquarium (with white-bellied sharks smiling through the glass and a 15-foot eel hiding in the filter system)?

Across the aerial walkway from Hemingway's is the old-fashioned Tall Tales Barbershop. There is original wildlife art, a museum of the outdoors, trophy animals by the hundreds, and the biggest live bass in captivity. You can buy a hand-knit sweater, get wet beside an indoor waterfall, practice with your new shotgun in the shooting range downstairs, and buy a pair of gym shoes or a fishing rod. Just plan on spending a couple of hours when you go in, and take a camera—there are photo opportunities indicated everywhere; you can pose with 10-foot black bears or tiny fawns. Call (417) 887–7334 or visit the Web site at www.basspro.com.

Springfield is a major city, but, as in most big cities, there are hidden treasures. Gary and Paula Blankenship's **Walnut Street Inn Bed and Breakfast** at 900 East Walnut, Springfield 65806 (417–864–6346 or 800–593–6346) has a quiet ambience to counter the big-city feel. Each of the twelve rooms includes a private bath, some with original porcelain antique fixtures, hardwood floors, and antique furnishings. Ozark specialties such as persimmon muffins and walnut bread are featured along

Civil War Strife

with a full breakfast. The inn now offers something even more tempting: in-room massage from Linda Stowe, an RN, BSN, LMT certified relaxation masseuse! They also have a two-person steam bath! What a fine weekend retreat this has turned out to be. Rates are $89 to $169 per night for two persons.

Missouri gave 109,000 men to the Union cause and about 30,000 men to the Confederacy. Vicious guerrilla action terrorized the state, especially near the Kansas border. The Battle of Wilson's Creek near Springfield was one of the bloodiest of the Civil War.

The inn caters to business travelers and an additional phone line is in each suite for computers. The suites also have VCR and CD players. If you want a more complete view, call up the inn's Web site at www.walnutstreetinn.com or e-mail the Blankenships at stay@walnutstreetinn.com. The fax number is (417) 864–6184.

The circa 1856 *Gray/Campbell Farmstead* in Nathanael Greene Park at 2400 South Scenic, 65807, is the oldest house in the city. Guides present the history of the farmstead and conduct tours of the log kitchen, granary, two-crib barn, and family cemetery. It is open during April and October on Sundays from 1:30 to 4:30 P.M.; May through September, Saturday and Sunday from 1:30 to 4:30 P.M. or by appointment. Call (417) 862–6293.

Also in this park is the *Japanese Stroll Garden,* a seven-and-a-half-acre stroll around three small lakes with extensive landscaping. There is a tea house, a moon bridge, and other features unique to a Japanese garden. It is open from April through October, Friday through Monday, from 11:00 A.M. to 7:30 P.M.

An outstanding nature center, designed by the Missouri Department of Conservation, is at 4600 South Chrisman (417–888–4237). Want to know how to tell a hawk from a heron when they're far overhead? David Catlin, manager of the center, or one of the volunteers will show you silhouettes suspended from the ceiling that correspond to identifying shapes on the floor. Another room invites you into the dark with displays that light up—or sing out—as you press a button or break a light beam. See a barred owl, hear a whippoorwill, watch a flying squirrel—it's all here—three miles of outdoor nature trails take you through Ozark woodlands—eighty acres of hilly wilderness—and a small bog; cross genuine suspension bridges and learn while you take in the fresh air.

Springfield is a mecca for watercolorists. For thirty-five years, the *Springfield Art Museum* (417–866–2716) has been the locus for Watercolor USA, one of the most prestigious shows in the nation. Every June and July the museum displays the best and the brightest; you may browse or buy at 1111 Brookside, Springfield 65807. (You'll know you're

Missouri was the twenty-fourth state to be admitted into the Union, and the second state (after Louisiana) west of the Mississippi. The "Missouri Compromise" of 1820 allowed this state to enter the Union on August 10, 1821, as a slave state, but no other concessions were made in states formed from the Louisiana Territory.

close when you see the large yellow sculpture called "Sun Target"; local kids call it "The French Fries.") The museum owns a fine permanent collection of original works. Visit at any time of the year. Museum hours are Sunday from 1:00 to 5:00 P.M.; Tuesday, Wednesday, and Saturday from 9:00 A.M. to 5:00 P.M.; and Thursday and Friday from 9:00 A.M. until 8:00 P.M.

The **Landers** at 311 East Walnut, Springfield 65806, is the home of the Springfield Little Theatre, which features talented actors from around the Ozarks. Kathleen Turner got her start here. In 1909 theater architect Carl Boller designed the theater to look like a jewel box and a cartouche. It has a high, curved ceiling resembling a crown. The theater has been refurbished to its original splendor. There are the original wooden armrests and floral ironwork on the seats. The ribs going up the cartouche are like a crown inset with jewels, where the lights sparkle surrounded by 14-karat gold leaf and sterling painted moldings. The baroque decor and heavy draperies give it an elegantly royal feel. The $400,000 renovation of this magnificent theater is worth seeing alone, but the fact that it also offers a six-show main season (each show running three weeks), the Springfield Opera, the Springfield Ballet, and the Mid-America Singers makes it all the more worthy of a visit. Call the box office at (417) 869–1334 for current productions.

The **Virginia Rose Bed and Breakfast** at 317 East Glenwood, Springfield 65807, is in a 1906 farmhouse with a red barn in the middle of a subdivision—sort of a country inn in the middle of the city. Owners Virginia and Jackie Buck offer guests a choice of five guest rooms all with private baths. Well, actually there is one suite with a connecting bath that is used for families with children or couples traveling together. A big breakfast awaits guests in the morning—all for $60 to $90. The Bucks' daughter Cindy manages the B&B. Call (417) 883–0693 or (800) 345–1412, or e-mail at vjrosebb@aol.com.

A world traveler once said that no matter where in the world he went, he always sought out an Italian restaurant. "You can count on it to be good," was his philosophy. Even if you are not an "accidental tourist," it is still a pretty sound idea. In Springfield there is **Teatro Ristorante** at 2160 West Chesterfield Boulevard, Springfield 65807. It offers authentic Northern Italian cuisine in an elegant setting that pulls you into the great Italian theater of the seventeenth century.

The sauces, pasta, and bread are made fresh daily. It doesn't get any better than that. There are good Italian wines to complement the meals and what they call "indulgent" desserts available. Dinner is served from 5:00 to 10:00 P.M. Monday through Saturday. Call (417) 887–2626.

You will also want to call Kathy Adamson and visit her shop, **Woodland Carvings** at 115 East Historic Main Street in **Ash Grove** 65604, 15 miles northwest of Springfield, while you are in the area. Kathy carves original and functional art—doors, screen doors, beds, fireplace mantels, lamps as well as gift and art items. Her hours are irregular because of her show schedule, but it is worth the effort to contact her at (417) 672–2791 and see what she does, or visit her new Web site at www.woodlandcarvings.com. Her outdoor and western art has evolved from hand-carved deck plates and yokes that are used as braces on canoes, as well as intricately carved canoe paddles. She carves river gods with long flowing beards (that resemble her husband Sonny) for

Author's Favorite Annual Events in Southwest Missouri

August

Springfield—Ozark Empire Fair, with live music, (417) 833–2660

Cassville—Old Soldiers and Settlers Reunion, (417) 847–2814

Carthage—Marion Days, annual religious events for Vietnamese Catholics, (417) 358–7787

September

Mansfield—Laura Ingalls Wilder Festival, (417) 924–8182

Silver Dollar City—Festival of America; Silver Dollar City and out-of-state artisans demonstrate and sell crafts, (800) 952–6626

Branson—Annual Autumn Daze Craft Festival, with over 150 crafters, (888) 322–2786

December

Silver Dollar City—Old Time Country Christmas, with lights, music, and special Christmas attractions for adults and children, (800) 952–6626

Branson—Candlelight Christmas in historic downtown Branson, where local merchants dress in nineteenth-century clothes and carolers are in the streets; tree and window decorations, (888) 322–2786

Branson—Trail of Lights at Shepherd of the Hills, a spectacular drive-through display of lights, (417) 334–4191

Springfield—Ozark Mountain Christmas/Festival of Lights, (800) 214–3661

the yokes of canoes. Kathy, however, doesn't just carve canoes: She works "relief carving" on flat wood and creates three-dimensional scenes. Her river series showing life along the river look real enough to walk into. She carves mantels, clocks, and doors. She began by carving pieces for her own canoe, and the results were so beautiful that others asked her to personalize their crafts.

Kathy uses teak, butternut, mahogany, cedar, and walnut, relying solely on her own strength and sharp tools to create the delicate layers in the wood. She uses earth-tone artist oils and stains to add a bit of color to the carvings while allowing the grain to show through.

Outdoor Playground

Just outside Springfield on Highway 65 is another kind of mecca—tiny *Galloway* is wall-to-wall antiques. It's as if the town had been invaded by aliens selling oldies; nearly every building and home is now a shop. Find everything from a vine-and-thorn-wrapped birdhouse (to discourage cats, of course) to European china, but don't stop before you get to the flea market a half-mile or so north of the other shops. Here are two floors of great bargain flea market antiques.

Kansas City isn't the only barbecue mecca in the state. *Hogwild BBQ,* 22 East Olive Street, Aurora 65605, is open Tuesday through Saturday from 11:00 A.M. until 9:00 P.M. to feed your barbecue passion. Aurora is 18 miles southwest of Springfield along the Ozark Mountain Scenic parkway en route to Branson. Owners Mark and Sarah Parker serve Memphis-style barbecue and play Memphis-style blues on the jukebox at Hogwild, which has not only a new dining room but also a finished outdoor dining deck. The meat is cooked slowly in specially designed pits. The meat is rubbed with Mark's secret blend of dry spices and cooked over charcoal and hickory. The "slab for two" is a huge portion of pork ribs with a generous helping of baked beans, coleslaw, or potato salad. There are other options—brisket of beef, pork shoulder sandwiches, and hearty salads with chunks of grilled chicken, pork, or beef. Pie a la mode with peaches, apples, or cherries is among the fine dessert choices. Call (417) 678–7443.

West of Springfield at 528 South Highway ZZ in *Republic,* you can tour *General Sweeny's Museum of Civil War History* and see thousands of items from the bloody war fought in Missouri, Arkansas, Kansas, and Indian Territory. In this area families were split between blue and gray uniforms, and bands of killers disguised in those uniforms raided cities and farms. More than fifty exhibits will show you the progression of the war here from the 1850s in "Bleeding Kansas" to the surrender of the last regiments of Confederate Missouri troops at Ft. Blakely, Alabama. There are rare photos, guns, swords, flags, uniforms, and more. The museum is open from March through October, Wednesday through Sunday from 10:00 A.M. until 5:00 P.M.; November through February, Saturday and Sunday, 10:00 A.M. to 5:00 P.M. Call (417) 732–1224.

Head north on Interstate 44 to *Lebanon,* a town loaded with surprises. Flea markets and antiques shops are all over the place, more than twenty-three at last count.

Nancy Ballhagen's Puzzles at 25211 Garden Crest Road, Lebanon 65536, may not be for everyone, but if you are a jigsaw puzzle fan, this is a must. Keith and Nancy Ballhagen have the only jigsaw puzzle shop in the Ozarks, with the world's smallest puzzle (2¼ inches by 2½ inches with 99 pieces) and the world's largest puzzle (3½ feet by 9 feet, 7,500 pieces). There are double-sided puzzles, round puzzles, and puzzles within puzzles, not to mention movie poster puzzles, postage stamp puzzles, and puzzles covering any subject you can think of. The most popular is the Route 66 puzzle (600 pieces). Nancy says they just always liked to do puzzles, especially when the children were young, and it sort of grew into a business. They have more than 1,200 puzzles displayed in their shop and now are carving wooden puzzles. To find puzzle paradise, take exit 135 (Sleeper exit) from Interstate 44 and follow the east outer road ³/₄ mile to the first mailbox on your left—you can see it from the freeway. Hours are 8:00 A.M. to 6:00 P.M. during the summer and 9:00 A.M. to 5:00 P.M. in the winter, or call (417) 286–3837. Visit their Web site at www.missouripuzzle.com.

Well, maybe they don't have the *only* jigsaw puzzle shop in the Ozarks. Their son, Richard Ballhagen, inherited the puzzle mania from Keith and Nancy and opened *Richard's Puzzles,* where he makes only hand-cut wooden puzzles at 26240 Pecos Drive, Lebanon 65538 (the north outer road, Historic Route 66, midway between I–44 exits 130 and 135). Although it's still all in the family, Richard's shop is different. Here he creates heirloom puzzles or puzzles from your favorite photograph or print. Just about anything you can imagine, he can carve. The intricately cut puzzles are made of ¼-inch wood and include a variety of special effects such as silhouette pieces, sculpted borders, or a name cut right into the puzzle for a personal touch. A slide top wooden box for storage is included with every puzzle. He keeps odd hours because he works a full-time job as well, so call ahead for an appointment, (417) 532–5355, or visit his Web site at www.rbpuzzles.com.

Welcome to the world of homemade chocolates! **Karen's Kandies** at 212 West Commercial, Lebanon 65536, has all the candy a true chocoholic could ever dream of. They even have sugar-free chocolates, and all the candy is handmade to order fresh and full of flavor. You can order candy Tuesday through Friday from 9:00 A.M. until 5:00 P.M. by calling (417) 533–3009 or toll free at (877) 545–9344. You can even fax an order to (417) 533–3009 twenty-four hours a day using your credit card. Visit the sweet Web site at www.nvo.com/karens_kandies.

A small side trip north on Interstate 44 will quickly take you to **Waynesville** and the **Big Piney River National Scenic Trail Rides** there. This is a chance to get off the roads and into the woods. Ride well-mannered horses over mountains, through beautiful valleys, along the edge of bluffs, through quiet forests, and along the famous Big Piney River. Half- and full-day trail rides are available seasonally (May through October). Evening entertainment includes horse shows, movies, square dancing, family games, and good, wholesome outdoor recreational activities. Campsites have a dining hall where Betty Laughlin does the cooking, modern rest rooms, showers, and electricity. Brothers Jimmy, Jay, Jeff, and Joey are all partners in the operation. Sunday church services are held in a dining hall and on the trail. Arrangements must be made in advance, so call (573) 774–6879.

If that is too primitive for you, head for downtown Waynesville, where there is a bed and breakfast. Find **The Home Place** at 302 South Benton Street, Waynesville 65583; (573) 774–6637. There are three bedchambers filled with antiques, and hostess Jean Hiatt will fix you breakfast in the morning. There's no place like "home place." Rooms are $55 to $65.

The **Benton Street Cafe,** at 103 North Benton Street, Waynesville 65583, would be a good choice for lunch. Owner Cheryl Jackson is justifiably proud of this place. Everything is made from scratch, and the menu changes every day. The house is circa 1800s and is one of only two original buildings left on the courthouse square. Its wooden floors and staircase give it a farmhouse feel. One wall has been stripped down to show the hand-hewn logs inside the walls (Cheryl put Plexiglas over that segment).

The dishes rely heavily on fresh vegetables. Cheryl describes the food as good "healthy home cooking." There is a fresh homemade soup every day that ranges from exotic Italian to just plain chicken noodle.

And, of course, the bread is freshly baked, too. The menu runs the gamut from seafood fettuccini to fried chicken (the cabbage rolls are good), and the desserts are scrumptious—fresh apple cake and cream pies). Hours are from 11:00 A.M. to 3:00 P.M. Monday through Saturday. Call (573) 774–6268.

Across the square is the **Old Stagecoach Inn Museum,** which has been totally renovated and is exactly as it was when the stage stopped here at the courthouse. It is listed on the National Register of Historic Places and is open April through September on Saturday from 10:00 A.M. to 4:00 P.M. Guided tours are available.

Caveman BBQ might be Missouri's most unusual place to eat. Park in the gravel lot at 26880 Rochester Road (65556) just a few miles from Richland, then board the "Batmobile" to where an elevator takes you up to the restaurant, located inside a cave. It took five years of incredible labor and five years of jackhammer and shovel to remove 160 tons of rock to make

Eminence is the home of astronaut Tom Akers and his family. Akers, who has had four space flights to date, holds the record for the number of hours of EVAs (extravehicular activities, or space walks), most of that time accrued while helping to repair the Hubble Space Telescope.

Col. Akers has experienced more than 800 hours of space flight, bringing his total EVA time to 29 hours and 40 minutes. He was a member of the first three-person EVA and the longest EVA—8½ hours—in history.

enough room to seat 200 people in this former resort dance hall. Renovators tried not to change the cave's appearance too much and were quite successful. A dehumidifier keeps the restaurant dry, and small waterfalls into a goldfish pond allow natural water to drip from the ceiling. The fare is BBQ. Specialties include slabs of smoked ribs and other meats. The restaurant is a destination for river traffic, too. You can float to the bottom and walk up the bank. The dress code is casual. They also operate Ozark Springs Resort, with fourteen log cabins that were built in 1919. They are the only canoe outfitters on about 50 miles of the river. To find it, go 6 miles east of the I–44/Highway 7 junction. Take exit 150 off of I–44, make a turn to the right onto W, and take W until the pavement ends. Turn left and go 1 mile down a gravel road to the resort. Shuttles to the restaurant leave every fifteen minutes. Call (573) 765–4554 for more information.

Fort Leonard Wood is the home of the U.S. Army Corps of Engineers. It is also the home of the Army Engineering Center and the **U.S. Army Engineer Museum.** The Fort covers about 63,000 acres in the Ozarks about 130 miles southwest of St. Louis on I–44 near Waynesville. A recipe for creamed chipped beef on toast, called S.O.S. by the soldiers who had to eat it, is tacked on the wall of a restored mess hall, one of several "temporary" wooden buildings built during World War II. A field kitchen lists the fort's daily food requirements in 1943. These included 4,750 pounds of bacon, 47 gallons of vinegar, and 105 gallons of syrup.

The oldest treasure is a signet ring that belonged to Lysimachus, an engineer general who served Alexander the Great in about 330 B.C. The museum walks people through a chronological history of the corps. There are several specialized galleries. Many of the temporary mobilization buildings, two-story wooden barracks familiar to soldiers at every post in the world and built to last about ten years, have been restored to create typical company areas. A supply room with a wood-burning stove, racks for M1 rifles and 45-caliber pistols, and entrenching tools would bring a tear to a supply sergeant's eye.

The history of the Corps, however, dates back to the Revolutionary War. There's a 1741 muzzle-loading cannon that the French lent to the Continental Army, and a shovel and ax dating from the 1781 battle of Yorktown, the first engineering victory of army engineers who built fortifications and trenches into British positions. The oldest unit in the U.S. Army is the 101st Engineer Battalion of the Massachusetts National Guard, established in 1636.

Another display demonstrates low tide at Omaha Beach during the D-Day invasion of June 6, 1944, with an engineer disposing of German mines that would have been a danger to Allied ships.

Children can take the wheel of a restored pilothouse, U.S. Snag Boat No. 13, which kept the Mississippi River clear for more than 50 years. Other hands-on activities include a land-mine detector. Gun enthusiasts will enjoy the nineteenth-century Gatling Gun, an 1819 Flintlock rifle, an 1816 Springfield 69-caliber musket, and many small arms from more recent wars.

The museum is at the corner of Nebraska and South Dakota Avenues. Hours are 10:00 A.M. to 4:00 P.M. Monday through Saturday. Admission is free but donations are accepted. Call (314) 596–0169 for more information.

Wander down Highway VV from Licking and enjoy the rugged countryside, which contains some of the largest springs in the world. The Jacks Fork River, Alley Spring with its restored *Old Red Mill,* and the Current River near *Eminence* provide year-round canoeing. (The spring water is a consistent 58° F degrees year-round.)

Highway 19 is a rustic stretch of the Ozark Plateau. The hills are steep and the road curvy, so your only choice is a slow drive across narrow bridges over gleaming waterways. You can't pass anyone on Highway 19, so you may as well relax and enjoy the view. It is a scenic highway and has its share of people there just to see the towering pines that create a lush green canopy that shades the roadway. The highway snakes from near Hannibal to the Arkansas state line. You can drive from Hermann to Eminence while stopping at little shops for ice cream, sandwiches, and shopping. The views are enchanting, so take your time and slowpoke along.

Alley Spring Mill sits along the crystal clear Jacks Fork River. It is open every day from Memorial Day through Labor Day from 9:00 A.M. until 4:00 P.M. Rangers are on hand to explain how the mill worked and the role it played in developing a community of Ozark settlers. The area still calls people together as it has for more than 10,000 years. Native Americans gathered here to hunt the abundant game and fish the rich waters. The first mill was built in 1868. A newer one replaced it in 1894. The latter was cutting edge in its technology, featuring a turbine rather than a water wheel, and rollers to replace the grist stones. Soon a blacksmith opened a shop and people began to gather here and camp with entire families while the grain was ground. Now it is a popular spot for family reunions, campouts, and fishing trips. Camping and canoe rentals are available at the mill, which is located 6 miles west of Eminence on State Route 106. For more details call (314) 323–4236.

Missouri's southwestern rivers—quick-running, spring-fed, and bone-chillingly cold—are so beautiful they bring a lump to your throat. In fact, the Current, the Eleven Point, and the Jacks Fork have been designated *Ozark National Scenic Riverways*.

Generations of canoeists and trout fishermen know these secluded waters. You can spend the day without seeing another soul, then camp on a quiet sandbar at day's end and listen to the chuck-will's-widows and owls call while your fire lights the riffles with bronze. Pick fresh watercress from these icy waters to garnish the trout that sizzles in lemon butter on your grill, and know that life gets no better than this. There are plenty of rental outfits; pick up brochures anywhere.

Springs gush from beneath solid rock, slowly carving themselves a cave. Early residents built mills here to produce flour, cornmeal, and sawn lumber. There's as much natural history as history along these bright rivers.

The crystal-clear waters of the spring-fed Current River drift past rocky bluffs and shorelines thick with wildflowers. Schools of darters flash by in the cold water (water temperatures range from 53° to 57° F degrees year-round). This gentle wilderness is a favorite canoeing and tubing area for Midwesterners. Even beginners can navigate the waters without getting too wet except by choice. Paddle hard around the occasional rootwad, an area of ripped-up tree roots that may create some white water—or simply get out and push the canoe past it. Most stretches of the river are rated Class I, as easy as it gets. The gravel bars are fine places to pull out and have lunch or even to camp for the night. Only owls and the leaf rustle of small creatures break the silence. The tranquil moss-covered hillsides are a peaceful escape from the busy world back home. At some points along the river, the water turns a rich blue-green as it gets wider and deeper, sometimes as deep as 25 feet.

The half-day trip from Weymeyer put-in to Van Buren is an easy and beautiful route. A few miles before the Van Buren Bridge is Watercress Park, the site of a single Civil War battle—with trenches and grave sites—where the Union Army held the Confederates at bay across the river one cold night. At the pull-out spot just past the Van Buren Bridge, you can leave your canoe on the beach and let the outfitters know you are back.

Alley Spring Mill is called the most picturesque spot in the state. Some eighty million gallons of water a day flow through here, and the Red Mill has been restored to working order.

Big Spring is the largest concentration of springs in the world, which is a mystery to hydrologists who do not understand the large volume of water. Beautiful rivers gush right out of the ground from the base of spectacular rock bluffs and create the most consistent, spring-fed, crystal-clear rivers in the country. Round Spring Cave is just off Highway 19.

If you have horses, **Cross Country Trail Rides** on Highway 19 East, Eminence 65466, has a week planned for you. You can take the whole family on a cross-country trail ride from April through December. Jim and Jane Smith have spent thirty-five years perfecting the week's adventure. You will camp for the week on Jacks Fork River. The ride leaves and returns to the base camp every night, where eighteen meals are served and entertainment is royal. Well-known country music performers entertain at a dance every night but Sunday. There are horse shows, team roping events, and other sports to show off your steed. Jane says they fill up months in advance; to ensure a spot for you and your steed ($10 per night), write P.O. Box 15, Eminence 65466, or call (573) 226–3492. This is a "B.Y.O.H." affair; no rental horses are available.

If you don't have your own horse, head for **Coldwater Ranch** on Highway 19 north of Eminence and turn right on Road 208. Jim and Kathy

Thomas have horses at their place and will arrange anything from an hour ride to a six-day pack trip. For the overnight trips, tents, sleeping bags, food, and beverages are provided, and your steed has a saddlebag for your personal stuff. Quarter horses and a few gaited horses range from mounts for the novice to those for the experienced riders. The ranch accepts all ages; they have had four-year-olds and eighty-year-olds. Horses are $20 per hour; a 9:00 A.M. to 5:00 P.M. all-day trip is $100. Overnight trips range from $125 to $200 a night and include three meals and about ten hours of riding. Recent expansion on the ranch includes cabins (starting at $75 per couple; $10 per additional person) and RV/camping sites ($15 per night). You can also bring your own horse and rent a stall for $15 a night. Call (573) 226–3723 for more information.

A winding drive along Highway 160 takes you to the beautiful Eleven Point River, with its many natural springs and lovely spots for picnics. You will be surprised at the excellent roads through these wooded hills. The Between the Rivers section of the Ozark Hiking Trail covers about 30 miles. The northern entry point to this section is on Highway 60, approximately 3½ miles west of Van Buren. Trailhead parking is provided for users at Highway 60 and at Sinking Creek Lookout Tower, about a mile west of Highway J.

The trail winds south for the first 13 miles across small tributaries that feed the Current River. Creeks with names such as Wildhorse Hollow, Devil's Run, and Big Barren flow through the area. Designed for both hikers and horses, the trail crosses a ridge that divides the Current River from the Eleven Point River along Gold Mine Hollow. The trail offers panoramic mountain views and deeply wooded areas to filter the summer sun. Deer gaze from the shadows, too. If you are a hiking enthusiast, this area is for you. Pick up a book with a listing of all the hiking trails on federal property, complete with maps, at the Federal Forest Service Office in Winona, grab your backpack, and head out.

Wooded Ozark roads stretch out before you now, with oak trees shouldering evergreens; the Doniphan Lookout Tower watches the national forest for fires here. Tune your AM radio to 1610 for Ozark Riverway information if you are headed for canoeing or camping at one of the many parks or rivers nearby.

No horses, no trails, you just want a bed-and-breakfast. The **Old Blue House,** 301 South Main Street, Eminence 65466, is just the place. Wanda Pummill owns this home built in the 1860s. It has been a pharmacy, beauty shop, grocery store, and children's clothing store. It has seen days as a sporting-goods shop and a gift shop. It was even the old telephone office for a while. You know that because the bedroom at the top of the narrow stairs has a glass door with a hand-painted sign that still reads TELEPHONE OFFICE. The rooms are filled with antiques and the comfortable kitchen has an old harvest cooktable. Large magnolia and maple trees surround the porches on both sides of the house, and the flower garden is filled with peonies, roses, irises, and lilacs. There are four bedrooms, three with private baths, and there's cable television in each room. Wanda keeps baked goodies for nibbling. Rooms range from $60 to $85. Call (573) 226–3498 or (800) 474–9695, or tour the home on the Web site at www.missouri2000.net/oldbluehouse/. E-mail at oldbluehouseb-b@webtv.net.

If you have a carload of children and want a resort, the *River's Edge Resort* is also near Eminence and offers not only rooms and cabins but also hot tubs, inner tubes, firewood, and lodging on the Ozark National Scenic Riverways Jacks Fork and Current Rivers. Rooms overlooking the river are from $39 (weekdays in winter) to $99 (weekends in summer). New are camper's cabins, priced at $40 per night weekdays in spring and fall, and $50 on summer weekends. You can visit the Web site at www.rivers-edge.com or call (573) 226–3233.

Because of the number of campers who take this route to the wilderness, the little town of *Van Buren* on Highway 60 is the home of several neat shops. *Jackie's Country Store,* 208 Ash Street, Van Buren 63965, is owned by Jackie Wilson, who has lived in Van Buren for more than twenty-five years. "It's a whole different lifestyle," she says of the tiny town. She is from the Kansas City area; now she lives in a house overlooking a river and says she wouldn't live anywhere else. She offers arrangements of dried or fresh flowers and gifts at this unique store in a beautiful old house.

The sign on the shop door says OPEN WHEN I GET HERE, CLOSED WHEN I GET TIRED, and that says something about the lifestyle here. The hours translate to around 9:00 A.M. to 5:00 P.M. six days a week; (573) 323–8560.

The *Hidden Log Cabin Museum* is the darling of Ozark historian Wanda Newton. For many years she knew that a log cabin lay at the heart of the neat, ordinary, frame house next door. She waited for the house to go on the market and spent the time buying antiques and refurbishing them. She also studied the history of the Ozarks and dreamed. Then in 1990, it happened. The old Bowen place was for sale, and she bought it and began removing decades of "improvements" from its interior.

A one-of-a-kind "yawning" fireplace of hand-cut sandstone with a huge arch rock was professionally rebuilt and the hearth made ready for cooking with a collection of early ironware. Layers of sheetrock, insulation, and ceiling tiles were removed to expose the original construction. The furniture and household goods from the 1800s were placed in the painstakingly restored home. By the spring of 1993, her work was complete. In addition to the original log cabin room, the museum also has a dining room, bedroom, kitchen, and summer kitchen, each room filled with artifacts and furnishings. But most important is the woman who has lovingly created its homelike atmosphere. Wanda knows every jewel in this jewel box. Many of the pieces of furniture are from families who lived here. The treasures span two centuries, from tools of the early 1800s, pre–Civil War books and toys, and willow furniture made by gypsies to a 1930s Zenith radio from the Depression years. Many of the items are dated—a rope bed is from 1838, and an immigrant trunk dates from 1869. Located in downtown Van Buren, the museum is a block west of the courthouse on the south side of the Float Stream Cafe at the corner of John and Ash, Van Buren 63965. Hours are Monday through Saturday 9:00 A.M. to 5:00 P.M. and Sunday from 1:00 to 5:00 P.M. April through November; (573) 323–4563. Adults $2.00, children $1.00.

The **Float Stream Cafe** is well worth a visit. Good food is served here. There is a special every day, seven days a week. Friday is fried catfish day and Sunday has chicken and dumplings. The cafe is open from 5:30 A.M. until 9:00 P.M. Call (573) 323–9606.

The main reason for being in the area is floating the Current River. There are plenty of places to rent canoes, tubes, and rafts, but one of the nicest is the **Rosecliff on the River Lodge** at 1 Big Springs Road, Van Buren 63965, at the Van Buren Bridge. You can spend a full day on the river with the 22-mile Log Yard trip, which leaves at 7:00 A.M. Or you can take a two-day camping trip to Eminence on the Jacks Fork River. There are short 3-mile trips or longer half-day floats. Then there is the fun of tubing along Chilton Creek. But whatever you do, slather a lot of sunscreen on your body because you can get a world-class sunburn in an aluminum canoe on the brilliant water of the Current. The voice of experience is telling you this.

Rosecliff Lodge has a good restaurant—The Blue Heron—and the Rosebud Room. For information about these rooms, which all have a river view, call (573) 323-8156 or e-mail at syl@semo.net. Rooms range from $50 to $150.

Big Spring Lodge (573–323–4332) is about 4 miles from Van Buren; it is a National Park Service site on the Ozark National Scenic Riverways.

Rustic log cabins with fireplaces that reflect a more relaxed pace and a dining lodge/craft shop were built by the Civilian Conservation Corps (the CCC, otherwise known as "Roosevelt's Tree Army") in the thirties. The lodge is on the National Register, and rightly so; log, timber, rocks, and cut stone materials and unique spatial arrangements make this an excellent example of the projects that brought work to so many in Depression-era America. Dining room hours vary with the season. For more information write Big Spring Lodge, P.O. Box 602, Van Buren 63965.

Big Spring State Park is nearby, as are the Mark Twain National Forest and the Ozark National Riverways Tourist Information Station. Call (573) 323–4236 or write in advance for an accurate list of trails and starting points (P.O. Box 490, Van Buren 63965). Also, any Missouri tourism office can provide a list of hiking trails.

Big Spring is the largest single spring in the world, pouring out 277 million gallons of crystal-clear water each day—a breathtaking natural wonder you will want to photograph or draw.

The beginnings of **Grand Gulf State Park** (Missouri's answer to the Grand Canyon) in Thayer go back 450 million years to a time when sediment was deposited by ancient seas, forming dolomitic rock. As the area uplifted and the sea receded, water percolated down through cracks in the rock and began to dissolve passageways underneath. Streams cut their own beds on the surface of the soft rock. As air-filled caves formed and cave roofs collapsed, streams were diverted underground. The collapse of the Grand Gulf occurred within the past 10,000 years—fairly recent by a geologist's reckoning.

Today the gulf is ¾ mile wide with side walls 120 feet high. Part of the cave roof that did not collapse formed a natural bridge 75 feet high that spans 200 feet, one of the largest in the state. The park contains handicapped accessible overlooks with spectacular views of the chasm, a ¼-mile loop trail around the gulf, and a primitive trail across the rock bridge (don't look down!). Call (573) 548–2525 for details.

West Plains is a starting point for canoeing on the North Fork River. Or you can strike off on foot into the wilderness of the Mark Twain National Forest.

Travel westbound from West Plains on Highway 160 to Highway 181 north to the little town of **Zanoni** if you want total peace, quiet, and privacy with nothing to disturb your sleep but the morning song of bluebirds and wrens.

Dawt Mill was established in 1897, and its water-powered buhr stone mill is still grinding grain. A hundred years ago teams of mules and horses would pull wagons filled with corn and wheat to the mill, and farmers would wait for their turn at the water-powered buhr stone mill. The cotton gin would be pumping out cleaned cotton ready to be sold or spun. While waiting for their grinding, the families would shop at the general store or use the blacksmith's skills repairing farm implements and shoeing animals. People gathered on the porch of the mill to play music in the evening and would fall asleep under their wagons while the mill ground into the wee hours of the morning.

The *Zanoni Mill Inn Bed and Breakfast,* on Highway 181, Zanoni 65784, is a modern home set beside the remnants of an Ozark pioneer village in a secluded valley with a private lake. It has four large bedrooms, two with connecting baths and two with hall baths. All rooms have queen-size beds, but that is only the beginning of the amenities offered here. How about an 18 x 36-foot indoor pool and a hot tub, where you can soak and watch the big-screen TV? There is Ping-Pong and pool in the game room. Most interesting is the old mill itself, powered since the Civil War by the spring still gushing out of the hillside, restored and now owned by the great-grandchildren of the original 1870 settlers, and maintained by the grandson of the man who built the present mill in 1905 (the first two burned) to grind corn and wheat. Dave and Mary Morrison turn out a big country breakfast every day, because the home is headquarters of a 1,750-acre working ranch, and that requires a large breakfast, served by the pool if you like. Call (417) 679–4050 or (877) 679–4050 toll free. You can e-mail at zanonibb@webound.com or visit the Web site at bbim.org/zanoni. Rooms are $65 to $70 per night, plus tax.

Deep in the Ozark hills near *Ava* a bell chimes in the early morning quiet. Trappist monks in white robes and cowls move quietly into the darkness of the chapel for morning prayer and meditation. A day begins at *Assumption Abbey,* one of only eighteen monasteries of the Trappist order in the country. The abbey is surrounded by 3,400 wooded acres. The monks seldom leave the abbey and by their simple lives of prayer, labor, study, and solitude seek a deeper personal relationship with God. So why mention a monastery in a travel guide, you might ask? Well, although man cannot live by bread alone, a visit to the Assumption Abbey bakery is in order. To be self-supporting as monasteries must, the monks discovered a market for fruitcakes. Now they produce more than 18,000 fruitcakes annually. The old English recipe is mixed in the tiny kitchen of the abbey. Each cake weighs two pounds and is generously filled with raisins, cherries, and pineapple marinated in Burgundy. Each one is bathed with an ounce of dark rum for moistness and flavor. They bear no resemblance to the ready-made kind you get from your aunt at Christmas. They are sold by direct mail to customers all over the United States and are carried at prestigious stores such as Williams-Sonoma and Neiman-Marcus.

The abbey extends hospitality to men and women of all faiths. If you need a restful weekend, or counseling from the monks, you are welcome. Guests get home-cooked meals served family-style by the brothers. There is no charge for meals or accommodations due to the monks' vows to remain poor and serve others. Advance reservations for overnight stays are requested and donations help with the expenses. The simple quarters contain wash basins, twin beds, shared bath/shower, and a small homemade desk. Monks bring fresh soap and towels. It is a simple life. If you would like to spend a few days at this retreat, call (417) 683–2258 or write Rte. 5 Box 1056, Ava 65608.

Guest ranches are fun whether you are with a vanload of children or alone. If the abbey is too quiet for your tastes and you still want to get some brain-clearing time, mosey over to the **Bucks and Spurs Scenic River Guest Ranch,** also in Ava. You can get some hands-on time on this thousand-acre horse-and-cattle ranch by helping Cecil and Sonya Huff with the chores. Or you can float down Big Beaver Creek in an inner tube and study the clouds and treetops. The choice is yours. The new lodge can be viewed on the Web at www.bucksandspurs.com. Four guest rooms sharing two baths are paneled in weathered barn wood. The dining room has a long table for chow time or the Huffs will set up a picnic site when you ride the trails. Horses, tack, guides, and canoes are furnished. There's fishing and swimming or a turbulent game of horseshoes for excitement. Weekend packages are $395 for adults, $380 for children under twelve (free for kids under three). Family discounts are available. Call (417) 683–2381.

North on Highway 5 is tiny **Mansfield,** home of the **Laura Ingalls Wilder–Rose Wilder Lane Museum and Home** (417–924–3626). Laura's home is just as she left it and there is a museum that contains four handwritten manuscripts. Author of the now famous (courtesy of television) *Little House on the Prairie,* among other books, Laura was encouraged to write by her daughter, Rose Wilder Lane, a well-known author in her own right from the early 1900s. They are buried in the Mansfield cemetery.

Friendship House at 210 West Commercial, Mansfield 65704 (417–924–8511), was built in 1939 as a boardinghouse, and innkeepers Charlie and Sharon Davis try to hold onto that '30s feeling—Sharon cooks in iron skillets on a 1948 Chambers gas stove and plays music from that era

Laura Ingalls Wilder–Rose Wilder Lane Museum and Home

in the evening. But it's not just sleeping rooms with Murphy beds and lace curtains anymore. There's a swimming pool outside this sixteen-room rock house, and the furniture ranges from Victorian to the 1940s. A wake-up coffee-and-juice tray is delivered to your door every morning. A full country breakfast follows in the dining room, and its most famous feature is side pork—since it is mentioned often in Wilder's books—accompanying fresh fruit, scrambled eggs, and jams made from fruit grown and gathered by Sharon. This is your chance to try not only side pork, but also wild-plum, crab-apple, and elderberry jam. Pets are welcome here and there are a couple of resident dogs and cats. Rooms or efficiency apartments are from $75 to $95 with breakfast. For dinner Sharon sends guests to nearby **Mountain Grove** for "great steaks" at the unusual **Club 60** on Old Highway 60. The license plate fence in front of this old 1946 tavern will catch your eye. Although drinks are served and there is a pool table, this is very much a family place.

Go west on Highway 60 to swing back into Springfield.

Mining Country

Head west on Interstate 44 to Halltown; then slip onto Highway 96 West for **Carthage,** where the majestic 1895 Jasper County Court House stands proudly on the square, turreted like a medieval castle. Settled in the 1840s, Carthage was burned to the ground in guerrilla raids during the Civil War. The Battle of Carthage was fought July 5, 1861—sixteen days before the battle of Manassas in Virginia—making it the first land battle of the Civil War. More than 8,000 men

How to Make a Spy

In her teens Myra Belle Shirley watched her town leveled by war. The Battle of Carthage was the first major Civil War battle, fought July 5, 1861. She became the infamous Confederate spy and outlaw, Belle Starr.

fought here, 1,000 of them German-American Union troops from St. Louis led by Colonel Franz Siegel. The rest of the soldiers were Southern sympathizers led by Missouri governor Clayburn Jackson. Destruction of the town was total. The 1849 home named Kendrick Place, built by slaves, was one of the few homes left standing after the war. In the late nineteenth century, all new homes were built; these are an abundance of Victorian homes and more than one hundred of them have been restored. This interesting piece of history can be researched more thoroughly at the **Civil War Museum** at 205 Grant Street, Carthage 64836 (417–237–7060) from 10:00 A.M. until 5:00 P.M., and at the **Victorian Era Powers Museum** at 1617 West Oak Street, Carthage 64836 (417–358–2667). The curator at the Powers Museum is Michele Hansford, and she is very knowledgeable about both the Victorian era in Carthage and the Civil War battles fought near here. Lead and zinc mines were developed after the war, and wealthy owners built magnificent homes away from the mining camps. Marble quarries provided Carthage gray marble for many large state and federal buildings. The fine old homes found here bespeak prosperity. It's still a beautiful city—the courthouse, high school, and many of the churches and homes are built of the stone quarried here. (The stone is not technically marble, but a limestone that takes a high polish.) Both the courthouse and high school contain murals by Lowell Davis, one of America's best-known nature artists and a native of Carthage.

Carthage has more than its share of well-known native sons and is becoming a center for artists in the area. About eighteen resident artists call it home. Internationally known zoologist and naturalist Marlin Perkins (remember *Wild Kingdom?*) was born here; you'll find a bronze sculpture of Perkins by artists Bob Tommey and Bill Snow in Central Park on Garrison Avenue.

Follow the historic drive markers for a tour of the magnificent old mansions that have been kept so beautifully over the years. Innkeepers Bonnie and Michael Melvin welcome you to their home, the imposing circa 1901 **Leggett House,** at 1106 Grand, Carthage 64836 (417–358–0683). They saw the house when they were visiting from St. Louis and mentioned to the owners that if the home were ever for sale they would be interested in it. In 1999 they received a phone call and the rest is history. Now this magnificent home is in its glory again with stained glass, a mosaic-tiled solarium with a marble fountain, finely crafted woodwork and—an elevator. Rates are $85 a night, which includes a full breakfast prepared by both Bonnie and Michael and served in the formal dining room.

The Melvins send guests to The Ranch House restaurant, which has something for just about any size appetitie, including big steaks; 2937 South Grand, Carthage 65836; (417) 359–5200.

Jim and Jan O'Haro invite guests to join them at the **White Rose,** 13001 Journey Road, Carthage 64836. The house was built in 1900 of Carthage marble and was originally a thousand-acre dairy farm. The front walk is 300 feet of Carthage marble leading to this beautiful three-story home. Rose, herb, cut-flower, and vegetable gardens lead you to the old carriage house. The White Rose is not an inn in the commercial sense, but a bed-and-breakfast of the European type. It is a private home open for guests to enjoy an atmosphere of warmth and comfort. As you might have guessed from the name, the family is proud of its Irish heritage. Not only do guests receive a full Irish breakfast, but tea is served at four o'clock, and guests are given a complimentary beverage in the evening. Full-course dinners are also included in "Bed and Banquet" reservations, and ingredients used include both imported and those grown in the vegetable garden out back. The O'Haros describe it thus: "The idea is seductive and yet so simple. Who hasn't wished after a truly superb dinner . . . the kind that lingers in the memory . . . that you could just go upstairs and sink into bed instead of getting in a car and driving somewhere else? To keep the magic that surrounds the very best meals alive, you need to be able to linger, maybe to take your coffee in another room in front of a log fire, knowing that your bed is only a few steps away. . . ." Call (417) 359–9253 or e-mail joharo@4state.com for reservations. Rooms are $76–$105. Visit the White Rose Web site at www.whiterosebed-breakfast.com.

Michael and Jeanne Goolsby have opened their 1893 Queen Anne Victorian to guests. The **Grand Avenue Bed & Breakfast** at 1615 Grand Avenue, Carthage 64836, has four original stained-glass windows. All guest rooms have private baths, cable TV, telephones, and coffee service. Two have computer hookups. The first-floor room has a king-size bed and Jacuzzi for $89. On the second floor, there's the new Hawthorne Room ($99) with a two-person jacuzzi, the Alcott Room ($79), and the Mark Twain Room ($84), which can also be made into a suite (priced

Trivia

The town of Noel gets popular every year at Christmas—at least its post office gets popular—as people send letters and cards here for postmarks. It's actually pronounced Nole. South of Noel is Bluff Dwellers Cave, a well-known tourist attraction that was 250 million years, give or take a million, in the making. It has drawn cave seekers since 1927.

from $99). The Goolsbys serve a full country breakfast (the specialty is orange nutmeg French toast) with sausage or bacon. You can call toll free (888) 380–6786, or (417) 358–7265. E-mail at reservation@grand-avenue. com, or check their Web site at www.grand-avenue. com for a view of this stately home.

Alba is a tiny hamlet where you might expect to find a small diner—if you were lucky. It's a town with no stoplights and fewer than 500 residents. Not a likely place for an authentic French restaurant. Chef Max Givone, a native of Marseille, France, moved to Alba from San Francisco to be closer to his wife Linda's elderly parents. He worked as a chef at the Lodge of the Four Seasons at Lake of the Ozarks, but what he really wanted to do was open his own place. The *Old Miner's Inn* began serving French cuisine a bit at a time in an area where fried chicken and pork chops—not escargot and sweetbreads—are expected on the menu. Local people lined up around the block the first night it opened almost twenty years ago and kept coming back as Givone slowly introduced them to French cooking. He moved from simple chicken entrees like lemon chicken and Chicken Provençal to Medaillon du Veau with demiglace sauce of mushrooms and cognac. Desserts then appeared on the menu: strawberry flambé and three-layer chocolate cake. A wine list offers an assortment of French and California vintages. Givone drives more than 100 miles to Kansas City to buy supplies because he won't compromise on authenticity, and word of mouth regularly draws customers from four states as well as Europe and the rest of the country. To find Alba, exit Highway 71 or Highway 96 near Carthage and follow farm roads for several miles. The inn is open Tuesday through Saturday for dinner only and reservations are required. Phone (417) 525–4332. Entrees run from $16 to $23.

Joplin is the end of the Missouri portion of old Route 66 and has been a stopping point on cross-country travel for many decades—in fact, since 1889, when Joplin City was named for the Rev. Harris G. Joplin, a Tennesseean settler. The abandoned tailing piles and mine shafts scattered about the town and the elegant homes just west of the downtown area are reminders of the mining era of Joplin. Mineral collectors are drawn to the abandoned mine dumps and chert piles and to the Tri-State Mineral Museum, one of the best museums of its kind in the state.

The Joplin Historical Society preserves much of the city's history at the *Dorothea B. Hoover Historical Museum,* located in Schifferdecker Park at the intersection of Seventh Street and Schifferdecker Park, Joplin 64853 (and adjacent to the Tri-State Mineral Museum). Hours are Tuesday through Saturday from 9:00 A.M. to 4:00 P.M. (Sunday from 1:00 P.M.). Call for holiday hours, (417) 623–1180 or (417) 623–2341. To learn more about the city of Joplin, contact its Web site at www.joplinmo.org.

Outside Joplin go east on County Highway V to Diamond. From Diamond drive 2 miles on V and then south about a mile to find the **George Washington Carver National Monument,** which commemorates a man who was more than an educator, botanist, agronomist, and "cookstove chemist." He was the man who wanted "to be of the greatest good to the greatest number of people," a man who refused to accept boundaries, who drew from science, art, and religion to become a teacher and director of a department at Tuskegee Institute in Alabama. He taught botany and agriculture to the children of ex-slaves and tried to devise farming methods to improve the land exhausted by cotton. Known as the "Peanut Man," Carver led poor, one-horse farmers to grow protein-rich and soil-regenerating soybeans and peanuts. The Carver Nature Trail leads from the birthplace site through two springs and ends at the Carver family cemetery.

Joplin is also the home of the **Spiva Center for the Arts** at 222 West Third (corner of Third and Wall) Joplin 64801. Call (417) 623–0183 or fax (417) 623–3805, or e-mail at artspiva@clandjop. com. You can visit their Web site and see the works of the artist of the month at www. clandjop.com/~artspiva/.

Just down Highway 71 is the **Real Hatfield Smokehouse,** 7329 Gateway Drive, Neosho 64850 (417–624–3765). Owner Nick Neece has a sparkle in his blue eyes as he talks about his "home-grown" hogs. "We smoke anything you can get from a hog," he says. Bacon, hams—you name it, he smokes it. He will mail hams anywhere in the United States and even has a regular customer in London. The small smokehouse uses a special sugar cure and hickory logs to give meats a golden-brown finish and good flavor without as much salt as other smokehouses. Hours are 7:30 A.M. to 6:00 P.M. Monday through Saturday. The smokehouse is closed on Sunday.

If you love ghost-storied and mysterious sights, visit "Spooksville," 11 miles southwest of Joplin. It is here that an eerie light has been appearing in the middle of a lonely road most nights since 1886. This almost

Trivia

Two major Civil War battles were fought in Newtonia—with total forces numbering in the thousands. The 1862 battle was one of very few encounters in which Native Americans fought on both sides. Southern forces had Choctaw, Cherokee, and Chickasaw soldiers, while other Cherokees fought with the Union forces. This was the first battle of Colonel J. O. (Jo) Shelby's famous Iron Brigade. The 1864 battle, also involving Shelby, was the last battle in the Civil War fought west of the Mississippi. A Civil War cemetery here houses the remains of thirteen soldiers, including the famous (or infamous to the Confederates) Robert Christian. Many slaves and their descendants are also buried here. The earliest stone is 1858.

supernatural spook light created panic in the small village of Hornet and is often referred to as the Hornet Ghost Light. Early settlers actually left the area in terror because of the giant ball of light bouncing over the hills and across the fields. Today the light seems to concentrate on one gravel road known as Devil's Promenade or Spook Light Road. The light has even been rumored to come right up to your car and land on the hood, then bounce off or go out and appear later behind you. It disappears whenever approached. If you have the nerve, take I–44 West from Joplin to Highway 43, then drive south on Highway 43 approximately 6 miles to Highway BB. Turn right. Drive approximately 3 miles to road's end. Turn right and drive another mile to a second dirt road to the left. If you haven't chickened out yet, you will now be headed west on Spook Light Road. The road is long. Park anywhere along the side of the road and wait. Try to find the darkest spot about 2 miles down the road. You can even venture down some of the very dark side roads. There is no charge for this thrill except the years of therapy it will take to get over it.

Pierce City on Highway 37 has a couple of neat little places to stop for a rest. But this is only a rest stop because what you really want to see is the **Jolly Mill.** You will be rewarded with a lovely wooded drive after you leave Highway 97 and turn on Highway 60. Go 1⁹⁄₁₀ miles to a sign on FR1010, then 1⁸⁄₁₀ miles across a creek with a bridge with no sides to FR2025, past an old white church and churchyard, then ⁷⁄₁₀ miles to the park.

This park is sort of a secret spot that the locals enjoy. Its history is fascinating. In 1848 George Isbell built a water-powered mill to serve settlers with grist mill products (and spirits). The new village that grew up around him was called Jollification, and it was a rest stop and resupply point for wagon trains headed west to Kansas and Indian Territory. When the Civil War came the area was ravaged, and two cavalry battles raged here. Bushwackers terrorized and burned the village but, here's a surprise, the distillery was spared.

A new village rose from the ashes and the distillery resumed operation. In 1872 a railroad was built to Indian Territory, eliminating wagons. At the same time George Isbell refused to pay the new tax on spirits, stopped making whiskey (much to the regret of travelers), and turned his attention to milling flour. The village faded and by 1894 the mill stood alone with the schoolhouse. But the mill prospered, flour was milled here until the 1920s, and grist mill products were ground out here for another fifty years.

A community effort was made to have the mill placed on the National

Jolly Mill

Register of Historic Places and the mill was rehabilitated. It is once again a working mill. The water still rushes by picnic tables, the covered bridge, and another wooden bridge. It is worth the drive to see.

Webb City's claim to fame, the *"Praying Hands,"* is in *King Jack Park.* This 32-foot concrete-and-steel structure is atop a 40-foot-high hill. The park is named for the ore called "jack" that made the city rich in the 1870s. There are no signs inviting the visitor to stop to see the huge sculpture, it just suddenly appears. The hands were created by Jack Dawson, an art instructor at the Webb City schools, and he intended it to be just a quiet reminder for people to turn to God. Webb City is off Highway 71.

When you get enough of sitting around indoors, you outdoor folks can go west on Highway 59 at Anderson to enter canoe heaven. Highway 59 runs along the Elk River, and the sudden appearance of the famous overhanging bluffs makes you want to duck as you drive under them.

Tri-Lakes Area

The last town on Highway 76 before you enter the Mark Twain National Forest is *Cassville.* Highway 76 is a long and winding road through the forest, so if you arrive at this point after dark, you might as well spend the night. Check out *The Rib* on Highway 112 South,

Missouri Divided

By the time the Civil War was approaching, Missouri was warring within itself. The governor and many legislators favored secession but were outvoted at the convention called to decide the matter. The governor's faction fled south to Cassville, where they signed an ordinance of secession and affiliation with the Confederate States of America.

Cassville 65625 (417–847–3600). It's a mighty fine restaurant that lives up to its name. Skip and Kathy White offer, among other items, BBQ ribs and steak, and on Friday and Saturday nights, there's a prime rib special. Hours are Tuesday through Friday 11:30 A.M. to 2:00 P.M. and 5:00 to 9:00 P.M., and Friday and Saturday 5:00 to 10:00 P.M. Closed on Sunday and Monday.

The *Devil's Kitchen Trail* winds from the valley to the top and down again, giving a close-up look at the geology and history of the area. Eleven of the park's fourteen caves are found along the rocky bench here. Shelters like these were used by Ozark bluff-dwelling Indians who lived here about 10,000 years ago. Artifacts such as food and fragments of clothing have been found to date this culture. The Devil's Kitchen was named for the stone formation that provided a hideout for Civil War guerrillas. Heading south on Highway 112, softly winding roads, tree-lined hills, and spectacular views pop up as you crest hilltops in this lovely national forest.

Roaring River State Park is the fountainhead of the Roaring River. There is a hidden spring in a cave filled with crystal-clear aqua-blue water that stays a constant 58° F year-round. More than twenty million gallons a day are pumped into the river. Here the state maintains a trout hatchery and stocks the river daily in season.

The park runs the *Roaring River Inn.* The inn, made largely of wood and stone, has twenty-six rooms and a view of the river valley below. Rooms range from $79 to $120. Cabins also are available from $75. To reserve a cabin or room, call (417) 847–2330. Other accommodations are available outside the park and in the town of Cassville. The *Parkcliff Cabins* are log cabins with loft, deck, fireplace, full kitchen, and two bedrooms for $125. Call (417) 236–5902. There are also several campgrounds in the Mark Twain National Forest, and about 20 miles east of the state park is the *Big Bay Campgrounds.* It has bathrooms and water and is geared mostly to tent campers. Rate are $10 a night. Call (417) 847–2144.

Roaring River State Park is part of the White River basin. From a geologist's point of view, the basin tells a fascinating story. The White River has cut into the flat Springfield plateau, creating deep, steep-walled valleys and exposing varied layers of rock—shale, limestone, dolomite, and chert.

Pastures fringed with woods are found along Highway 76 East through the Piney Creek Wildlife Area. Mile after mile of ridge roads and startling views unfold until finally, over the crest of the last hill, beautiful Table Rock Lake appears before you. It feels like the top of a ferris wheel from this vantage. The occasional small farm or Ozark stone cottage dots the roadside. Valleys with pastures, ponds, or a lone barn sitting starkly against the sky are the only traces of civilization.

At the town of Cape Fair you can turn right on Highway 76 to Table Rock Lake or turn left to **Reeds Spring.** Because of the proximity of Silver Dollar City, there are quite a few artists in residence. Mark Oehler's **Omega Pottery Shop** (417–272–3369) on Highway 248 East (at the south edge of town) is one of them. Mark crafts each piece of wheel-thrown stoneware and finishes it in a gas-fired kiln at 2,350 degrees—that makes it safe for oven, dishwasher, microwave, and moon missions. He travels occasionally but says it's "too much of a bother to pack everything up and move it." He would rather stay here in Reeds Spring. "Pottery is a craft that needs space to display it," he says. "That's why potters have studio-galleries."

Mark enjoys doing custom work—such as lamps, sinks, and dishes. He points to other craftspeople—Tom Hess, another potter; Lory Brown, a pine-needle basket maker; Ed Seals, who does copper work; and Kay Cloud and her wonderful Sawdust Doll Houses—all in the Reeds Spring area. Omega Pottery is open from 10:00 A.M. to 4:00 P.M. every day except Wednesday. Visit his elaborate Web site at www. omega-pottery-shop. com not only to see his wares but also to learn how pottery is made.

Hess Pottery on Highway 13 North, a mile north of Reeds Spring, is where potter Tom Hess and basket maker Lory Brown have built a unique twelve-sided Mongolian yurt for their workshop and gallery. The natural surroundings offer the perfect atmosphere to enjoy the work these two fine artists produce. Tom's pottery is handmade, using natural red clay. Each piece is sealed with a coating of very fine clay and then fired in a kiln. It is oven proof, dishwasher safe, and can be used in a microwave.

Lory's pine-needle baskets are made with 18-inch southern Yellow Pine needles and 10-inch Ponderosa Pine needles. These baskets must be seen to be loved. Each coil of pine needles is stitched with raffia palm leaf to the preceding coil using closely spaced stitches. The finished baskets are sturdy and durable and retain their wonderful pine scent. Call (417) 272–3283. The shop is open from 10:00 A.M. to 5:00 P.M. in the summer and "most days" in the winter. Visit their Web site at www.hesspottery.com.

Table Rock State Park is one of the most popular (meaning crowded) state parks in Missouri. Off the beaten path here means wilderness, on the path means bumper-to-bumper in summertime. As in most resort areas in the state, early spring and late fall are perfect times to roam without the huge crowds summer brings.

Author Harold Bell Wright came to these hills for his health in the early part of the twentieth century and was so taken by the beauty of the area that he settled in to write. *The Shepherd of the Hills* is his best-known and most-beloved book; it captured the imagination of generations and even became one of John Wayne's early movies (which, incidentally, borrowed only the name from the book—the script was unrecognizable!).

Highway 65 is an old-fashioned, uncrowded Ozark highway. You can still see the view as you crest hills here, but the ***Shepherd of the Hills Inspiration Tower*** offers an incredible one. The tower's first observation level is at 145 feet; the tower is 230 feet, 10 inches tall, with two elevators or 279 stairs to the top. But rest assured it is stable. It is designed to withstand 172 mph winds (gusts of 224 mph), and it cost $1.5 million to build; this is not surprising since it contains 92,064 pounds of steel and is set in forty-three truckloads of concrete. It also contains 4,400 square feet of glass, for a breathtaking view from the highest point around the Tri-Lakes area.

If you've heard of Silver Dollar City (and you will if you stay in Missouri for long), you've heard of ***Branson.*** Once a quiet little town pocketed in the weathered Ozark Mountains near the Arkansas border, the town has seen business pick up considerably of late.

Branson has changed in the past several years from the strip of country music "opries" and related foofaraw crowded cheek-by-jowl along Highway 76 to the country music capital of the Midwest, giving Nashville a run for its money. Twenty-seven theaters in town now feature such stars as Wayne Newton, Johnny Cash, Loretta Lynn, Andy Williams, Mel Tillis, and Roy Clark, who join regulars such as Boxcar Willie, Moe Bandy (the show President Bush and his staff stopped to see after the '92 GOP convention), and, possibly the most popular show in town, Japanese hillbilly fiddler Shoji Tabuchi.

Branson is trying to keep up with the demand of more than four million tourists a year, but as you would suspect, about an hour before the matinee or evening shows begin, the traffic is much like a long narrow parking lot. How bad is the traffic? Well, women have been seen leaving their husbands behind the wheel on Highway 76 while they get out and shop, buy things, and rejoin their spouses in the car a block or so up the street. We are talking gridlock here. The secret to getting around is learning the back roads. Just knowing that the quickest route from Andy Williams's Theater to Ray Stevens is Forsythe Street to Truman to Shepherd of the Hills Expressway—and not 76 Country Boulevard (a road to avoid if at all possible)—can save you enough time for dinner.

There are other little secrets, too. The Chamber of Commerce will give you a free, easy-to-read map showing the shortcuts from one end of the 5-mile strip to the other. The recently repaved back roads can make life a little easier, even though you can't avoid the traffic altogether. The city now has a trolley system on the strip and that helps a bit. (Disney scouts have been looking at land around Branson for a theme park, too. That should make things even more interesting.)

Do flea markets interest you? You're in the right place; downtown Branson has five of them. If you don't find something in this lineup, you aren't looking very hard, or you have a good deal more self-discipline than most of us!

Even before you start your day, you can order a three-egg omelette at the **Hard Luck Diner** in the Grand Village Shops at 2800 76 Country Boulevard in Branson 65616 and have someone sing a country song. The singing waitstaff makes sure your day begins with a song. Call (417) 336–7467.

Because Branson is in the throes of a building boom and the traffic can be a genuine pain, the best thing to do is to find a bed-and-breakfast somewhere away from Branson and then just go in when you are psyched up to do it. (Avoiding the whole place might be more to your liking.) But you've come this far, so the first order of business is to get that map (the Chamber of Commerce or many hotels will have them) and use all the traffic shortcuts you can. The side roads that loop off Highway 76 do reduce travel time and frustration. If you are not attending a show, stay off the streets around the 7:00 P.M. and 8:00 P.M. curtain times when about 1,500 people per theater are all on Highway

Trivia

The Shepherd of the Hills Theater is the longest-running theater in the country. It began with a stage with its audience on blankets on the hillside, upgraded to folding chairs, and now is an outdoor amphitheater that seats around 2,500 people. The year 2002 is its forty-third year in nonstop operation. In 1998 there was a big fire in the dressing rooms and it was announced that there would be no show that year. People poured in with stage props (antique guns, for example) to help, and the theater was up and running in time for the annual performance.

Trivia

Children can attend several shows, such as the Osmonds and comedian Yakov Smirnoff, at no cost. If you wait until after 3:00 P.M. to visit Silver Dollar City, you get in free with the same ticket the next day.

76 and the local police are issuing tickets for driving in the center turn lane.

Branson traffic lulls roughly before 8:30 A.M., between 10:00 and 10:30 A.M., and from around 2:00 to 2:30 P.M. Branson drivers are very courteous, though, and it won't be long before someone lets you pull out in front of them onto the strip. Do yourself a favor and enjoy the *original downtown* Branson while you are in the area. It is filled with family-owned businesses. They are thriving *in spite of* the theaters, not because of them. Traffic veers off Highway 65 to the right and, unfortunately, downtown is left across the overpass. But while that is bad news for the merchants there, it is good news for you if you hate crowds and traffic.

Or take the devil by the horns: Stay on the strip and walk to everything. You can stroll along the strip and take the trolley. Then you can leave the driving to someone else and have fun with your friends. You and the kids can "Ride The Ducks," vintage WWII amphibious vehicles that go along the strip, through an outdoor military history museum, and then splash into the lake.

The Branson/Lakes Area Chamber of Commerce will send you information packets. The one to ask for is the *Branson Roads Scholar: Mastering the Back Roads of Branson.* It contains a map of alternative routes and traffic tips. Call (800) 214–3661 or visit www.branson.cvb.com.

The most exciting part of visiting Branson is how easy it is to get up close to the stars, the music legends who are playing golf (10:00 A.M. on Wednesday at Pointe Royale Golf Course on Highway 165 often has Mel Tillis, Andy Williams, and Moe Bandy teeing off together) or shopping at the grocery store. That constellation of stars is only the beginning. Other stars are scheduled to shoot through Branson for performances, too.

So you never know whom you will see sitting in one of the many restaurants (most of which are down-home sorts of places, not exactly low-calorie eateries) in town. For the best ambience, though, drive across the lake to the **Candlestick Inn** at 127 Taney Street, Branson 65616, on Mt. Branson, where the food is more upscale. The atmosphere is romantic, the view of downtown Branson is sensational (especially during the Christmas season's Festival of Lights), and you never know who will be at one of the tables. The menu features such delicacies as crab-stuffed trout. You can see the humongous neon candle sign (it says "steak and seafood") from downtown, but it's tricky to find if you don't know to just follow Highway 76/68 across the bridge. Call (417) 334–3633 for reservations or visit the Web site at www.candle stickinn.com.

Needless to say, there are many motels around Branson. You can escape the motel rut with a bed-and-breakfast if you plan ahead a little. Plus, the people in the B&Bs tend to know their way around the town and can give you the shortest, fastest routes to wherever you are planning to go. Call Ozark Mountain Country Bed-and-Breakfast Service at (800) 695–1546 and let Kay Cameron find you one of the more than fifty B&Bs in the Tri-Lakes area near Table Rock Lake, Lake Taneycomo, Branson, Silver Dollar City, or just across the border in Arkansas. She has about a hundred bed-and-breakfast inns to direct you to in the Ozarks, from cozy hideaways for couples to family-friendly accommodations, some with their own hot tubs or swimming pools. Kay also has the number of a show service that will deliver tickets to any bed-and-breakfast inn for you.

The easiest way to reach Branson is from Highway 65, which runs through the east end of town. The West Missouri 76 exit will put you on the strip, where you will watch pedestrians speed by your slowly moving car. Or you can use the back entrance and take Highway 248 to the Shepherd of the Hills Expressway to the west side of town, where things will not be much better. You can reach the Branson/Lakes Area Chamber of Commerce at (900) 884–BRANSON for a guide that lists the shows in town and the ticket office phone numbers. There is a $1.50 per minute charge for that call (average three minutes) and you get a recording to leave your name and address. It is sometimes cheaper to call the visitors information number at (417) 334–4136, but that line is often busy and you can be put on hold for about ten minutes. They have a computerized service listing the hotels and motels with vacant rooms. For show tickets you can call BransonTix, a private company that handles about a dozen theaters, at (800) 888–8497.

The *Branson Scenic Railway,* reminiscent of the passenger train era that ended some thirty years ago, made its first run in 1993. Four trains operate daily from the historic railroad depot at 206 East Main in old downtown Branson. Two of the trains go south past the Hollister depot and into the wilderness of the Ozarks. The unspoiled beauty of this unpopulated land has been inaccessible to sightseers until now. Two trains also travel north to James River at Galena. Right now, however, the trains take whatever track is clear, because it's an active rail line. Most often, it's the southern route. Rides are one hour and forty-five minutes long. The trains feature rebuilt passenger cars with silver-domed vista cars. The wail of the whistle warns the people of Branson that the brightly painted diesel engine is nearing a tunnel, curve, or bridge. It sounds continuously as long as the train is in town. Behind the last passenger car another engine tags along. There is no place to turn around, so when the train reaches the end of the line, the other engine comes alive and pulls the train back to Branson. For more information call (417) 334–6110 or (800) 287–2462. The price is $20.25 (plus tax), for adults; $10.25 (plus tax) for ages three through twelve, and kids under two travel free. Trains depart the depot from Monday through Saturday at 9:00 A.M., 11:30 A.M., 2:00 P.M. and 4:30 P.M. (depending on the season). The last train offers a family special when children under twelve ride free. Food is available on the train, from morning muffins to hoagies for lunch. The dinner train is a grand old experience, beginning the first Saturday in May. It departs at 5:00 P.M. and costs $42.50 plus tax.

Want a memory that will stay with you forever? Find **Nonie Lani's Tattoo Art Studio** at 1931 South Business Highway 65. David K. is the artist in residence, and he will do any design you can dream up. But you don't have to have a dragon or a heart with "Mom" inscribed in it. No, you can have permanent cosmetics for your eyes or lips done by Winona Martin, the cosmetic specialist. Call (417) 336–8535 for an appointment. The shop is open from noon to 9:00 P.M. seven days a week.

The **Stone Hill Wine Company** (417–334–1897), on Highway 165, 2 blocks south of Highway 76 West, is open Monday through Saturday 8:30 A.M. to 6:30 P.M. and 11:00 A.M. to 6:00 P.M. on Sunday for wine sales and tastings (open until dusk in the summer). The gift shop also sells sausages, cheese, and wine-related items.

Slow down 2 miles outside town and turn west on Highway V. There's something here you won't want to miss: the **School of the Ozarks** (417–334–9961 or 334–6411) in **Point Lookout.**

It's a college campus, all right, but wait! What's going on here? Everybody looks so . . . busy. This is a different kind of college—a fully accredited, four-year school where each full-time boarding student works at one of sixty-five campus jobs or industries to pay in part for his or her tuition. It calls itself "the campus that works." The rest is provided through scholarships. The campus fruitcake and jelly kitchen is open during business hours weekdays. Student workers bake some 20,000 fruitcakes a year and produce delicious apple butter and many flavors of jelly.

Students built the college itself—it's a pretty one—and run the Ralph

Foster Museum and the Edwards Mill (a working replica of an old-time gristmill) as part of their tuition. If you're hungry while you're here, stop at the student-run Friendship House and Gift Shop. It's an all-you-can-eat smorgasbord where the little ones under five can eat for free—can you pass it up? You can get a mighty prime steak here, they tell us. Friendship House is open between 7:00 A.M. and 7:30 P.M. Monday through Saturday and Sunday until 3:30 P.M.

The campus is beautiful, perched on its hill; don't miss the view from Point Lookout. Stand here at dusk when the bells of the carillon roll out over the mist-shrouded river below, if you want goosebumps up and down your arms. When the sun slides down the sky, that sound of bells on the crisp evening air is unforgettable. Williams Memorial Chapel is a

On a Very Personal Note

The first time I saw Nonie Lani's Tattoo Shop, my husband and I had driven to the Branson area to see Willie Nelson and Wayne Newton. I pointed the shop out to him and told him I wanted to go back the next day to interview the owner for the book. He went off to play golf that day, and when he came home I proudly showed him a new tattoo of a butterfly on my, uh, hip.

He was not amused. In fact, he was not pleased at all. He began to get surly about it. Then he smiled and accused me of getting a "stick-on" tattoo. He led me into the bathroom to rub it with soap and water. It did not come off. I expected him to tell his golf buddies about it the next day, but he never mentioned it to anyone. He was truly embarrassed for me. Every night when I undressed, he glared at me. Now mind you, I had just turned 50 years old and we had been married nearly 25 years. To say he did not like surprises is putting it mildly. He is very conservative.

Of course, so am I. The tattoo was not done by David K. but purchased in the five-and-dime downtown. But I was having so much fun I decided to carry on with the fiction. Before the butterfly began to wear off, I used alcohol to remove it and applied a new one—on the other side this time—and waited for him to figure it out. He didn't. This went on for four weeks—first on the right, then on the left—the butterflies remained on my backside, and impossibly, he did not notice their change of address. But the good news was that on the fifth week when I replaced the butterfly with a dragon, he did notice.

It was probably the best practical joke I have ever managed. My husband believed me, my best friends and my mother believed me. Only my dad (who never saw it) never believed it. He said he simply knew me too well to believe I would have a butterfly permanently placed on my derriere. Now the dragon maybe . . . .

fine place to stop for a moment; the tourist bustle slows to a halt here and there's room to breathe.

Big Cedar Lodge at 612 Devil's Pool Road in **Ridgedale,** 9 miles south of Branson, is off the beaten path literally, but is very well-known by people all over the country. You can stay in the lodge itself (winter from $69 weekdays) or in private cabins (winter from $169 weekdays), and there is a Jack Nicklaus–designed executive golf course called *Top of the Rock.* It is an Audubon Signature Course, the first in the state and only the sixth in the country. The distinction means the course meets Audubon's environmental guidelines on natural habitat and water life. Big Cedar also has a fine trout stream and waterfalls all over the place. Devil's Pool Restaurant offers a level of dining not found easily in the Ozarks—maple-glazed quail with white bean ragout, prime rib, and a champagne brunch on Sundays. Call (415) 335–2777 or visit their Web site at www.bigcedarlodge.com.

January is spawning season at **Shepherd of the Hills Fish Hatchery,** 6 miles southwest of Branson on Highway 165 in the White River Valley, just below Table Rock Dam. The Missouri Department of Conservation produces 1.2 million fish annually, 80 percent of which go into nearby Lake Taneycomo. There is a visitors' center filled with exhibits and aquariums, and four trails ranging from 3/10 mile to about 1½ miles. Call 417–334–4865. Hours are 9:00 A.M. to 5:00 P.M. seven days a week (except Thanksgiving, Christmas, and New Year's Day). Visit on the last Saturday in February for "Vulture Venture" (noon until 6:00 P.M.) and see hundreds of vultures enjoying their winter roosting spots. There are fun activities for the kids, too.

If you want luxury in the European style, the **Chateau on the Lake,** 415 North State Highway 265, Branson 65616, is high-dollar elegant. This ten-story hotel sits on a hill right next to Table Rock Lake and has 302 rooms and suites. A standard room with a mountain view begins at $169 and goes even higher if you want to see the lake. The murals that decorate the ballroom are of castles in Europe, and you can scuba dive, parasail, water-ski, fish, play tennis, or work out in a twenty-four-hour fitness center. There's a Sweet Shoppe and a deli, and the Chateau Grille offers fine dining. If you want to check it out first, visit the Chateau's Web site at www.jqh.com/chateau.html. Call (888) 333–LAKE.

This you have to see to believe. **Cathedral Church of the Prince of Peace** is the world's smallest cathedral. Situated in **Highlandville,** it's 3 miles off Highway 65 and 1,500 yards off Highway 160 (take County Road EE to Highlandville.) It is the cathedral of the very, very small Christ

Cathedral Church of the Prince of Peace, Highlandville

Catholic Church, which claimed the title of "the Catholic Peace Church" in 1965. The beautiful Garden of Saints displays statues of about a dozen saints among the flower beds, with many varieties of geraniums surrounding the Ozark-stone building. The garden has a shrine to Our Lady of Guadalupe with angels on either side of the opening. Red roses fill the area. A pond and fountain honoring Our Lady of Mt. Carmel floats lily pads and is home to large goldfish and blue herons.

The cathedral also showcases a well-known oil painting by Tomás Fundora, "Cristo de Espaldas"—"The Back of Christ"—which has raised a bit of controversy wherever it is shown. Bishop Pruter ends his homily with the command to "follow Christ" and finds the painting of Jesus walking away just the right statement. A 1,500-foot trail meanders through the woods and meadows by the 14 Stations of the Cross. But walk right up there and open the door. Inside is a cathedral—complete with pews, candles, altar, tabernacle, and prie-dieu. A rich stained-glass window catches the sunlight. If you are lucky you will hear the world's smallest cathedral pipe organ, custom built for the cathedral, with forty-two pipes and the full range of the human voice. The woodwork is old-world craftsmanship at its best. Sunday morning service is at 11:00 A.M. During the week Mass is said every morning at 11:00 A.M., and a litany for peace is offered every day. Bishop Karl Pruter is the presiding bishop. Built of native stone, the cathedral measures 14 feet by 17 feet and seats a congregation of fifteen; it is mentioned in the *Guinness Book of Records*. The blue onion dome suggests the church's Eastern rite affiliation. Bishop Pruter suggests knocking on the door of the house attached to the church by a covered walkway if you want to talk about the Catholic Peace Church. Call (417) 443–3951.

Long Creek Herb Farm is nestled deep in the woods on the Long Creek arm of Table Rock Lake. Jim Long calls it an "old-fashioned working herb farm in the heart of the Ozarks" and that describes it pretty well. Guests sip herb tea on the shady porch and listen to the tree frogs. On the twenty-seven-acre farm, skullcap, foxglove, and horehound are grown, and goats, chickens, guineas, geese, and steers are raised. Jim grows 400 cultivated and native herbs; many of them, such as sweet goldenrod and horsetail, are unique to the Ozarks.

There is a meticulously groomed demonstration garden with winding paths and a bentwood gazebo. After twenty years as a landscape architect, Jim decided that his love of plants needed a new outlet, and he wanted to share the experience of herbs with people.

He also has a gift shop where you can buy about eighty products, including seasonings, teas, and herb blends both medicinal and culinary. You can buy a Dream Pillow to induce dreams that are relaxing, romantic, or action-packed, depending on the herb blend.

The farm is open on Wednesdays in the summertime (May through October) and other days by appointment. You must call first. You will need directions or a map to find the place because you must cross two state lines and three county lines to get there. Visit their Web site at www.longcreekherbs.com. Call (417) 779–5450.

The *Golden Pioneer Museum* in Golden can be found between Branson and Eureka Springs on Highway 86. The owner of this museum is Winfred Prier, and the curator is Murry Carmichael. The museum is home to Arlis Coger's collections from the Trail of Tears Museum, which used to be in Huntsville. The 5,200-square-foot museum contains pots (800 clay pots to be exact), weapons, tools, and clothing made by the Arkansas Osage Indians and found in the War Eagle (Arkansas) mounds. Here is the largest collection of Dalton points (more than 1,000), arrowheads knapped around 8000 B.C. by Native Americans living along the White River south of Huntsville. On display also is the world's largest collection of Tussinger points. The extensive mineral collection includes the world's largest quartz and crystal cluster— 4,200 pounds—found in Hot Springs and displayed in its own glass case. Other displays show rocks that look ordinary until ultraviolet light reveals the vibrant fluorescent color within them. There is also an incredible collection of baseball cards. The guns on display include one of only three or four derringers like the gun that killed President Abraham Lincoln. It also has one of the largest collections of carnival glass in the Midwest, more than seventy-two collections, and it's still growing. There is a gift shop, too. Call (417) 271–3299 to arrange for a tour (open April through November).

Dogwood Canyon Nature Park on Highway 86 West and Highway 13 near Lempe 65681 is the dream come true of Johnny Morris, the Bass Pro Shop founder. This 10,000-acre property preserves an Ozark wonderland that he now shares with the public. Three creeks flow through the canyon—Dogwood Creek, Little Indians Creek, and Hobbs Creek—creating one of the best trout streams in the Midwest. Strategically placed weirs, or dams, and a series of short spillways form terraces in the stream and aerate the water. Each dam creates a pool for the trout. Wet-season, spring-fed waterfalls from bluffs above the stream bank were made year-round attractions by the addition of pumps to recirculate water to add oxygen for the trout. Stone walkways and wrought-iron railings built by Bass Pro's staff blacksmiths guide visitors, and 5 miles of paved road pass the most interesting sights in the canyon. There are twenty-nine stream crossings on the property, and most fords are located at the base of a weir so that passengers in vehicles can view cascading water at eye level. Other crossings include stone bridges built by a local mason, and a post-and-beam-covered bridge built by Amish craftsmen. The park is open to the general public year-round, and for tram tours from March 9 through November 30. Horseback trail rides are offered ($35.00), and bicycle tours are also available ($14.95 adults, $6.95 children). Half-day guided trophy fishing excursions on Dogwood Creek are $195.00 (ages 13 and up), or two hours of unguided fishing will cost you $25.00 ($12.50 for kids) for catch-and-release or $20.00 ($9.50 for kids) plus $3.50 a pound for those who (must) keep their catch. Tour guides relate the history of the area during the two-hour tram ride ($25 adults, $15 children), pointing out caves where workers discovered ancient burials. One site high on a bluff contained the remains of a Native American who died more than a thousand years ago—predating Missouri's Osage tribe. Other remains (a child and two adults) at another site were dated to 6000 B.C. by scientists—making them the oldest human remains ever found in the state. The tour crosses into Arkansas and travels among herds of bison, longhorn cattle, and elk. The visitors' center has Civil War and Indian artifacts. Reservations are required for tram tours, trail rides, and fishing excursions. Call (417) 779–5983 for more information.

Trivia

Table Rock Lake *has its own Loch Ness monster, they say. For years scuba divers have claimed to have seen "Bubba," a 200-pound catfish swimming around the dam's waters where currents suck bait fish down to the dam's turbines, creating a fast-food drive-in for the cool cats that hang out there. One diver describes him as "as long as me," but to date, no one has ever caught a 6-foot catfish (the record, however, is 5 feet 3 inches, which is as long as me, and weighing in at 117 pounds).*

Just a mile east of Highway 65 on Highway 14, the town of *Ozark* is a haven for antiques buffs. The largest collection is housed at the *Maine Streete Mall,* 1994 Evangel, Ozark 65721, a warehouse along Highway 65 and home to 108 antiques dealers. There are even antique cars inside. The mall is open seven days a week from 9:00 A.M. to 6:00 P.M. Call (417) 581–2575 for information. You will find a couple dozen more shops—filled with a gazillion items—in the town of Ozark itself. This town, 15 miles south of Springfield and near enough to Branson to draw its crowds, is a mecca for folks who love old stuff.

Dear's Rest Bed and Breakfast, 1408 Capp Hill Ranch Road, Ozark 65721, is tucked in a beautifully natural Ozark setting where you can enjoy unexpected visits from deer, raccoons, and wild turkey, and bird song will wake you in the morning. The rustic house was built for innkeepers Allan and Linda Schilter by local Amish builders and is filled with family antiques and old toys. The greatroom has a cozy fireplace, and since the home is open to only one family at a time, it becomes your fireplace, too. The all-cedar home has art-stenciled walls. The broad deck, hot tub, and covered porch are ideal places to enjoy the woodsy view or take your breakfast. You can hike on the old ranch roads and come back to steam away the cricks in a large hot tub in the woods. Birders enjoy the beautiful mountain views and the 250 varieties of birds that have been sighted in the area. There is a resident bluebird that frequents the water provided there. The pristine, spring-fed creek provides the perfect spot for "stream snorkeling" and the Schilters will provide the snorkel gear. Dear's Rest is actually 10 miles south of Ozark in the Mark Twain National Forest, so there is a world of outdoors waiting.

The bedroom contains two full-size beds and a crib and can accommodate parties of two to six. The additional people in your party will share a bath and sleep in a cozy loft for an additional $10 for each child and $15 for each adult. The room with a private bath is $95. Allan and Linda will fix you a full country breakfast in the morning and send you on your way to nearby Springfield or Branson. You can visit the B&B's Web site at www.dearsrest.com and e-mail the Schilters at info@dearsrest.com. To find the house, take Highway 14 to Highway W and then to W-27-A. Call (417) 581–3839 or (800) 588–2262.

What was once the largest dairy farm in this area is now home to Mark and Susan Bryant. They share it as the ***Barn Again Bed and Breakfast Inn,*** 904 Church Street, Ozark 65721. The five-acre farmstead overlooks the Finley River. The centerpiece is the two-story plank-and-stone structure, which is their home and where breakfast is served to guests. A nearby white clapboard house built in 1910 provides two guest suites. A wraparound porch leads to a deck with a hot tub. There's even a small wedding chapel near the brick pathways that wind through the shady grounds. A renovated milking parlor built in the 1920s houses three more rooms, and a swimming pool is nearby. Each room and suite has a private bath and entrance. A spring-fed creek flows just below the house, and often you will see deer, foxes, blue herons, or wild turkeys. Rooms are from $89 to $109 with full breakfast. Call (877) 462–2276 for reservations.

The ***Smokey Hollow Lake Bed and Breakfast*** at 880 Cash Spring Road, Ozark 65721-6185, is a country retreat sitting on 180 acres of Ozarks hills and hollows. The suite is a private barn loft that includes a kitchen, two baths, and a two-person whirlpool bath. There's a six-acre lake for fishing, canoeing, or paddle boating and a creek for wading. Hosts Brenda and Richard Bilyeu will fix a good breakfast for you. The suite is $75 to $150. Call (417) 485–0286 or (800) 485–0286, or visit the Web site at www.bbim.org/smokey/.

PLACES TO STAY IN SOUTHWEST MISSOURI

SPRINGFIELD
Super 8 Motel,
3022 North Kentwood Avenue, 65803;
(417) 833–9218
or (800) 800–8000

Days Inn,
2700 North Glenstone, 65803;
(417) 865–8600 or (800) DAYS INN

Holiday Inn, 2720 North Glenstone, 65803;
(417) 862–9415 or (800) HOLIDAY

Best Western Deerfield Inn,
3343 East Battlefield Road, 65804;
(417) 966–1963 or (800) 528–1234

Park Inn,
1772 South Glenstone, 65804;
(417) 882–1113 or (800) 749–PARK

Ramada Inn, I–44
2820 North Glenstone Avenue, 65803;
(417) 869–3900

VAN BUREN
Smalley's Motel,
Business 60, 639365;
(800) 727–4263 or (573) 323–4263;
(tube floats leave from motel)

WEST PLAINS
Ramada Inn, Highway 61 and Highway 160, 65775;
(417) 256–8191

Holiday Inn Express,
1605 Imperial Drive, 65775;
(417) 257–2830

LEBANON
Best Western Wyota Inn,
Business Loop 44, exit 130, 65536;
(417) 532–6171

Holiday Inn Express, I–44
and Highway WW
Corner, 65536;
(800) HOLIDAY

EMINENCE
Shady Lane Cabins and
Motel, 65466;
(573) 226–3893

CARTHAGE
*Econo Lodge,
1441 West Central, 648367
(417) 358–3900 or
(800) 553–ECONO

Best Budget Inn, East
Highway 96, 64836;
(417) 358–6911 or
(800) 357–4953

Days Inn,
2244 Grand, 64836;
(417) 358–2499 or
(800) 325–2525 or

*Precious Moments Best
Western Hotel,
2701 Hazel (Northeast
corner of Highways HH
and 71A), 64836;
(417) 359–5900 or
(800) 511–7676 or

CASSVILLE
Super 8, Highway
37/76–86, 65625;
(417) 847–4888

Sunset Motel, 65625;
(800) 798–2904

JOPLIN
*Holiday Inn, 3615 Range
Line Road, 64804;
(417) 623–4093

Days Inn, 3500 Range
Line Road, 64804;
(417) 623–4206

NOEL
Bell Aire Motel, Highway
59 South, 65854;
(417) 475–3851

SHELL KNOB
Campbell Point
Resort, 65747;
(800) 304–3169

REEDS SPRING
Mountain Country
Motor Inn, 65737;
(417) 739–4155 or
(800) 753–2755

BRANSON
Econolodge,
230 S. Wildwood, 65616;
(800) 542–3326

KIMBERLING CITY
Kimberling Arms Resort,
Highway B, 65686;
(417) 739–2461 or
(800) 528–1234

**PLACES TO EAT IN
SOUTHWEST MISSOURI**

SPRINGFIELD
Nonna's Italian Cafe,
306 South Avenue, 65806
(417) 831–1222

McGuffey's (Chesterfield
Village), 2101 West
Chesterfield Boulevard,
Ste A–100, 65807;
(417) 882–2484

WINONA
Nu-Way Foods, Highways
60 and 19 North, 65588;
(Deli) (573) 325–4522

WEST PLAINS
Figaro's Restaurant,
Highway 61/160, 65775;
(417) 256–8191

EMINENCE
Ozark Orchard, Main Street
(across from the court-
house), 65466;
(573) 226–3604
(closed January and
February)

Ruby's T&T Family
Restaurant,
Main Street, 65466;
(573) 226–3878

Selected Chambers of Commerce

Branson, (417) 334–4136

Kimberling City, (800) 595–0393

Van Buren, (800) OZARKVB
www.semo.net/vanburen
(e-mail) vbcoc@semo.net

* has restaurant

REEDS SPRING
Ledgestone Grille & Pub,
1600 Ledgestone
Way, 65466;
(417) 336–1777 or
336–1781

BRANSON
Beverly's Steak House &
Saloon, 225 Violyn, 65616;
(417) 334–6508

KIMBERLING CITY
The Bearded Clam Lounge
and Eatery,
Highway 13, 65686;
(417) 739–4440

**HELPFUL WEB SITE
FOR THE QUEEN OF THE
OZARKS REGION**

www.springfieldmo.org

Central Missouri

Welcome to America's Heartland, where the Mighty Mo marks the end of the glaciated plains, and hill country begins. Remnant prairies tucked between the hills remind us that once these seas of grass covered a third of the state. In this area there are not one but three big lakes, and from Kansas City to the Lake of the Ozarks lie tiny towns built on gentle ridges, waiting to be discovered. Rough gravel roads wind through dogwood forests, along tentacled lakeshores and into towns that seem to have been protected from the rush like the wild morel hidden under a leaf. The big city here is Kansas City: the birthplace of jazz, the homeland of barbecue, and the Heart of America.

Lake of the Ozarks is not only a tourist area, it is a second home site for people from both Kansas City and St. Louis. The eastern shore, known as the St. Louis side, has million-dollar homes in the Land of the Four Seasons resort area. Six Mile Cove (the 6-mile marker means you are 6 miles from Bagnell Dam) is called Millionaires' Cove by boaters and has some of the most opulent homes in the Midwest. A houseboat business has sprung up on that side, and visitors can now cruise the lake and see both shores without the long drive around the lake.

The Heart of America

Describing **Kansas City** as a city with "manure on its feet and wheat in its jeans" was a fair assessment at one time. Its two major industries were meat and wheat—all because a man named Joe McCoy convinced the local powers-that-were in 1871 that the newfangled "bobwire" (barbed wire) made it impossible to herd Texas cattle east. A central shipping point was needed, and the Kansas City stockyard was born (where a fine steakhouse, the **Golden Ox,** is within sniffing distance at 1600 Genessee, Kansas City 64102; 816–842–2866).

Kansas City is known as the "Heart of America," not because of its location in the center of the country but because of the people who call it home. Kansas City has a symphony, a lyric opera, the Missouri State

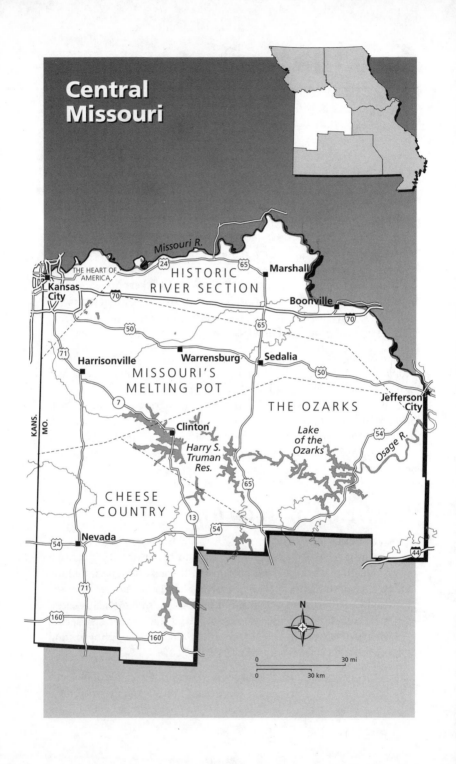

Central Missouri

Missouri R.

THE HEART OF AMERICA

Kansas City

HISTORIC RIVER SECTION

Marshall

Boonville

Harrisonville

Warrensburg

Sedalia

MISSOURI'S MELTING POT

THE OZARKS

Jefferson City

KANS. MO.

Clinton

Harry S. Truman Res.

Lake of the Ozarks

Osage R.

CHEESE COUNTRY

Nevada

N

0   30 mi

0   30 km

Ballet Company, baseball's Royals, and football's Kansas City Chiefs. Enclosed in the very heart of the city is Swope Park, the second-largest city park in the nation, with quiet, tree-shaded picnic areas and a modern zoo now upgraded to world-class. If you haven't been to KC lately, be sure to drive by the new futuristic Bartle Hall sculptures at night, beautiful in a strange space-age way.

Charlie "Yardbird" Parker's grave site is in Lincoln Cemetery, at 8604 Truman Road. The road to the bedraggled cemetery is narrow and unmarked. There is an entrance from Blue Ridge Boulevard.

The Nelson-Atkins Museum owns one of the finest collections of Oriental art in the world and has a beautiful outdoor sculpture garden. The Kansas City Museum has a planetarium and an old-fashioned ice-cream parlor where you can order a phosphate or a sundae. The Kansas City studio of artist Thomas Hart Benton is now a state park.

Of course, **Country Club Plaza,** the country's first shopping center, is a must-see place if you are from out of town. This is particularly true at Christmastime, when each building is intricately outlined in colored lights. The new Brush Creek renovation is also worth a trip if you haven't been here in a while. There are walkways and gardens and even a fountain in the middle of the creek. Boats cruise the creek in summer.

The first question most visitors ask when they get off a plane at the Kansas City International Airport is "Where's the best barbecue?" That's for you to judge: The oldest contenders are **Arthur Bryant Barbecue** at 1727 Brooklyn, Kansas City 64103 (816–231–1123), and **Gates and Sons Bar-B-Q** at 1221 Brooklyn, Kansas City 64127 (816–483–3880). Both offer carryout, so you can do comparison tests with their different sauces until you are all "pigged out."

Gates's and Bryant's owe their fame, in part, to the fact that they used to be located next to the old Kansas City Royals baseball stadium. Not only were they favorite places to eat before and after games, the announcers would all be happily noshing barbecue and talking about it during the games. Then writer Calvin Trillin declared KC the barbecue capital of the planet and made Bryant's even more famous. But there are between eighty and ninety barbecue restaurants in the Kansas City area, and most of the best are just joints tucked away somewhere, and "best" is defined by what kind of sauce you favor. **Little Jake's** at 1227 Grand, Kansas City 64106 (816–283–0880), for example, has a sign in the window that reads EAT IT AND BEAT IT, which tells you something about its size, popularity, and attitude. **B.B.'s Lawnside Bar-B-Que** at 1205 East 85th Street, Kansas City 64131-2556, is a fun spot with wooden floors that slope and old blues posters on the walls. There is a definite Louisiana influence in the food there—great gumbo as well as some of the best barbecue in town. B.B.'s is as famous for the blues jam sessions as it is for the food. Sunday nights are the best. The Lonnie Ray Blues Band plays rockin' blues from 8:00 until 11:00 P.M., but Sunday night is jam night, and so many other blues players join in that you can lose count. Entire groups show up to play during breaks. Another favorite is the Tawny Dang Poodles, an all-woman band that rocks at B.B.'s on other nights and often shows up Sunday night in the jam. The music is loud, the food fantastic, the crowd enthusiastic, and it is just more darn fun than you can stand. Call (816) 822–7427 to see who is playing tonight.

While you are in this neighborhood, you should know about *Stroud's* at 1015 East 85th Street, Kansas City 64131, just 1 block west of B.B.'s. This old restaurant, located under an overpass, has been serving the best

Author's Favorite Annual Events in Central Missouri

July

Osage Beach—Fireworks on the Water, Tan-Tar-A Resort/Four Seasons Resort, (800) 826–8272

Lexington—July Fourth Celebration, skydiving

Gravois Mills—Annual Osage Indian Heritage days and Crafts Festival, (573) 378–4373

Sedalia—Annual Garden Party, Bothwell Lodge, state historic site, roaring twenties party, (660) 827–0510

August

Laurie—Village of Laurie Annual BBQ Cook-Off, (573) 374–8776

Sedalia—Missouri State Fair, (660) 530–5600

September

Independence—Santa-Cali-Gon Days Festival, celebrates the Santa Fe, CA, and Oregon Trails, (816) 252–4745

Osage Beach—Annual Fall Festival of Color Hot Air Balloon Race; (573) 365–6663

October

Kansas City—American Royal Barbecue, 300 teams of BBQers, music, dancing, and food, (816) 221–9800

Versailles—Annual Old Tyme Apple Festival, (573) 378–4401

Cole Camp—Low German Theatre, (573) 668–4970

Lake Ozarks—Annual Lake of the Ozarks Dixieland Jazz Festival, Four Seasons Lodge, (573) 392–1731

Sunrise Beach—Annual Missouri State Buddy Bass Championship, (573) 374–5500

November

Kansas City—Plaza Lighting Ceremony, (816) 274–8444

AUTHOR'S TOP TEN FAVORITES
IN CENTRAL MISSOURI

Cascone's Grill

Harling's Upstairs

Sun Ray Cafe

Joe D's Winebar and Cafe

Arrow Rock

Lyceum Theatre

Evergreen Restaurant

*Dutch Bakery and
  Bulk Food Store*

Wheel Inn

Der Essen Platz

fried chicken in the Kansas City area for years and years. It's served family style—huge platters of chicken, mashed potatoes, green beans, and rolls—and you will be taking as much home as you eat there. Stroud's is open Tuesday through Sunday for lunch and dinner. Call (816) 333–2132.

Here and there, drowsing on old streets, pocketed in small shopping centers, crouching behind buildings, or even tucked inside buildings, you're likely to find places that definitely qualify as out of the mainstream. After barbecue, Kansas City is famous for jazz.

Eighteenth and Vine in Kansas City was really jumping from the 1920s to the 1950s. There were smoky joints filled with baseball players from the Kansas City Negro League team, the Monarchs, and jazz musicians signing autographs for fans and talking and laughing over drinks. There were restaurants and nightclubs there—the Mardi Gras, Blue Room, and Subway Club—and baseball and jazz are forever linked in Kansas City. An untouched memory of that time can still be found at the **Mutual Musicians' Foundation,** in the old Musicians' Union Hall—a hot-pink bungalow in the historic jazz district around Eighteenth and Vine. It is, in fact, the only building inside the city limits that is on the National Register of Historical Places. It is located at 1825 Highland Avenue, Kansas City 64108. Tours are available, but the place really jumps on Friday and Saturday nights when musicians from all over Kansas City gather here to jam after their regular gigs around the city. The traditional jazz jam starts at midnight. There is no cover charge, but donations are always welcome to keep this place open. Call (816) 471–5212 to find out more.

Now the area is coming alive again, and the link is still strong. At the **Kansas City Jazz Museum,** 1616 East 18th Street, Kansas City 64108, visitors can listen to the music of such greats as Louis Armstrong, Julia Lee, Duke Ellington, Ella Fitzgerald, and Charlie "Yardbird" Parker. In fact, the museum is the final resting place of Yardbird's saxophone. The museum has an extensive exhibit honoring Ella Fitzgerald, "The First Lady of Song," with thirty of her most identifiable personal effects, including her famous cat-rim, rhinestone-covered glasses and silver pumps.

This is one of the most interactive museums in the country. Music fills the air as the story of jazz is told through sight and sound. Visitors can listen to

Trivia

While you are downtown in Kansas City, look for the "cow on a stick." The huge bull used to be atop the American Hereford Association, but the organization has since moved. Now the giant bovine watches over the area from his perch on a pylon above Argus Health Systems. They decided to keep it so folks could find them easily.

performances while a giant video wall projects early performances by some of these famous artists. The museum offers something for every level of jazz understanding. You can putter in a mixing station and create your own mix of sounds or enter the Wee-Bob children's activity center. Shop for a CD or tape, T-shirt or poster in the Swing Shop.

Museum hours are Tuesday through Saturday 9:00 A.M. to 6:00 P.M. and Sunday from noon to 6:00 P.M. Admission to the museum is $6.00 for adults, $2.50 for children, or you can buy a combination ticket to both the Jazz and Baseball Museums for $8.00 for adults, $4.00 for children under twelve; kids under three, free. For more information call (816) 474–VINE.

The new **Negro League Baseball Museum** is at 1616 East 18th Street, Kansas City 64108, too, and it remembers the other half of the jazz and

Something Old, Something New

*A*lthough not off the beaten path by any means, there's something old and something new in Kansas City. The old Kansas City Union Station—site of an infamous gangster massacre and formerly one of the largest and busiest rail centers in the country—at 2300 Main Street in Kansas City 64108, has been restored to its glorious original beauty and is now an urban plaza and entertainment center. There are several restaurants, evening entertainment at City Nights with live performance theater, motion pictures, and laser and magic shows as well as music and theater performances. There are also shopping areas and, best of all, especially for the kids, Science City featuring more than fifty hands-on environments for all ages to explore. Science City is a city-within-

a-city on multiple levels with streets and alleyways. Each exhibit is a realistic environment that offers interactive experiences with costumed citizens who live and work in the "city's" Festival Plaza, Uptown, Downtown, Southside, and Old Town. You can even explore an excavation dig site in Prehistoric Kansas City or assist a surgical team in the Operating Room. Want a chance to be on TV? You can broadcast news from the Television Station. You can bake a cake in the Test Kitchen or try your hand at being an astronaut in the Space Center. Or you can board a real locomotive located just outside the station. Science City's Web site is at www.sciencecity.com. Science City is open daily. Call (816) 460–9372 or (800) 556–9372 for times and shows.

OTHER ATTRACTIONS WORTH SEEING IN CENTRAL MISSOURI

Kansas City:
  Country Club Plaza at Christmas
  Worlds of Fun/Oceans of Fun
  Crown Center

Camdenton:
  Bridal Cave

Osage Beach:
  Outlet Mall

baseball love affair—the league that played in the 1920s and '30s before the all-white major leagues would accept black players. Black players formed their own league, and some of the best athletes ever to play the game got their start there: Satchel Paige, Ernie Banks, Josh Gibson, and "Cool Papa" Bell. Do these names sound familiar? How about Willie Mays, Hank Aaron, Roy Campanella, or the incredible Jackie Robinson? The Kansas City Monarchs were considered the Yankees of black baseball. The Negro National League drew more than 50,000 spectators from coast to coast. Then in 1947 a guy named Jackie Robinson stepped up to bat for the Brooklyn Dodgers and smashed the color barrier right over the fence. The rest is baseball history.

The museum is more than just a collection of pictures and memorabilia: it re-creates the look, sound, and feel of the game in the heyday of the league. Its centerpiece main gallery has a three-station interactive computer module with video games, historical vignettes, and coaching tips. The museum covers the history of black baseball from its beginning after the Civil War through the end of Negro Leagues play in the 1960s, and features a custom-designed database to search for the play-by-play of league games. There is a gift shop featuring autographed baseballs, Louisville slugger bats, T-shirts, caps, and jackets. Take a look back at Negro League baseball by visiting the Web site at www.kansascity.com. Hours are Tuesday through Saturday 9:00 A.M. until 6:00 P.M., Sunday noon to 6:00 P.M. Call (816) 221–1920 for more information.

Right across the street is the historic *Gem Theater Cultural and Performing Arts Center* at 1615 East Eighteenth Street, Kansas City 64108. As early as the 1920s, Kansas City's vibrant theatrical community was known around the world. This newly reconstructed theater still has the trademark neon marquee hanging outside and once again presents first-class entertainment. The latest in lighting, sound, and acoustical design have been added. The Alvin Ailey Dancers perform here along with renowned jazz groups and theater ensembles. Call the ticket office at (816) 842–1414 for a schedule filled with multimedia events.

At 2033 Vine, Kansas City 64108, is the *Black Archives of Mid-America,* where you can find documents, artifacts, paintings, and exhibits that explore the lives of African-Americans in Kansas City, including musicians, artists, writers, and leaders in many other fields. The first-floor exhibit features the Tuskegee Airmen of World War II, and the second floor is dedicated to the Buffalo soldiers of the Civil War. There are plans to run the trolley from the Crown Center, which is only five minutes away, to this historic district. Call (816) 483–1300.

Downtown (way downtown) is the *City Market,* where you can shop outdoors with a big wicker basket for just-picked produce in the wonderful atmosphere of a European marketplace. You can buy everything from morel mushrooms in early May to late-harvest turnips in October.

Wearin' o' the Green, Italiano

*T*he North End is where I grew up. We lived with my grandmother, "Nana" Randazzo, until I was about twelve years old. I went to the Catholic school a couple of blocks from our home—Holy Rosary School—and rarely left the neighborhood. My grandma spoke Sicilian, my parents were bilingual, and I grew up knowing just enough Sicilian to stay out of trouble with my Nana. Everyone in the neighborhood was Italian. There was a penny candy store on one corner, an Italian bakery on the other, and a park with a bocce court and a swimming pool a half block away. A good restaurant served the area, and we could open fire hydrants on hot summer days and play kick-the-can in the streets. Yelling "first light!" when the street lights came on was a nightly contest. We even had lightning bugs. Why would anyone want to leave a neighborhood so wonderful? It was safe. It was home.

But one of my earliest childhood memories, kindergarten or first grade, was of walking to school on March 17—a day that meant absolutely nothing to my family—and finding everyone else dressed in green. Now remember, this was an Italian neighborhood. There was not a drop of Irish blood anywhere for miles. Suddenly everyone was Irish, and I was the one who got pinched dozens of times—for not wearing green—before the bell rang to begin classes. I was terrified, and when the lunch bell rang, I took off for home with my lunch tucked under my arm like a football. (We wrapped our lunch in newspaper, sacks didn't exist for us.) When I arrived home unexpectedly, crying, my Nana couldn't understand what the problem was. I refused to go back to school until she found me something green to wear. When she saw that I was adamant, she began to rummage in the closets muttering "manacia l'America!" under her breath. (That is phonetically spelled and is some sort of Sicilian-American slanguage [sic]. It means "blame it on America" and was used whenever things American got to be too much for her.) I returned to school wearing green but not understanding why. I noticed that nobody pinched Sister Mary Margaret. Although she was wearing black, she had a green shamrock pinned to her habit.

There are always fresh eggs and chickens, and on Saturday mornings local farmers and buyers meet over the freshest produce this side of the garden. The area by the Missouri River has undergone restoration, complete with a riverboat museum.

The year was 1856 when the steamboat *Arabia* set out for the West, loaded with trade goods and passengers. As the folks at the **Steamboat Arabia Museum** say, you'll find axes, awls, and augers to zillions of other treasures restored to near-mint condition. How did they manage to amass all this in one place? Well, the *Arabia* hit a cottonwood snag in the Missouri River and sank like a stone. There it rested from 1856 to 1988, a time capsule waiting to spill its treasures, both everyday and exotic, into the present. But, of course, even the everyday from over one hundred years ago is exotic now. You'll find spurs, tinware, perfume (that retained its scent after its sojourn under 45 feet of mud and water), wine, whiskey, and champagne (still bubbly), canned goods, hair pins, inkwells, and clothing.

The Hawley family excavated the boat and spent untold hours painstakingly restoring the artifacts they found. To our good fortune, rather than selling off the bounty they opened a museum, and this treasure trove now tells casual visitors, school kids, scholars, living-history reenactors, and just plain history buffs volumes about what life was like on the frontier; civilization was built with the bits and pieces of trade goods carried by packets like the *Arabia*. A short film introduces you to the museum and to the excavation and restoration process. See what frontier life was like for $8.50 for adults, $6.00 for seniors, $4.75 for children four to twelve, free for younger kids. Hours are Monday through Saturday, 10:00 A.M. to 6:00 P.M. and Sunday from noon to 5:00 P.M.; for information call (816) 471–4030. The museum is at 400 Grand, Kansas City 64106.

Inside the Fifth Street market building is **Cascone's Grill**, 20 East Fifth Street, Kansas City 64106, where the market crowd eats. The Cascone family cooks up the most amazing early-morning Italian breakfasts (Italian breaded steak, fried eggs, hash browns, and Italian bread toast) and late-in-the-day lunches featuring Vita Cascone's own spaghetti sauce. They open and close seasonally with the rhythm of the market crowd. But Tuesday through Saturday 6:00 A.M. to 2:00 P.M. will usually find them open. Call (816) 471–1018.

Catty-corner from the market, across the street at 513 Walnut, Kansas City 64106, is **Planters' Seed and Spice Co.** Step inside this old building and inhale the wonderful odors of fresh bulk herbs and spices, the scent of old wood, the aroma of exotic teas and coffees, and the clean smell of seeds. Need a watering can? They've got 'em. Want to buy a pound of dried bay leaves? Look no further. It's a delightful place. Call (816) 842–3651.

Just down the street from the City Market at 400 East Fifth Street, Kansas City 64106, is a French bistro—admittedly a most unlikely spot to find such a place—but it is as authentic as it can be, with an outdoor cafe in the alley just as they are in Paris. *Le Fou Frog* isn't really faux at all, as owner and chef Mano Rafael will tell you. He is from Marseilles and made his reputation as head chef in some New York hot spots (Petrossian and Casanis). He met and married Barbara Bayer from Kansas City, and the rest is history.

The real test of a French bistro is the *soupe a l'oignon gratinee* with a bubbly top of Gruyère cheese ($5.50). This one passes with gold stars. Of course, it is impossible to taste everything on the menu, but give it a good try. The *poussin aux olives et herbes de provences* (whole baby chicken roasted in a fragrant sauce of olives and fresh herbs and served with garlic mashed potatoes) ($19.75) is excellent, but if you are feeling adventurous you might try the *cote de porc au Richard*—grilled pork chops that have been marinated in anise-flavored *pastis,* Ricard, and *herbes de Provence*. It is served with Panisse and baby vegetables for $24.

There is an excellent wine list with some very good and inexpensive wines available, just as there should be in a bistro. Call (816) 474–6060 for reservations.

Keep going east on Fifth Street to Harrison, and on the corner is a restaurant that has changed hands a few times but has always been Italian, because this is a neighborhood simply known as "The North End." It is the Little Italy that many big cities have. *Garozzo's Ristorante,* 526 Harrison, Kansas City 64106, has soft music by Frank Sinatra, a lively bar, and really, really huge servings of pasta. Do not, repeat, do *not* order spaghetti and meatballs unless you want to eat it for a week or can share it with several other people. The other dishes are more moderately proportioned but excellent. If you like, no, *love* garlic, order some olive oil to dip your Italian bread into and you will get a bowl of oil smothered in garlic and Parmesan cheese. Hours are Monday through Thursday 11:00 A.M. to 11:00 P.M. and Saturday 4:00 to 11:00 P.M. Call (816) 221–2455.

As long as you are in the River Market area, visit *Cheep Antiques River Market Emporium,* 500 West Fifth Street, Kansas City 64106. The store carries furniture in every price range and features antiques from Belgium, France, Germany, England, and Holland. A specialty is making entertainment centers from old armoires. Hours are 9:00 A.M. until 3:00 P.M. Tuesday through Friday and until 5:00 P.M. on Saturday and Sunday. Call (816) 471–0092.

Just south of the Paseo Bridge at Independence Avenue is *Scimeca's* Italian grocery store and deli. While not in the fanciest part of town, it is a good place to buy real imported Italian cheeses, olive oil, and olives. Their own Italian sausage is the best in town, and it is one of the few places to buy Italian bread from the Roma bakery.

St. Mary's Episcopal Church is a grand old church at 1307 Holmes in downtown Kansas City 64106. The red brick church has been there forever (since 1888) and as with many old churches, it has some interesting history and a good ghost story. Amazingly, the building was spared when the neighborhood around it was razed during urban renewal in the 1960s. It is a wonderful Sunday morning experience to follow the sound of the carillon and to hear organist Bruce Prince Joseph make the huge pipe organ sing for the Solemn High Mass celebrated every Sunday at 10:00 A.M., complete with incense and bells. The congregation is an interesting and varied collection of people from the urban area as well as suburban people who make the drive into the city every Sunday. Call (816) 842–0975 for the times of other services.

Strange As It Seems

The ghost of St. Mary's is believed to be that of Father Henry Jardine, who was rector of St. Mary's in 1879. A crypt was built under the altar for Father Jardine's body before his death. Because he suffered from a painful facial nerve disorder, he took laudanum (tincture of opium) and used chloroform to help him sleep. One night he died of the combination. The bishop declared it a suicide and therefore Father Jardine's body was buried in unconsecrated ground rather than in his beloved church. There have been several ghostly incidents. An acolyte saw a priest, in vestments, who stood facing the altar when he arrived at the church. He hurried to the sacristy thinking he must be late, only to find the rector waiting for him there. When they went back to the sanctuary, no one was there. Several people have sensed a presence in the gallery where his restless ghost hovers. St. Mary's Rector, The Reverend Dr. Bruce Rahtjen, is attempting to have Father Jardine's remains moved from the cemetery to the new columbarium in the church, perhaps allowing his spirit to rest in peace at last.

Along Southwest Boulevard the scent of chili peppers fills the air. This is Kansas City's Hispanic neighborhood, and the restaurants here are very popular, especially at lunchtime.

If you are looking for homemade tamales wrapped in corn husks, go to *La Posada Grocery* at 722 Southwest Boulevard, Kansas City 64108. They sell about any Mexican ingredient you could want—chilies, spices, corn husks, even Mexican coffee. Hours are Monday through Saturday 8:00 A.M. to 7:00 P.M. and Sunday 8:00 A.M. to 5:00 P.M. Call (816) 842–1891.

Casa de Fajita at 423 Southwest Boulevard, Kansas City 64108 is the spot to be for lunch or dinner in this area. The food is authentic and delicious. There are many Mexican restaurants on The Boulevard, but the best chili rellenos are here, handmade every day. Call (816) 471–7788. Hours are Monday through Thursday 10:00 A.M. to 9:00 P.M., until 10:00 P.M. on Friday, Saturday 10:00 A.M. until 10:30 P.M., and Sunday noon to 9:00 P.M.

Carmen's Cafe at 520 Southwest Boulevard, Kansas City 64108, is different from the typical Mexican restaurants that populate this area. Carmen's is actually an Italian dining establishment with what has been described as "a Latin flair." Hours are Monday through Thursday 11:00 A.M. to 10:00 P.M., Friday 11:00 A.M. to 11:00 P.M., and Saturday 4:00 P.M. to 11:00 P.M. Call (816) 471–4944 for more information.

Creative Candles (816–474–9711) is at 2101 Broadway, Kansas City 64108, at the corner of Southwest Boulevard and Broadway. Creative they are indeed. Duane Benton got into the candle business in the '60s like a lot of other idealistic entrepreneurial dropouts; the difference is that Duane kept at it and now sells candles throughout the United States.

On the edge of town in what is known as the West Bottoms, a community of artists is growing. They live in lofts in old factories and warehouses in what was once the heart of Kansas City's economy. They paint and sculpt and create art and live on the edge. Their galleries are not fancy, but their work is unique. Many are graduates of Kansas City's Art Institute. Most galleries don't keep regular business hours, so it's best to call ahead for an appointment if you want to view the art. They are typically open evenings and weekends. Among some of studios in this area is the *Old Post Office* at 1229 Union Avenue, Kansas City 64101 (816–221–1184).

This is an old industrial area with some pretty good eating places hidden away in it.

One of them, *Lydia's* at 101 West 22nd Street, Kansas City 64018, is located in a converted warehouse. Lydia's is very well known around town—there are three in New York—and beautifully done. The food, of course, is quite good, as is the wine list. Call (816) 221–3722 for reservations. Hours are 11:00 A.M. until 2:00 P.M. weekdays for lunch and 5:00 to 9:30 P.M. for dinner. Saturday dinner hours are from 4:30 until 10:30 P.M.

The perfect place to cool off on a sweltering summer day used to be the corner drugstore in any small town. It was a perfect spot to meet your favorite sweetie and the only place to get a fizzy chocolate phosphate, an ice-cold cherry Coke, or a tall ice cream soda. The *Kansas City Museum* at 3218 Gladstone Boulevard, Kansas City 64123, has re-created that spot for the children of the city. What the heck's a phosphate? A combination of flavored carbonated water and ice. Why is that chocolate-covered dip of vanilla called a sundae? Old "blue laws" made it illegal to sell soda water on Sunday, so it had everything an ice cream soda had except carbonated water. Most soda pops were originally hawked as health tonics. In fact, Coca-Cola was invented by a pharmacist. The cherry-wood pharmacy dates from 1886, the marble-topped soda fountain counter and stained glass lamps with spigots from about 1910. All were donated from the Kirby Drugstore in Modena. The museum hours vary according to season, so call ahead to make sure they're open on the day you want to visit. Regular museum admission is $2.50 for adults and $2.00 for kids and seniors. Call (816) 483–8300.

Just south of the busy interstates that ring downtown Kansas City proper is *Central Park Gallery* 110 East Missouri, Kansas City 64108, at the corner of Seventeenth Street (816–471–7711); it's a newly renovated, 110-year- old, three-story schoolhouse. Peter McCoy bought the old grade school and converted it into a showcase of Midwestern fine art, highlighting lithographs, raku ware, and original paintings. Hours are 10:00 A.M. to 6:00 P.M. Tuesday through Friday, and from 10:00 A.M. until 4:00 P.M. on Saturday.

The Thirty-ninth Street area of Kansas City is a wonderful old area in which to stroll. There are antiques shops, crystal shops, and just a lot of interesting places. There are also some of the city's best restaurants. *Cafe Allegro* at 1815 West Thirty-ninth Street, Kansas City 64111, is one of the best and most pricey restaurants. Owner Steve Cole, who still does some of the cooking himself, makes it worth every cent with a meal unlike anything you will find elsewhere. His wine list is superb. Call (816) 561–3663 for reservations, which you *will* need. Seating for lunch begins at 11:30 A.M. until about 2:30 P.M., and dinner is served from 6:00 P.M. until 10:00 P.M.

Around the corner at 3906 Bell Street is the **Genghis Khan Mongolian Barbecue,** an eat-all-you-can meat, seafood, and vegetable grill that is well worth its modest prices. Lunch is served Monday through Friday from 10:30 A.M. to 4:00 P.M., Saturday from noon to 4:00 P.M. Dinner hours are Monday through Thursday 4:00 to 9:30 P.M., Friday and Saturday from 4:00 to 10:30 P.M. Closed Sunday. Call owner Ling Chang for more information at 816–753–3600, or visit their Web site at www.mongolian.com.

Another interesting eating establishment on Thirty-ninth Street is quite different but worth seeking out if you are adventurous. **Hot Tamale Brown's Cajun Express** at the corner of Thirty-ninth and Main (10 West Thirty-ninth Street, Kansas City 64111) traces its name back to a slave named, simply, Brown, who won his freedom and then his fortune as a boat captain in the South. He became known as Cajun Brown and owned a boat called the Cajun Express. His son met and married a Mexican woman who sold tamales to the local fishermen. Their son was called Hot Tamale Brown and the rest is family history. A secret family recipe is known only to the restaurant's owner, Hot Tamale Brown III. He and his wife, Rosalind, opened the restaurant in an old bank building, where much of the business is done through the drive-in teller's window. You walk through a cast-iron fence under the light of a three-globed street lamp and into this bistro to hear the sounds of Louis Armstrong playing New Orleans music. You will find not just the true Bourbon Street tamale here, but Rosalind's own recipes for jambalaya, gumbo, and crawfish étoufée to be followed by key lime cheesecake. Call (816) 561–2020. Hours are 11:00 A.M. until 10:00 P.M. Monday through Saturday.

Drive on toward Main on Thirty-ninth Street and you will dead-end into an old art deco building, and the only clue you will have that you have found the right place is the occasional neon beer sign in the second-floor windows. You have found **Harling's Upstairs** at 3941-A Main, Kansas City 64111 (816–531–0303). The best time to search out Harling's is between 1:00 and 6:00 P.M. on any Saturday when Diane "Mama" Ray and her blues band pour their heart into a jam session that packs the house every single Saturday. A long list of Kansas City jazz and blues musicians join her to jam on any given Saturday. (It's a good idea to stop at **Antonio's Pizza** down at 3814 Main Street, Kansas City 64111 [816–561–1988] and get a thick slice or two of pizza to eat with your beer, because if you give up your seat, you will never get it back.) There are other things going on at Harling's at night, including Irish music on Thursdays. But Mama Ray is worth the trip on a Saturday afternoon, and if you love the blues, you will get there early and

Has Anyone Seen Dan's Nephew?

you will not leave until the band leaves at 6:00 P.M. Drive around back to park and climb the steep wooden stairway to the second floor. The dress is very, very casual, and blues lovers come from every part of the Kansas City area. (Someone described it as "kinda like the *Star Wars* bar," and what makes it fun is that people fill up the tables and before the evening's over, you have made new friends.

Kelly's in historic Westport at 500 Westport Road (816) 561–0635 is a good place to sip a brew. This is a very popular Kansas City nightspot. In fact, Daniel Boone's nephew used to hang out here. Well, he once ran a trading post in the building, which is the oldest in Kansas City. He hasn't come in lately.

There is more good jazz and blues in Kansas City than anywhere in the country. While you are in Harling's pick up a copy of *JAM (Jazz Ambassador Magazine),* with listings of all the jazz clubs in town and who is playing where. Then you can search out night life at places like the **Levee** at 16 West Forty-third Street, Kansas City 64111 (816– 561–2821), with wonderfully loud rock 'n roll to dance to on Saturday afternoons until 8:00 P.M., or **The Phoenix** downtown at 302 West Eighth Street, Kansas City 64105 (816–472–0001) where, if you are lucky, you might hear vocalist Karrin Allyson and her group. She is probably the finest young jazz voice in the country.

Mediterranean food with a Greek flavor is presented in the tiny **Sun Ray Cafe** at 813 West Seventeenth Street, Kansas City 64108, by Yannis Vantoz, who brought his native Greek dishes to the Kansas City area not long ago. The appetizer menu offers a selection of ten typically Greek choices, including hummus, calamari, tzatziki, spanakopita, feta cheese, and an absolutely wonderful marinated octopus.

Main courses include lamp chops, salmon, and different fresh fish daily. Yannis does not have a liquor license, so bring a favorite bottle of wine and he'll provide the wine glasses. With no corkage charge, you'll get a dinner as good as any in the best restaurants of Kansas City, at very reasonable prices. The appetizers are about $3.00 each, and entrees range from $14.50 to $17.50.

The cafe is open for lunch Tuesday through Saturday from 11:00 A.M. to 2:00 P.M. and for dinner from 5:30 to 10:00 P.M. on Friday and Saturday. Yannis will also serve small private parties on other nights. Call (816) 221–5757.

At the corner of the block at 1700 Summit, Kansas City 64108, the **Bluebird Cafe** serves lunch Monday through Saturday—great homemade soups and interesting sandwiches on crunchy sunflower-seed bread. This corner cafe is much larger than it looks from the outside and fills up quickly at lunch time. The tin ceilings and antique cabinets make the high-ceilinged rooms cozy. A long bar along one wall is a fine spot to wait for a table. Lunch is available from 11:00 A.M. to 2:00 P.M. Monday through Saturday. Dinner is served Wednesday through Sunday from 5:00 to 10:00 P.M. Call (816) 221-7559.

Historic Westport, some 40 blocks south of downtown, was the whole city at one time. Some of us think it still is. Check out the *Classic Cup* (816-756-0771) at 4130 Pennsylvania, Kansas City 64111, owned by Charlene Welling. Originally the spot in Kansas City for gourmet coffee beans, it now offers a selection of imported cheeses, pâté, and preserves. The bakery, ruled by pastry chef Paul Frazier, offers incredible edibles.

The Cup now runneth over; you can pick from one of the finest wine lists in the city and stay for a wonderful lunch. Chef Brenda Sweeny is the creative engine behind the apron. The menu changes daily but is always based on fresh ingredients.

The all-time favorite entree is the raspberry–Dijon mustard sauce on grilled pork tenderloin (sometimes it's blueberry, blackberry, or tart cherry–Dijon sauce). Hours are Monday through Friday from 7:00 A.M. to 10:00 P.M., Saturday from 8:00 A.M. to 11:00 P.M., and Sunday from 10:00 A.M. to 3:30 P.M. for brunch, and 5:00 to 10:00 P.M. for dinner.

Three Dog Bakery at 612 West Forty-eighth Street, Kansas City 64112, has tasty-looking cookies arranged in a bakery case. You might be tempted to buy a bagful to munch on as you walk. What you need, however, is a doggie bag, because owners Mark Beckloff and Dan Dye are serving freshly baked treats for your pooch. You can buy your canine a pupcake or a cheese pizza. For the vegetable course there is "collie-flower," and for dessert there are "snickerpoodles," always a favorite. A portion of the price goes to help abused dogs. The treats have no salt or chemicals and are low-fat (your dog will thank you). You can also order your loving pet its own specially decorated birthday cake to share with other dogs on the block. Hours are 10:00 A.M. to 7:00 P.M. Monday through Saturday (Thursday until 8:00 P.M.) and 11:00 A.M. to 5:00 P.M. on Sunday. Call (816) 753-3647 to order that special pal a special cake.

Let's get small. If you love tiny things (or if you haven't quite grown up), don't miss the *Toys and Miniatures Museum* at 5235 Oak Street, Kansas City 64112 (816-333-2055). Childhood friends Mary Harris Francis and Barbara Marshall started the museum in a Mediterranean-style mansion built in 1906. It has been expanded to 21,500 square feet.

The mansion and the surrounding property is owned by the University of Missouri–Kansas City, but the toys and miniatures belong to a private nonprofit foundation. Miniatures are not toys, scale is important in a miniature—everything in a miniature room must look exactly like a full-size room. Toys are a separate collection.

Tucked upstairs is a Victorian nursery with a brass cradle made in Paris in 1850. It has been in Mary's family for several generations. Barbara's father, Hallmark Cards founder Joyce C. Hall, had a dollhouse built for his daughter at a local high school. When it was time to pick it up for Christmas, it was too big to take out of the school, so she did not get her dollhouse. Now they have a museum recognized as one of the largest miniature museums in the world. There are more than eighty-five antique furnished dollhouses at least one hundred years old, scale-model miniature rooms, and toys. The museum is open Wednesday through Saturday 10:00 A.M. to 4:00 P.M. and Sunday from 1:00 to 4:00 P.M. It is closed for two weeks following Labor Day. Admission is $4.00 for adults and $2.00 for children. Every Saturday at 1:00 P.M. you can enjoy storytellers, and at 2:30 P.M. on the first Saturday of the month there's a magician to entertain you.

Of course, in cities the size of Kansas City there is something for everyone if you know where to look. Sometimes just finding the first place is the key. For example, if your taste leans to designer clothes but your money leans more toward off-the-rack, you might enjoy browsing in some of KC's consignment shops. After pricing new clothes at Country Club Plaza, check out **B-Bax Consignment Shoppe** at 1201 West Forty-seventh Street, Kansas City 64112, just 3 blocks west of the Plaza. It is a boutique where you will discover Plaza style at much better prices—everything from silk blouses to fur coats. They also have a list of the eleven other consignment shops in the Kansas City area (816–531–0067). Hours are Monday through Friday from 10:00 A.M. until 5:30 P.M. and Saturday until 5:00 P.M.

South of Country Club Plaza, in Brookside, in an old Texaco station, is a small wine bar and cafe called **Joe D's Winebar-Cafe & Patio** (6227 Brookside Plaza, Kansas City 64227). It was the first wine bar in the country. Owner Joe DiGiovanni, one of the leaders of Les Amis du Vin (Friends of Wine), is a personable young man who will sit down and talk wine anytime.

He has the largest by-the-glass wine list in Kansas City, and his house wines are excellent. His menu changes each day, depending on what seasonal fresh produce and meat the chef has discovered. Unusual entrees such as breast of chicken with strawberry-peppercorn sauce, orange cream fettucine, or fresh marlin with coconut-banana-curry sauce are written on a chalkboard. The pizza du jour on fresh Italian Boboli bread (artichoke and crab pizza? Yes!) changes with the chef's mood. Joe D's (816-333-6116) opens weekdays at 11:30 A.M. and serves lunch until 2:30 P.M. Between 2:30 and 5:00 P.M. only appetizers and salads are served; dinner is served after 5:00 P.M. Joe D's closes at 11:00 P.M. on Monday and Tuesday, midnight on Wednesday and Thursday, and 1:00 A.M. on Friday and Saturday. After dinner be sure to try the bread pudding with hot caramel sauce, just like grandma used to make. Entrees range from about $8.00 to $18.00.

You can buy The **Best of Kansas City** at the shop of the same name at Crown Center, 2450 Grand Avenue, Kansas City 64108. Everything from apple butter (Stephenson's) to Zarda barbecue sauce is sold here. Call (816) 842-0200. Order gift baskets at (800) 366-8780. Hours are 10:00 A.M. to 9:00 P.M. (Sunday until 5:00 P.M.).

The piano bar seems to be a dying breed of nightclub, which is what makes **Inge's Lounge** at 8410 Wornall Road, Kansas City 64114, such a great find. Long-time piano player Dave McCubbin can play any song you can think of—old standards, '50s hits—it is almost a challenge to try to ask for a song he will not know. Inge's is a comfortable neighborhood bar in a strip mall. But don't be fooled by its quiet storefront: Dave invites people to pick up the mike and sing. This is not a karaoke bar, however, and the people who come up to stand by the mike are regulars and, for the most part, have the voice and style of professionals. Inge's is open Monday through Saturday from 10:00 A.M. to 1:30 A.M. Dave plays Wednesday through Saturday nights from 8:30 P.M. until 12:30 A.M. Call (816) 363-8722.

The city of **Independence,** just east of downtown Kansas City on Interstate 70, could be a day trip in itself: There's Harry S Truman's home, now a national park, and the **Truman Presidential Library,** at 24 Highway and Delaware, Independence 64050 (816-833-1400), is open 9:00 A.M. to 5:00 P.M. Monday through Saturday and noon to 5:00 P.M. Sunday (closed Thanksgiving, Christmas, and New Year's Day). There's a special program night on Thursdays, when the museum is open until 9:00 P.M. Admission is $5.00 adults, $4.50 seniors, $3.00 ages six to eighteen, under six free. Self-guided tours.

You'll also find the world center for the Reorganized Church of Latter-Day Saints and the RLDS Auditorium. There are also Civil War battlefields, as well as the beginnings of the Santa Fe Trail, still visible in the worn earth. (Sometimes it seems as if half the towns on this side of the state claim the trail, but in Independence they still celebrate the

Santa-Cali-Gon, where the Santa Fe, California, and Oregon trails jumped off into the wilderness.) The National Frontier Trails Center is a fine place to learn more about the hardships and adventures of those who dared to leave civilization behind and strike out across the wilderness to a new life. It's in the historic Waggoner-Gates Milling Company building. Call (816) 254–0059 for further information.

The *Rheinland Restaurant* at 208 North Main, Independence 64050, serves a scrumptious *Zigeunerschnitzel* (Gypsy Schnitzel), a pork cutlet with a spicy pepper sauce and a side of *späetzle* (tiny dumpling or noodles). A large dark beer will help the digestion. Heinz and Rosie Heinzelmann are the owners and they suggest the *Jaegerschnitzel* (hunter-style), which is less spicy and covered with a creamy burgundy-mushroom sauce. These and the *Rouladen* with *Rotkoiil* (beef filled with bacon, pickles, and onions, served with red cabbage and *späetzle*) are available for dinner only; however, the lunch crowd can try the *Schnitzel à la Holstein* or many kinds of sandwiches (the Strammer Max is a favorite—thin-sliced Black Forest ham on rye topped with a fried egg). The Rheinland is open Tuesday through Saturday from 11:00 A.M. to 9:00 P.M. and on Sunday from noon to 8:00 P.M. Most evenings there is music from a hammer dulcimer and guitar. On Friday nights it's sing-along accordion music. Call (816) 461–5383.

If you are an old-movie buff, head for the *Englewood Theater* at 10917 Winner Road, Independence 64052. You can call (816) 252–2463 and get the list of movies for a couple of months. The 1949 art deco theater has been restored to its original luster with a huge 50-foot screen and an outstanding sound system geared to handle every type of movie sound made. More than a thousand neon lights glitter outside. The theater seats 670 people and is patterned after the beautiful Radio City Music Hall in New York City. Tickets are cheap on "two-buck" Tuesday and not bad the rest of the week at $3.00 before 6:00 P.M. and $5.00 after. The really neat thing is that you can call ahead and buy tickets at the amazing price of six for $18 to see movies like *A Night to Remember* (the original *Titanic,* circa 1958), Fred Astaire–Ginger Rogers movies, or old sci-fi thrillers. Movies are at 7:15 P.M. on weeknights, with matinees on Saturday and Sunday.

There are antiques stores, B&Bs, and dandy places to eat—in short, there's entirely too much to include in a single volume. We've narrowed it down to these few, which are off the beaten path by virtue of location, arcane historical significance, or ambience. Of course, the best tenderloin in town is at the *Courthouse Exchange,* 113 West Lexington, Independence 64050. The portion is huge. Call (816) 252–0344.

Strange As It Seems

Want to see the mantel Jackie Kennedy started a feud over? When Harry Truman moved this mantel to the Truman Library in Independence, the former first lady had a fit and wanted it returned to the White House.

Don't miss **Clinton's** on the square, at 100 West Maple, Independence 64050. When he was on the campaign train in Independence, President Bill Clinton visited here; they have photos and a thank-you letter to prove it! (He's wearing a Clinton's sweatshirt.) Just how long has it been since you've had a real chocolate soda or cherry phosphate? While you're there, ask them to make a chocolate-cherry cola; it's like a liquid, chocolate-covered cherry with a twist. This is a real old-time soda fountain, complete with uniformed soda jerks and a marble counter with a mirrored back; the malts still whir in those tall, frosty metal containers as they did when we were kids. Call (816) 833–2046 for more information. Clinton's is open daily.

And if all this hedonistic revelry doesn't get you, maybe the historical angle will: Truman's very first job was at Clinton's. You don't have to be a soda jerk first to be president, but maybe it helps. Harry was one of our most popular commanders-in-chief.

You think celebrity prisoners in our jails are pampered now. When Frank James was held at the jail in Independence, his cell sported an Oriental carpet; he had guests in for dinner and served them fine wines. For that matter, so did William Quantrill when he was incarcerated here.

Although the dank cells with their monolithic stone walls were decorated when company called, they were still jail. More than a hundred and thirty years after the fact, the cells are still dark, forbidding holes that look impossible to escape. The 1869 **Jail Marshall's Home and Museum** (816–252–1892) are at 217 North Main, Independence 64050. The museum is open April through October, 10:00 A.M. to 5:00 P.M. Monday through Saturday, 1:00 P.M. to 4:00 P.M. Sunday; November, December, and March, 10:00 A.M. to 4:00 P.M. Tuesday through Saturday, 1:00 P.M. to 4:00 P.M. Sunday; closed January and February. Admission is $4.00 adults, $1.00 ages six to seventeen, and free for children under six.

Several interesting B&Bs are in Independence. **Serendipity Bed & Breakfast** at 116 South Pleasant Street, Independence 64050, is a step back in time. This three-story, 1887 brick house is full of Victorian details. An authentic-looking iron stove hides an electric range, and tall glass-door cabinets are full of antique food containers and plates. Even the brick-edged flower beds in the garden are alive with color from spring through fall. The most modern item is the 1926 Studebaker in the carriage house, which is driven to take guests on a tour of

Independence. Rates are $45 to $85, which includes a full breakfast in the dining room. If there are six or more in your party, you can arrange for a Victorian Tour and Tea for $15 a person. Call Susan for more information (816-833-4719).

Perhaps you remember the nineteenth-century painting of two trappers in a long wooden canoe. A big black animal—perhaps a bear—sits in the bow gazing enigmatically at the viewer. Or maybe "The Jolly Boatmen" is more your style, with the rivermen dancing at the dock, playing instruments, and generally raising a ruckus. Artist George Caleb Bingham painted both, along with many others depicting life along the Western Frontier.

Bingham made his home for a time at the elegant *Bingham-Waggoner Estate* at 313 West Pacific, Independence 64050, where he watched two Civil War battles rage across his front lawn (not conducive to painting a decent picture. Think what that would do to your concentration!).

Visit from April to October, Monday through Saturday from 10:00 A.M. to 4:00 P.M. and Sunday 1:00 to 4:00 P.M., to find out how "the other half" lived in the last century—or rent the mansion for a festive event and make the past your own. The mansion is also open from late November through December for the Christmas season; they decorate all twenty-six rooms. Admission is $3.00 for adults, $2.50 for senior citizens, $1.00 for children six to sixteen, and free for children under six, with slightly higher winter fees to defray the cost of all those decorations. Call (816) 461-3491 for more information.

Another beautiful visit is to the *Vaile Mansion* at 1500 North Liberty in Independence 64050. It is open from April 1 to October 31, Monday through Saturday from 10:00 A.M. until 4:00 P.M. and from 1:00 to 4:00 P.M. on Sunday. Admission is $3.00 for adults, $2.50 for seniors, $1.00 for children six to sixteen. Call (816) 325-7430.

There is great antiques shopping in this region. Independence was the jumping-off point for pioneers heading west, so this is as far as a lot of their furniture got. Shlepping across the country with a wagon full of sideboards and armoires didn't seem practical, so Independence is where many pioneers began jettisoning large pieces of furniture. (Rocking chairs often made it as far as the Platte River.)

National Frontiers Trails Center exhibits commemorate the Santa Fe, California, and Oregon trails, all of which passed through or began in Independence. The Trails Center doesn't feel like a museum, because it presents the trails through the words of the pioneers who traveled them. The layout of the center is patterned after the trails. At one point, a fork in the path forces visitors to choose between taking the Santa Fe or the Oregon-California routes. One route dead-ends, so if you choose that route, you have to go back and try again. Voice-activated boxes tell stories of how the West was settled, and the murals by Charles Goslin show how it was accomplished. There are many pioneers' journals which make fascinating reading, and there is a theater with a trails film. The center is located at 318 West Pacific Street, Independence 64050. Call (816) 325– 7575. Hours are 9:00 A.M. to 4:30 P.M. Monday through Saturday, 12:30 to 4:30 P.M. Sunday. Closed Thanksgiving, Christmas, and New Year's Day. Admission is $3.50 for adults, $3.00 for seniors, $2.00 for ages six to seventeen, and free for those under five.

The **Woodstock Inn Bed & Breakfast** at 1212 West Lexington, Independence 64050 was originally a doll and quilt factory. It features eleven uniquely and beautifully appointed guest rooms. Innkeepers Todd and Patricia Justice have completely refurbished the place, which now features a fenced-in courtyard and garden area, thermo-massage spa tubs, fireplaces, and a wealth of fine collectibles, rare antiques, and priceless artwork from around the world. Rooms range from $75 to $189 and all rooms have private baths. Call (816) 833–2233 for reservations.

A maze of interstates has left old Highway 40 very nearly off the beaten path. Find the highway just south of the intersection of Noland Road and Interstate 70, and turn east to **Stephenson's Old Apple Farm Restaurant** at Lee's Summit Road, Independence 64136. This one is well worth a stop, as happy eaters from presidents to movie stars have discovered. A large barrel of their famous cider keeps waiting diners happy. Stephenson's is sprawling but done in small rooms to keep the feeling intimate; some rooms are elegant, others are like dining in a rustic wine cellar. Enjoy an apple daiquiri (or peach or strawberry in season) and their famous smoked chicken. Meals are served with almost too many choices (savory green rice, frozen fruit salad, several types of muffins, and Stephenson's own apple fritters). Call (816) 373–5400 for reservations.

And 2 blocks east of Stephenson's is one of the dandiest antiques malls you'll ever want to explore—**Antiqueland** (816–373–0410), at 4621 Schrank Drive, Independence 64055 (don't worry, you can see it from Highway 40). It's huge, upstairs and downstairs; plan on taking plenty of time. More than 200 dealers show off their wares in 40,000 square feet of space.

An antiques mall is an antiques mall is an antiques mall, right? Not in this case. There's also a tearoom, if you get hungry; if a powerful thirst is upon you and you just need a treat, there's an old-fashioned soda fountain adjacent to the tearoom.

For heaven's sake, don't leave town without visiting The *Angel Lady* at 216 South Spring Street, Independence 64050 (on the southwest corner of the route around the square). Owner Carolyn Pratt has thousands of angels, in this four-room brick gift shop. More than 2,000 seraphim, cherubim, and their brethren—ranging in price from $1.00 to $500.00—fill her little shop just south of the square. Glass angels hang from the windows and reflect the sunlight; golden angels glimmer on tables; pictures of angels hang on the walls. A wonderful stained-glass window with an angel was rescued by Carolyn from an old church and destruction. The shop is open Monday through Saturday 9:00 A.M. until 5:00 P.M. Call (816) 252–5300.

Every town tries to have the weirdest little museum, and *Leila's Hair Museum* gives Independence a lock on that title. (Ow! Sorry!) You can see a 14-inch-high tree made of human hair. There are more than 1,000 pieces of jewelry and art all made from hair and dating before 1900. The Hair Museum is at 815 West Twenty-third Street, Independence 64050. It is open Tuesday through Saturday, 8:30 A.M. to 4:30 P.M. There is a $3.00 admission charge. Call (816) 252–HAIR for more information.

Independence is the center of the Reorganized Church of Latter-Day Saints, and the new temple is something to behold. Inside the 1,600-seat sanctuary at 201 South River, Independence 65050, is a 102-rank, 5,685-pipe organ built by Casavant Frères Limitée in Quebec, Canada. That is only the beginning. The rest you have to see for yourself. It is truly magnificent. The building is open to the public for guided tours from 9:00 A.M. to 5:00 P.M., Monday through Saturday and from 1:00 to 5:00 P.M. on Sunday. You can attend free organ recitals at the auditorium from 3:00 to 3:30 P.M. daily from June to August, and on Sunday only the remainder of the year. Also open to the public is a daily prayer for peace at 12:30 P.M. in the temple sanctuary.

At the old RLDS auditorium, the one with the green dome at 1001 West Walnut, Independence 64050, you can take your children to the nondenominational Children's Peace Pavilion. There they can play games that help them learn cooperation, communication, and self-esteem, and have a good time. The peace pavilion is on the fourth floor; admission is free. Call (816) 521–3030 for information. Hours are 9:00 A.M. to 5:00 P.M. daily; closed Christmas and New Year's Day. Admission is free. There are guided tours and free organ recitals on Sunday at 3:00 P.M. (and daily in June, July, August at 3:00 P.M.).

What Goes Around, Comes Around

William Clark returned from the historic expedition with Meriwether Lewis to become administrator of the Missouri Territory. Respectful and fair, Clark was accorded similar courtesies by the tribal chiefs, sparing the state some of the woes brought upon other areas by mismanaged dealings with the Native Americans.

Just outside Independence is the town of **Sugar Creek,** where a small girl named Caroline Rozgaj discovered America in 1914 when her family came from their native Croatia. She met and married Michael Kobe in 1927 and raised a family in a home filled with the delightful aroma of warm *povitica* bread. The children learned the art from their mother. Her philosophy, "If you put good things in it, it'll taste good," still works today at the **Kobe House Bakery** at 212 South Sterling, Sugar Creek 64054. Caroline's children also will indulge you with mama's strudel and other Croation favorites. It's the same tradition and the same house where Caroline raised them. Hours are 7:30 A.M. to 6:00 P.M. Thursday and Friday, 7:30 A.M. to 4:00 P.M. Saturday. Call (816) 254–3334 or toll free (888) 254–3334 if you are out of town and want to order *povitica* bread.

Martin City is pretty small, but it has a fine melodrama theater that is popular with folks in the Kansas City area. Judy Thompson has opened a pottery shop in Martin City as a retail outlet for local artists. The **Potter's Obsession** has become a thriving business because she also decided to offer pottery-making classes, too. The shop is at 512 East 135th Street, Martin City 64145, in an old but charming building. The front portion is retail space where you can buy handmade ceramic pottery created by Judy and other artists. The back section is a pottery-making studio, where students of all ages learn to use a potter's wheel to shape pieces, then fire and glaze them. Call (816) 941–2555.

Historic River Section

How about a day trip back in time? It's 1803, the year of the Louisiana Purchase: Imagine Missouri nearly empty of "civilization," as it was when it became part of the United States. Early fur trappers traded necessities—like tobacco, tomahawks, blankets, fabrics, and cookware. The Osage peoples were the most common Indians in this area, and they did business amicably with both French and American trading posts.

East of Independence you'll explore **Fort Osage,** a National Historic Landmark and the westernmost U.S. outpost in the Louisiana Purchase; its site was chosen by Lewis and Clark; construction was originally supervised by William Clark himself. Strategically overlooking the

Fort Osage, Sibley

Missouri River, the fort was reconstructed from detailed plans preserved by the U.S. War Department. The factory building stands today on its original foundation. Artifacts unearthed during the excavation are on display in the visitors' center.

You may find a living history reenactment in progress, complete with trappers and military men, Indians, explorers, storytellers, and musicians. Clothing displayed is authenticated down to the last bit of trim, and guides learn their alter egos' life and times so thoroughly that you forget you are only visiting the past. Sit inside the blockhouse looking out at the river, watch arrowheads being made from local flint, or visit the gift shop to purchase unique items with a sense of history (like real bone buttons).

Rustle up a group to enjoy one of the after-hours programs offered by the Jackson County Heritage Program. You can reserve a place at a hearthside supper in the factory's dining rooms, for example. Enjoy an authentic nineteenth-century meal by candlelight; then cozy up to the fireplace and savor the entertainment.

Several weekends a year, special events such as the Sheep Shearing (May) or Militia Muster and Candlelight Tour (October) are offered, or spend the Fourth of July as our forebears did—the fort's a great place for it.

To find Fort Osage (816–650– 5737) take Highway 24 from Kansas City east to Buckner; turn north at Sibley Street (Highway BB); follow the gray signs through the tiny town of Sibley. The fort is open year-round on weekends from 9:00 A.M. to 4:30 P.M. You can explore on your own Wednesday through Sunday April through November. Admission is

$3.00 for adults and $2.00 for senior citizens and children ages five through thirteen. Children under five are admitted free.

A more historic (and scenic) route between Fort Osage and Lexington will take you down the Highway 224 spur through Napoleon, Waterloo, and Wellington. This is Lafayette County—beginning to get the picture here? Must have been history buffs around this area since dirt was young. The road runs along the Missouri River, sometimes almost at water level, other times from a spectacular river-bluff view.

Don't miss the turnoff to tiny downtown *Napoleon;* it's a lovely place to pick up a bit of lunch in a real old-fashioned general store. The *G&S General Store* celebrated its centennial in 1992. This is no upscale yuppie fern bar; you'll find hardware, horse liniment, and canned goods on the aisles leading back to the deli area. And what a deli—it's an old-time meat case where owners Rex and Jacie Ryan will make you a sandwich while you wait—maybe a fresh pink pastrami on rye with the works. A big case full of soft drinks, milk, and juices completes the offerings. Hours are 9:00 A.M. to 7:00 P.M. Monday through Friday, 9:00 A.M. to 6:00 P.M. Saturday, and 11:00 A.M. to 4:00 P.M. on Sunday. Call (816) 934–8222.

Across the street is *Ma & Pa's Riverview Antiques Mall* (816–934–2698), and a wonderful view. The Missouri River shines like a mirror far below, and rich bottomland fields fill the rest of the space to the far hills. Vicki Merritt welcomes you Monday through Saturday 9:30 A.M. to 5:00 P.M. and Sunday from noon to 5:00 P.M.

Ride On By

The Pony Express house at 1704 South Street is not open to the public, but it is interesting that one of the founders of the Pony Express, William Bradford Waddell, built it, and family members have lived there ever since. The person who now occupies the house—Katherine Bradford Van Amburg—is his great-great-granddaughter. Members of the Waddell family have lived in the house since 1840.

A bit farther on is Waterloo, just between Napoleon and Wellington—the obvious place, don't you think? There's not much here but a sign and a few houses, but it would be perfect even if it were only the sign!

On the way into *Lexington,* watch for colorful sights guaranteed to make you smile, like the A-frame wedding chapel overlooking the river, the old Peckerwood Club, and a grain silo painted to look like a lighthouse—and that glorious old river.

Once you enter historic Lexington, soak up the antebellum ambience. The homes along Highway 24 and on South Street are wonderful examples of Victorian charm—and, remember, we're not just talking 1890s gingerbread here. The Victorian era began in the 1840s. You'll itch to get inside some

And the State Motto Is...

of these beauties; check with the Chamber of Commerce for dates and times on historic homes tours. Lexington has four national historic districts and 110 antebellum and Victorian homes and shops. There are several good B&Bs, too.

The state motto is a quotation from Cicero: "Salus popali suprema lex esto." (Let the welfare of the people be the supreme law.)

The Victorian, at 1522 South Street, Lexington 64067 (660–259–2868), is the labor of love of Shirley Childs and Mary Ault. This lovely Victorian was built in 1885 by the town banker. It has thirteen rooms and ten beautiful fireplaces. Shirley and Mary have done a lot of renovation and added an enclosed gazebo and hot tub in the garden. There's a carriage house with one room and a private bath. It is almost like an apartment, with a refrigerator filled with soft drinks and a sitting area with a wicker couch and television. Two more rooms are in the main house. Rates are $75 with continental breakfast. E-mail at ms16@iland.net.

The carriage house is also home to Shirley's **Mistiques** antiques shop. Both the house and the shop are filled with interesting things. Mary is a Hummel collector. Shirley has an original Vincent Price drawing and a Steve Balboni autographed baseball bat. The house has been on the homes tour, and last year 5,000 people came through. Tours of the downstairs are available for $2.00.

Shirley and Mary also own the local pub. **Riley's Irish Pub and Grill,** at 913 Main Street, Lexington 64067, is a pub tucked into a historic building, a pub in the real sense of the word—families gather there to eat and the bar is open until closing time. There is an Irish menu as well as food cooked on the grill, so it is an interesting place to stop. It is open Wednesday through Saturday from 11:00 A.M. until 10:00 P.M. Call (660) 259–4770.

The area around the courthouse has plenty of places to browse in. Probably the neatest place in town is the **Victorian Peddler Antiques Shop and Tea Room** at 900 Main Street, Lexington 64067. Rebecca Hooser and her daughter Melissa Clark carry fine Victorian furniture but you can also have lunch there. The tearoom has an eclectic assortment of antique tables and chairs. As Rebecca says, "If you like your table, you can take it home with you." The menu changes each day, but there is always a quiche, a soup, and a gourmet sandwich available to eat before you order a piece of homemade pie. Everything is made from scratch. The tearoom is open Tuesday through Saturday from 11:00 A.M. to 2:00 P.M., Friday and Saturday for dinner from 5:00 to 9:00 P.M., and Sunday from 11:30 A.M. to 2:00 P.M. Call (660) 259–4533 for more information.

The **Velvet Pumpkin Antiques** shop is at 920 Main Street, Lexington 64067. Owner Georgia Brown keeps regular hours from Monday through Saturday from 10:00 A.M. until 5:00 P.M. and Sunday from 11:00 A.M. to 4:00 P.M. Call (660) 259–4545.

Ma & Pa's Bakin' Place (660–259–6612) is a little farther down the block at 929 Main, Lexington 64067. This place is full of cookies, cakes, potato and salt-rising bread, and other freshly baked treats. It is open from 6:00 A.M. to 2:00 P.M. Tuesday through Saturday, so you can stop in before you hit the road. James Covey and the aptly named Karen Baker are the owners; these game young people have been known to attend local fairs in period costume, baking their delights outdoors in an old-fashioned wood stove.

Be sure to stop by the restored **Log House Museum** at 307 Broadway, Lexington 64067. This 1830s home was discovered in a rundown condition and was moved and rebuilt log by log by the volunteer efforts of local citizens. Now it is surrounded by wildflowers and paths as it might have been when it was new. Spinning wheels, quilts, and other items of the era fill the little cabin, and a gift shop is in the back; admission is $1.00 for adults and 50 cents for children under twelve. Hours are Wednesday through Saturday 11:00 A.M. to 4:00 P.M. and Sunday noon to 4:00 P.M. From November to April, however, the house is open only by appointment; it's too expensive to keep it warm through the winter months on a day-to-day basis. Call the Log House at (660) 259–4711 during open hours. The Battle of Lexington was fought in September 1861 when General Sterling Price moved his Confederate troops north after the Battle of Wilson's Creek and the fall of Springfield. After fifty-two hours of fighting, Union troops surrendered to the invaders. General Price took 3,000 prisoners and broke the chain of Union-held posts along the Missouri River. Remnants of the battle endure; a cannonball remains lodged in a pillar of the courthouse. You can still find earthworks out behind **Anderson House State Historic Site** (660–259–4654) overlooking the Missouri River. This red-brick house served as headquarters and hospital for both sides and is now a Civil War museum.

Along Highway 24 toward **Waverly,** the land undergoes a change from fenced, row-cropped fields to orchards. The peach crop is always at risk in Missouri's unpredictable weather. Blossoms are often teased out early by a mild February to be punished by an April freeze. It is a dangerous business, but the area around Waverly perseveres. The best peaches from this area are huge and sweet and dripping with juice. A bad year for the peach business is when the fruit is too big, too juicy, and not nearly plentiful enough to make shipping profitable. This is bad for orchard owners but wonderful for anyone lucky enough to be driving through.

Highway 24 is the old Lewis and Clark Trail along the river. Now it is filled with markets where orchard owners sell their bounty to travelers. Pick up peaches and apples or honey, homemade sausages, cheese, and cider along this scenic drive.

The Santa Fe Trail ran through here at one time, and it is still a trail of sorts for people living in the area: It is Missouri's apple and peach country. The Santa Fe Trail Growers Association is made up of seventeen members in the area. On a drive along Highway 24 you will see a bountiful expanse of apples, peaches, nectarines, strawberries, raspberries, and blackberries—and all for sale if the season is right. Schreiman and Burkhart are just two of the orchards you will pass along the road. Greenhouses along the way are filled with vegetables, sweet corn, cider, and honey. In July, *Peters Market* is worth the drive from Kansas City for many people.

Eleven miles south of Arrow Rock you may see some beautiful animals grazing in a field. Jim and Marcia Atkinson breed show-quality llamas on their farm. If you have never seen a llama close up, it is well worth the short drive. These animals are strong and intelligent as well as quiet and gentle. They have expressive faces and long, lovely wool. Their gentle temperament makes them good companions. They are bred as pack animals in South America, and the Atkinsons' llama Kong is one of the largest herd sires in this country.

About a mile outside the town of *Arrow Rock* on Highway 41 stands a comfortable white Victorian house shaded by old trees. It is now the home of Bob and Chris Rappold's *Evergreen Restaurant* (660–837–3251), a good spot to have a quiet dinner during the season at Arrow Rock's Lyceum Theater. Warm antiques and a fireplace in every room create a cozy ambience in which to enjoy really fine country cooking. Chris's Chocolate Mousse Cake is a sinful way to finish a meal; if you want to feel more virtuous, order the seasonal fruit tart. Evergreen closes after Christmas and opens again in the spring.

Bob and Chris used to be proprietors of Cafe Europa in Columbia. If it's any indication of how good their food is, former happy customers still drive all the way from Columbia to find them. They've kept some of the old Evergreen's recipes while adding favorites from Cafe Europa.

On matinee days—Wednesday and Saturday—during the theater season, hours are 11:30 A.M. to 3:00 P.M. for lunch, and 5:30 to 8:30 P.M. for dinner, and 4:00 to 7:00 P.M. on Sunday. In the winter Evergreen is open weekends by reservation only. If you have a group and let Bob know ahead of time, they'll open any time for private parties. Historical gossip has it that Jesse James once hid upstairs; listen quietly and you may hear his ghost. The Rappolds' emphasize the importance of having reservations because the location of the Evergreen is so far off the beaten path that finding extra help for unexpected crowds is impossible.

Pioneers stopped at historic Arrow Rock on their way west; it was a Santa Fe Trail town, a river port, and a meeting place for those who shaped history. More than forty original buildings remain. Arrow Rock is still a real town, with permanent residents, a grocery store, a gas station, and a post office, but it is also a state park and historic site. The population is only 70 (and the historic district so tightly controlled that someone has to die before someone new can move in, they say) but the place is packed in the summertime when the Lyceum Theatre is active. The state leases out the Old Tavern Inn, and it draws people from all over the state. Fried chicken, ham, blueberry cobbler, and wonderful bread pudding make people come back again and again. There is more, too. The 160-year-old tavern (that word was synonymous with hotel then) was home to travelers on the Santa Fe Trail or people bound for Independence and the Oregon Trail. Some died here of the cholera and typhus that stopped the westward trek of many. And so, the place is haunted. Beds used in exhibits on the second floor have been found mussed, quiet voices have been heard as well as the cries of a child whose mother died here; photos show strange images that are not really there, and once, a mysterious cloud of smoke appeared in the manager's upstairs bedroom. They seem to be friendly spirits, though. Dinners are bounteous and amazingly inexpensive ($10.95 will buy a huge meal, from salad to dessert). The museum is upstairs.

Arrow Rock looks like a normal town, but normal for a hundred years ago. Streets and gutters are made from huge blocks of limestone; board sidewalks clatter with footsteps. The old bank acts as ticket office for the Lyceum, and the tiny stone jail still waits for an inmate. You may camp at Arrow Rock State Park; sites are available for groups or individuals. Contact the Web site at www.arrowrock.org.

Today, the *Lyceum Repertory Theatre* (660–837–3311) offers performances throughout the summer in an old church building; it's Missouri's oldest repertory company. Call ahead for a list of plays and their rotating dates.

Borgman's Bed and Breakfast at 706 Van Buren, Arrow Rock 65320 (660–837–3350) is a nineteenth-century inn with five bedrooms and a common game room. Play a quick round of Scrabble, or enjoy a fireside chat with the Borgmans. Mother-and-daughter team Helen and Kathy Borgman did much of the restoration work themselves; take a look at the fascinating "house book," which shows step-by-step what's been done. Helen will fix you a generous breakfast, and Kathy will give you a tour of the town—she's an official Arrow Rock guide. Additional meals are available if you make prior arrangements. A cat and bird are in residence, so no other pets are welcomed. Rates are $55 to $60 for a double.

Artist George Caleb Bingham's home is here (remember him from Independence?), as is the home of Dr. John Sappington, one of the first to use quinine to treat malaria. Kathy Borgman will tell you all about it.

Miss Nellie's Bed and Breakfast is an elegant home built in 1853. It is walking distance from everything at 633 Main Street, Arrow Rock 65320. Innkeeper Linda Hoffman knows her way around the town and will set you on your way exploring. The home has two rooms for guests, one with a fireplace. The rooms are spacious and have sitting areas. One is on the first floor with semiprivate bath, the other is upstairs, where there are two full shared baths. A Steinway grand piano is in the parlor, and the home is furnished with period antiques. A continental breakfast is served in the formal dining room each morning. The home has a large wrap-around porch with a swing and wicker furniture. Rooms are $60. Call (800) 795–2797.

Cupid's Arrow Indian-Style

Legend has it that the town of Arrow Rock was named after a bow and arrow competition between Indian warriors vying for the hand of a chief's daughter. One arrow—the winner's, no doubt—shot from a sandbar in the river flew so far that it lodged in a distant bluff above the river.

There are seven B&Bs in Arrow Rock. It is quite a draw for Missourians in the summertime when the theater is going.

At *Boonville,* following the river east, the western prairie meets the Ozarks. The town was settled in 1810 by the widow Hannah Cole, who, with her nine children, built cabins on the bluffs overlooking the Missouri River. During the War of 1812 the settlement was palisaded and named Cole's Fort. It became the main river port for all of southwestern Missouri.

The older residential section of Boonville has an unusually well-preserved collection of antebellum brick residences with wide halls and large rooms. Modest neoclassical homes are mixed with more flamboyant Victorian ones; many are on the National Register of Historic Places.

While in Boonville visit the *Old Cooper County Jail and Hanging Barn* at 614 East Morgan, Boonville 65233. The jail was built in 1848 and used until 1978 when public hanging was declared cruel and unusual punishment. Prisoners' quarters resemble dungeons, where the inmates were sometimes shackled to the wall with metal rings. Outside the jail is the hanging barn where nineteen-year-old Lawrence Mabry was executed in 1930, the state's last public hanging (as told in historian Bob Dyer's folk song, "The Last Man to Hang in Missouri").

Thespian Hall at 522 Main Street, Boonville 65233 is the oldest theater still in use west of the Alleghenies. Originally built in 1857, it has been used as an army barracks, Civil War hospital, and skating rink, among other things. It featured gymnastics, opera, and movies in its day and is now the home of the Boonville Community Theatre.

If you have come to town for one of Boonville's many bluegrass festivals—where musicians play everything from harmonicas to paper bags—Thespian Hall is the center of the activity. The folk music tradition lives on here through the efforts of the Friends of Historic Boonville. If you can, try to coordinate your visit with one of these festivals. The Big Muddy Folk Festival is in April, and the Missouri River Festival of the Arts is in August.

If you are out walking around, search out Harley Park, where Lookout Point sits atop a bluff over the Missouri River, and get a feel for what early townsfolk saw along the long bend of the river. An Indian burial mound surmounts this high point; imagine the prospect of immortality with such a view.

At 611 East Morgan Street, Boonville 65233, is a circa 1869 home that has been elegantly restored and filled with antiques. Hosts of *Morgan Street Repose,* Robert and Doris Shenk, serve an extravagant breakfast in the formal dining room or in the secret English garden. Rooms are $86 to $120. Call (660) 882–7195 or (800) 248–5061 for reservations.

In nearby New Franklin on County Road 463, the *Rivercene Bed and Breakfast* will take you back in time to the 1869 home of a riverboat captain, Joseph B. Kinney, who ran a line of twenty-one sternwheelers up and down the Missouri River. The three-story brick Second Empire or Baroque revival home has survived flood after flood because of Kinney's understanding of the river and its architect's foresight in building it upon a pyramidal, floating foundation that kept water away from the first floor. Marble fireplaces warm the rooms, and hosts Jody and Ron Lenz wake the guests in the seven rooms each morning with the aroma of breakfast. You can spend the day on the one of several porches watching the birds and wildlife or take off on the KATY Trail. If you do, one of the rooms has a Jacuzzi, which feels fine after a day on the trail. Rooms are $90 to $140. Call (816) 848–2497 or (800) 531–0862, fax (816) 848–2142, or e-mail at rivercene@showmestate.com. Visit the Web site at www.riverscene.com and see the rooms online.

The mid-Missouri area was the site of many of the key battles of the Civil War. The first land battle of the war was fought 4 miles below Boonville on June 17, 1861. State troops under the command of Confederate Colonel John S. Marmaduke were defeated by federal forces led by Captain Nathaniel Lyon. Military historians consider this victory important in preserving the Union.

Jefferson City, Missouri's capital, is smack in the center of the state on Highway 50, handy to legislators and lobbyists. Built on the steep southern bluffs of the Missouri River, the city and the surrounding rural landscape offer considerable scenic variety. Large streams are bordered with steeply sloping and heavily forested hills. Bottomland here is rich with alluvial and yellow loess soils that don't look the way you expect fertile topsoil to look but support more wheat and corn than any other section of the Ozarks.

Here also is Jefferson Landing, one of the busiest centers of the nineteenth century. It's still busy; the Amtrak station is at the landing, as are the Lohman Building, the Union Hotel, and the Maus House.

The State Capitol is certainly on the path; however, once inside the House Lounge, you will find a mural painted in 1935 by Thomas Hart Benton. This mural stirred controversy in 1936 because some of the legislators said it lacked refinement. Always quick with an answer, Benton retorted that he portrayed "people involved in their natural, daily activities that did not require being polite."

Whether you are riding the KATY Trail or doing political business in Jeff City, you can enjoy the pampering of a bed-and-breakfast. The *Jefferson Inn* is at 801 West High Street, Jefferson City 65101. Innkeeper Geri Sims will welcome you (and your guests if you are having a fete of some kind) to her 1920s brick home, just 5 blocks from downtown. All three of the rooms have private baths and amenities like queen-size beds and hot tubs. Guests are invited to use the spacious common areas and enjoy the Victorian ambience of the antique furniture and decor. A full breakfast is served in the dining room. Rooms go for $75 a night. For reservations you can call (573) 635–7196 or (800) 530–5009, or visit the Web site at www.bbim.org/jefferson/rooms.html.

Central Dairy at 610 Madison Street, Jefferson City 65101-3131, still has old-fashioned ice cream and old-fashioned ice cream prices. This is a must-stop place for people on the KATY Trail on a hot summer's day and for everyone else, for that matter. Hours are Monday through Saturday from 8:00 A.M. until 6:00 P.M. and Sunday from 10:00 A.M. to 6:00 P.M. Gale Hackman and his son, Chris, are the owners, and they will make you one of their specialties, called the Rock and Roll. It's like a banana split but with four, count 'em, four flavors of ice cream and toppings. Betcha can't eat one! Call (573) 635–6148.

Arri's Pizza at 117 West High Street, Jefferson City 65101-1515, is a favorite with the members of congress in the capital city. Call (573) 635–9225.

Missouri's Melting Pot

Head west to *California* (that's California, Missouri) on Highway 50, and go south on Highway 87, 2½ miles to *Burgers' Smokehouse,* 32819 Highway 87, California 65018, if you fancy a ham to carry home. It is open from 7:30 A.M. to 5:00 P.M. This family-owned smokehouse has been in business for over twenty-five years and is one of the largest country meat-processing plants in the United States, producing 200,000 hams annually. You can take a tour of the plant any day but Sunday between 7:30 A.M. and 4:00 P.M. There is a toll-free number for ordering a ham: (800) 624–5426. Call (573) 796–4111 for information if you are in the area. Visit the Web site at www.smokehouse.com.

What you wouldn't expect to find here are the seasonal dioramas, which show the beauty of the Ozarks with great care for botanical and zoological detail. These scenes by artist Terry Chase depict the influence of Ozark geography and changing seasons on the process of curing meat.

If you feel in the gallery mood—or just in the mood for a fascinating chat with a man who always has time to sit down and have a cup of coffee—check out *Beryl White's Studio and Gallery* at 401 North High Street, California 65018 (573–796–2303). Beryl has been restoring this old Victorian storefront building for some time; it is now on the National Register. It's just the place if you're running short of sketching supplies while dawdling off the path. Beryl stocks everything from books to brushes and offers oil painting classes as well.

Leave California on Highway 87 and travel about 12 miles to *Jamestown,* if it's between June and fall, and pick some berries at *Missouri Highland Farms* at 17071 Garrett Road, Jamestown 65046. Growers Dan and Mary Brauch begin the year with asparagus and follow it up with berries of about any color you might be craving: blackberries, blueberries, and raspberries in three colors (black, red, and yellow). Hours are from 8:00

A.M. until about 5:00 P.M. in the summer and from 10:00 A.M. in the fall when the raspberries are ripe. Call (660) 849–2544 for more information. To find the farm, turn right off Highway 87 in Jamestown and follow "Y" Road (the one next to the post office) to the end.

Highway 50 will take you to the town of **Tipton**. Follow the signs to the **Dutch Bakery and Bulk Food Store** (660–433–2865). Located on Highways 5 and 50 at the west end of Tipton 65081, the shop is owned by Leonard and Suetta Hoover. Suetta does all the baking right here in the house while minding their six children and seems unruffled by it all. Old Order Mennonites, they came here from Pennsylvania and speak Pennsylvania Dutch when alone in the shop or talking to the children. Her pies are baked from homegrown berries and fruit; fresh vegetables from their garden are available in season. Homemade breads (a favorite is a wonderful oatmeal bread) and rolls fill the shelves along with bulk foods. But the primary reason for stopping here is the "Dutch letters"—crisp, thick pastry rolled and filled with almond paste and shaped into letters. They are cheaper if you buy five, and you might as well so you won't have to turn around and come back in an hour.

While in Tipton try to visit the **McClay House** on Howard Street and B Highway on the second or fourth Sunday of each month. This beautiful old three-story house has been restored and contains the original furniture. It is the site of the annual Fourth of July ice-cream social and features dinner and entertainment in September. The first Saturday in July is called Super Saturday around here and draws a thousand visitors for the barbecue contest, volleyball, and three-on-three basketball contests. Call the Tipton Chamber of Commerce (660) 433–6377 for more information about the McClay House and Super Saturday. Be sure and notice the newly-painted "Eight-Ball" water tower. There's a Fischer's Pool Table manufacturing plant in town.

You can find the Web site for the town of Tipton at www.tiptonmo.com.

At the intersection of Highways 50 and 65 in **Sedalia** is an old-fashioned 1950s drive-in called the **Wheel Inn** at 1800 West Broadway, Sedalia 65301. You must try their Guberburger; a hamburger grilled with peanut butter and served with mayonnaise, tomato, lettuce, and pickles. Before you shout *"Yuck!"* try it. They are deadly good and habit-forming. Note: The Wheel Inn is closed on Tuesdays. Call (660) 826–5177.

If you're in the mood for some really good barbecue, however, turn south on Highway 65 at that intersection and drive to 1915 South Limit to **Kehde's Barbecue,** Sedalia 65301 (660–826–2267), where John and

Trivia

The cemetery in the little town of Belton on Highways 71 and 58 might be worth a stop if you want to see the graves of Carry Nation and Dale Carnegie. The museum in the old city hall is fraught with memorabilia of the two leaders.

Chelsea Kehde (pronounced *K.D.*) serve the best barbecue in the area. But that's not all, Kehde's also has jalapeño fries (french fries dipped in some kind of spicy coating) and a grilled tenderloin sandwich that is as good as the fried kind but without all the fat. Kehde's is a regular stop for folks headed to or from the Lake of the Ozarks and Kansas City. Kehde's added a railroad dining car to the building to handle the extra crowds from the state fair and summertime Lake of the Ozarks crowd. It's fun to sit up in the old dining car and watch the traffic go by while enjoying the best barbecued ribs in the area. Take home a bottle of the sauce. In fact, take a couple or you will have to send for more when you get home.

If you drive into Sedalia on Highway 65, you will probably pass (off to your left and way up) a beautiful stone mansion overlooking the highway. It is Stonyridge Farm in **Bothwell State Park,** 19350 Bothwell State Park Road, Sedalia 65301. Bothwell chose limestone as his primary building material for the lodge and cliff house. There are more angles to this place than a Chinese puzzle—it must have driven the roofers crazy. The original carriage road rises almost 100 feet but in a gentle ascent, with the lay of the land; hand-laid stone culverts allow water passage under the road. Take the first left after you pass the house on Highway 65 going toward Sedalia (or, driving north, watch very carefully for the small sign marking the turn or you will have to turn around and go back when you finally see it). It is worth the trouble to find; there are spectacular views and wonderful walking trails near the house.

There are several antiques malls in Sedalia, but remember that in August this is the home of the **Missouri State Fair,** which attracts more than 300,000 people. The path gets beaten smooth, but it leads to midway rides, big-name entertainment, livestock shows, and car races—good, clean, all-American fun.

Sedalia's Web site is www.chamber.sedalia.mo.us.

In the little community of **Georgetown,** just outside of Sedalia (22166 Highway H, Georgetown 65301) stands a three-story girls' school built in 1842 by General George R. Smith, who founded the town of Sedalia. He built the girls' school for his own two daughters. The ten-room, white-brick beauty now houses Lorene Downing's **Georgetown Bed and Breakfast.** Three (or four) guest rooms, two with private baths, come

Bothwell State Park, Sedalia

with a big "farmer's breakfast" and are priced form $65 to $75. You can call Lorene at (660) 826–3941.

The KATY Trail snakes along the river for 83 miles from Sedalia east to Jefferson City, burrowing through its only tunnel at Recuperate. The trail also treats you to the only Missouri River railroad bridge near Franklin and goes past glittering Burlington limestone bluffs containing millions of fossils from the sea. The Mighty Mo has been out of banks twice since the trail was begun, once in the Great Flood of '93 and again in the almost-great flood of '95, but work is progressing to connect the trail here with its other end in St. Charles. When the river is behaving, you can look "across the wide Missouri" and have a magnificent view of the river traffic of barges and boats.

Western Missouri waited a long time for a botanical garden; St. Louis, in the east, has one of the finest in the country. Finally, after much hemming and hawing among folks in the Greater Kansas City area and those just over the Kansas border, the people of ***Powell Gardens*** couldn't wait any longer and began their own. Hurrah for private initiative! This is a beautiful, not-for-profit, 807-acre garden and natural resource center where you can wander among the flowers and indigenous plants, learn about "S-s-s-s-snakes!," make an all-natural wreath, or learn how to plant, prune, and harvest your own backyard botanical garden—you get the idea. The new chapel at the gardens was designed by E. Fay Jones, a nationally honored and recognized architect who built Thorncrown Chapel in Arkansas. Hours are from 9:00 A.M. to 6:00 P.M. daily. Workshops and seminars are scheduled year-round. There are also a cafe and a gift shop. Powell Gardens (816–566–2600) is just south of Highway 50 at Kingsville.

The KATY Trail

The KATY Trail is named for the MKT (Missouri-Kansas-Texas) Railroad tracks laid down over a century ago. The MKT came out of Fort Riley, Kansas, in the mid-1890s and shot into Indian Territory. It was the heartline of the area, rumbling in and bringing the lifeblood of freight, newspapers, and passengers needed to make the Midwest part of the Industrial Revolution. By 1892 the KATY had a direct route to St. Louis and connections to the eastern seaboard. Many of the small towns along the trail were born— and died—with the railroad.

Watch for signs from Interstate 70 (or Highway 291) for **Fleming Park** and **Lake Jacomo**. You'll find the usual sailing, swimming, and fishing as well as the **Burroughs Audubon Society Library** (816– 795–8177). Learn about the birds, take a hike, browse through the books, and discover how to turn your backyard into a wildlife sanctuary. The library is open from 12:30 to 4:30 P.M. Tuesday through Saturday.

Stop in your tracks. The world is moving altogether too quickly, but there's an antidote: *Missouri Town 1855* in Fleming Park. Managed by the Jackson County Parks Department, one of the two largest county parks departments in the United States, it is a collection of original mid-nineteenth-century buildings moved on-site. They now make up a brand-new old town founded in 1960.

A wide variety of architectural styles add to the historical significance of the town. It's just that sort of progression from rugged log cabins to fine homes that would have taken place in the last century as settlers arrived and commerce thrived. You'll find antebellum homes, a tavern, a schoolhouse, a church, a lawyer's tiny office (apparently the law was not quite so lucrative then), and the mercantile, where settlers would have bought outright or bartered for their goods. It has even been the setting for several movies, including the television version of *Friendly Persuasion* and the more recent movie *Across Five Aprils,* a story of a family split by the Civil War.

If the buildings alone aren't enough to pique your interest, this is a "living history" experience. You're liable to see the blacksmith at work, watch oxen tilling the soil, or be followed by the resident flock of geese. You can wander around a real herb garden and discover how many herbs were used as medicinals in the past century—hospitals were rare in those days, and medical insurance was unheard of.

Missouri Town 1855 is on the east side of Fleming Park. Take Colbern Road east to Cyclone School Road. Turn north (left) and follow the signs 2 miles to the entrance. Admission for adults is $3.00, $1.00 for youths, and children under four get in for free. The town is open Wednesday through Sunday from 9:00 A.M. till 5:00 P.M. from April 15 through November 15 and on weekends only from November till April.

Now it is dinnertime, and you are in for a surprise! Find **Chicken and Blues** at 235 S.E. Main Street in the historic Strother's District of **Lee's Summit** (64063). The restaurant specializes in pan-fried chicken. The "blues" part of the restaurant name comes from the music that is played in the background. Hours are Wednesday through Sunday, 11:00 A.M. to 8:00 P.M., Friday and Saturday until 9:00 P.M. The restaurant is closed Monday and Tuesday. Next door at 217 S.E. Main Street is **Strother's,** a neat little 1860s restaurant and microbrewery serving sandwiches and twenty-five microbrew beers on tap. Call (816) 246–0600 for information for both places.

Ray Julo's place is always full of ice-cream connoisseurs, people who know how special frozen custard is. **Custard's Last Stand** at 111 S.E. 291 Highway, Lee's Summit 64063, has been in town since 1989, and business is fine even with the competition. Frozen custard is a super premium ice cream with one-third less air than regular ice cream and is served at 28° F instead of 10° F as is regular ice cream. It doesn't freeze your taste buds. And, Ray points out, it has eggs in it, which makes it creamier—creamy and very thick—so thick it is handed to you upside down.

Custard's Last Stand was voted best ice cream in the Kansas City area two years in a row by a local magazine. There are forty-five flavors to choose from, with flavors like peanut butter, bubble gum, or the ever-popular "Berry, Berry, Berry" (a combination of strawberry, blueberry, and raspberry). Call a member of the Julo family (there are three generations working there) at (816) 524–7677. Hours are 11:00 A.M. until 10:00 P.M. (10:30 P.M. on Friday and Saturday) and from noon to 10:00 P.M. on Sunday.

Across the street stands a one-hundred-year-old church at 509 West Main. It is no longer a place of worship unless you worship the God-of-Good-Things-to-Eat. It is now the **Cafe Petit Four,** a deli and bakery where Lynn Phelps creates some wonderful meals. But the atmosphere is unique because of the 14-foot ceilings with the original brass chandelier lighting the room and seating for about ten in the choir loft.

Lunchtime people find all manner of home-cooked soups, quiches, and sandwiches on fresh bread. There is a vegetarian menu, too, and the veggie burger is quite good. Dinnertime brings out the big appetites, and they are satisfied with items like steaks or shrimp Creole. The desserts are handmade delicacies, the favorite being peanut butter pie, that will tempt you right off that diet. Not only can you go there for lunch

In 1868, when fifty-one pioneer families settled in the area, they applied for a post office and name for their town. Excelsior was suggested, but it was already taken. More names were sent and more had already been assigned. Finally, the frustrated citizens of this settlement on the east branch of the Grand River sent one last request: "We don't care what name you give us, so long as it is sort of 'peculiar.'" Well, that's exactly what they got: Peculiar, Missouri.

or dinner, but there is a grand Sunday brunch. Hours are Tuesday through Friday 9:30 A.M. until 3:00 P.M., and Saturday 8:00 A.M. to 4:00 P.M. That Sunday brunch is served from 9:30 A.M. to 2:00 P.M. Call (816) 537–5983.

Unity Village, on Highway 50 just west of Lee's Summit, is an incorporated town with its own post office and government. It's a peaceful setting with an old-world feel; spacious grounds contain a natural rock bridge, Spanish Mediterranean-style buildings, and a formal rose garden with reflecting pools and fountains. People of all faiths use the resources at Unity. The restaurant, bookstore, and chapel are open to the public, and you may arrange an overnight stay by calling (816) 524–3550.

Little *Greenwood* is just south of Lee's Summit on Highway 291, then east on Highway 150. This was once a bustling place with not one but two train stations. It was a major shipping center for cattle and lumber. It still has two explosives factories and a rock quarry nearby, accounting for the heavy trucks rumbling through this sleepy town.

An old wooden bridge marks the end of downtown proper; watch for signs to find any number of little antiques stores and factory outlets. *Greenwood Antiques and Country Tea Room* at 502 Main Street, Greenwood 64034, is a mall-type operation hard by the railroad bridge and just full of small booths. More than seventy shops occupy 15,000 square feet of space. The food is excellent; add your name to the waiting list when you go in the door, and they'll find you. Hours are 10:00 A.M. to 5:00 P.M. Monday through Saturday and Sundays noon to 5:00 P.M. Call (816) 537–7172 for more information.

Lone Jack is another unlikely spot for an upscale restaurant, but the *Cafe Periwinkle,* at 103 West 50 Highway, Greenwood 64070, offers casual yet elegant dining in a new plantation-style home. The menu features such interesting items as French pepper steak in a Parisian pepper sauce, chicken al pesto, and shrimp thermidor. A good wine list complements the menu. The front room is formal, with table linens; the back room is more masculine, a back-from-the-hunt feeling. For private events or for busy nights there are three additional rooms upstairs: the

Louis XIV, Flag, and Southwestern. There is even a gift and antiques shop. Call (816) 697–3599 for information. Hours are Tuesday through Saturday from 11:00 A.M. to 2:00 P.M. for lunch and 5:00 to 9:00 P.M. for dinner. Sunday brunch is served from 11:00 A.M. to 4:00 P.M.

There is a winery in Lone Jack, too: **Bynum Winery** at 13520 South Sam Moore Road, Lone Jack 64070.

If you still haven't gotten enough of the War between the States, head south and east of **Warrensburg** to **Cedarcroft Farm** at 431 Southeast County Road, Warrensburg 64093, a farm getaway B&B where Bill and Sandra Wayne have an 1867 farmhouse on eighty scenic acres to share with you. The house was built by Sandra's great-grandfather who was a Union soldier. Bill is a Civil War re-enactor and historian who can tell you a lot about the history of this area. He even has a uniform you can try on and a musket he will teach you to shoot. Sandra turns out a "more-than-you-can-eat" country breakfast accompanied by cookies, fudge, nut bread, and a table full of country cooking. These are five private rooms with three beds, perfect for ladies on an antiquing adventure, for just $125 each (for one to three people). The price includes a complimentary evening snack and a large five-menu breakfast. Bill and Sandra have added a secluded romantic cottage with spa, fireplace, and king-size bed; it costs from $185 to $210 a night. They will even pick you up at the Amtrak station. Horseback riding is available, nearby, too. For information call (660) 747–5728 or (800) 368–4944. The Web site is www.cedarcroft.com.

The farmstead is on the Historic Register and dates from the 1860s. The basement barns for the horses are unique because the horses sleep downstairs and the loft is at ground level. This prominent farmstead has what Sandra calls "a little Garden of Eden on the back 40," so consenting adults can walk in the woods, play in the creek, and "do some smooching." It's a good place to get away from the kids for the weekend. As you might suspect, this B&B fills quickly, so call early. Sandra can direct you to the nearby Amish community in Windsor and lots of other interesting places in the area. E-mail them at bwayne@cedarcroft.com or visit their Web site at www.cedarcroft.com.

Warrensburg is the home of Central Missouri State University. It is a fair-to-middlin'-size city now as it grows with the university. Coming into town on Highway 13 or Highway 50, you may have noticed several life-size animal sculptures made of scrap metal or pieces of wood. These are the handiwork of sculptor Jim Myers. Jim says he has been making scrap-wood sculptures since he was a kid; his dad owned a lumberyard.

He studied at the Hollywood Art Center in California and the Paris American Academy in France before returning to open his *Contemporary Gallerie* (660–429–2107) in 1982, where he displays his smaller wood sculptures and oils.

The *Camel Crossing Bed and Breakfast* at 210 East Gay, Warrensburg 64093 (660–429–2973) belongs to Joyce and Ed Barnes. It is a lovely turn-of-the-century home in the residential area near the university. Tastefully decorated with Middle Eastern and Oriental accents gathered while the couple lived in Saudi Arabia, the place has a unique flavor, including a collection of several hundred camel figures. A camel crossing sign is used as their logo. Rates are $70 to 90 with private bath. E-mail them at camelx@iland.net. Visit their Web site at www.bbim.org/camelx/index.html.

If you are headed north on Highway 13, there is a little surprise waiting for you about 4 miles north of Warrensburg near Fayetteville. Standing patiently near the highway are Ogbid and his wife Ishtar watching traffic roll by day after day. Ogbid and Ishtar are made of old oil drums, engine pistons, metal buckets, and assorted springs and reflectors, giving them a nightlife of sorts. Their son Nimrod joined them a few years ago. Nimrod resembles his parents, although he is unique because his head is an old metal chamber pot. Then Cousin It joined the family. He is made from an old water heater with a freon canister for a head, and he's covered with thousands of yards of baling wire, each strand individually attached. Cousin It, with 150 pounds of hair, looks more like a furry family pet than a relative.

Trivia

Warren Goodall invented the power rotary mower in Warrensburg and sold them for $100 a piece.

The creator, J.C. Carter, lives up the hill. He's had fun with his hobby of creating "assembled metal sculptures," sort of recycling-gone-bonkers. He has visions when he sees industrial junk—freon canisters and chamber pots take on a life of their own. But he pulls the whole community into the fun. When locals complained that Ishtar and Ogbid looked lonely standing out there, he threw a wedding complete with preacher, cake, reception, and birdseed to throw (instead of rice) there at the corner, then carted the 1,400-pound wedding couple off for their honeymoon. A couple of weeks later they returned with Nimrod. (Gestation period of robots is sort of undetermined at this time.) It wasn't long (how long is a mystery) until little Offazzie joined the family, and a cute little thing she is, too. Cousin It was then joined by "The Reaper," and the happy family spent its days watching the road. But this is the real world, and there are bad people in

Jim Myers sculpture, Contemporary Gallerie

it. One dark and stormy night, little Nimrod was kidnapped. J.C. and his wife, Karen, offered a reward for his return, but to no avail. Then a neighbor called. He had found Nimrod in a field beaten to a fare-thee-well. J.C. took the pickup out there and brought him home. He was in intensive care for a long time as J.C. worked to bring him back to life. Since the street isn't safe anymore, Carter brought little Offazzie and the cousins home, leaving Ishtar and Ogbid lonely sentinels by the road, their sheer weight making them safe from kidnappers, or so they thought. Bad guys came again and vandalized the brave twosome. This time they were nearly killed off, but J.C. managed to unscramble them once again. The Carters' insurance paid off once again but then they said "nevermore." Now the recovered family lives its life in **Carter's Gallery,** just up the road from where the two stood. But they are very lonely, so please, if you plan to drive by, call J. C. at (660) 747–5506 and see these wonderful, gentle creatures. A visit to the gallery would make both J. C. and his "family" very happy. There is no charge.

The Web site for Warrensburg is www.warrensburg.org.

Bristle Ridge Winery, between Warrensburg and **Knob Noster,** is ½ mile south of Highway 50 at Montserrat and produces high-quality wines that range from subtle dry whites to bright sweet reds. It sits on a hill with a panoramic view, the perfect spot to picnic with a bottle of wine, bread, cheese, and summer sausage—all sold at Bristle Ridge. Open daily (except Monday) 10:00 A.M. to 5:00 P.M. and Sunday noon until 5:00 P.M. Call (660) 422–5646.

Look up while driving through Knob Noster, because there are interesting things in the air above Whiteman Air Force Base. The previously very, very, top-secret Stealth Bomber calls this base home, and its eerie Batmanlike silhouette can be seen low in the sky on approach to the

Trivia

Concordia is the birthplace of internationally known Christian evangelist and faith healer Kathryn Kuhlman. She was born in a farmhouse 4 miles south of the city. She began preaching when she was sixteen and worked for twenty years among poor farming communities in the Midwest. See the historical marker in downtown Central Park.

base's runway. If you see it, you might as well pull off to the side of the road—as everyone else is doing—to watch it land.

North of Knob Noster on Highway 23 is the town of *Concordia,* where they take their German heritage very, very seriously. The *Plattdutsch Hadn Tohopa* (Low German Club) of Concordia has an annual Low German Theater at the Concordia Community Center at 802 Gordon Street. This lavish fall production is compiled and written by people of the town. Saturday night offers a dinner theater serving German delights such as peppered beef and bratwurst. Sunday is usually matinee theater only. Lavona Larimore will know the dates for this year. She can be reached at (660) 463–2454, the Chamber of Commerce office.

Concordia's rich German heritage draws thousands of visitors each year for the annual Concordia Fall Festival in September. There are exhibits, carnival rides, and German food and beer at the "Heidelberg Gardens" in one of the two beautiful parks in town. Across the street from one park is *Mrs. G's B&B* at One South East Fourteen Street in Concordia 64020, which is patterned after British B&B's. The Cotswold Village Room on the main floor, Welsh Garden Room, and Scottish Highlands Room have clawfoot tubs, decorative fireplaces, and coffee- and tea-making facilities. This ranch-style home with a loft is decorated with antiques in a charming eclectic style that proprietor Nancy Gilbertson (Mrs. G) calls "stocking feet cozy." Rooms are $50 to $60. Call (660) 463–2160 or e-mail regilbertson@almanet.net.

The Ozarks

Cole Camp is a tiny town that would be easy to miss, but don't. The first place to stop, if you have planned this right and it is lunchtime, is *Der Essen Platz,* Cole Camp 65325 (660–668–3080). It's on the corner—you can't miss it, the town is small—and it's open seven days a week. Owner Larry Shackelford's German-style restaurant features imported beers and food and a Friday buffet from 5:00 P.M. to 9:00 P.M., April through December. Cream pies of a variety not found elsewhere (unless you come from a German neighborhood) are a specialty; try German chocolate pie with coconut, or lemon pie with sour cream, crumb

Winter Solace

*T*he Missouri Ozarks are a quiet labyrinth of rugged hills and deep valleys, as famous for its folk culture as its beauty. Our home was perched high above a lake looking down at the very tops of the old oak trees with dozens of dogwoods sprinkled among them. The glass front let us watch the summer people on the lake; the screened porch was a perfect spot for breakfast. A telescope allowed us a view of the other side of the lake, a toll call away by road.

The chimney of the stone fireplace rose to the second-story ceiling, a loft above the one-room living area held our bed. The change of the seasons moved like a kaleidoscope across north window glass, the spring dogwoods and wild pear trees splashed white and pink across the barely budded trees. Bright daffodils popped up in the woods where earlier settlers must have planted them. Summers were intensely green, with ivy taking over the woods around the house. Deer and almost-tame raccoons and fox shared the woods around the cottage with us. The roar of the boats and shouts of the skiers began early and continued until after sunset.

When the leaves changed in the fall, the quiet made the woods a private place. The color, not so garishly bright as New Hampshire's maples, but a rustic red and gold of Missouri oak, gave the hills a new texture, a different feel. The leaves fall—some years slowly, one by one, other years it seems, all at once—leaving the view unobstructed and breathtaking when the cool, early-morning lake fog hangs over the still-warm water.

The most beautiful spectacle I remember took place deep in winter. One special day, the sun was warm, the air crisp and cold. We built a huge fire in the fireplace and grilled steaks and baked potatoes there that evening. In the morning, the whisper of snowflakes woke us. The sleeping loft was bathed in the reflected light of a deep snow. The quiet was almost tangible; I could feel it, taste it, touch it. We threw more logs on the smoldering fire and curled up on the couch with the down comforter and a cup of hot coffee. We were treated to the sight of a bald eagle perched on a tree limb outside the window. We watched him dive for fish twice and carry them off to a nearby nest.

Putting the FOR SALE sign by the roadside of our little wooded acreage was a sad day. But like the seasons, the times of our lives change, and with those changes come new colors and new sights. Our lives move in new directions, just as the winds change from south to north and back again. The memories, though, will be mine forever.

topping, and whipped cream. Joyce Schlesselmann, dining room manager, brought out samples of the wurst sandwiches (a pun—laugh, don't groan!) they offer. The menu includes *kasseler rippchen* (smoked boneless pork chops served on sauerkraut), *sauerbraten* (marinated beef on a bed of spätzle and gingersnap gravy), and if you are a schnitzel fan, *schweines-schnitzel, wiener schnitzel,* and *jaeger schnitzel.*

Local artist Neil Heimsoth show his oils and watercolors at the **Handel House,** 101 South Maple, Cole Camp 65325. Neil has the lower level of this large antiques shop, which can be reached at (660) 668–9952. Stop in to chat with Neil and he will tell you about the German singing groups he is a part of and of the German Music Festival called "Saengerfest" the third weekend in July. It's all free. There's German food and beer (a small donation is requested for this) and hundreds of singers (180 singers in 1999) to keep the music going all day and into the night. You can call Neil at (660) 668–3157 or e-mail him at heimat@iland.net for more information about the festival or singing groups.

Looking for a mighty fine pizza with homemade crust and a cold beer? Travel to 104 South Maple, Cole Camp 65325 and meet Michael and Marcy Cash at *Jak's Pizza.* There is no Jak—the name comes from the couple's three children, Jane, Alice, and Katie. You can add some homemade cheesecake to your menu after the "not-so-plain cheese pizza" or the "double-double pepperoni pizza" you are having. Hours are Tuesday through Sunday 11:00 A.M. to 8:00 P.M. (Friday until 9:00 P.M.) The restaurant is closed on Mondays. You can taste a virtual pizza at their web site www.mcleodusa.com or call (660) 668–3393.

Next door at 104 South Maple, Cole Camp 65325 is Michael's mom, Shirley Cash, who runs the **Katzen Jammer Gift and Antiques Shop.** What makes this little shop unique is that most of the antiques are from the Cole Camp area. Hours are Monday through Saturday 10:30 A.M. to 4:00 P.M. Call (660) 668–2357.

Pick up a copy of the *Antiques and Shop Guide* and stroll around town. You will find many, many places to poke around.

While you are in Cole Camp, stop by *Maxwell's Woodcarving,* 113 Main Street, Cole Camp 65325, right around the corner from Der Essen Platz, and take a look at Jim Maxwell's caricature woodcarvings. The finely detailed carvings feature Missouri coal miners, gangsters, artillery men from the Civil War, and doughboys of World War I. The limited-edition carvings are original pieces of art sought after by collectors. Maxwell is the author of two woodcarving books and creates a variety of subjects from casually styled Ozark Hill people to very accurately detailed caricatures of other bygone eras. Call (660) 668-2466 for more information.

A really, really good little spot is the *Maple Street Cafe* in Cole Camp, owned by a Mennonite family. A specialty is fresh trout from nearby Troutdale Farm in Versailles.

Highway 52 runs into Highway 5 at the city of *Versailles* (pronounced just as it looks, not the French way). Versailles is the gateway to the Lake of the Ozarks area. Here you make the decision to go east on Highway 52 to the St. Louis side of the lake or southwest on Highway 5 to the Kansas City side.

Just ½ block southeast of the square a brick walkway leads to a two-story white Victorian home that has now become the *Hilty Inn Bed and Breakfast,* 206 Jasper, Versailles 65084. This elegant home built in 1877 has four rooms with private baths. Owner Doris Hilty knows her way around the area and can guide you in your shopping or lake fun. If a quiet afternoon is what you want, though, there is a sitting room and a gift shop in which to browse. Doris carries books by local writers (this book can be purchased there) and crafts by area Mennonites. The East bedroom has a private front porch, and there is a screened side porch with swings for the other guests. A good breakfast with gourmet coffee and tea is part of the package. Doris also serves dinner in the dining room of her home—lovely, candlelight gourmet dinners. Simply call her twenty-four hours in advance to reserve a seat any night of the week. She can accommodate parties as large as twenty people or as small as two. Doris's gift shop specializes in A. Rebecca Nightwear, soft, all-natural sleepwear. Rates are $65 to $85; suites are $105. Call (573) 378–2020.

Just around the corner from the Hilty Inn is *J&S Enterprises* at 100 North Fisher, Versailles 65084, in the building that used to house Omi's Apple Haus. This nice little gift shop makes custom gift baskets and has a year-round Christmas room. Call (573) 378–6733 for more information.

World Craft and Thrift Shop at 123 East Newton Street, Versailles 65084 is owned by the Mennonite Church. Crafts are imported from all over the world, and you can browse in the thrift shop in the back room for great used stuff as well. Call (573) 378–5900.

Stop for lunch at *Bromley's,* a little gourmet restaurant at 112 East Jasper, Versailles 65084. DeeDee Bromley and Lisa Spence will serve you lunch Tuesday through Saturday from 11:00 A.M. until 2:00 P.M., and dinner on Friday and Saturday from 5:30 until 8:00 P.M. Call (753) 378–6995.

There's also a—believe this?—costume shop in Versailles: the *Party Odyssey Costumes and More* at 110 West Newton Street, Versailles 65044. By slipping into Millie Bebermeyer's shop, you can be Maid Marian or

Uncle Sam. With more than a thousand costumes there, you can send in the clowns, or become one of the three little pigs, or disguise yourself as a pirate complete with hook. And there's more than costumes. Hours are Tuesday to Saturday 10:00 A.M. until 5:00 P.M. Call (573) 378–6683 or fax (573) 378–5251.

The *Lake of the Ozarks* area is called the "Land of the Magic Dragon." If you look at the lake on a map and go snake-eyed, it has a dragon shape; hence the name. The Ozark heritage stems from the first immigrants here who were from Tennessee, Kentucky, and nearby parts of the southern Appalachians. The Upper-South hill-country folks were descended from Scottish-Irish stock.

For many years the Ozark Mountains sheltered these folks, and few outsiders entered the area; you may have heard of the Irish Wilderness. Because of the rough topography, the railroads avoided the area, and this extreme isolation until about fifty years ago created the "Ozark Hillbilly." The values, lifestyle, and beliefs of those first settlers are still much in evidence.

The building of Bagnell Dam to form the Lake of the Ozarks eroded that isolation and turned the area into the Midwest's summer playground. Because it is not a Corps of Engineers lake, homes can be built right on the water's edge; the 1,300 miles of serpentine shore has more shoreline than the state of California!

Miles of lake coves, wooded hills, and steep dusty roads are still unsettled. Most undeveloped areas have no roads at all leading to them. The east side of the lake, which houses the dam, has become the drop-in tourist side. The track is beaten slick over here. There are restaurants, shopping malls, and water slides galore.

Some of the unique places on the east side deserve a mention before you head to the west side of the lake, where the more fascinating spots hide. If you go to Bagnell Dam from Eldon, watch for wintering eagles—here and at most of the lake crossings. They retreat from the Arctic chill up north, following flocks of migrating geese.

You may not have thought of Missouri as a big state for bald eagle watching—and spring through early fall, it's not, though a captive breeding program of the Missouri Department of Conservation has been in effect since 1981 to reestablish a wild breeding population. But come winter, these big birds take up residence wherever they can find open water and plentiful feeding. One recent year, more than 1,400 bald eagles were counted, making this state second only to

Washington in the lower forty-eight states for eagle sightings. At most Missouri lakes, their main diet consists of fish—they have far better luck with fishing than most humans.

Taking the back way around the lake along Highway 52 to Eldon and then Highway 54 to Bagnell Dam is more interesting than the much-traveled and very crowded Highway 5/54 route.

A left turn (north) on Highway 5 puts you in the middle of the Mennonite community. On the roads around Versailles, horse-drawn buggies carry Mennonite citizens on their daily tasks. They are less strict than the Jamesport Amish—the somber black attire is uncommon—and most of the homes have telephones and electricity, though many don't. Old Order Mennonite women wear prayer bonnets but dress in printed fabrics. Some families have cars, but many of the cars are painted black—chrome and all. To get a good tour of the area, begin where Highway 5 splits into Highway 52. Follow 52 to Highway C on the left.

Mennonite Barbara Lehman used to serve people wonderful dinners in her parents' home on C Highway near Versailles. The place was so popular with locals and tourists alike, she outgrew it and moved to a new building on Highway 5 just north of Highway 52 in Versailles (65084).

The food is still fabulous, with the same wonderful family-style service, home cooked with farm-fresh everything from the garden and barn, prepared daily by Barbara. Call (660) 433–2646 for more information about *Lehman's.*

The vegetables are fresh by season, this morning's eggs are just in from the barn, and the jam, of course, is homemade. In the winter the vegetables come from the Lehman farm by way of the freezer. Barbara serves two kinds of pie with the meal, and when the season is right, fresh strawberry and peach pie or cobbler. Smoked turkey, ham, beef, or chicken are part of the three-course meal, which includes six salads, two veggies, homemade rolls, and desserts.

Follow Highway C about 6 miles to *Pleasant Valley Quilts.* There is a sign by the road where you can turn and drive about three quarters of a mile on gravel. The Brubaker family gathers a fine selection of quilts and crafts from Mennonite families in the area. Their daughters, Lydia and Lucille, handle the quilt shop, where quilts of all sizes and colors are hung for display. In fact, quilts will be made to order for you if you have a particular color or style in mind. Quilts made by local Mennonite ladies join aprons, dolls, and other hand-crafted items for sale here. The store is open from 8:00 A.M. to 5:00 P.M. every day but Sunday. Call (573) 378–6151.

Follow the sign off Highway C down a gravel road to the **Dutch Country Store,** which carries bulk foods as well as a huge selection of freight-damaged groceries and toiletries. There are usually buggies parked out front along with the automobiles. The store always has a good selection of name-brand cereals and canned goods, shampoo, and dog food, just about anything. The selection is different every week.

Turn north on Highway E, then follow E to Highway K (this sounds harder than it really is), but watch closely for horse-drawn buggies and bicycles on these hilly back roads. Highway K leads east to the tiny, tiny town of **Excelsior** and **Weavers' Market,** serving this community of about 250 Mennonite families. Weavers' carries fresh-frozen farm produce, frozen homemade pies ready to pop into your oven, an enormous assortment of teas and spices, and other bulk foods, including homemade noodles. Nearby (follow the signs) is **Excelsior Fabric,** where Anna and Sam Shirk and their family carry an extensive collection of quilting fabrics.

If you decide to turn left back at Highway E on some pretty Sunday morning about 10:00 A.M., you will come to the Clearview Mennonite Church and see dozens of horse-drawn buggies tied up in stables and at hitching posts around the church. It's quite a sight.

Now find your way back to Highway 52 and go east past the Highway C Junction, 3 miles after the Save-a-Lot store at 16151 Old Marvin Road in **Barnett** to Leah Zimmerman's bake shop (a sign on the highway says FARMER'S MARKET). Leah's is the first house on the left; a large sign in her yard reads **Shady Oak Market.** Her buggy is near the barn, where her horse Jessica waits for excursions to the grocery store, Weavers' Market, or church on Sunday. Leah has produce from her own wonderful garden, but she also is the source for eggs from free-range chickens, fresh fruit from family orchards, and a whole range of baked goods she turns out daily. Cinnamon bread, pies with whatever fresh fruit is in season, cookies, jams, and canned goods deck her shelves in the pantry just off the front porch. The sign says COME IN and that's just what it means. She's usually in the kitchen baking something tasty—she does custom baking for regulars—and comes out when she hears the door slam. And say "hi" to Joshua, her loveable sweetheart of a German shepherd, and Patches, the cat. Call (573) 378-6401 to order something special (in the fall her apple dumplings are wonderful!).

The difference between the east and west sides of the lake has been described as like "flipping channels between *Hee Haw* and *Lifestyles of the Rich and Famous.*" Welcome to the St. Louis side, a road more traveled but

Shady Oak Market

still lots of fun. The Ozark Web site has plenty of information about the area: www.ozark-missouri.com.

Highway 54 through *Osage Beach* is, in a word, touristy. The path here is not only beaten, it's three lanes wide and heavy with traffic in the summer—the bumper-to-bumper gridlock type you came here to get away from. The road is filled to overflowing with craft shops, flea markets, bumper cars, and water slides. There are plenty of good eating places, from fast-food chains to little places like the *Peace-'n'-Plenty Country Cafe* in Poverty Flats Village (near State Road KK at 5837 Highway 54, Osage Beach 65065), specializing in homemade soups, sandwiches, breads, and salads. Call (573) 348–1462.

Cliff House Bed & Breakfast in Osage Beach on State Road KK (at the 25-mile marker by water) is a truly unforgettable and romantic spot. Each of the four suites has fabulous lake views, and all have private entrances and baths, a Jacuzzi, fireplace, television, and stereo. Cascading decks lead to the water's edge, where a gazebo and hot tub await, as well as a dock for fishing, swimming, and boating. Not only do you get a 180-degree view of the lake from your private deck, you can also charter a wonderful 37-foot teak-and-mahogany trawler, complete with captain, to cruise the lake. Innkeeper Anne Baker fixes a complete breakfast served in your room in the morning. This romantic spot is not just another Lake of the Ozarks experience! Rates are $105 to $120 weekdays, $125 to $140 on weekends (two-night minimum). Off-season rates are $95 to $130. Contact Anne at (573) 348– 9726 or e-mail her at annieb@usmo.com. Cliff House is on Osage Beach 65065. Visit it on the Web at www.lakecliffhouse.com.

Gray's Country Home Bed and Breakfast is on Highway D at the junction of Highways 42 and 54 near Osage Beach. Marti Gray built this two-story blue home with its wonderful wrap-around porch on five acres of woods. The house cannot be seen from the road in the summertime. Although it is not on the water, the ambience is pure lake country. You can get comfortable in the white wicker furniture on the screened porch and enjoy the quiet or head for the state park just 6 miles away, on Highway 42, where you can rent boats, ride horses, hike on the trails, or swim at the public beach. In the evening guests are welcome to use the parlor with its Ozark stone fireplace. Breakfast is served there in winter. Two comfortable suites await you in the evening. From the Dogwood Suite you will step down, through French doors, into a marble and tile bathroom. The large bedroom has country antiques, and the queen-size bed has a carved headboard. You can step out onto your private porch in the morning. The Dolly Suite offers an extensive doll collection as well as a sitting room with a window seat and private bath. Marti serves a full breakfast every morning. Call (573) 348–5564 for detailed directions. Gray's is at 24 High Ridge Court in Kaiser 65047. Visit the Web site at www.countryhome.odd.net. Rates are from $89 to $110.

Joe Orr is a Missouri artist who is gaining a well-deserved reputation. You can see why for yourself at his elegant gallery/studio/home right next to TanTara at 1405 Highway KK, Osage Beach 65065. The *Orr Gallery and Studio* also features Rita Orr's wonderful silkscreens and monoprints. But that's not all that is tucked away in this second-floor hideaway. Displayed here are Ron Schroeder's sculptures, Paul Clervi's bronze sculptures, Steve Johnson's contemporary free-form pottery, and Rhonda Cearlock's raku pottery. Joe is the founder of the National Oil and Acrylic Painters Society, which has a national exhibition here in November with more than 600 artists from thirty states entered for exhibit. Joe's and Rita's studios are on the gallery level of their home, too, and open if you want to watch them at work. Hours are from 10:00 A.M. until 5:00 P.M. daily, but Joe is quick to add that it's "sort of by chance or appointment, too," so calling ahead (573–348–2232) might be a good idea.

The *Potted Steer Restaurant* (573–348–5053) is in a comfortable-looking wooden building tucked in at the west end of the Grand Glaize Bridge on Highway 54 in Osage Beach. Owner Joseph Boer, a native of Holland who came to this country on refugee status on Christmas Day in 1956, opened the restaurant in 1971. It is a very laid-back place where casual clothes are the rule and long waits are expected. But the crowd is vacation-loose and fun. The specialty here is deep-fried lobster tail (which sounds like heresy to a seafood lover). Boer says he has never tasted the creation that made the restaurant famous. You see, he hates seafood. To tide you over until dinner arrives, order the massive onion rings. Boer also has one of the finest wine lists in the state. The restaurant is closed from the middle of November until the third Friday in March.

If you have taken the route along the west side of the lake, you will begin to see the real Ozarks now. Missouri has surprisingly diverse wildlife, from the blind cave fish to the black bear, which still forages in the heavy woods. The pileated woodpecker (the size of a chicken, no kidding!) will certainly wake you up in the morning if he decides to peck on your shake shingles. The west side of the lake is still undiscovered except by Kansas City people, who have tried to keep it quiet. Here, great eating places abound and small shops hide off the beaten path.

Highway 5 cuts like a razor slash through the hills between **Gravois Mills** and Laurie. There are some quiet, low-key places not to be missed.

Spring Lake Lodge and Antiques on Highway 5, Gravois Mills 65037 (573–372–2201), owned by James Marci and Gordon Stallings, is no flea market. Open March to October, the shop contains fine antiques, art objects, jewelry, and decorative accessories that are as nice as those at big-city shops but priced more reasonably. The shop is closed in the winter so that the two men can travel around the country finding and buying the elegant pieces they show there. People who know about the place try to be the first ones there in the spring when the shop opens. Large walnut sideboards, Victorian sofas, and unique lamps are part of the hundreds of items in the two floors of showroom.

The bright yellow place with the two huge, hairy gorillas standing out front is the **Gorilla Burger,** on Highway 5 in Gravois Mills 65037, and although the Gorillaburger is good, the turkey fries (don't ask) are a seasonal treat not to be passed up. Call (573) 372–5499.

As you continue along Highway 5 through the town of Gravois Mills, you will notice a large sign pointing to **Troutdale Ranch** on Troutdale Road. It is not the spot for experienced trout fishers, but it is the perfect spot to teach the children how to cast a line (guaranteed catch) and it is the perfect place to pick up some sweet, pink-fleshed trout for dinner. There has been a trout farm here since 1932. Current owner Dorothy Gates and her son, Lorin, haven't changed things much. Someone will simply go out the door and net you some of the freshest trout you will ever taste. They will clean and bone it for you and pack it in ice, too. The water here is 56° F, colder than most trout waters, so the trout grow more slowly and that means better. They are farm-fed, making them safe and some of the best you will ever eat. Many of the best restaurants in the metropolitan areas serve trout from the ranch. Try the smoked trout that is also for sale at the ranch. It is excellent. In fact, it's on the menu at the Blue Heron—served cold—and is a popular summer dish. Troutdale is open year-round from 7:30 A.M. until 4:30 P.M. (from November until March 1, they are closed on Sunday). Call (573) 372–6100 for information.

After Gravois Mills you will come to the tiny **Ozark Hills Senior Citizens Craft Shop** on Highway 5 in Gravois Mills 65037. The store carries lovingly hand-crafted crochets, knits, and pieces of needlework made by the local seniors. Also sold here are hand-carved items and almost any other kind of craft you can imagine. Call (573) 372–2465.

Just outside of **Laurie** on Highway 5 is St. Patrick's Catholic Church. Father Fred Barnett is the pastor here. This unique church sits on acres of outdoor gardens that feature waterfalls, fountains, and a shrine dedicated to mothers, the **Shrine of Mary Mother of the Church.** You may add your mother's name to the list to be remembered in ongoing prayers. On summer Sundays, Mass is at 8:30 A.M. at the shrine, and casual dress is in the spirit of a Lake of the Ozarks vacation. The outdoor candlelight procession and Mass on Saturday nights at 8:30 P.M. at the shrine are beautiful and open to anyone. Times change in winter, so call Father Barnett (573–374–7855) for a current schedule.

Hungry in Laurie? Right there on Highway 5 is a great restaurant. **Ivor's** at 630 North Main Street, Laurie 65037, is a favorite with the locals and is just the right combination of casual and nice for lake living. You can have a steak, seafood, or a really good fettuccine. Call (573) 374–2866.

In the town of Laurie you can turn right on Highway 135, which wanders back to Stover and Highway 52, over some genuine roller-coaster dips and beautiful unpopulated Ozark country.

The **Buffalo Creek Vineyards and Winery,** 2888 Riverview Road, Stover 65078 is a bit of a surprise in the lake area. Owner Jim Stephens has five acres of vines growing near Stover. His tasting room is accessible by water at the 70-mile marker between Little Buffalo Cove and Big Buffalo Cove. (Watch for the signs.) The Concord grape wine is light and not too sweet. He also bottles a Foch, Seyval, Vignoles, and a ruby Cabernet that is aged in oak. The most popular wines are the fruit wines: pear (also aged in oak) and persimmon. Another favorite is the Show-Me Red, a blend of Foch and Concord grapes, aged in Missouri oak. It is a semidry wine with a pungent finish.

The tasting room is located above the water in a remodeled old farm barn and offers a panoramic view of the lake. Boat visitors can dock in the five-well dock and call the winery to be picked up and transported up the hill. The atmosphere is relaxed and comfortable on the hill. A large lounging deck sits right on the crest of the hill overlooking the water.

Overnight accommodations are available, too. The snug guest cottage with panoramic views of the lake can accommodate up to six people. The winery also sponsors live music, special dinners, and other "happenings" throughout the summer. It is open year-round Monday through Saturday from 10:00 A.M. until 5:00 or 6:00 P.M., depending on the season, and Sundays from 11:00 A.M. to 5:00 or 6:00 P.M. For reservations call toll-free (888) 247–1192 or (573) 377–4535.

To find the winery by car, take Highway 135 (6 miles east of Stover, or 16 miles west on Highway 135 from Laurie). Turn southwest on T Road and continue 9 miles to the winery.

Near the town of **Greenview** on Highway 5 stands a hand-hewn oak log building. Known as the **Old Trail House** (573-873-5824), it overlooks the lake at the spot where one of the wagon trails going from Old Linn Creek to Arnholdt's Mill on the Big Niangua River ran across the ridge. Wagons drawn by oxen and horses forded the river at the mill. The spot is said to be an old Indian lookout point, and you can see for about 20 miles to the west from the deck, where dinner is served in good weather. A beautiful, antique oak mantel surrounds a log fire in winter. It is a favorite spot of locals. Hours are from 5:00 to 9:00 P.M. during the week, and 5:00 to 10:00 P.M. on weekends. Winter hours may vary, so call ahead.

If you are looking for a bed and breakfast instead of a resort on the Lake of the Ozarks, check with Kay Cameron at Ozark Mountain Country Bed and Breakfast Service at (417) 334–4720 or (800) 695–1546 or e-mail at mgcameron@aol.com. Kay has listings for cottages on the water in Camdenton, Osage Beach, Sunrise Beach, and other small towns around the lake. For more lake information contact www.funlake.com on the Web.

Either way you circle the lake, east or west, you will end up in **Camdenton** at the intersection of Highways 5 and 54. Continue west on Highway 54 and turn on Highway D to **Ha Ha Tonka State Park.** High on a bluff overlooking an arm of the Lake of the Ozarks, poised over a cold, aqua blue spring that bubbles out from under a limestone bluff, are the ruins of a stone "castle" with a story to tell. There is a European feel to the ruins; it's as if you have stumbled on a Scottish stronghold here in the Missouri woods. The place was conceived in 1900 as a sixty-room retreat for prominent Kansas City businessman Robert Snyder. But

Ha Ha Tonka State Park

tragedy struck; Snyder was killed in an automobile accident in 1906 and construction halted. Later, the castle-like mansion was completed by Snyder's son, but in 1942 a fire set by a spark from one of the many stone fireplaces gutted the buildings. All that was left were the ghostly stone walls thrust up against the sky. Ha Ha Tonka is now a state park, although the mansion is still a ghostly ruins half hidden in the trees.

The park is a classic example of karst topography, with caves and sink-holes, springs, natural bridges, and underground streams. (This typical southern Missouri geology is responsible for the many caves in the state.) There are nine nature trails here; explore on your own or check in with the park office (573–751–2479) for a naturalist-guided tour; programs are available all year long.

Missouri places second nationwide for the largest number of caves, but the state beats number one Tennessee in the number of "show caves" that are developed for touring. The state records more than 5,000 caves. The southern half of Missouri—in the Ozarks regions—is where most of the caves are because of the limestone deposits there. The complex of caves, underground streams, large springs, sinkholes, and natural

Strange As It Seems

Native Americans valued caves for their shelter and storage capabilities. They would mark the location of caves by creating thong trees—forcing a sapling white oak to a horizontal position using green, forked limbs thrust into the earth. Throughout the Ozarks, these thong trees can still be seen.

bridges at Ha Ha Tonka State Park makes it one of the country's most important geologic sites.

About halfway between Warsaw and Clinton on Highway 7 is the town of **Tightwad** (population 56). There's a UMB Bank in Tightwad, and the branch manager says that people from as far away as Florida have accounts there just to get the checks with "Tightwad" on them.

The city of **Clinton** is every Chamber of Commerce's dream come true. It has one of the most active squares in the country, filled with over 150 shops and services, and there is lots of parking. You can't miss the wonderful old courthouse and outdoor pavilion in the center of the square. The town has changed little since 1836, when it began as an outpost in the heart of the Golden Valley.

History buffs will find plenty of research material at the **Henry County Museum** at 203 West Franklin Street, Clinton 64735, just off the northwest corner of the square. The building itself was owned by Anheuser-Busch from 1886 until Prohibition. Huge blocks of ice (often cut from the nearby lake) were used to chill the kegs in the cooling room. The second room contains a skylight and double doors leading to the old loading dock and courtyard. Quick dashes in horse-drawn wagons were necessary to transport the beer while still cool to the depot where there was access to three railroads. The building houses the Courtenay Thomas room, commemorating the Clinton native who became an international operatic soprano.

Find Commercial Street in **Harrisonville** and hit the antiques jackpot. There are too many antiques and flea markets to mention, but it looks like three cherries on the antiques slot machine for flea-market gamblers.

Cheese Country

o west on Highway 54 to **El Dorado Springs** (*Da-RAY-do,* this being a very non-Spanish speaking part of the country) as a shortcut to the Osceola area.

Large dairy barns and silos built around the turn of the century are still in use, and dairy cattle—Holsteins and Guernseys—graze alongside beef cattle. Surprise! Missouri is the third-largest cheese-producing state in the nation.

El Dorado Springs, just east of Nevada (pronounced *Ne-VAY-da*) off Highway 54, is a pretty little town complete with a nostalgic bandstand in the tree-shaded park at the center of town. It looks like something straight out of *The Music Man*. There's a band here every Friday and Saturday night and Sunday afternoon; a local band has played in the park for more than a hundred years. The old spa town was crowded with bathhouses and hotels, but the spa business ended long ago for most towns like this one. El Dorado Springs has done a great job of preserving itself anyway.

While in El Dorado, you can see the free museum above *Carl's Gun Shop,* 100 North Main Street 64744. Owner Carl McCallister and his son, Terry, have more than 1,000 guns in glass showcases and a fine collection of trophy-size taxidermied animal mounts, including two full-body bears—one a Giant Kodiak—in a gymnasium-size room. The gun shop takes up ½ block and has one of the most complete private collections of firearms in the state. You won't find any assault rifles for sale here, and there's no survivalist gear on display. The well-lighted display rooms have a staff of people who knows guns. Carl even has toy guns for sale for customers' children. The family environment makes women and children feel comfortable. Terry's wife, Terri, also works at the store. Carl's is open six days a week from 9:00 A.M. to 5:00 P.M. Monday through Saturday. Call (417) 876–4168 for more information.

Walnuts are big in the state and if you are nuts about walnuts, visit *Hammons Pantry* at 414 North Street in Stockton 65785. Hammons Products is the world's largest processor of black walnuts, and its retail store is open Monday through Friday. Try walnut brittle or chocolate-covered walnuts for your sweet tooth, or a nutty breakfast with black-walnut pancake and waffle mix and a bottle of walnut syrup. Call (800) 872–6879 for a free catalog.

If you don't take the shortcut, you will continue down Interstate 71 to *Lamar;* history fans will find *Harry S Truman's Birthplace* here. (No, there is no period after the S, because the president didn't have a middle name—his folks just put an S in there.) It's a long way from this little house at 1009 Truman Street in Lamar 64759 to the big white one on Pennsylvania Avenue in our nation's capital. Hours are Monday through Saturday 10:00 A.M. to 4:00 P.M. and on Sunday from noon to 4:00 P.M. Call (417) 682–2279.

In *Golden City* bicyclists know a place called *Cooky's* at 529 Main, Golden City 64748 at the junction of Highway 126 and 37 south and east of Lamar. Out of season it's a small-town cafe on the south side of the main drag. During bike-riding season, though, Cooky's is the place to dream about when you are 300 miles out on the trail. Bikecentennial, Inc., of Missoula, Montana, put Cooky's on the map—the Transamerica Trail map, that is—and riders have flocked here ever since for some serious carbohydrate loading. It's not uncommon to watch a rider from Australia chow down on three or four pieces of Jim and Carol Elred's terrific pies; you can be more moderate, if you like. A steak dinner costs only $8.75; the home-raised beef will keep you going down the trail whether you come by car or bike. Hours are 6:00 A.M. until 8:00 P.M. Tuesday through Thursday and Sunday. On Friday and Saturday night it is open till 9:00 P.M. Call (417) 537–4741 for information.

Jerry Overton, president of the Missouri Prairie Foundation, puts in a good word for *Golden Prairie,* designated a National Natural Landmark by the federal Department of the Interior. It's not reclaimed prairie or replanted prairie—this is a virgin remnant of the thousands of acres of grassland that once covered the Midwest, important not only for the historic plants it contains, but also for the varieties of wildlife that inhabit it. Here you can still hear the sound of the prairie chicken. Listen for them exactly 3 miles west of Golden City on Highway 126 and exactly 2 miles south of Highway 26 on the first gravel road.

A roadside park just outside *Osceola* on Highway 82 West will show you what attracted Indians and settlers to the area: the breathtaking view of the white bluffs where the Sac and Osage Rivers meet. Highway 82 also has a Sac River access point and boat ramp if you are hauling a boat to the Truman Reservoir.

Highway 13 bypasses the town square but is home to *Osceola Cheese Shop* and *Ewe's in the Country* (417–646–8131). Mike and Marcia Bloom own both shops, which share the building. The Blooms buy the cheese in bulk and smoke and flavor it in the former cheese factory; they have been at this same location for more than forty-five years. They now offer more than sixty-nine varieties of cheese, mostly from Missouri, with each type cut for sampling. Try jalapeño (extra hot), instant pizza, or chocolate (yes!) cheese. Pick up a catalog; they ship cheese anywhere in the world—except from April to September, when it might arrive as hot cheese sauce. Hours are variable depending on the season.

Take a right at the sign on Highway 13 and wander into Osceola. On the northeast corner of the town square is *Dwell's Coach Stop.* There are many stories to be told here, if the walls could talk. With the help of artist M.E. Norton, they do. Harry Truman ate here, Jesse James slept here, and Dr. Ruth Seevers practiced here until she was ninety and had delivered more babies than anyone in the state. She died at 102, no doubt of exhaustion. The Butterfield Stage Line stopped here, and the Corps of Engineers built the Truman Dam nearby. Owners David and Lorraine Lackey will explain each section of the montage if you are interested: the Seminole chief who never surrendered (Chief Osceola), or the time the town was burned to the ground by Jim Lane, just after the Civil War—it's wall-to-wall history. Call (417) 646-2378 for more information.

On the southwest corner of the square is the 111-year-old Commercial Hotel, recently renovated and opened as a craft shop. *Colby's* at 107 Chestnut on the north side of the square (also in a renovated building), serves good, old-fashioned home cooking (including homemade bread, fried chicken, and pies) seven days a week from 6:00 A.M. to 6:00 P.M. Call (417) 646–2620 for more information.

Nearby in the Old Commercial Hotel, there is a neat little pre-owned clothing store and a surprise in the form of an espresso bar and gift shop. Owner Lynette Bullock invites you to drop in after lunch. Call (417) 464–8602 for more information.

Attics always have a trunk or two hidden away. Why not? They are fine for storing the other things we hate to throw away. When families moved here from the east, they brought their belongings in trunks and would use them as dressers, chairs, and tables until real furniture would be built. Chuck Burton and Elsa Hickethier have taken it upon themselves to restore trunks to their original splendor at the *Trunk Shop,* just south of Lowry City on Highway 13. Today Chuck stocks more than 100,000 trunk parts and not only restores trunks but builds them from scratch. The showroom has many antiques on sale, including some in like-new condition. He can pick locks and get your trunk open and then make a key for it, too. Chuck also does all manner of furniture repair, including caning and stripping. Call (417) 644–2846. The Trunk Shop is open from 8:00 A.M. until 5:00 P.M. every day but Tuesday—his "running around day." On Saturday the shop closes at 4:30 P.M.

PLACES TO STAY IN CENTRAL MISSOURI

KANSAS CITY
Quarterage Hotel at Westport,
508 Westport Road, 64112;
(816) 931-0001

Raphael Hotel and Restaurant, Country Club Plaza,
325 Ward Parkway, 64112;
(816) 756-3800 or
(800) 821-5343

Historic Suites of America,
612 Central, 64105;
(816) 842-6544

INDEPENDENCE
Sports Stadium Inn,
9803 East 40 Highway
(near the sports complex),
64055; (816) 353-0005

BOONVILLE
Days Inn, 2401 Pioneer,
65233; (660) 882-8624

Super 8 Motel, I-70,
exit 103, 65233;
(660) 882-2900 or
(800) 800-8000

JEFFERSON CITY
Best Western Inn,
Highway 54 (Ellis exit),
65109; (573) 635-4175

Capitol Plaza Hotel,
415 West McCarty Street,
65101; (573) 635-1234

Super 8,
1710 Jefferson Street,
65109; (573) 636-5456

LEXINGTON
Lexington Inn,
Highway 24/13, 64067;
(660) 259-4641

KNOB NOSTER
Whiteman Inn,
2340 West Irish Lane,
65336; (660) 563-3000

SEDALIA
Bothwell Kensington,
103 East Fourth Street,
65301; (660) 826-5588

Best Western State Fair
Motor Inn, 3120 South
65 Highway, 65301;
(660) 826-6100 or
(800) 528-1234

WARRENSBURG
Days Inn,
204 East Cleveland Street,
64093; (660) 429-2400

Best Western University
Inn, Highway 13/50, 64093;
(660) 747-5125

OSAGE BEACH
Tan-Tar-A Resort
and Golf Course,
P.O. Box 188TT, 65065;
(800) 826-8272

LAURIE
Millstone Lodge,
18106 Road O, 65038;
(573) 372-5111 or
(800) 290-2596

LAKE OZARK
Lodge of the Four Seasons
(spa and golf course),
65049; (888) 265-5500

PITTSBURG
Golden Dawn Motel,
Highway 64B, 65724;
(417) 852-4811

WHEATLAND
Sunflower Resort,
Rout 2, Box 2681, 65779;
(800) 258-5260

CLINTON
Days Inn, Highway 7
and Rives Road, 64735;
(660) 885-6901

NEVADA
Rambler Motel,
1401 East Austin, 64772;
(417) 667-3351

The Welcome Inn,
2345 Marvel, 64772;
(417) 667-6777

PLACES TO EAT IN CENTRAL MISSOURI

KANSAS CITY
Savoy Grill (seafood),
219 West Ninth Street,
64105; (816) 842-3890
(expensive)

Papagallo, (Middle Eastern
cuisine) 3535 Broadway,
64111; (816) 756-3227
(moderate prices)

ARROW ROCK
Historic Arrow Rock Tavern, P.O. Box 23, 65320;
(660) 837-3200

Old Schoolhouse Cafe,
65320; (660) 837-3331
(open summers)

BOONVILLE
Stein House,
421 Main Street, 65223;
(660) 882-6832

JEFFERSON CITY
Yen Chings,
2208 Missouri Boulevard,
65109; (573) 635–5225

Das Stein Haus,
1436 South Ridge Drive,
65109; (573) 634–3869
(behind the Ramada Inn)

Madison's Restaurant,
216 Madison Street, 65101;
(across from parking
garage),
(573) 634–2988

RICHMOND
The Brass Eagle,
907 Main Street, 64085;
(660) 259–6668

BELTON
Oden's Family Barbecue,
1302 North Scott, Belton,
64012; (816) 322–3072

Nichol's Bar–BQ,
110 Cunningham Parkway,
Belton, 64012;
(816) 331–4363

GRAVOIS MILLS
Frogs, Highway 5 to
Lake Road 5–15, 65037;
(573) 372–6566

OSAGE BEACH
Lucky Duck Cafe, HH to
Point of Cherokee Road
(3 mile marker), 65065;
(573) 365–9973

PITTSBURG
Chuckwagon Restaurant
65724

LAMAR
Lamarti's, 54 Southeast
1 Lane, 64759;
(417) 682–6034

Quatro's, 1201 Parry, 64759;
(417) 682–5677

**HELPFUL WEB SITE
FOR THE OZARKS**

---

www.funlake.com

Selected Chambers of Commerce

Arrow Rock, (816) 837–3443

Independence, (800) 748–7328 or
www.usachamber.com/independence

Jefferson City,
www.jcchamber.org/index.html.

Kansas City,
www.kcchamber.com
e-mail: chamber@kcity.com

Ozarks, (800) 769–1004

Northwest Missouri

I t does get cold in northwest Missouri—make no mistake—especially near the northernmost border, where the plains are chilled by every stiff wind howling down from the frigid north. Alberta Clipper, Siberian Express, whatever you call it, Missouri catches hell in the winter, bringing to mind that old joke: "There's nothing between here and the North Pole but two bobwire (barbed wire) fences, and one o' them's down." In 1989 all records were broken—along with that fence—when the nighttime temperature bottomed out at -23° F (wind chill made that -60° F). It also gets hot in Missouri; August days can soar over the 100° F mark.

But at its temperate best, Jesse James country is a great place to visit that's filled with great hideouts. (James knew them all. It seems that, like George Washington, Jesse James slept almost everywhere—in northwest Missouri, anyway.)

Not that that's all there is to this section of the state; we'd hate to say we're living in the past on the rather unsavory reputation of our own "Robbing" Hood. There is a national wildlife refuge on the central flyway that is absolutely essential to migrating waterfowl. There is Excelsior Springs, where folks once came to take the waters and where Harry S Truman heard he had lost the presidential election to Thomas Dewey—at least according to the *Chicago Tribune.*

The Northlands

J ust across the Missouri River from the town with a similar name is **North Kansas City.** This is a separate city, with a healthy industrial tax base and a coordinated downtown shopping area complete with plazas, fountains, and wide streets. "Northtown" has its own mayor, its own police department, and its own quirky charm. There are cafes and delis and bakeries; North Kansas Citians know how to eat. Northtown has a Web site at www.nkc.org.

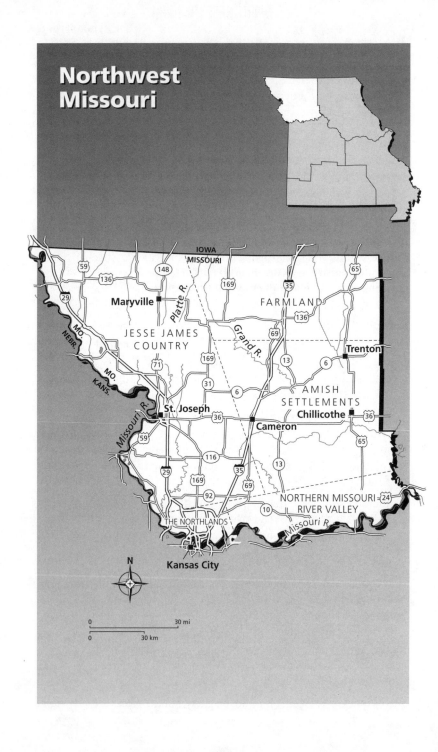

Northwest
Missouri

About forty-two years ago Rafael Jimenez and his wife Socorro opened a little restaurant in Kansas City serving the Mexican food they knew so well. He never advertised, but day after day the place was full of people. They came for lunch, they came for dinner, they came on a whim, because they were craving something. And business was good at the Acapulco. The Jimenezes turned out dishes based on old family recipes, and people filled the little restaurant every day and stood in line on weekends. Today the new and larger **Acapulco Restaurant** is at 1041 Burlington Avenue in North Kansas City 64116-4122. Rafael is more or less retired (he still shows up often) and his son, Gustavo, now owns the restaurant. Gus is more modern. He is thinking seriously about doing some advertising. The best advertising he does, though, is word of mouth. Once your mouth gets around the food he serves—Mexican chili made with big chunks of pork served with thick, soft, corn tortillas; tamales with rich masa surrounding shredded pork; and paper-thin tortilla chips with fresh salsa—you tell friends about it. And the secret, somehow, gets out. For more information call (816) 472–8689.

Tiny **Avondale** is slightly off Highway 210 as you leave North Kansas City. Here you'll discover **Nichols Pottery Shop and Studio** at 2615 Bell, Avondale 64117 (816–452–0880). Deanna Nichols handcrafts stoneware that is both beautiful and functional. "You can hang it on a wall, or take it down and serve from it," she says. The studio is filled with examples of her work, and not only mugs and platters, but also intricate, earthy fountains some 32 inches high. She does custom work, lamps, and dinnerware. Browse through the shop Tuesday through Friday from 10:00 A.M. to 5:00 P.M., until 4:00 P.M. Saturday. A garden full of shrubs and trees interesting in all four seasons has been added to the side of the building.

As long as you are here, check out **Avondale Furniture and Antiques** at 2600 North Highway 10, Avondale 64117. Hours are catch-as-catch-can; call (816) 452–2690 for an appointment if you prefer. Owner Lillian Waskovsky has an auction service and warehouse and likes to move pieces quickly. This place may not be glitzy, but the prices are very right.

AUTHOR'S FAVORITE ANNUAL EVENTS IN NORTHWEST MISSOURI

May

Excelsior Springs—The Gatsby Festival, always the weekend after Mother's Day, (816) 630-0753, www.epsi.net/gatsby/welcome.htmSo

Richmond—Morel Mushroom Festival, parade, food and craft booths, model train show, carnival, (816) 776–5304 or 5306, www.richmondchamber.org/festival.html

September

Excelsior Springs—Waterfest, second Saturday of September, arts, crafts, and food booths; games, music, and rides, (816) 630–6161, escoc@epsi.net

December

Lee Summit—Christmas in the Park, (816) 524–2424

Hayes Hamburgers at 2502 N.E. Vivion Road in suburban Kansas City 64119 (at Antioch Road) serves the kind of hamburgers that you could order before "fast food" was invented. This is the place to go for a hamburger after a football game or late at night on a date you don't want to end. The hamburgers are small and made of fresh chopped meat rolled into a ball and mashed onto the grill with a handful of onions. The aroma of onions and hamburger grilling together sparks an appetite. People buy them by the bag and have been known to eat a dozen. The chili is all-American good, too. The diner is open all the time—twenty-four hours a day.

Take the Highway 435 exit north off Interstate 35 and keep an eye out for Highway 152. A right turn will take you to *Hodge Park,* a fine place to get away from the "two Ps": progress and people.

Those big, hairy critters you spot as you enter the park are American bison; the Kansas City Zoo maintains a small herd here, where once there were thousands. Elk and deer share the enclosure; you may be able to get "up close and personal" with some of the Midwest's largest indigenous animals.

If human history is more your thing, park your car in the lot and keep walking. *Shoal Creek* (816–444–4363), is a restored frontier town at Hodge Park, full of historic buildings moved here by the Kansas City Parks and Recreation Department. The tiny, two-story jail built of monolithic limestone blocks (how did they lift those things?) came from nearby Missouri City. What a place for a lockup! Local ne'er-do-wells slept off Saturday night festivities here some one hundred years ago. Other buildings include square-hewn log cabins, a one-room schoolhouse, a barn, a replica of an old mill complete with mill wheel and race, and some pretty fine houses for the gentry. Stop by during one of their living-history weekends for a recreation of frontier life; you'll feel as if you've stepped back a century. Fine nature trails lead into the woods from Shoal Creek.

If you are interested in archaeology and the peoples that inhabited this land before Europeans moved in, get yourself to Line Creek Park at 5940 Northwest Waukomis. This is a Hopewell Culture site, where Native Americans lived and worked from approximately 50 B.C. to A.D. 200. The museum houses artifacts found on the spot and in the surrounding areas.

The Kansas City Parks and Recreation Department operates the site, and schoolchildren from grade four up come for mock "digs" (artifacts are salted back into the ground so that the kids have the excitement of

AUTHOR'S TOP TEN FAVORITES IN NORTHWEST MISSOURI

Hayes Hamburgers

Hardware Cafe

Martha Lafite Thompson Nature Sanctuary

Jamesport

Candyman's Mule Barn

The Hall of Waters

The Elms Hotel

Church of St. Luke the Beloved Physician

The Inn on Crescent Lake Bed and Breakfast

Weston

discovery). Hours may vary; call (816) 444–4363. You can also take your chances; the museum is usually open Saturdays and Sundays from 11:00 A.M. to 4:00 P.M. There's no charge for the museum, but for reservations for group programs, call the above number; there is a small fee for groups.

Do you want to have some real *fun* now? Well, there is a most unusual place in Kansas City to do just that if you are up to trying something different. *Jaegers Subsurface Paintball,* deep in the caves at 9300 N.E. Underground Drive in Kansas City 64161, is the place to find. For $25, manager Chris Morin will give you a safety briefing, helmet and goggles, and a semi-automatic weapon with 130 rounds of ammunition—i.e., paintballs.

The caves are spooky—dark stone walls and dirt floors—littered with washing machines, wire spools, and a beat-up delivery van to hide behind or trip over. Old paintball pellets and shards of exploded ones are debris on the floor. Fluorescent lights illuminate parts of the cave; other parts are dark. The color of your helmet designates the team you belong to. You are the hunter—and the hunted—on a field that consists of the cave's labyrinthine stone passages and lots of sand.

"Paintball . . . may be an inherently dangerous activity that can result in loss of life, eyesight, or hearing," says the waiver you sign before entering the field, and, although harmless, those little pellets *hurt* when you are hit. So it is easy to follow the next rule: When hit, you raise your gun above your head and yell "I'm hit!" and run off the field while the referee counts to ten. Aficionados of the game find the rapid-fire shooting under pressure and the thrill of catching the enemy unaware exciting and exhilarating (along with the satisfaction of hitting a moving target). You can spend a lot of money on more advanced equipment (like ear-mouth pieces to communicate with your partner or teammates, or an RT Automag semi-automatic airgun for $700) in places like the Irish Brigade Paintball Proshop and Supplies of Kansas City, or just drop in at Jaegers. Hours are Monday through Friday 5:00 P.M. to 10:00 P.M., Saturday 9:00 A.M. to 11:00 P.M., and Sunday noon to 8:00 P.M. Jaegers is just off of Interstate 435 near Worlds of Fun. Take Interstate 435 to the Highway 210 exit. Turn right at Randolph Road and go south to Underground Drive. Call (816) 452–6600 for more information, or e-mail at jaegersp@ earthlink.net.

Northern Missouri River Valley

ead east back on Highway 152 and you'll come to historic **Liberty.** The downtown square has been restored to Civil War–era glory, with authentic paint colors and fancy trim—most of it original.

On the south side of the square is the **Hardware Cafe** at 5 East Kansas, Liberty 64068 (816–792–3500), the latest incarnation of the old Boggess Hardware Store. Soups and salads are hearty and delicious, and entrees are never boring; if you like tearoom-style food and plenty of it, this is the place. Dessert lovers skip the meal and go right for the goodie tray. Try the "Robert Redford." We won't tell you what's in it, but once you sink your teeth into this confection you'll never miss the real thing. Prices are reasonable; two can lunch for just over $10. Hours are Monday 11:00 A.M. to 2:00 P.M., Tuesday through Thursday 11:00 A.M. to 9:00 P.M., and Friday and Saturday 11:00 A.M. to 10:00 P.M.

How Many Tons of Silt a Year?

As the Missouri River cut through mountains and prairie, it gathered huge quantities of silt and sand. It earned its nicknames—"the Muddy Mo" and "the Big Muddy"— because it used to dump about 200,000,000 tons of silt a year into the Mississippi River.

The restored **Corbin Mill Place** at 131 South Water, Liberty 64068, is now a compendium of six specialty shops housed in an old brick mill, among them the **Liberty Quilt Shoppe** (816–781–7966). Hours at the quilt shop vary each day: Monday and Thursday from 10:00 A.M. until 7:00 P.M., Tuesday, Wednesday, Friday, and Saturday until 5:00 P.M. You can also shop **With a French Accent,** a shop full of gifts and French antiques (816–792–8320) or play **Finders Keepers** in a gift shop there, too. Call (816) 792–5515. Also there is the **Old Mill Stitchery** (816– 792–3670). Behind the mill is **Bratcher Cooperage,** where you can watch the cooper turn out kegs and churns. It is open Monday through Saturday from 10:00 A.M. until 5:30 P.M.

Under the same roof is **Corbin Mill Restaurant,** where Sandy—of the antique shop—and her daughter turn out home cooking for the lunchtime crowd in Liberty from 11:00 A.M. to 2:00 P.M. Monday through Saturday. They make a fabulous Reuben sandwich, and prices are moderate.

Sandy and Tom Williams opened the mill in 1986 as an outgrowth of their original antiques store a few blocks away, and now they offer a great place to spend an afternoon—it just keeps growing. The mill, with its 24-inch-thick limestone foundation and 18-inch brick walls, is built on an original land grant from President James Monroe for relief from the 1811 New Madrid earthquake (that event had far-reaching consequences!). Corbin Mill Place is open at 131 South Water from 10:00 A.M. to 5:00 P.M. Monday through Saturday.

There are three museums in downtown Liberty, either on the square or within easy walking distance, among them the *Jesse James Bank Museum Historic Site* (816–781–4458) and the *Historic Liberty Jail* at 216 North Main Street, Liberty 64068 (816–781–3188). The museum provides exhibits, audiovisual presentations, and art to help visitors understand the significant events that took place in the jail. It is sponsored by the Church of Jesus Christ of Latter-Day Saints. Hours are daily from 9:00 A.M. to 9:00 P.M.

The "Heatherly War" of 1836 made it into the history books. Some sources list this as an Indian war; in fact, it was a family of white outlaws who killed their neighbors and laid the blame at the feet of the Iowa Indians. Several companies from Clay and Ray Counties were dispatched to investigate and/or quell a supposed uprising. Ma Heatherly instigated the murders that were carried out by her brood of mixed-blood offspring.

The town is chock-full of antiques and craft shops, so plan on browsing. You can pick up a map at Corbin Mill or check out the Web site at www.ci.Liberty.mo.us.

The *Martha Lafite Thompson Nature Sanctuary* (816–781–8598) offers a wonderful place to watch the wildlife, take a naturalist-guided walk, or enjoy special programs—from making your own bird feeder to learning about the constellations on a night hike. More than 600 species of plants and many fish, reptiles, amphibians, and mammals make their homes here, and more than 160 species of birds have been sighted. Worn out? Take in the lovely new sanctuary building with its displays of indigenous plants, or watch snapping turtles and catfish in the creek-habitat aquarium. Enjoy one of their many programs. Relax on the spacious deck in redwood Adirondack chairs, or buy a book, a bird feeder, or bird call to take home. Watch for the sanctuary sign at 407 North La Frenz Road.

North Water Street is in the Lightburne Historic District and contains a diverse collection of structures built during the late-nineteenth century, such as Lightburne Hall, an elaborate 1852 mansion, and the 1898 Simmons house. These are all private homes. But the *James Inn Bed and Breakfast and Day Spa* at 342 North Water, Liberty 64068, is in the High Gothic Saint James Catholic Church. Built in 1913 and in use as a church until 1981, it stood empty for about ten years. It was made into a bed-and-breakfast inn by new owners in 1992 when it was purchased by David and MaryAnne Kimbrell. The beautiful high ceilings of the old brick structure give it a unique feel. The five bedrooms have private baths. All rooms have Jacuzzi tubs, pedestal sinks, and separate showers. The rooms contain many antiques as well as queen-size beds, television (with cable and HBO), and telephones. Rates for these rooms are $85 to $145 Sunday through Thursday, $145 to $199 on weekends. The bedroom on the main floor is handicap-accessible and has a single Jacuzzi. Some of the rooms have fireplaces and there is an outdoor tub and sauna. Prices include dinner on Friday night. But this is more than just a bed-and-breakfast, as the name implies. It is also a day spa featuring facials, massage, manicures, pedicures, and body wraps. One romantic specialty is the couples massage for $79. You can find more information and pictures at the Web site www.thejamesinn.com. Day spa prices vary with the services. Call for more information at (816) 781-3677.

Take Highway 210 through the tiny towns of Missouri City, Orrick, Fleming, and Camden, which are dotted along the Missouri River. The views are spectacular, especially from the observation stop just this side of Missouri City. At your back is Nebo Hill, an important site for prehistoric Indians who found this a perfect place for ceremonies and camps; the site was in use for hundreds of years. After a good spring rain you're liable to see artifact hunters out in the fields nearby.

Highway 210 will take you to *Richmond.* Here the *Ray County Museum* occupies a beautiful old brick home on West Royle Street, Richmond 64085 (816–776–2305). The Y-shaped building is unusual in itself, and the contents will tell you much about this area, from pre–Civil War days to the present. A special natural history section highlights indigenous wildlife.

To find the museum, go past the four-way stop at the edge of town on Highway 210 to Royle Street, and west to the large brick building atop the hill on the left. The library is open Wednesday through Sunday from noon until 4:00 P.M., but call for the museum hours, which changed after its remodeling. If you are here the first weekend in October, you'll find mountain men, trappers, and traders as well as old-time arts and crafts at the Old Trails Festival on the grounds of the museum.

Just 5 miles north of Richmond on Highway 13 is *Die Brok Pann Bakery,* at 14711 Highway 13, Richmond 64085, where you can buy high-quality baked goods as well as bulk foods and cheese. This friendly Mennonite shop is run by Paul and Delores King. It has homemade cookies, pies, and wonderful cinnamon rolls. Doughnuts are fresh every morning. It is open Tuesday through Saturday, 7:30 A.M. to 5:00 P.M. Call (816) 776–3275.

Time to eat? Find **Darcy Ann's Restaurant and Pub** in downtown **Norborne** at 112 South Pine. It is in a hundred-year-old bank building, which has been returned to its original appearance and updated with modern conveniences. The food is good, and it is open for breakfast, lunch, and dinner. The pub is open until midnight on Friday and Saturday nights. There is a Sunday brunch from 10:00 A.M. to 2:00 P.M. The Union Depot Variety Stage showcases local talent and big-name entertainers. The stage productions are always new. Call (816) 594–3807 to see what's going on this week.

Amish Settlements

For a visit to a very special small town, spend some time in **Chillicothe;** don't pass it by. (It has a Web site at chillicothemo.com.)

Remember that gorgeous blonde of 1930s movies fame, Jean Harlow? The folks in Chillicothe do, every time they dine at **Harlow's,** 609 Jackson Street, Chillicothe 64601 (660–646–6812). The lady's photos adorn every wall, reminding us what glamour was all about. It's tablecloth dining at 609 Jackson, but it's casual. Cliff and Kathy Harlow are proud of their blue-ribbon-winning batter-fried turkey breast. Entrees range in price from $5.95 to $18.95. Hours are 11:00 A.M. to 9:30 P.M. Monday through Friday. It's dinner Tuesday through Saturday from 4:00 until about 10:00 P.M.

For sheer indulgence, Francine Davenport can bake some triple chocolate muffins—something so sinful you will repent for days—or you can indulge without the guilt with her low-fat peaches 'n cream muffins. Whatever you choose, **Francine's Pastry Parlor,** tucked away inside a plain white storefront at 1007 Bryan, Chillicothe 64601, is the place to go if you are looking for some warm, fresh-from-the-oven treats. Call Francine at (660) 646–3333.

The **Grand River Historical Society Museum** is also in town at Forrest Drive and McNally. Hours are 1:00 to 4:00 P.M. Tuesday through Sunday (April through October).

North on Highway 65 is the town of **Trenton.** Don't mistake Trenton Cemetery Prairie for a neglected eyesore, with its rough grasses obscuring some of the old tombstones. Established in 1830, its protected status as a cemetery happily resulted in one of the few precious parcels of native prairie remaining in the state. Today it is maintained by the Missouri Conservation Department. Preservation is especially crucial; prairie north of the Missouri River is scarce. These patchwork remnants produce the seeds adapted to the northern Missouri climate that are essential to reestablishing prairie ecosystems.

This is an area of oddities; what you see may not be what you get. *Riverside Country Club* (660–359–6004), Trenton's golf course, has tree stumps carved into life-size animals around the fairways. (If you hit a birdie or an eagle around here, it may be a wooden one.) Former greens keeper Don McNabb was an artist with a chainsaw and has salted the nine-hole course with bears and other critters. The club is open for golf to anyone for the cost of a greens fee (and cart rental, if you wish), but nongolfers are welcome to check out the carvings.

What's it like to live like a governor? You can find out for yourself. Hosts Robert and Carolyn Brown offer lodging in former Governor Arthur Hyde's mansion at 418 East Seventh Street, Trenton 64683 (660–359– 5631). The 1950s *Hyde Mansion Bed and Breakfast* was completely renovated by the Browns. The large dining room contains several small tables for more intimate breakfasts. Carolyn takes individual orders for country breakfasts, unless there is a full house. Then a buffet breakfast is served from the commercial-size kitchen. There are five bedrooms; the living room and its baby grand piano are all yours. In fact, they added a 9-foot-long pool table. Rooms, all with private baths, are $55 to $110. Hyde's is near enough to Jamesport to fill up on festival weekends, so make your reservations early.

Drive north on Highway 65 about as far as you can go in the state, and Glen Mock will welcome you to *Mockville Land & Cattle Company,* Corn Place, Mercer 64661, 3 miles outside *Mercer.* Glen has an 1880s bed-and-breakfast. Actually it's more like a bread & staples. You are taken to this rustic cabin in the rolling hills by horse and wagon to begin your 1880 adventurous stay as the old settlers did years ago. Glen stocks the cabin with a chilled bottle of wine, fresh fruit, homemade bread, and all the makings for breakfast—eggs, bacon, potatoes, and homemade jam. The only food you need bring is the necessities for lunch and dinner. A fireplace provides warmth. There is a fine outhouse and an outdoor shower with water that you pump yourself. Glen breeds horses—paints to be exact—so there is unlimited horseback riding included in the price. He has 250 acres, and the neighbors will let you ride their land, too. So, if you really want to get away from it all (including telephones and electricity) and ride in a beautiful hardwood forest, this is the place for you. The price is $300 for a three-day, two-night weekend. You can bring friends because the cabin will accommodate four people. The price for four is $500. There's not another place like this, and it is sometimes booked a year in advance for the colorful fall season. It is now open for turkey season, and you will soon be able to hunt buffalo here. Call (660) 382–5862 for reservations and directions. There is one other amenity: For a little extra, Glen will cook dinner for you. Ask about menu selection when you call or visit the Web site at www.turkey huntings.com.

Jamesport is a different world. It is the largest Mennonite settlement in Missouri and home to the most orthodox "horse-and-buggy" Mennonites. Here the Amish wear black, fasten clothes with pins, and allow no electricity in their homes. Don't ask the Amish to pose for pictures, though; it's against their beliefs.

Before spending a day wandering around Jamesport's Amish community, you might want to stay at the *Marigold Inn* on Highway F in Jamesport and browse through *Marigold's,* a pretty marigold-colored home-cum-shop just 3 blocks west of downtown. Nancy Tracy will be at the shop and will show you quilts, folk art, and collectibles galore. She knows her way around the community and can give you a map to get you started. She and her husband, Larry, are the innkeepers at the inn

"Real World" Experience

*I*t was a warm and wet November day, the color gray and dismal. Yellow leaves had begun to stick to the raindrops and fall with them, cluttering the streets with mats of browning vegetation. We were looking for a day trip from Kansas City and chose Jamesport. Saturday is a busy day in this Amish community. Local residents were hurrying by in their horse-drawn carriages—wooden boxes with tiny windows in the back—headed for the nearby bulk food stores.

Books give only the minimum information about the Amish, the strictest branch of the Mennonite Church. The founder, Jacob Amman, was a Swiss religious reformer who laid the foundation for the difficult lives the Amish lead. It is strange to see the farmhouses sitting unattached to the life-giving power poles we are so accustomed to seeing in neat rows down the roadway. Forbidden modern conveniences, the Amish live in a sunrise to sunset world. The absence of television antennae or satellite dishes transport the little farms' appearances back to simpler times. The people shun vanity. Their clothes are black and fastened with straight pins—they are forbidden the vainglory of buttons—their hair is hidden under bonnets and hats. They will not allow themselves to be photographed.

We bought handmade quilts and hand-loomed rugs. We drove away in our fast car, back to our modern lives, stocked with every possible convenience, from zippers to microwave ovens. So why do the women of the Amish community have the time to quilt by the light of a kerosene lamp while we are so busy we barely have time to sew on a lost button? Ah, vanity. It is such time-consuming sin.

next door, which has twelve delightful rooms with hand-stenciled walls and handmade quilts. The rooms have a king-size bed ($59) or two queens ($69). Call (660) 684–6122.

Now, with map in hand, let's tour Jamesport. Remember, just about everything in town is closed on Thursday and Sunday. You can begin and end where Highway 6 meets Highway F and leads into the western part of downtown. *Anna's Bake Shop* off of Highway F in Jamesport would be a good place to start with fresh-baked donuts, pies, breads, or cinnamon rolls. It opens at 8:00 A.M. so you can get an early start. It stays open until 6:00 P.M. (closed from Christmas until February).

Fern Rosenbaum manages *It's a Hoot* on South Street (second block west of the four-way stop), and she knows more about the Amish people than just about anyone. Tell her what you are looking for and she will tell you how to find it. Her shop is full of fun stuff, too. Need a broom? *Colonial Rug and Broom Shop* is just 2½ blocks west of the four-way and has handwoven rugs and brooms made daily. You can purchase them already made or have them created to your own needs by artisans Larry and Jane Martin; (660) 684–6211 or (800) 647–5586.

Still in the city square just past the four-way on South Street is *Downhome Oak & Spice,* specializing in oak furniture, woodcraft, teas, and spices. But the real reason for finding it is the hand-dipped ice cream. It's open 9:00 A.M. until 5:00 P.M. Monday through Saturday; (660) 684–6526.

The Mennonite-owned *Ginerich Dutch Pantry and Bakery* is right at the four-way in Jamesport and has real, Amish-style meals with lots of wonderful homemade food and baked goods. It is open Monday through Saturday from 6:00 A.M. until 9:00 P.M.; (660) 684–6212.

Now let's get out of town a bit. The roads here are described as "gravel roads," but gravel would be a big improvement. You won't need an all-terrain vehicle to find them, but driving slowly is definitely in order unless you want to disappear into a pothole never to be seen again. The horse-and-buggies pack down a couple of very strong little paths in the center of the roads, but the rest of the road is pretty much shot. It makes passing another car going the other way a bit of an adventure and the buggies, understandably, won't leave the path under any circumstances. But aside from a bit of horse poop on your tires, you will emerge undamaged if you go slowly. Remember most of these shops are closed on Thursday and Sunday and have no telephones or electric lights.

Kerosene lamps light the *H & M Country Store* just south of Jamesport.

It's a good place to stock up your kitchen. You'll find bulk groceries at great prices (wonderful high-gluten flour for your bread machine), dried fruit, beans, homemade mixes for just about anything you want (biscuits, pancakes, muffins), and spices and herbs by the wall-full. You want noodles? Every kind you can imagine is here. You can buy fresh produce and brown eggs here, too.

To find a nice selection of hand-quilted pieces, venture out of town east on Highway F and 1 mile south on U Highway for **Sherwood Quilts and Crafts,** which has a large selection of handmade quilts, rugs, and baskets. It has a bed piled high with beautiful quilts; dig through until you find the one you can't live without. It is open from 8:00 A.M. until 5:00 P.M.

South of town on Highway 190 about 1¼ miles you can stop in to cure that headache or backache. **Ella's Reflexology** will take an appointment or even welcome drop-ins for a technique of acupressure that has been alleviating pain for 4,500 years. Call (660) 684–6502. Also nearby is the **Rolling Hills Store,** offering sturdy dry goods at excellent prices and lots of natural fiber fabrics, plus boots and shoes.

A pretty place to spend the night if you want to get out of town and into the country is the **Oak Tree Inn** on Highway F. This three-story home was built by the Amish in a twenty-acre grove of trees. If you love to walk in the woods or play with the animals, this is the place because Carolyn Huston raises miniature horses.

You can stay at the **Country Colonial Bed and Breakfast** and allow hosts Myrick and Janet den Hartog to tell you a little bit about the area. After shopping, you can return to this early 1900s home and enjoy playing the baby grand piano, and when night falls again snuggle back into the featherbed. You will awake to the aroma of a large country breakfast being prepared, and if the weather is fine, it will be served in the flower garden. Rooms are $75 to $95. Call (660) 684–6711 or (800) 579–9248.

So many places to see, so little time! If you leave town the way you came in, you can stop at the **Country Cupboard Restaurant,** in downtown Jamesport 64648, which is open Tuesday through Sunday from 6:30 A.M. until 9:00 P.M. and always has a daily special and homemade pies and breads (660–684–6597).

The Mormons settled in western Daviess County in the 1830s. Just north and west of Gallatin (take Highway 13 north and turn west on Highway P) is the historic **Adam-Ondi-Ahman Shrine,** believed by Mormons to be the place where Christ will return. Northwest Missouri is important historically to the Mormon people; there were once thousands of them here. The majority were forced out during the Mormon Wars, when the state militia was ordered to drive them out of Missouri. The town of Far West, now no more than a historical marker, comprised 5,000 souls, all exterminated or driven from their homes. Many died during a forced march in this land of religious freedom. The marker is off Highway 13, west on Highway HH and north on Highway D, near Shoal Creek (just northwest of Kingston).

Ever wonder where retail giant J.C. Penney got his start? No, not New York, or even Chicago. It was right here in *Hamilton* in 1895 that he got his first job at Hale's Department Store. By the time he returned to Hamilton to buy his old employer's place of business in 1924, it was number 500 in his chain of stores. His company motto was: "Honor, confidence, service, and cooperation"—no wonder he did so well.

The *J.C. Penney Memorial Library and Museum* (816–583–9997), uptown on Davis Street in Hamilton, is open Tuesday through Saturday from 10:00 A.M. to 5:00 P.M. You'll love the displays of early merchandise—makes you wonder who wore the stuff. The Penney farm cottage has also been restored.

Even cattlemen like this area's history. J.C. Penney once raised great herds of Angus, and at the Penney farm there is a monument—a big monument—to Penney's prize bull.

In the town of *Winston* (64689), on Highway 69 just before I–35, is *Winston Station Antiques,* which is open Tuesday through Saturday from 10:00 A.M. to 5:00 P.M. for antiques and useful junk. Call (660) 749–5334.

Jesse James Country

Take the Business 69 exit to *Excelsior Springs.* Once a magnet for people who wished to "take the waters," this old spa has enough moxie to try for a comeback. The health-spa ship was scuttled in the 1950s when an article in the *Saturday Evening Post* declared mineral waters an ineffective form of treatment; the demise was clinched when Missouri passed a bill prohibiting advertising by doctors, so now we enjoy the waters—and the baths and massages—for the lovely, hedonistic fun of it. The town was founded in 1880 for the waters. Even the Native Americans living here valued its healing properties.

Visit the *Hall of Waters* at 201 East Broadway, Excelsior Springs 64024, the world's longest mineral-water bar, and sample some of the waters that attracted thousands near the turn of the century. There are more naturally occurring types of mineral waters here than anyplace else on earth except the German city of Baden-Baden, which ties Excelsior Springs.

For a truly sybaritic experience, check the schedule for baths and massage, also at the Hall of Waters (816–630–0753). You can once again "take the waters," as they used to say. The bathhouse is open by appointment from 9:00 A.M. to 5:00 P.M. Monday through Friday (the spa is closed on Tuesday) and 10:00 A.M. to 5:00 P.M. Saturday and Sunday. A sampling of the available treatments includes: *light vapor bath:* with forty-four sixty-five-watt light bulbs to warm joints and muscles and open pores to the steam; *mineral water bubble tub:* soak in a deep bath of mineral water aerated by powerful bubbles; *salt rub:* a scrubdown with sea salt, Epsom salts, and a loofah sponge to exfoliate and stimulate; *massage:* a classic deep tissue Swedish massage with reflexology acupressure by a licensed massage therapist (a water-based cream is used while you lie on a padded table, and eucalyptus candles and soft music relax you); *steam bath:* opens your pores at 115° while you rest on a bed; and last, and best, the *Fango mud bath:* black mud painted over the body is left to dry followed by a thorough rinsing. There are all kinds of special packages of these services ranging in

Taking the Waters

*E*xcelsior Springs has long been famous for its waters. Native Americans were aware of the benefits of the springs, but the settlers called them "pizen." The medicinal uses of the waters were responsible for the founding of the town in 1880. There are five categories of mineral water, and each has a medicinal purpose. Excelsior Springs is one of only six cities in the world to have all of them—one of two in the United States—and you can still experience most of them at the Hall of Waters there. They are: iron manganese, which as the name suggests, is a source of iron; sulfo-saline, which is a very, very strong laxative (given a two-ounce cup, people were told not to drink it in the elevator but to wait until

they got to their rooms. This was no joke!). The next is soda bicarbonate, which was naturally carbonated and, as you might suspect, was used to settle a queasy stomach. The fourth category used to be the last—the neutral waters which could be drunk in unlimited amounts—until it was discovered that they had very different compositions and served different purposes. These were calcium and lithium waters. The lithium water had properties that soothed depression (the most famous and best-tasting water in the world was Blue Rock Lithia) and of course, the calcium water, which is the only water still bottled today in Excelsior Springs and an excellent no-calorie source of calcium.

Hall of Waters

price from $20 to $399, with plenty of options in between. Call (816) 630–0753 for an appointment.

The lovely Art Deco–style building, built in 1937 as "the finest and most complete health resort structure in the U.S.," is a fine example of a WPA project begun during the Great Depression. Moreover, how many towns have city offices that are shared with mineral baths and massage rooms—not to mention a 25-meter indoor pool?

The *Paradise Playhouse* is a brand new dinner theater done in Hawaiian theme. It's right across from the Hall of Waters at 101 Spring Street Excelsior Springs 64024. The buffet is cooked right there in the shiny-new, cutting-edge kitchen. Tables are tiered for best view of the stage and the plays are very well done. Call (816) 630–3333 for show times.

If you like old-fashioned burgers, don't miss *Ray's Lunch,* at 231 East Broadway, Excelsior Springs 64024. The hash browns are *killer* good, and the secret chili recipe is a favorite with locals. Call (816) 637–3432.

Across the street from Ray's Lunch is the *Tropical Mexican Restaurant and Cantina* at 244 East Broadway, Excelsior Springs 64024. This restaurant is in an unlikely spot downtown with little traffic, and yet it is full every day at lunch and packed for dinner. Why? Because the food is great, that's why. Bill, Marco, and Eva Pither serve lunch Monday through Saturday beginning at 11:00 A.M. and continue on with dinner until 8:00 P.M. on weeknights and 9:00 P.M. on Friday and Saturday nights. Try the chili relleños—a long chili stuffed with cheese, coated with batter and cooked until the cheese melts. Call (816) 630–5355.

New to town is the wonderful *Olde English Garden Shoppe* at 115 East Broadway, Excelsior Springs 64024, cultivated by Jim and Ginger Nelson. This overlooks the river and has waterfalls and garden delights. It is stocked with all kinds of garden ornaments and gifts for gardeners, from large engraved paving stones to little seed-row markers. The Nelsons carry some books as well. The shop is open Tuesday through Sunday from 10:00 A.M. to 6:00 P.M. Call (816) 630–5060.

Other places to shop in the Olde Towne area include the *Enchanted Frog Antiques* at 219 East Broadway, Excelsior Springs 64024, where you can find art pottery, furniture, books, glassware, and porch and garden decor. You can find prints and a frame for that print as well. Owner Laveigh Rooney will tell you how she came to name the shop after a reptile that is the symbol of health and prosperity in many countries of the world. So if she can bring a little of the magic and mystery back into today's high-tech world, then so be it. Drop in for a free smile, at least, from 10:00 A.M. until 5:00 P.M. Monday through Saturday, and on Sunday from 11:00 A.M. to 3:00 P.M. Call (816) 630–6933.

The *Old Bank Museum,* 101 East Broadway, Excelsior Springs 64024 (816–630–6161), in a former Bank Building, circa 1906, and itself an interesting architectural achievement, preserves spa-town history. (Check out the dentist's office and thank your lucky stars this is the present.) Look up to find a pair of murals; they're wonderful copies of Jean-François Millet's "The Gleaners" and "The Angelus," painted by an itinerant artist with more talent than fame. You can buy postcards, homemade lye soap, or a museum membership (for $1.00); you may find the Women's Auxiliary of the museum quilting or weaving rag rugs when you visit on a Wednesday. The Chamber of Commerce is here; Pat Wilson will fill you in on local happenings.

There are several other antiques shops in the area. *Mary's Tiques and Treasures* is around the corner at 451 South Thompson Avenue, Excelsior Springs 64024. George and Mary Pasalich will show you around from Monday until Saturday 11:00 A.M. until 5:00 P.M. and on Sunday from 1:00 until 5:00 P.M. (816–630–2215). There's always a free cup of coffee, so you can take your time prowling about in this shop, which goes on and on through several rooms. The front of the shop has

Jesse James Farm

Mineral Water Well, Excelsior Springs

Trust Falls

Octagonal Schoolhouse, Watkins Mill

Elms Hotel, Excelsior Springs

Attractions in and around Excelsior Springs

a baker's rack filled with fresh baked goods from Die Brot Pann, the Mennonite bakery in Richmond, and a display of Pasta Bella flavored pastas from the local pasta plant.

There are shops within this shop, too. *Rozart Pottery* is displayed here. It is handcrafted by George and Rosie Rydings. The *Wacky Wagon's Lady Bug* is also in here. This is a collection of rubber stamps and all the accessories that go with them.

Next door at 455 and 457 South Thompson, Excelsior Springs 64024 is *Colleen's Cottage* (816–630–8844), owned by Colleen Rhodus, which has recently expanded.

Around the corner, the *Olde Towne Mall* has antiques galore at 414 South Thompson, Excelsior Springs 64024, where Leonard Jones, Pat Leatherman, and Phil Broadbent have opened a huge space and filled it with lots of stuff. This "Olde Towne" area is bursting with new shops since the Elms has reopened, and it is a fine place to walk on a Saturday afternoon.

Across from the mall is an old-fashioned hardware store that has withstood the test of time. The newest generation of *Brunke's Supply* at 423 Thompson, Excelsior Springs 64024, is exactly like the old one—row upon row, deep into the bowels of the store, lined up in some kind of order only John Brunke knows, are thousands and thousands of *things*. Stuff. Gadgets. Cast-iron pots. Aluminum pans. Screws. Bolts. Signs. Anything. Everything. A real if-we-don't-have-it-you-probably-don't-need-it kind of place. You're gonna love it. Call (816) 637–3155.

What do Harry S Truman, Al Capone, and Franklin D. Roosevelt have in common? They all stayed at the *Elms Hotel* at Elms Boulevard and Regent Street, Excelsior Springs 64024. You can, too. The elegant old hotel—built originally in 1888—and the beautiful grounds around it underwent a complete ($8 million dollar) renovation in 1998. The hotel has been a resting place for the famous and the infamous, from Presidents Franklin Roosevelt and Harry Truman to Al Capone, who hosted all-night drinking and gambling parties here during Prohibition. The new look celebrates the time of that bygone era. In fact, the workers in the renovation process claim to have seen the ghost of someone who looks a lot like Al Capone drifting down the hall of the fourth floor.

Look for the 1948 Chevrolet Stylemaster out front of the hotel. President Truman arrived in just such a car on election night in 1948. He came to avoid the press on a night when everyone thought he would be defeated by Thomas Dewey. He went to bed thinking he had lost the election and was awakened at 3:00 A.M. to learn that he had been reelected. The famous photo of him gleefully holding an early copy of the *Chicago Daily Tribune* carrying the blatant headline DEWEY DEFEATS TRUMAN was taken in front of the Elms Hotel.

The original tile floor and the huge "walk-in" fireplace in the lobby, as well as the Art Deco designs and stained glass in the Monarch Room, make this magnificent hotel worth a visit. It is, of course, on the National Register of Historic Places.

The Elms offers 153 guest rooms and suites, and the feeling of Truman's genteel time is augmented with such modern amenities as a communications system with voice mail, dataport, and cordless phones. There is twenty-four-hour room service and concierge service. A gourmet shop features coffees, espresso, cappuccino, entrees, and homemade ice creams. A beauty salon for hair and scalp treatments, facials, manicures, pedicures, and makeup is also available.

Boxer Jack Dempsey used the hotel as a training center. Now a new and complete fitness center on the grounds has tennis courts, riding stables, jogging trail, mountain biking, and, of course, an outdoor pool. Indoors there is a European swim track and banked jogging track. This indoor pool is shaped like a paper clip, with two sides extending the length of the room, and then curling back through two short rounded ends so that you can swim laps without having to turn around. The small islands in the middle of the pool are set with brightly painted giant flowers and playing-card symbols—hearts, spades, clubs, and diamonds—and bright bursts of color hang above the pool. Classes in yoga and t'ai chi, and nutrition and health programs including wellness cooking, are featured.

Strange As It Sounds

Mormon travelers on the old trails left legends and stories. There is still a site inside the Excelsior Springs city limits that is visited by pilgrims. Mormons were being chased from the country and took refuge in an old church; such a storm came up that it spooked their pursuers' horses, the river rose, and the pursuers gave up and went home, leading the Mormons to believe they had been delivered by a miracle.

The new spa is the real center of this elegant hotel. Look at this list of possibilities: body treatment rooms for mud, aloe, and seaweed-algae wraps, salt glow, and body-polish exfoliation, and hydrotherapy; Swiss and Vichy showers; massage rooms for reflexology, sports, signature, and couples massage; and relaxation facilities with sauna, steam, mineral baths, and whirlpools. Rooms and suites begin at $99 (rooms Sunday through Thursday) to $299 (Friday and Saturday) and all include breakfast and dinner. Various golf, spa, and honeymoon packages are also offered, or just stop by for the magnificent Sunday brunch. Call (800) 843–3567.

The beautiful little stone church across the street from the Elms, at the corner of Regent and Kansas City Avenues, Excelsior Springs 64024, is the *Church of St. Luke, the Beloved Physician.* The Episcopal congregation began having services in Excelsior Springs as far back as 1905, but it was 1933 when the church was built on property donated by Major W.A.J. Bell of Blechingly, England. The church is built in the English style, similar to The Church of St. Mary the Virgin (A.D. 1090) in Bell's home parish. It is built of stones quarried on Major Bell's property nearby. The inside of this remarkable church is so lovely that it is often requested for weddings. Guests at the Elms are frequently visitors on Sunday mornings. You will be most welcome, so sign the guest book and plan to stay for coffee and refreshments in the undercroft.

Right down Kansas City Avenue at Chillicothe Street—beside the Elms Hotel—is an old depot where trains brought guests from Chicago and Kansas City to the hotel. Now it is the *Wabash Barbecue,* 646 South Kansas City Avenue, Excelsior Springs 64024. The meats smoked in the old brick garage out back are very good and so is the secret barbecue sauce. Jim McCullough and his wife, Cheri, have restored the building to its 1925 charm. Between its days as a depot, which ended in 1933, new owners converted it into a dairy, delivering milk to the residents of Excelsior. The dairy sold milk shakes and burgers, too, and Jim—whose family goes back six generations in town—remembers hanging out here in the 1960s. He and Cheri looked at the walk-in coolers that once held cans of fresh milk and knew they would be perfect for slabs of meat, the big garage fine for smoking. On summer weekends you can enjoy music out on the patio. Call (816) 630–7700 for carryout, too.

The *Antique Tulip* across the street from the Elms Hotel at 564 Kansas City Avenue, Excelsior Springs 64024, has pretty bentwood furniture and hand-painted birdhouses on the front porch and much more inside.

Excelsior Springs Fine Art Gallery at 520 Kansas City Avenue, Excelsior

Springs 64024 was built in 1909 as a boardinghouse. Later it became a convent for the nuns who taught at the Catholic school across the street. Then it stood empty for years and years. Now it has found rebirth as a home and art gallery. Keith Bowman and his wife, Jeri—who are both art teachers in the local school district—bought the old building and with hard work and a little money have begun to restore it to its original beauty. Inches of tar and tiles were removed from the hardwood floors, staircases and sliding doors were painstakingly rebuilt. Beautiful stained-glass windows grace the entryway. Now the gallery and studio show the works of local artists Tuesday and Friday 4:00 to 7:00 P.M. and Saturday 10:00 A.M. to 4:00 P.M. You're also welcome to call for an appointment. There's even more: The Armchair Film Society shows old movies on the second or third Friday of each month. Call (816) 630–5671 for information about the movies and art shows held at the gallery.

Downtown the old *Mill Inn Restaurant* at 415 St. Louis Avenue, Excelsior Springs 64024, looks vaguely south-of-the-border. Inside you'll find wonderful cinnamon rolls (if you can beat the local farmers to them!), peanut butter pie, and, on Wednesday and Saturday only, homemade bread pudding. Call (816) 637–8008.

Anne Higdon and Bruce Libowitz met at New York's French Culinary Institute, so the breakfast part of the new bed-and-breakfast in Excelsior Springs is guaranteed good. The *Inn on Crescent Lake* is a three-story Georgia colonial mansion on twenty-two acres at 1261 St. Louis Avenue, Excelsior Springs 64024. The home was built in 1915 and still has the crescent-shaped moat encircling the estate for which it was named.

The guest rooms all have private baths (some have whirlpool tubs) and individual temperature control and cable television. Bruce and Anne shared a dream of having the perfect country inn where people could

Hometown Notes

I call Excelsior Springs home. I have always been very active in the community, beginning with a few years as PTA president when my children were young, and moving on to become the Honorable Patti DeLano, Mayor of Excelsior Springs. I was elected to two terms on the City Council and served on the Planning and Zoning Commission and the Road and Bridge Commission. I have also served on the Board of Directors of the Missouri Municipal League. For three years I wrote a weekly column for the Daily Standard, the local newspaper. I then went back to school at William Jewell College in Liberty and earned my B.S. in Communications.

unwind. This is a good place to do it. The swimming pool is a fine spot for cooling off, and the ponds are great for fishing. Paddleboats are available for tooling around the little lakes.

Breakfast may be served in the dining room, living room, or in the sun-filled solarium (or even in your bedroom if you are so inclined). The dining room is available for guests of the inn for dinner, too, with a little advance notice. Rooms are $135 to $150. Call (816) 630–6745 for reservations, e-mail at ahigdon@aol.com, or visit the Web site at www. crescent.com.

Excelsior Lake Springs also has one of the most beautiful old golf courses in the Kansas City area, and it's a municipal course, so it's affordable. Rolling hills, big trees, and surrounding woodlands make it challenging; watered fairways and paved cart paths make it pleasant year-round, and it is an "English-type" course, unique because it has no sand traps or bunkers, which keeps play moving smoothly (so leave your sand wedge in the car). If you go into the snack bar for a cold drink, don't miss the tiny log cabin tucked *inside* the clubhouse. It's one of the original structures in this old town and lets you see how Missouri settlers once lived. The Battle of Fredericksburg, a Civil War skirmish, was fought along the southwest sector of the course, and a monument commerating the event stands near the 15th tee. At the bottom of Golf Hill Drive in East Valley Park, you can stop and take a walk along the Fishing River path to see a new view of this old town— here you'll find one of the original mineral water wells towering over the park. Visit the Web site at www.exsmo.com.

On the eastern edge of Excelsior Springs on Highway 10, which is also called Isley Boulevard, is *Angie's Beanie Babies, Collectibles, and Decorating* at 1016 Isley Boulevard, Excelsior Springs 64024. You will find all the Beanie Babies you could ever want here. Everything from porcelain dolls to Franklin Mint plates are here, too. Fragrant essences of potpourri and scented candles fill the air, and handmade Victorian-style decor and artistry is everywhere. Hundreds of lavish gifts and designer accents for your home are here waiting for you from 10:00 A.M. until 5:00 P.M. Wednesday through Saturday. Call (816) 630–2488.

Follow the signs to the *Watkins Woolen Mill State Historic Site* west off Highway 69 onto Highway 92 near Larson and get ready to walk back in time. The decades fall away like leaves as you wander down the footpath from the parking area. You pass deep Missouri woods, then a tiny stone-walled cemetery where the gravestones are encrusted with lichen. Farther along the path a brick giant rises to your right, and a graceful mansion crowns the hill to your left. A young belle could make quite an entrance down the lovely, curved walnut staircase in the entry-way—and probably did, more than once.

Waltus Watkins built his empire here around 1850, in the years before the Civil War. Quite an empire it was: The three-story brick mill employed dozens, providing woolen fabrics to the area. The milling machinery, from washing vats to looms, is still intact, providing pristine examples of early industrial ingenuity. The house and its outbuildings reflect a gracious life—the reward for hard work and hard-headed business sense.

Before it became a state park, the mill seemed destined for destruction. The family was selling it after more than a century of occupancy, and the place was on the auction block. Representatives from the Smithsonian were on hand to bid on rare equipment—but the day was saved, along with the integrity of the mill complex, when private individuals bought the site lock, stock, and barrel (and there were a few of those about). Eventually they were able to pass the mill complex along to the state of Missouri, and now you can tour the mill and the elegant home on the hill, participate in living-history weekends (try not to miss the Victorian Christmas), or watch an ongoing archaeological dig intended to discover still more about day-to-day life one hundred years ago and more. Tours are given Monday through Saturday from 10:00 A.M. till 4:00 P.M. and Sunday from 11:00 A.M. till 4:00 P.M. Winter hours are 11:00 A.M. till 4:00 P.M. Admission is $1.25 for adults, and 75 cents for children under twelve. Special events are usually free. A new interpretive center opened in 1992 and acts as museum and buffer between now and the nineteenth century. Call (816) 580–3887 for more information.

A brick church and an octagonal schoolhouse are nearby, both restored to their original condition. The Watkins children and those of mill workers and local farmers attended to their readin', 'ritin', and 'rithmetic here. See the schoolhouse when it's open, if you can; call (816) 296–3357. The ventilation system of windows high in the octagonal clerestory turret is ingenious. Sunlight reflects softly around the white-painted walls inside; not much artificial light would have been necessary, with the tall windows on every side.

The park also has a 5-mile-long bike path through the woods as well as a sandy beach for swimming in the lake.

History buffs should look for the ***Jesse James Farm Historic Site*** (816–628–6065) just off Highway 92 on Jesse James Drive, between Excelsior Springs and ***Kearney*** (watch for signs). The white house with its gingerbread trim and cedar roof sits just over a rise, a little way back

Trivia

Frank and Jesse James's dad was a preacher at the Pisgah Baptist Church in Excelsior Springs. They moved to the farm in 1843.

from the road; the new asphalt drive and path make the place handicapped accessible. The original part of the house is a log cabin, which was recently rescued from a precarious slide into decay. The cabin contains, among other things, the remains of Jesse's original coffin, which was exhumed when the body was moved to nearby Kearney; the family originally buried him in the yard to keep the body from being disturbed by those bent on revenge or souvenirs. The coffin is odd by today's standards; there was a glass window at face level—presumably for viewing the body, not for providing a window on eternity for the deceased!

July 17, 1995, was a big day in Kearney. The body buried in Jesse's grave was exhumed for DNA testing to finally settle the debate about who, exactly, was buried in the James family plot. Jesse's ancestors offered DNA samples, and another man who claims that his grandfather is buried in Jesse's grave also offered his DNA for testing. People who believe that James died in 1950 at a very old age as well as people who believe it is Jesse's body in Mt. Olivet Cemetery brought folding chairs that morning to watch. "You goin' to the digging?" was the question asked at Clem's Cafe when it opened early that morning. By closing time, lots of people were wearing "We Dig Jesse" T-shirts that Pat Dane, the enterprising owner of *Maggie's Attic* across the street from the cemetery at the intersection of Highways 92 and 33, had sold to all the network cameramen and reporters gathered there. Maggie's, at 190 West Sixth Street, Kearney 64060, carries the ususal gift items—candles, dishes, and such—but Pat also has a more unusual stock along with the silk flowers and antiques. A wine cellar is on the premises with all sorts of offerings including a large selection of Missouri wines. Hours are Monday through Friday from 10:00 A.M. until 5:30 P.M., and on Saturday from 9:00 A.M. until 4:00 P.M. Call (816) 628–6355. Be sure to visit the James Farm and see where he called home. The newer section of the house was a Sears & Roebuck mail order. Mrs. James decided that the old place was getting too run down—not to mention crowded—and she sent for the two-room addition, assembled on the spot. It still sports the original wallpaper.

This is the famous outlaw's birthplace, the place where his father was hanged and his mother's arm was lost to a Pinkerton's bomb. Enjoy the new on-site museum, which includes a gift shop full of James memorabilia, books, and local crafts, or stick around in August and September for the play *The Life and Times of Jesse James*. Brother Frank was there, too. Oh, you want to know about the DNA test, do you? It was Jesse all right.

Admission to the museum and home is $6.50 for adults, $4.50 for seniors, and $3.00 for children ages eight to fifteen. The hours are from 9:00 A.M. to 4:00 P.M. seven days a week, Sundays from noon to 4:00 P.M.

On a less grim note, visit the **Claybrook Mansion** across the road from the James Farm in Kearney 64060. This delightful pre–Civil War home owned by Jesse's daughter and her husband was the last word in modern convenience and elegance. Fairs and historic re-creations bring Claybrook alive several times a year. Purchase tickets at the James Farm; the price is included in the James Farm tour admission, but it is open only during warm weather; the place is like a barn to heat.

And if you've ever wanted to lay a flower on the outlaw's grave, it's located in **Mt. Olivet Cemetery** on Highway 92, ½ mile east of Interstate 35 in Kearney (pronounced *CAR-ney*). Look for it near the cedar trees at the west end of the cemetery, which is open during daylight hours year-round.

Legend has it that Jesse, Frank, and/or Cole Younger visited darn near every fallen-down log cabin in this part of Missouri—not to mention the surrounding states. The James gang would have had to be in three places at once, the way their exploits were reported, but no matter. That's the fun thing about legends; they're much more elastic than the truth.

Fast-growing Kearney still hangs on to its small-town charm. At **Clem's Cafe,** 119 East Washington, Kearney 64060 (816–628–4044), Charlie Davis (not Clem—you'll have to ask Charlie for that story) serves great homemade pies; in fact, everything is homemade. Clem's has really great biscuits-and-gravy and homemade cinnamon rolls, so it is very popular for breakfast around these parts. For great steak, burgers and sandwiches, try next door at **Cattlener's Steak House** (this time Charlie got his name on it), which is owned by the same folks; (816) 635–4545.

There's a tiny beauty shop in town, **Total-e-Clips,** at 205 East Fifth Street in Kearney 64060, where you can spend some relaxing time being pampered with manicure, pedicure, massage, and, best of all, an hour facial by Nita Hopkins. Call (816) 628–4611 for an appointment.

Bob and Fern Buhlig have opened their circa 1907 home to guests passing through Kearney. The **Buhlig Hospitality Inn** is a bed-and-breakfast at 400 South Jefferson, Kearney 64060. This is a B&B the way they were meant to be. You will feel right at home here because guests are invited to use the living room for relaxation. The home is touched with antiques, and the breakfast is a crowd pleaser. The rooms are $65, but the "Sweetheart Room" is $85. It has a private entrance, whirlpool tub, fireplace, and a king-size bed and lives up to its name. Call (816) 628–3922 for

reservations if you will be in Kearney or visit the Web site at www.
bedandbreakfastkearny.com.

You might want to visit **Cezanne's Garden** at the junction of Highways
92 and 33 in Kearney 64060 and look at Cathy Breshear's custom sten-
cilwork. There are some large garden scenes that are quite lovely, and
owner Jana Barnhart's shop is full of framed prints, silk and dried flo-
rals, chenille afghans, and upholstered pieces in a soft-traditional look.
Hours are 9:30 A.M. to 5:30 P.M. Monday through Friday (open Thursday
until 8:00 P.M.) and from 10:00 A.M. to 4:00 P.M. on Saturday. Call (816)
415–0055 for more information.

Western Way Bed & Breakfast, 13606 Henson Road, Holt 64068, is new
to the area as a B&B, but the Over the Hill Ranch 4½ miles north and
west of Kearney has been Connie and Bill Green's home for more than
twenty years. Not only do they take care of people in a wonderful way,
but they will also board horses overnight. That is one reason their first
year in the B&B business was such a raging success. The production
company filming the movie *Ride with the Devil* in the Kansas City area
spent time here with their steeds and, in fact, Connie and Bill make
appearances in the movie as wagon drivers. Country singer Shania
Twain is one of the bed and breakfast's most famous guests. The singer
spent three days at the ranch with her horse while appearing in Kansas
City. The Greens are raising draft horses now, too, so carriage rides are
available for guests in the secluded log home and guest house. There's a
hot tub on the property to soothe away your aches. The guest house
offers all the privacy you could want. A suite with a king-size bed and
double jacuzzi goes for $125 a night. The other room has a smaller hot
tub and rents for $100. A room in the main house is $100. Horses stay for
$20 a night per stall. Call (816) 628-5686 for information and directions
(the driveway is ½ mile long and in the woods).

Highway 9 will lead you to the charming little college town of **Parkville.**
This is a bustling crafts and antiques center, with longtime shops inter-
woven with new establishments. **English Landing,** across the tracks
from the old town, houses the **Cafe Cedar** at 160 South Main, Parkville
64152, serving Mediterranean cuisine. It is not only luscious food but
healthy as well. Owners Osama Aburas and Jahad Saleh are rightly
proud of their creations. They offer plenty of vegetarian dishes and any
kind of kabob—lamb, chicken, shrimp, beef—you could want. The
entrees cover a range from rack of lamb to baked salmon or stuffed
Cornish hen. Nothing is fried, everything is baked or broiled. There are
six different kinds of salads, lots of sandwiches, and appetizers. On nice
days you can eat on the deck overlooking the Missouri River. Hours are

Monday through Saturday from 11:00 A.M. until 10:00 P.M., Sunday noon to 9:00 P.M. Call (816) 505–2233 for more information.

Just past the shopping complex is quiet English Landing Park on the banks of the Missouri. Look for the historic ninety-five-year-old Waddell "A" truss bridge, one of only two of this type left in the country. It was salvaged and moved to its present location. Now it's the focal point of the park, providing a walkway across a small feeder creek leading to the big river.

Cecil Doubenmier is a prize-winning Parkville potter who sells his pottery mostly at craft fairs—there's not room at his place for visitors. If you don't want to follow him around the Midwest, then look for his work at the **Peddler's Wagon,** a downtown quilt shop at 115 Main, Parkville 64152 (816–741–0225). This little shop sells anything a quilter may need as well as new, handmade quilts and some country gifts. There are also classes in quilting and silk embroidery. Hours are Tuesday through Saturday from 10:00 A.M. until 5:00 P.M., year-round, and Sundays October 1 through December 3 from 12:30 to 4:00 P.M.

Of course there is a magnetic attraction when chocolate is mentioned, so you will be irresistibly drawn to **Parkville Coffee & Fudge** at 113 Main Street, Parkville 64152. Owner Bill Norton has added even more to tempt you, especially if you can resist the siren call of chocolate. Also for sale are items from his, and co-owner Kris Norton's, collection of sporting collectibles—gun shell boxes, duck calls, tobacco tins, decoys, and powder tins—to entice you. Winter hours are Wednesday through Saturday 10:00 A.M. to 5:00 P.M. and Sunday 1:00 to 4:00 P.M. Call (816) 587–4200 for more information on hours of operation.

You can't miss **Home Embellishments** at 102 Main, Parkville 64152 (816–505–1022). Just look for the yellow building with the purple awning and a metal naked lady out front. Inside you can find brass hardware, furniture, and art from nearly fifty local craftspeople. There is jewelry, metal sculptures, handmade kaleidoscopes, hand-blown lights, fused lights, and lamps made of truck parts (talk about one-of-a-kind gifts!). Jan Gunn knows her way around Parkville, too. She can direct you to the **Garden Goddess** at 5 Main Street, Parkville 64152 (816–505–0225) where you can look at handmade garden pottery. Then head for **Stone Canyon Pizza** at 15 Main Street, Parkville 64152. Well, you see, there is plenty to do to make Parkville a fine day trip.

Down to Earth Lifestyles is the quiet eighty-five-acre country place of Bill and Lola Coons just outside of Parkville at 12500 N.W. Crooked Road, Parkville 64152. It is a contemporary earth-integrated home that gives guests the luxury of total peace and quiet. There are four rooms, each with a private bath and color television. You can fish the stocked ponds or swim in an indoor heated pool. Skylights and picture windows allow in sunlight and provide a nice view. The rooms are furnished with country antiques. There are horses, and cows, and it is fine for birdwatching. Country breakfasts of omelettes, biscuits, pancakes, and country-cured ham and sausage await you in the morning. You can even get breakfast in bed with a flower on the tray and a little bell to ring for extras. It's close to the airport and popular for honeymooners who spend their wedding night here and catch a plane for someplace exotic the next morning. Rooms cost $89 for one person (plus tax), or $99 for two. Call (816) 891–1018 for reservations and other information.

If you are a devotee of fine baked goods, you'll want to stop by *Fannie's Restaurant* in *Platte City* 64079 (816–431–5675), at Interstate 29 and Main Street. Fannie's can serve 150 diners at once, and it's a good thing because there is a steady business from the officers sent for schooling at Fort Leavenworth, Kansas, just across the Missouri River. Homemade bread comes with the meal, or you can buy a giant, fluffy loaf to take home; try the pies, cinnamon rolls, and cobblers as well. Oh, yes, the meals are fine, too. They run from $5.95 to $13.95, or enjoy the smorgasbord every day. The breakfast buffet is $5.25, lunch is $5.95, dinner during the week is only $7.95. On Friday and Saturday nights it is $13.95, but the seafood buffet and barbecue smorgasbord are worth every penny. Fannie's also features lots of preserves, relishes, and fresh spices from the Amish in Jamesport. Hours are from 7:00 A.M. to 9:00 P.M. every day of the week.

A former millionaire's estate on seventy-three acres is now the *Basswood Country Inn Resort* at 15880 Interurban Road, Platte City 64079. This 1935 lakeside home has six suites—each with two bedrooms and a mini or full kitchen, some with fireplaces and all in country French decor. There is television, VCR, and a phone in each room. Hosts Don and Betty Soper can direct you to nearby golf courses and antiques malls. Rates are $79 to $149. Call (816) 858–5556 or (800) 242–2775.

Just off Highway 45, *Weston* is a beautiful town tucked between rounded hills, its past shaped as much by the nearby Missouri River and its thread of commerce as by the orchards, vineyards, distilleries, and good tobacco-growing soils here. After the signing of the 1837 Platte Purchase, it attracted settlers who recognized its rich soil—and appreciated the low prices.

Historic preservation in Weston has been a high priority for many years; the place exudes charm as a flower exudes scent. A beautiful old

Catholic church overlooks the town, and tobacco and apple barns stand tall on many of the surrounding hills. It has a foursquare flavor that just feels historic—and in fact, Weston bills itself as the Midwest's most historic town. There are more than one hundred historically significant homes and businesses from before the Civil War alone. Book a tour of the homes (advance reservations are required for the tour; call (816) 640–2650 and ask Marion Gaskill to arrange a mini-tour for groups of fifteen or more of two of the homes), or visit the **Weston Museum** at Main and Spring Streets, Weston 64098. Hollywood has discovered Weston, and it's not unknown for movie cameras to roll on Main Street. Life in Platte County goes way back, long before these neat homes were built or the first still was cranked up; the museum will take you from prehistoric times through World War II. Hours are from 1:00 till 4:00 P.M. Tuesday through Saturday, and on Sunday from 1:30 to 5:00 P.M. (closed January and February). This one is a bargain; admission is free. Call (816) 386–2977. It's a day trip all by itself.

Weston's **McCormick Distilling Company** (816–640–2276) is a rare treat, 1¼ miles south of town on Highway JJ. They say this is the oldest continually active distillery in the country—or at least west of the Hudson River. It was founded in 1856 by stagecoach and Pony Express king Ben Holladay.

You can't tour the distillery anymore, but be sure to visit the **McCormick Country Store** at 420 Main Street in Weston 64098, where Terri French handles all McCormick goods. You can find mugs, T-shirts, and other gift items as well as a fine line of cigars. There's a tasting room in which you can taste the products of the distillery for 25 cents. Call (816) 640–3149 for more information.

Pirtle's Weston Vineyards Winery (816–640–5728) is one of Missouri's most interesting wineries, located in the former German Lutheran Evangelical Church at 502 Spring Street, Weston 64098. Jesus made wine, why not Pirtle's? Owner Elbert Pirtle's striking stained-glass windows depict the winery's logo and a wild rose—the math professor from the University of Missouri at Kansas City is quite the Renaissance man.

Northern Platte County soil is conducive to some fine viticulture; taste the products of these rolling hills Monday through Saturday from 10:00 A.M. to 6:00 P.M. and Sunday from noon to 6:00 P.M. The Pirtles love to talk wine and vines. Schedule a wine-tasting party here, and don't forget the mead, a honey-based beverage once thought to be a "love potion." (So what have you got to lose?) It's sweet and smoky—and so it should be, because it's aged in McCormick Distillery oak barrels. Newest in the mead line are sparkling and raspberry mead. Great stuff and just as romantic as the original. They say that originally the church was upstairs and a cooperage was in the basement where barrels were made to serve northwest Missouri. The winery now has a wine garden where you can take a basket of cheese, sausage, and bread to enjoy with your wine.

Across the street at 505 Spring, Weston 64098, you'll find *The Vineyards* (816–640–5588). The restaurant features country Continental cuisine and is considered one of the finest places to eat in the Kansas City area. With that reputation, you'd best call for reservations; the place is charming but small, seating only thirty-six . . . well, forty-two in a pinch, if they push the tables together. The kitchen is tucked into every nook and cranny in the basement. Duck, lamb, salmon, and white perch are just some of the featured items on the menu. Appetizers of baked brie with roasted garlic and fresh fruit give you some idea of the restaurant's Continental style. Patio dining during fine weather is a treat. There's a nice mix of art and music in the tiny 1845 Rumpel House. Lunch is served Wednesday through Saturday from 11:00 A.M. until 2:00 P.M. Dinner is from 6:00 until 8:30 P.M. Owner Cheryl Hartell says reservations are a must on weekends. There is a Sunday brunch, too, from 11:00 A.M. to 4:00 P.M., then early dinner from 4:00 until 7:00 P.M.

Just around the corner northwest from the Vineyards is the *American Bowman Restaurant* in Weston 64098 ("where the Past is Present"), the oldest continually operating pub in Weston at 150-plus rollicking years old. It offers Irish-style food and entertainment, pewter mugs, and kerosene lamps on the tables. There's O'Malley's 1842 Pub, the Post Ordinary, the Heritage Theater, and malt and hops cellars in the same building (as well as an antiques mall).

At Christmas try the Dickens Dinner; during other seasons, 1837 Dinners, Civil War Dinners, and Nineteenth-Century Irish Banquets are yours for the ordering. For reservations call (816) 640–5235. Hours are from 11:30 A.M. until 3:00 P.M. every day but Monday. On Friday and Saturday dinner is served until 9:00 P.M. Reservations are required.

Steamboat Gothic describes Julie and John Pasley's place, the *Benner House Bed and Breakfast* (816–640–2616) at 645 Main Street, Weston 64098 (Sierra the dog lives here, too). With its double-deck, wraparound porch and gingerbread trim, the jaunty, turn-of-the-century mansion looks as if it could steam away like the nearby riverboats. Brass beds, baths with pull-chain water closets, and claw-foot tubs add to the interior decor and to your mood. There is a private bath for each room. The view from the second floor rooms is spectacular. You can see the wide

Missouri across the floodplain. Julie's candlelit breakfasts star cinnamon twists and delightful little pastries filled with cream cheese. A double room costs $90. If you are missing your pets, Sierra the dog will keep you company while you are downstairs. The well-behaved Sierra won't intrude in your room. A new hot tub has been added that guests may use. E-mail the Benner House at bennebb@msa.com.

The **Missouri Bluffs Boutique & Gallery** is full of quirky, unique clothes, jewelry, and paintings at 512 Main Street, Weston 64098 (816–640–2770). It's like a maze, with rooms opening off rooms, but the clothing is delightful and the art is worth the search. Owner Ann Bollin obviously enjoys shopping to stock the boutique. Hours are Monday through Saturday 10:00 A.M. to 5:00 P.M. and on Sunday noon to 5:00 P.M.

Getting hungry? Find the **Weston Cafe** at 407 Main Street, Weston 64098 where the locals eat (along with the visiting film crew here to make a movie about President Harry Truman, appropriately named "Truman"). The Cafe Melt is excellent, and the coffee is plentiful and good. Call (816) 640–5558 for details. Hours are Monday through Thursday from 6:00 A.M. until 2:30 P.M. and on Friday and Saturday until 8:00 P.M., Sunday hours are 7:00 A.M. until 2:00 P.M.

If you're in the mood for something a bit more upscale, the **Avalon,** across the street from the museum, offers an *excellent* beef tenderloin with a bourbon sauce. Kind of a salute to Weston's distillery history, but as tender and flavorful as it's possible to be. A little bar area opens onto a charming outdoor courtyard. Owners/chefs Kelly Cogan and David Scott grill a fine salmon and offer an entire wild game section on the menu. There are pasta dishes and salads and sandwiches for the lunchtime crowd, too. Hours are Tuesday through Sunday from 11:00 A.M. until 3:00 P.M. and dinner seating is from 5:30 until 8:30 P.M. Tuesday through Thursday, and Friday and Saturday until 9:00 P.M. Call (816) 640–2835.

Take a short jaunt west of Weston back on Highway 45 to see a view worth going way out of your way for. **Weston Bend State Park** is one of Missouri's newest, and the scenic overlook that spreads a panorama of the Missouri River and rolling fields, wooded loess hills, and Leavenworth clear across the river in Kansas is simply not to be missed. There's also camping, picnicking, hiking, and bicycling, if that's your pleasure. Call (816) 640–5443 for more information.

There is a shop called **End of the Trail Native American Arts and Crafts** at 509 Main Street, Weston 64098, where Richard Janulewicz and Connie Behymer share with visitors a fine collection of authentic, high-quality products of fifty different tribes. Want a wooden Indian?

This is the place. Bead work, kachinas, pottery, and sand paintings are only the beginning. Also available are knives, drums, pipes, and CDs, just to name some of the items on display. Hours are 10:00 A.M. to 5:00 P.M. Tuesday through Saturday. Sunday hours are noon to 5:00 P.M. Call (816) 640–5460 or e-mail the shop at nativecrafts@endofthetrail.com. The business is closed in January and February while they go on hunting expeditions for more things. But you can always look at the Web site at www.endofthetrail.com.

A bit farther west at the junction of highways 45 and 92 and almost to the bridge to Kansas is the *Beverly Hills Antiques Mall*—in Beverly, definitely not in California. Sure, there are plenty of antiques malls across the state, some better than others. This one's one of the best, with high-quality goods and plenty of variety from fifty-five dealers. No garage-sale stuff here, thank you. The mall is open every day from 10:00 A.M. to 5:00 P.M. You can't miss it; it's in the old two-story Beverly Lumber Company building at 24630 Highway 92, Beverly 64079, and there's virtually nothing else there—but if you get lost, call (816) 330–3432, and they'll send out the Mounties.

Snow Creek Ski Area (816–640–2200), just north of Weston, is open seven days a week through the cold months. There's plenty of manmade snow (up to 4 feet), lifts, a ski rental, and a cozy lodge for après-ski. Normal costs include a Snow Pass (a lift ticket), plus rental equipment if needed. (Yes, there is downhill skiing in Missouri; the big hills near the Missouri River are satisfyingly steep, if not long. You can still break a leg if you're so inclined.) Snow Passes are sold thirty minutes before each session, which are Monday through Friday noon to 9:00 P.M., Saturday from 9:00 A.M. until 3:00 P.M., and Sunday from 9:00 A.M. to 8:00 P.M. Beginning in early January every year, there is a special midnight ski on Friday and Saturday from 10:00 P.M. to 3:00 A.M at the bargain price of $40, including rental. The regular rates vary so much that calling (816) 640–2200 and listening to the recording is a good idea. Snowboards are available, too, and are $28 per session, but a Visa card and a $200 deposit are mandatory for snowboards. To reach Snow Creek from the north, take Interstate 29 South to exit 20 (Weston) then go to Highway 273 and drive about 5 miles. When you reach a flashing red light at Highways 273 and 45, turn right on 45 and go 8 miles north. Snow Creek is on the right. There is a restaurant and bar, so you can stay for dinner. Lessons are available, too. Check out the Web site at www.skipeaks.com for prices and more information.

Iatan Marsh near the water treatment plant is the place to be in winter if you're a birder. The warmer waters here attract flocks of migrant waterfowl; who knows what you might spot.

Nearby Bean Lake and Little Bean Marsh catch the birds—and bird-ers—year-round. You may see rails and bitterns, yellow-headed black-birds, green herons, and egrets along with the ducks and geese. An observation tower makes sighting easier; Little Bean Marsh is the largest remaining natural marsh in Missouri, a remnant of our wetlands heritage.

This is a test: What are emus raised for? Bet you don't know the answer. In fact, bet you have never even seen an emu. Well, here is your chance to see seventy of them at **Nature's Own Emu Products,** 1611 Vincent Road S.E. near **Faucett** 64448 (between Weston and St. Joseph on I–29), where Jennifer and Michael Snook raise these beautiful birds. They are a lot like ostriches, which are raised for their meat, but emus are more valuable for their oil. Oil of emu is the world's best moisturizer. It is used in lotions, soaps, lip balm, and other products.

These leggy birds are a bit smaller than ostriches. They reach 6 feet in height and weigh in at around 150 pounds. The meat is 97 percent fat-free and tastes like lean beef, as does ostrich meat, and if you stop in and there's any cooked, Jennifer will let you taste it. But she really wants to sell you some handmade soap or lip balm that will leave your skin feel-ing like velvet. There are a lot of other all-natural products, too. Bath salts, insect repellent, even a therma-jell to rub into sore joints are some of the other products made with oil of emu. You can try samples of the products here and make up your mind for yourself. Now that would be

Nature's Own Emu Products

an interesting gift to take home from your trip, wouldn't it? Even the beautiful emerald-green eggs are used for works of art and are in demand. Call toll free (877) 3–EMUOIL to let them know you are coming. They love to have people stop by.

If you've read Lewis and Clark's journals, you'll remember the description of an oxbow they dubbed "Gosling Lake." This is now thought to be Sugar Lake in *Lewis and Clark State Park* (816–579–5564), just off Highway 59. There's a huge fish hatchery here; you can see anything from fry to fingerlings to lunkers.

St. Joseph is a river town that lost the race to Kansas City when KC was first to bridge the Muddy Mo with the Hannibal Bridge. Still a big and bustling town, it has plenty for the day-tripper to do and see. Consider this: St. Joe has eight (count 'em!) museums. The *Albrecht-Kemper Art Museum* (816–233–7003) has a collection of some of the finest American art in the country, including works by Mary Cassatt, William Merritt Chase, George Catlin, and Missouri's own Thomas Hart Benton. Traveling shows are often exhibited at the Albrecht, including an excellent George Catlin exhibit. Remember Catlin? He's the artist who gave up virtually everything to record the Indian tribes in the early 1800s. It's the best record we have. Housed in an old Georgian manse, the museum at 2818 Frederick, St. Joseph 64506 has been in operation since 1966. Hours are Tuesday through Friday from 10:00 A.M. to 4:00 P.M., Saturday and Sunday from 1:00 to 4:00 P.M. Entry fees are $3.00 for adults, $2.00 for seniors, and $1.00 for students with any type of ID. Children under six get in free. Go to the museum's Web site at www.albrecht-kemper.org or e-mail to akma@sleepy. ponyexpress.net.

Then of course there's the *1858 Patee House.* St. Joseph's only National Historic Landmark, the magnificent old hotel was the original headquarters for the Pony Express. It houses a tiny village *inside* a downstairs room, plus a steam engine that almost pulls into the rebuilt "station." Admission is $3.00. Also there are the *Jesse James Museum* (816–232–8206), *Roubidoux Row,* and the *Doll Museum.* Admission to each is $2.00. The *Pony Express Museum* at 914 Penn Street, St. Joseph 64503, chronicles the history of these early mail runs. Admission is $3.00, and it is open April through October from 9:00 A.M. to 5:00 P.M.

There's a morbid fascination to this next one, the *Glore Psychiatric Museum,* 3406 Frederick, St. Joseph 64506 (816–387–2310). The museum is housed in an old, rather forbidding wing on the hospital grounds. If you get a little shaky mentally, consider yourself fortunate that it's now

2000+; the museum features twenty display rooms of arcane treatments for psychiatric disorders, from prehistoric times to the recent past. (What did cave men do, you ask? Knocked a hole in your skull to let out the evil spirits. Some patients even lived!) The museum is handicapped-accessible, and admission is free.

Missing a museum? It's the *St. Joseph Museum* at Eleventh and Charles Streets, St. Joseph 64501, founded in 1926. Enjoy displays of North American Indian crafts and Midwestern wildlife as well as the trading post exhibit. Admission is $2.00.

As long as we are on the subject of museums, here's a bizarre one that might interest you: The *Heaton-Bowman-Smith & Sidenfaden Funeral Museum* at 3609 Frederick Boulevard, St. Joseph 64506, displays the state's oldest funeral home, circa 1842, belonging to the state's first licensed funeral director. It is free, but you have to call first (816) 232–3355 or –4428.

The 1885 Queen Anne mansion at 809 Hall Street, St. Joseph 64501 draws you into the Victorian elegance of another era. The *Shakespeare Chateau* welcomes visitors with beautiful stained glass, wonderful fireplaces, and ornately carved woodwork. Seven guest rooms are available, and a sumptuous gourmet breakfast is part of the package. Rooms range from $110 to $175. Call (816) 232–2667 for reservations. See for yourself at the Web site at shakespearechateau.com.

For a taste (and smell) of old St. Joe in its cattle days, leave Interstate 229 and take Highway 59 South to Illinois, then turn west and go a block to the *Old Hoof and Horn Steakhouse* at 429 Illinois Avenue St. Joseph 64504 in the stockyards. This steak house has been here since 1889 and is the oldest restaurant in town. Stockyard employees ate here so often that a tunnel was built to the restaurant's front door so that hungry workers didn't have to wait for the trains to pass between the two locations to devour the sizzling steaks they craved. The tunnel is closed now but the plain brick building still serves the best steaks in town. Of course it was a saloon and brothel first, but a retired do-gooder (a policeman, actually) bought it and turned it into a cafe in 1907. Since 1963 Jack and Rosie Miller have built a reputation of quality steaks the likes of which you have never tasted. There is an in-house butcher shop, and the steaks are only choice aged Dugdale beef. Their son, Rick, is now the owner/operator and he has kept up the tradition. If you are a steak lover, a real meat-and-potatoes kind of person, this is the place for you. You might also like the fried chicken or pork chops, too. Regulars always order the fresh spinach salad with its tangy-sweet dressing. Of course if you are not quite stuffed, there's dessert—black-bottom pie or chocolate-raspberry mousse torte.

The high-ceilinged walls are covered with murals of scenes from the early days of the city, days when it boomed as an outfitting post for covered wagons headed west. Simple wooden tables and chairs that remind you your grandmother's house aren't fancy but serve the purpose. It is open Monday and Tuesday 11:00 A.M. until 9:00 P.M., Wednesday and Friday until 10:00 P.M., and Saturday from 4:00 to 10:00 P.M.

Harding House Bed and Breakfast at 219 North Twentieth Street, St. Joseph 64501-2444, is a gracious turn-of-the-century home with beveled glass windows, oak woodwork, and many antiques. Hosts Glen and Mary Harding serve tea or sherry by the fire in cool weather and on the porch during the warm months. There's a full American breakfast, topped off with homemade pastries. Rates are $65 (plus tax) with private bath. For reservations call (816) 232–7020 or e-mail at inn_keeper@hotmail.com.

Jerre Anne Cafeteria and Bakery (816–232–6585) has whipped up home-style cooking since 1930. Everything is made fresh here. Try the gooseberry pie or the fruit salad pie, originated in the '30s and still sold today to an enthusiastic clientele. The chicken and dumplings are better than Grandma's, and the pork tenderloin is breaded and fried to perfection. They also do a brisk carryout business; the apricot nut bread is wonderful. Jerre Anne's is open Tuesday through Saturday from 11:00 A.M. to 7:00 P.M. at 2640 Mitchell Avenue, St. Joseph 64507. If you want to check out St. Joseph on the Web, it's at www.stjomo.com.

For sheer spectacle visit *Squaw Creek National Wildlife Refuge* (660–442–3187) during the fall migration. You may see up to 350,000 snow geese fill the air like clouds. These clouds, though, are full of thunder; the sound of that many wings is deafening. Snow, blue, and Canada geese, migrating ducks and attendant bald eagles (as many as 150 representatives of our national symbol), plus coyote, beaver, muskrat, and deer make this a wildlife-lover's paradise. At least 268 species of birds have been recorded on the refuge. It's an essential stop on the flyway for migratory waterfowl and it has been for centuries; this area was described in the journals of Lewis and Clark. There are now 7,193 acres on the refuge just off Highway 159; watch for signs. Unusual loess hills that look like great dunes, reddish and fantastically eroded, are threaded with hiking trails.

Most visitors stay in nearby St. Joseph but there are antique-filled guest rooms beginning at $60 at the circa 1881 *Hugh Montgomery*

Squaw Creek National Wildlife Refuge

House at 410 East 6th Street in *Mound City* 64470, 4 miles north. Innkeepers Rick and Darla Saxton invite you to warm up by the fireplace and enjoy a tray of candy and soda that awaits you in your room. Call (660) 442–5634 or (660) 939–4530 for more information. Grab a hearty sandwich for lunch at *Quackers Bar and Grill* in Mound City (660) 442–5502. Four blocks west of the inn are a handful of brick-fronted antiques shops on the town's main street.

Maryville is home to *Five Mile Corner Antique Mall* at 30622 Highway 71 South, Maryville 64468 (660–562– 2294). Hours are 10:00 A.M. to 5:00 P.M. Monday through Saturday. Gailen and Twilla Hager have 5,000 square feet of antiques to peruse. There's more to do here than just shop, of course. For instance, you can visit the Mary Linn Performing Arts Theater to hear a concert or watch a play performed by the Missouri Repertory Company.

If all this antiques hunting has you ready for a bit of quiet, retreat from the world at *Conception Abbey* at the junction of Highway 136 and Highway VV in Conception Junction 64433. Benedictine monks run The Printery House (660–944–2218), where they make greeting cards and colorful notes (ask for their catalog) when they are not going about their real work. Benedictines consider their true work to be prayer—but the work of their hands is prayer, too. Stay over at the 1,000-acre retreat, 900 of which is productive farmland; visit with "the weather monk," or learn along with the seminarians. The Romanesque Basilica of the Immaculate Conception (1891) adjoining the monastery has examples of Beuronese art. Tours can be arranged by calling the guest master at (660) 944–2211 to make a reservation. Visit the Web site at www.conceptionabbey.org or e-mail at communications@conceptin.edu.

As you near **Lathrop,** your sweet tooth will begin to ache. It's **Candy-man's Mule Barn,** 7950 East Highway 116 in Lathrop 64465 (816–528–4263), 600 feet off Interstate 35 at the Lathrop exit. An odd name for a candy place, you say? Owner Alma Collins bought the shop because it resembles one of the mule barns that put Lathrop on the map; the town was once the mule capital of America, selling hundreds of these sturdy animals at the turn of the century. Foreign buyers flocked to Lathrop, and nearly all the pack animals for the Boer War were from this little Missouri town. All the barns are gone now, and there's no trace of the busy hotels that housed the buyers; so the original builders decided to re-create a bit of history. The candy factory began more than twenty-five years ago, making the best hand-dipped chocolates to come down the pike. Alma does the same; you can watch the kitchen-fresh candy being made Monday, Tuesday, and Thursday from 10:00 A.M. to 4:00 P.M. Retail shop hours are the same. The gift shop also handles other "Best of Missouri Hands" products, including hillbilly bean soup. Lunch is served at the **Hungry Mule Cafe** on Highway 116 (816–528–6294).

In **Plattsburg,** Shirley and John Grant's **Curiosity Corner** (816–539–2666) specializes in silver, coins, tools, and furniture at 216 North Main, Plattsburg 64477. **Tiques & Stuff** (816–539–3232) is Charles and Michele Spease's place on the east side of the courthouse at 108 Maple, Plattsburg 64477. It is open Monday through Saturday from 10:00 A.M. to 5:00 P.M.

If antiques excite you—really nice antiques—visit **Spease Antiques** at 205 Northeast Street, Plattsburg 64477 (816–539–3170), which specializes in Victorian walnut furniture. They recently sold a walnut bedroom set for $15,000. This is no junque shoppe.

There is also a bed and breakfast in town. **Le Belle Maison Bed and Breakfast** at the corner of Broadway and Second Street (200 West Broadway, Plattsburg 64477) has private baths and offers a full breakfast (and a traditional apple dessert every evening). The innkeepers have opened their circa-1910 Victorian home to guests. Not just the bedrooms but the parlor and dining room are for guests, too. Rooms are all $60 a night. You can reach the bed and breakfast by calling (816) 930–3243 or by e-mail at appleinn@aol.com or check out the Web site at www.bbonline.com/mo.

There are several good places to eat in town, depending on what you are looking for, and all of these have been recommended. **Bert and Ernie's** at 108 Broadway, Plattsburg 64477 (816–539–3136), has the best food, they tell me. **Kelly's Bakery** at 117 North Main, Plattsburg 64477 (816–539–

2198), opens at 6:00 A.M. Tuesday through Saturday. They start baking at 3:00 A.M. so everything is fresh and warm.

A little southwest of Plattsburg on Highway 169 and Z Highway is the town of **Edgerton.** Here **Harmer's Cafe,** 501 Frank Street, Edgerton 64444, has long specialized in old-fashioned favorites such as pan-fried chicken, mashed potatoes, and cobbler. Karen Belt, who took over the restaurant from her mother, hasn't changed it much. You don't mess with success. The green beans are done in the traditional Midwestern way with bacon, brown sugar, and onions and slow cooked for hours. They alone are worth the trip. Call (816) 790–3621 for more information. Hours are Monday 6:30 A.M. to 2:00 P.M., Tuesday and Wednesday until 7:30 P.M., and Thursday through Sunday 8:00 A.M. to 2:30 P.M.

Gower is north of Plattsburg on Highway 169. Every Friday night people from the surrounding region flock here to hear old-time music at a place called **Gower Good Timers Hall.** They come dressed in overalls or jeans; some carry pillows or chairs. Some carry musical instruments. There is no charge to get in, and none of the musicians will be paid. If it were jazz music, it would be called a jam session. What it is is a regular old-fashioned hootenanny, because only bluegrass music is allowed. No electrical instruments or drums are used, and anyone who wants to participate is welcome.

On an average Friday night, 300 people may show up. Everyone joins in the free potluck dinner while the musicians warm up. The music always starts at 7:00 P.M., when Jim Snyder rings an old cow bell that hangs over center stage. Jim is the power behind this get-together. In

President for (Less Than) a Day

*T*he Greenlawn Cemetery in Plattsburg is the final resting place of a man who served as president of the United States for one day—Sunday, March 4, 1849. Outgoing vice-president George M. Dallas had already resigned from office the Friday before. The term of President James K. Polk expired at noon on the fourth. The incoming Zachary Taylor refused to take his oath on the Sabbath, waiting until 11:30 Monday morning. For that 23½-hour period, the nation had no elected chief executive. The Succession Law of 1792 stated that the head of the Senate automatically became president should the top two offices be vacant. David Rice Atchison was that man. They say the president slept through much of his term of office. There is no presidential library here, but there is a statue of Atchison at the entrance of the Clinton County courthouse in Plattsburg.

1986 he started to call everyone in the area who played an instrument and invited them all to his house to play. He wanted to re-create on his farm the family get-togethers he remembered as a child. His dad, his uncle, and many of their friends would sit around with their guitars, fiddles, mandolins, and harmonicas to play until it was time to do evening chores. Within a year they had to rent the American Legion Hall. When that became too small, they raised some money and built their own place. Now it has a full stage, sound equipment, and a kitchen. But the generous applause is still there to encourage even the youngest or rankest beginner. Applause and good food and it's all free—what more could you want?

Smithville is near the intersection of Highways 169 and 92, and if all you know about the place is that it used to flood, you're in for a nice surprise. The town is close by the new Smithville Lake for summer fun, and there are plenty of shops to browse in.

Smithville Lake is a fairly recent addition to Missouri's array of man-made lakes. Constructed by the U.S. Army Corps of Engineers to control the flooding that Smithville residents have lived with since there was a Smithville, the lake is also a magnet for water-lovers. Turn north off Highway 92 (between Kearney and the town of Smithville) for sailing, fishing, boating, or just messing around.

Also at the lake is Missouri's own *Woodhenge,* a re-creation of a Woodland Indian site that may have been used as an astronomical observatory around 5,000 years ago. The original location of Woodhenge was uncovered during the building of the lake, and dredging was halted until archaeologists could study the area. It was important enough that the present site was reconstructed as an aid to further study; scientists from Woods Hole, Massachusetts, have come here to observe the solstice and equinox.

Near the new dam at Smithville Lake, one of the largest glacial erratics in the area squats like a patient dinosaur under an accretion of graffiti. A large, pink Sioux-quartzite stone, this elephant-sized monster was brought here by the last glacier some 15,000 years ago. It may have been an important landmark for the Paleo-Indians who lived in the area.

At the Jerry Litton Visitors' Center (816–532–0174), also near the dam, you can find out about these earliest inhabitants, about visits by Lewis and Clark as they came through on the nearby Missouri River, about the pioneer settlers, and about the birds and animals that make this area home. Admission is free. Stop for lunch at the *Brick House Cafe and Pub,* 111 North Bridge, Smithville 64089. Call (816) 532–8865.

About 3½ miles north of Smithville on Highway 169, you can turn right on Highway W and drive 2 miles across the east side of the lake to *Paradise*. This community is home to about twenty-five families and *Ed Gilliam's Shop*. Gilliam carves Father Christmas, some sixty-seven styles of Santas, and, coincidentally, looks as though he should be surrounded by elves himself. Perhaps it is because he was born on Christmas Day. Ed has been carving since he was twelve years old—that's more than fifty years now—and still fills his shop with piles of Missouri and Minnesota basswood, sugar pine, cottonwood bark, and driftwood bits that drop from the hundreds of carvings lining the shop. Santas of every style line the walls. There are fat Santas and thin Santas, Black Santas, and Uncle Sam Santas. Or how about a German Belznickle, a rather stern-looking Santa who carries a switch.

They are not all Santas, though. Ed turns out cigar store Indians, folk art, cowboys, and all manner of Americana ranging from 4 inches to 4 feet in height. Ed is usually at his house in Paradise, but it is a good idea to call first, (816) 873–2592. To find Ed's house find *Clyde's General Store* (which has a fountain for ice-cream treats in the summer), a two-story brick building, then turn right at the end of the building and go two blocks to Holmes Street. Ed's place is at 18403 Holmes Street, Paradise 64089.

PLACES TO STAY IN NORTHWEST MISSOURI

KANSAS CITY
Super 8 Motel, 6900 N.W. Eighty-Third Terrace (Barry Road and I–29), 64152; (816) 587–0808

Holiday Inn, 11832 Plaza Circle (airport), 64153; (816) 464–2543

KANSAS CITY NORTH
Inn Towne Lodge, I–35 North and Antioch, 64117; (816) 453–6550

LIBERTY
Super 8 Motel, 4032 South Lynn (I-35/Highway 152), 64068; (816) 833–1888

Best Western Hallmark Inn North, 209 North 291 Highway, 64068; (816) 781–8770

Fairfield Inn, 8101 North Church, 64068; (816) 792–4000

CHILLICOTHE
Grand River Inn, 606 West Business 36, 64601; (660) 646–6590

Selected Chambers of Commerce

Excelsior Springs, (816) 630–6161

Kansas City (Visitors and Convention Bureau), (913) 663–9797

Platt City, (816) 858–5270

Richmond, (816) 640–2909

St. Joseph, (800) 785–0360

Best Western Inn,
1020 South
Washington, 64601;
(660) 846–0572 or
(800) 646–0572

GALLATIN
Sandman Motel,
512 South Main, 64640;
(660) 663–2191

EXCELSIOR SPRINGS
Monterey Motel,
217 Concourse Avenue,
64024; (816) 637–3171

**PLACES TO EAT IN
NORTHWEST MISSOURI**

KANSAS CITY
Cascone's Italian
Restaurant and Lounge,
3733 North Oak
Trafficway, 64116;
(816) 454–7977,
(moderate)

Stroud's, 5410 N.E. Oak
Ridge Drive, 64119;
(816) 454–9600
(moderate)

Rembrandt's Restaurant,
2820 N.W. Barry Road,
64154; (816) 436–8700,
(expensive)

AVONDALE
The Depot Saloon & BBQ
2706 Bell, 64117;
(816) 452–2100
(inexpensive)

LIBERTY
The Fork 'N Spoon Cafe,
12 West Kansas St.
(1 block off the Liberty
square) 64068;
(816) 792–0707

RICHMOND
Olde Towne Restaurant and
Lounge, 106 West North
Main, 64085;
(816) 776–2328

JAMESPORT
JJ's Cafe, South Street,
64648; (660) 684–6608

**HELPFUL WEB SITE
FOR KANSAS CITY**

www.kansascity.com

Northeast Missouri

orth of St. Louis the land changes. Hills are gentler; they are the legacy of a wall of glacial ice that smoothed rough edges and brought with it tons of rich, deep soil some 15,000 years ago. Thanks to that gift, quintessentially Mid-American towns are dotted with the docile shapes of cows; barns are large and prosperous-looking; fence rows blossom with wildflowers; and bluebirds and meadowlarks sing.

Northeast Missouri is rich in history as well. That consummate storyteller Mark Twain was born here; he has endowed us with more colorful quotations than any writer before or since. You've heard of Mark Twain Cave and his boyhood home in Hannibal, but did you know that near Florida, Missouri, you can explore Samuel Clemens's birthplace? General Omar Bradley's birthplace is in this area, too, along with General John J. Pershing's boyhood home and a monument to General Sterling Price. (Generally speaking, it seems to be a great place for great men.)

> **How Many States Does Missouri Border?**
>
> *Missouri borders eight states. Only Tennessee touches as many neighbors.*

The Civil War raged from St. Louis to the Iowa border, where the Battle of Athens took place. Tiny Palmyra was the site of an atrocity that presidents Abraham Lincoln and Jefferson Davis called the worst of war crimes.

All along the Missouri River valley are tiny, picturesque towns, many with a German heritage, and many with wineries where you may taste the best the United States has to offer. (Mt. Pleasant's Port won the gold in international competition.) Lewis and Clark passed by these town sites on their way to the Northwest Passage and remarked on them in their journals.

The mighty Mississippi is busy with commerce, as it has been for more than 200 years. Barges churn by, and the power of that mile-wide channel vibrates under you as you stand on a riverboat's deck. The Great River Road, which runs along the Mississippi from New Orleans to its source, is so picturesque that plans are afoot to make it a National Scenic Roadway.

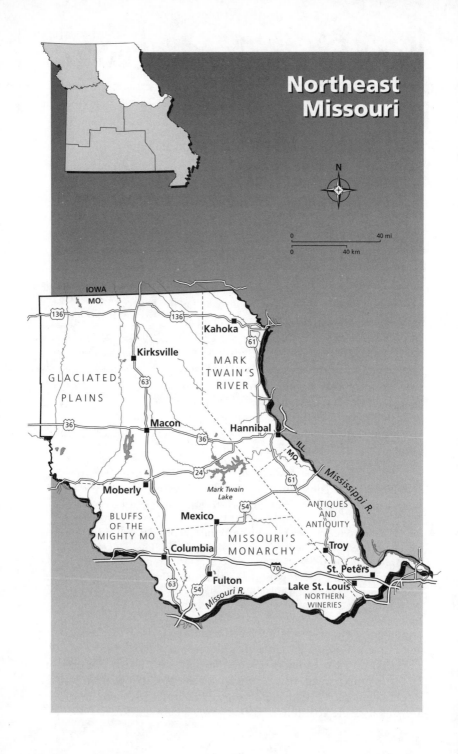

Northeast
Missouri

N

0   40 mi
0   40 km

IOWA
MO.

Kahoka

Kirksville

MARK
TWAIN'S
RIVER

GLACIATED
PLAINS

Macon

Hannibal

ILL.
MO.

Mississippi R.

Moberly

Mark Twain
Lake

ANTIQUES
AND
ANTIQUITY

BLUFFS
OF THE
MIGHTY MO

Mexico

MISSOURI'S
MONARCHY

Troy

Columbia

St. Peters

Fulton

Lake St. Louis

Missouri R.

NORTHERN
WINERIES

Bald eagles feed along both rivers in winter, drawn by open water and good fishing below the locks and dams. Amish communities, college towns, museums, eateries, petroglyphs, wildlife refuges—whatever your interest, you'll find it satisfied in northeast Missouri, where literally everything is off the beaten path.

Antiques and Antiquity

Just north of St. Louis is *St. Charles.* The first capitol of Missouri is located at 208–216 South Main Street (636–946–9282); legislators met here until October 1826, when the abandoned buildings began to settle slowly into decay. In 1961 the state of Missouri began a ten-year restoration project that sparked the revitalization of St. Charles. Shops, restaurants, and delightful little surprises abound. Take a walking tour of history; the St. Charles Convention and Visitors' Bureau (636–946–7776) can get you started.

Boone's Lick Trail Inn, at 1000 South Main Street, St. Charles 63301 (636–947–7000 or 800–366–2427), is in St. Charles. This 1840 Federal-style home is on the Boone's Lick Trail, right where it has crossed Main Street for more than 155 years. Five guest rooms are decorated in regional antiques, and there are two gathering rooms for the use of innkeepers V'Ann and Paul Mydler's guests. The rooms range from $120 to $135 weekdays, $135 to $165 on weekends. (On festival or other special weekends there is a two-night minimum stay.) It is close to the airport, the KATY Trail, and the casino. Fax (636) 946–2637 or visit the Web site at www.inbrook.com/inns/boones.

The city is the state's largest National Register Historic District with 10 blocks of mid-1800s buildings authentically restored. Stroll along cobblestone streets, watch the river flow by and, enjoy fine dining, antiquing, and history.

If your sweet tooth kicks in and you've a dime or two in your pocket, satisfy that craving the old-fashioned way at *Pop's General Store,* 322 South Main, St. Charles 63301 (636–723–6040). Imagine an old-style emporium with a potbellied stove, brass cash register, and advertising

---

Author's Favorite Annual Events in Northeast Missori

July

Hannibal—National Tom Sawyer Days (and National Fence Painting Contest), (573) 221–2477

Macon—Annual Demolition Derby, (660) 385–2811

September

Macon—Annual Buzzard Run, car show, (660) 226–5286

Kirksville—Annual NEMO Tri-Fed Midwest Regional Triathlon, (660) 626–2213

November

Columbia—Fall Craft Show, Missouri's largest indoor craft show, (573) 874–1132

The Missouri River flows north—the wrong way and against all natural order—along St. Charles County. It flows north for several miles, then turns east to join the Mississippi River. This is one of the few places in the Western Hemisphere where a major river flows north.

memorabilia from soap powders to nostrums; that place is here. Richard House (otherwise known as Pop) sells horehound candy, peppermint drops, and other old favorites by the pound or by the piece. Hours are 10:00 AM. to 5:00 P.M. every single day.

With your sweet tooth satisfied, you can head for the riverboat and some casino fun.

Both of our big rivers claimed more than their share of casualties. Steamboats sank with dismal regularity, and to this day—locks and dams notwithstanding—riverboat captains watch their charts and take their soundings much as Samuel Clemens did when he sang out, "Mark Twain." The channels of both the Missouri and the Mississippi are graveyards for boats, from tugs to stern-wheelers; the rivers are not to be taken lightly. Our Lady of the Rivers Shrine, a lighthouse-like monument at Portage de Sioux, is a reminder that brave travelers needed all the help they could get. That said, it's time to board at the **Ameristar Casino St. Charles,** 1260 South Main, St. Charles 63301 (636–940–4300). The station is off Interstate 70 just ten minutes west of Lambert Airport and gives you two action-packed casinos. The casino on the boat is open from 8:00 A.M. until 5:00 A.M. during the week and twenty-four hours Friday, Saturday, and holidays. Take the Sixth Street exit (229a) just across the bridge.

If you enjoy a little wine tasting, try the **Winery of the Little Hills** at 427 South Main Street, St. Charles 63301. Call (636) 946–9165. If beer is more to your liking, head over to **Trailhead Brewing Company,** at the corner of Main Street and Boonslick in historic downtown St. Charles 63302. Trailhead crafts its own beer and carries a variety of other brands. It's a good place to find a sandwich, salad, or burger, too. Hours are 11:00 A.M. to 10:00 P.M. seven days a week (Friday and Saturday until 11:00 P.M.). Call (636) 946–2739.

People who like to have just a salad or soup for lunch so that they can justify indulging in dessert will love **Miss Aimee B's Tea Room,** 837 First Capitol Drive, St. Charles 63301. Hours are 8:00 A.M. to 3:00 P.M. Tuesday through Saturday. If you're there in the spring or summer, be sure to try a seasonal dessert like the chocolate-strawberry pie. Call (636) 946–4202 for more information.

The **Mother-in-Law House** at 500 South Main Street, St. Charles 63301, must first have its name explained. In 1866 a French bride so missed her mother that her understanding husband built her a home with a dividing

AUTHOR'S TOP TEN FAVORITES

KATY Trail

St. Charles Historic District

Hannibal

Mount Pleasant Winery

Gail Shen's Chinatown

Poppy

The 63 Diner

Buck's Ice Cream

Les Bourgeois Vineyards

Rocheport

wall down the center so his mother-in-law could come to America and move in with them. Donna Hafer found the red-brick beauty on Main Street in the historic district of St. Charles and gave it the TLC it needed to become the gracious, antiques-filled restaurant it is today. The dining room has the original oil lamps. Glittering prisms pour a soft glow on the antique furnishings. Fresh flowers adorn each table and the staff wears dainty pinafores. The recipes have been in Donna's family for over a century and make the salad bar a delight. Her coconut cream pie is renowned in the area.

The restaurant is open for lunch Monday through Saturday and for dinner Tuesday through Saturday. Hours are Tuesday through Saturday with lunch from 11:00 A.M. until 2:30 P.M. and dinner from 5:30 to 9:30 P.M. Monday is lunch only. Reservations are recommended; call (636) 946-9444.

This is an area with more than one hundred quaint shops and restaurants plus many art, crafts, and historical festivals offered throughout the year. Be prepared to spend at least a day here. St. Charles is also right on the KATY Trail. If you didn't bring your bike, you can rent one at the *Touring Cyclist* at 104 South Main, St. Charles 63301. The cost is $10 for the first hour, and $5 per additional hour. Call (636) 949-9630.

Jesse James is a popular legend in Missouri, and the *Jesse James Cafe* in Foristell 63383 is the place to go for James fans. The cafe is decorated à la Jesse, and there's a free museum with artifacts from the James family. Exit I-70 at 203 and you can't miss it. Call (636) 673-2315 for more information.

Right down the road, the *Elvis Museum* at I-70 and Main Street in *Wright City* 63390 is a shrine to the King. A Cadillac that Elvis rode in is parked out front, and inside there is a replica of his tomb at Graceland and a video called "The Elvis Files," which denies his death. Of course, there is a large gift shop. Hours are 10:00 A.M. to 5:00 P.M. Monday through Saturday. The museum is free; donations are accepted. Call (636) 745-3154 for more information.

Winfield, Clarksville, Louisiana—the names are strung like beads along the Great River Road (now Scenic Highway 79) between St. Louis and Hannibal. These little towns harbor more antiques shops than you know what to do with. There are so many, in fact, that we only have room to include those towns that have additional attractions. Don't let

Snaking Frolics

Clarksville was called Appletown by river men because of the huge quantity of apples it shipped on the river each fall. But "Snakeville" would have been more accurate, because the really big feature of the town was its rattlesnake population. During its early years Clarksville was a choice place for a popular sport called "snaking frolics." The record was set by the town constable, who, along with others in town, killed 9,000 rattlers on one of the town's annual spring hunts.

that stop you, though; Missouri is a mecca for affordable goodies. If you can't find what you're looking for, you just haven't found the magic spot yet, and isn't the search as much fun as the finding?

Age-old traditions of quilting, stained glass, blacksmithing, and furniture-making are found in Clarksville. Much of the town is on the National Register of Historic Places, and it has a good museum.

Little **Eolia** has **St. John's Episcopal Church** and cemetery, the oldest Episcopal church west of the Mississippi.

Bowling Green features antiques shops along Business Highway 61. **Honeyshuck** is the restored home of House Speaker Champ Clark. Several miles outside Bowling Green on Highways Y and M is a thriving Amish community. It is filled with talented craftspeople who carry on the traditions passed down to them by their parents. Several families make and sell handmade crafts and bakery goods. A woodworking shop creates beautiful handmade furniture and cabinets. You can arrange for a tour of the area by calling the Bowling Green City Clerk at (636) 324–5451.

If your sweet tooth needs satisfying while you're in Bowling Green, be sure to visit **Bankhead Chocolates.** They've been making candy for eighty-three years, and experience does make a difference! Owner Laura Portwood says most people tell her that candy is an impulse item, not a destination—"Not with us!" she laughs. Bankhead Chocolates is open from 9:00 A.M. to 5:00 P.M. Monday through Friday, and 9:00 A.M. to 3:00 P.M. on Saturday. The shop is located at 1415 Business 54 in Bowling Green 63334. Call (573) 324–2312.

Lock and Dam No. 25 on the Mississippi is a fine place to watch the eagles feed in the winter. Or take the old Winfield Ferry across the river to Calhoon County, Illinois. (Don't worry, you can come right back if you're not through antiques hunting.)

If you fancy a bit of wilderness about now, a short detour west on Highway 47 will take you to spectacular **Cuivre River State Park** (636–528–7247). More than 31 miles of trails will let you discover one of the state's most rustic parks. The rough terrain is more like the Ozarks than the rest of glacier-smoothed northern Missouri, and like the Ozarks, it encourages many plants found only farther south, such as flowering dogwood, Missouri orange coneflower, and dittany. Frenchman's Bluff overlooks the Cuivre River Valley. The Lincoln Hills region, where Cuivre River State Park is found, formed millions of years ago when intense pressures caused the earth to buckle. Erosion cut even deeper; the resulting springs, sinkholes, and rocky cliffs make this an outdoor-lover's paradise. Archaeologists speculate that the region was home to prehistoric humans as early as 12,000 years ago; a 1937 dig unearthed a stone chamber containing a skeleton and pieces of a clay pot.

Clarksville is finding its way back—but back toward the past. With about the same population that it had in 1860, this spic-and-span town has new life in its old veins. A historic preservation effort mounted in 1987 has saved many of the delightful buildings in record time. There are also some new antiques and gift shops open to explore.

The *Clifford Wirick Centennial House* at 105 South Second Street, Clarksville 63336 (573–242–3376), is on the National Register of Historic Places. If you love stained glass—old or new—you'll find this place to your liking. They also do repairs, should you have a favorite piece that needs attention. Owner/historian Vernon Hughes is here to answer your questions about Clarksville or provide you with fine examples of American dinnerware, glass, china, pottery, and prints. There is a fine collection of antique furniture, too. The house is open seven days a week from 10:00 A.M. to 5:00 P.M. (The house opens a little later on Sundays.) It is closed July, August, and September.

The town commands an 800-square-mile view of the valley of the Big Muddy from an aerie on the highest point overlooking the Mississippi. Surprisingly, barge traffic on the river below is constant—you don't expect to see so much action. See ice-formed drumlins (those are hills) in this panoramic view.

Clarksville is a great place to observe wintering eagles; the Missouri Department of Conservation's Eagle Days, held here the last weekend of January, can swell the town's normal population of 500 to over 5,000. Is it worth it? You bet it is. Even the *New York Times* visited to check out the bald eagles, which can number from the hundreds to the thousands, depending on the weather. (The colder the winter has been, the more eagles gather here.) The Clarksville Eagle Center offers information, a museum, and spanking-clean rest rooms. Call (573) 242–3132.

The entire business district of downtown *Louisiana* is on the National Register of Historic Places and is well known for its antiques shops along Georgia and Main Streets. There are two museums—the

Louisiana Historical Museum and the *Phillips Museum.* But most interesting is the fact that it has the most intact Victorian streetscape in the state. Dozens of historic homes line Georgia and Main Streets and it still, of course, has a town square. Also worth a visit, perhaps, is the old *Gates of Peace Jewish Cemetery* off Highway 54.

There are many antebellum homes in this old river town. The *Louisiana Guest House Bed and Breakfast* at 1311 Georgia Street, Louisiana 63353, is a one-hundred-year old Cape Cod that offers spacious rooms, private baths, cable television, and a queen-size bed. You are welcomed by your hosts, Mett and Betty Jo Bryant, with a cheese tray and something to drink, and a full breakfast will be ready for you in the morning. Betty Jo will be happy to give you a map and some good directions to find the nearby Amish community and its many places to shop. Rates are from $75 to $85. Call (573) 754–6366 or (888) 753–6366.

There is some good antiquing in Louisiana. Right down the street at 515 Georgia Street is *Kate's Attic Antiques and Mini Mall* with forty booths to look over. Hours are from 10:00 A.M. until 4:30 P.M. every day except Sunday, when hours are 11:00 A.M. to 4:00 P.M. Call (573) 754–4544.

Mark Twain's River

For tourists, *Hannibal* is not exactly "off the beaten path." Half a million people annually come through this picturesque little town. Everybody knows about the Mark Twain Boyhood Home. Everybody's seen that fence—or at least pictures of it—where Tom Sawyer tricked his buddies into doing his work for him. (The original fence was 9 feet tall and a lot longer than the one that stands here now—no wonder the kid didn't want to paint it by himself.) You may even know about Margaret Tobin Brown's home (remember *The Unsinkable Molly Brown*?) and the fine dinner cruise on the Mississippi riverboat, the *Mark Twain.* So we'll let you find them on your own—it's easy.

But did you know that right across the street, at 211 Hill Street, Hannibal 63402, is the *"Becky Thatcher" House?* Actually Becky was Laura Hawkins, who lived here in the 1840s and attended school with young Sam Clemens. She was his childhood sweetheart, immortalized in print as Tom Sawyer's Becky Thatcher. The upstairs parlor and bedroom of the home are restored and are open to the public at no charge. The main floor features a bookshop carrying the largest selection of books by or about Mark Twain anywhere. First editions and out-of-print books are sometimes available. Call (573) 221–0822.

While you're in the historic district, look for *Ayers Pottery.* Steve Ayers does beautiful work, primarily using Missouri clays, and the shop is set up to encourage your involvement. There's a hall around three sides of the workshop, so you can see every step in the process. He also stocks a selection of beautiful kites, porcelain jewelry, baskets, and hand-forged things—goodies he picks up while on the craft-show circuit.

Even when Steve's out of town, the shop is open at 308 North Third, Hannibal 63401, seven days a week in the summer from 8:00 A.M. to 6:00 P.M. (573-221-6960). It's only half a block from the Mark Twain Museum. Steve has opened another shop, aptly named *Fresh Ayers* at 213 North Main Street, Hannibal 63401 (573-221-1017), where, along with pottery, Steve also carries coffee beans in many flavors. If you want to try some of them, there is a delightful cappuccino bar in the back of the store. Steve is involved in a project to list all of the artists living along the river route. While you sip your espresso, Steve can give you directions to many other craftspeople to visit along the way.

One of the first places you will find is *Hammon Glass* nearby at 115 Hill Street, Hannibal 63401. It is the shop of John Miller, a third-generation glass blower who grew up tending the furnaces for his uncle and grand-father. His shop is in a former bottling plant, all concrete and perfect for his trade. John's grandfather blew lamp chimneys, communion glasses, railroad globes, and functional glassware back when it wasn't so much an art as a functional craft. His father grew up working in a glass shop. Drop by the shop and look at the unique items he makes now. Marbles are his biggest sellers, believe it or not, but there is a wonderful collection of perfume bottles, paperweights, and oil lamps as well as striking free-form sculptures. Of course there are glasses and bowls, candy dishes, and all manner of beautiful glassware. Call (573) 221-3900 for more information. Hours are Monday through Saturday 10:00 A.M. to 5:00 P.M., Sunday noon to 4:00 P.M.

If elegant Victoriana is your weakness, stay in gingerbread heaven at the *Garth Woodside Mansion.* This one's on the National Register, and it deserves to be. Mark Twain was often a guest of the Garths. Built in 1871, this stunning Victorian summer mansion is on thirty-nine acres of gardens and woodlands at 11069 New London Road, Hannibal 63401.

You won't believe the three-story flying staircase with no visible means of support; you might not trust it, either, though they say it's quite safe. Enter the walnut-lined library through 9-foot doors, or check out the extra-wide hostess's seat in the dining room (no, the hostess wasn't that wide; it accommodated the voluminous petticoats

Garth Woodside Mansion

of the era). The eight bedrooms still have the discreet opulence of Twain's era. The aroma of freshly baked pastries and muffins draws you to the dining room, where the eight-leaf walnut table is just as it was then. You can spend the day rocking on the veranda, watching deer or fox from the library window, and spend the evenings leisurely near a fire. Christmas is an especially fine time to visit, when the mansion becomes a fairyland of authentic Victorian decorations. Rates are from $109 to $295. Call (573) 221–2789 or (888) 427–8409 for more information or e-mail the inn at garth@nemonet. com. Visit the Web site at www.garthmansion.com.

Innkeepers Julie and John Rolsen say that the new featherbeds make people sleep later. Julie serves hot chocolate-chip cookies every day at 4 o'clock. Not only do the guests congregate for this, even the UPS delivery person and the mail carrier show up. The mansion is in a beautiful country setting—thirty-nine acres of meadows and woodlands that retain the feel of early Hannibal countryside.

Don't miss the mansion where Mr. Clemens addressed the cream of Hannibal society on his last visit here in 1902. It's ***Rockcliffe Mansion*** (573–221–4140), at 1000 Bird Street, Hannibal 63401, a wonderfully quirky place full of art nouveau decor, which was a breakaway style from the established Victorian. It, too, is on the National Register of Historic Places.

There are guided tours daily from March through November, 10:00 A.M. till 5:00 P.M., and from December through February, noon till 3:00 P.M. There's a small admission charge.

Mrs. Clemens Antique Mall is at 305 North Main Street, Hannibal 63401, and is one of the largest antiques malls in the area. More than forty booths offer a great selection of glassware, dolls, primitives, and all manner of collectibles. The ice cream parlor features Blue Bunny Ice Cream. Check out the website at www.hannibalmo.com/MrsClemens. htm or call (573) 221–6427.

If you're at all Irish (and who isn't, at least one day of the year), don't miss *St. Patrick,* the only town in the world (with a post office) named for everybody's patron saint. If you like, send a package of mail containing stamped, addressed envelopes to Postmaster Mike Lewis, St. Patrick 63466, to get the special St. Paddy's Day cancellation.

It's more fun to visit the post office, though. The letter boxes are antique, and the hospitality is the old-fashioned kind you'd expect in a town of fourteen souls. Hours are 9:00 A.M. till 1:00 P.M.

The *Shrine of St. Patrick* is fashioned after the Church of Four Masters in Donegal, Ireland; the style is ancient Celtic. There's a round bell tower with a circular staircase of the kind used on the Auld Sod. Dublin-made stained-glass windows are patterned after the famous illuminated manuscript, the Book of Kells; the most unusual has St. Patrick surrounded by the symbols of Ireland's four provinces: Ulster, Leinster, Munster, and Connaught. Perhaps you are beginning to catch the flavor of the place.

Oh, yes, there's another unusual attraction: geodes. What's a geode, you may ask? You must not be a rock hound, if you are wondering. A geode is a rather undistinguished blob that looks like a rounded river rock. But inside—ah, inside—there is magic. Beautiful crystal formations fill the hollow center of a geode like a Fabergé egg; they're considered gemstones.

Some of the world's finest geodes are found in this small area. You can buy one at Buschling Place 3 miles north of Dempsey; the Buschlings specialize in country crafts, turquoise, and, of course, geodes. Or you can find your own at *Sheffler Rock Shop and Geode Mine* (660–754–6443), located 2 miles south of Wayland on the Highway 136 Spur, from April to December. This is the only geode mine in the U.S. that is registered with the Federal Bureau of Mines. Watch for the round rock building made entirely of sixty tons of mineral specimens. This shop is open year-round and has been selling minerals, agates, and jewelry-making supplies for more than thirty years. If you come to dig your own geode, bring a rock hammer and a bit of muscle; these treasures don't come without sweat

Trivia

The word "twain" means "two" when used as a mark or measurement of the depth of the water. "Mark Twain" therefore means two fathoms.

equity. The mine is open in the winter from 9:00 A.M. to 5:00 P.M. and in the summer from 8:00 A.M. to 5:00 P.M. Tim Sheffler will be there to help you. He has expanded the shop and added a huge collection of fossils.

Bethel is the kind of place you dream about when you're feeling nostalgic for "the good old days," when things were simpler and the world was more easily understood, when people could meet one another's eyes directly and a handshake meant everything. Bethel old-timers say, "When you get it right, why change?" And here, they've pulled it off.

It's not all old-time ambience and down-home goodies. Bethel has a thriving art colony. The town plays host to frequent festivals, workshops, and seminars celebrating its agricultural, cultural, and social heritage throughout the year. Thousands of people flock here for the World Sheep and Wool Festival (ouch! a pun!). Other festivals throughout the year draw folks for antiques, fiddlers, music, and Christmas in Bethel. If you see a line on the sidewalk downtown, likely it's for the family storefront bakery that opens only during festivals. Breads, cinnamon rolls—they've got it. Get in line!

Founded as a utopian religious colony in 1844, the whole town is listed on the National Register of Historic Places. The museum can fill you in on the details; it's open daily.

Bethel is friendly; you're family as soon as you arrive. And it's best to arrive hungry. The **Fest Hall Restaurant** on Highway 15 in Bethel 63434 (660–284–6493) serves "good food and plenty of it," the folks say, at reasonable family prices. They also serve homemade pies that make it worth jettisoning a diet for, seven days a week. Hours are from 6:00 A.M. until about 8:00 P.M.

If you want to stay over, the **Bethel German Colony Bed and Breakfast** (same telephone number as Fest Hall) welcomes visitors to four rooms furnished in a simple country style above the Colony Restaurant. Incredibly affordable rates of $15 per person include a country breakfast blessed with home-baked bread and the Fest Hall's own apple butter. (Close your eyes. Imagine the rich, sweet aroma of bubbling apples and spices in an old copper kettle. That's what goes on your breakfast muffins.) If the restaurant is closed when you arrive, pop over to the grocery store on the corner for room keys.

Northern Wineries

Take a different loop to see the Missouri River and the little wineries that sprout like vines along its banks. There's a lot of history along the Missouri; whatever your interest, you'll find plenty to see and do.

Take Highway 94, for example. It's for people who don't like their roads straight and flat: mile after mile of two-lane blacktop that curves and winds from St. Charles to Jefferson City. It is one of the most beautiful and exhilarating drives in the state and is a practical route to mid-Missouri for those of us who don't enjoy the mind-numbing 65 mph of the interstate. Since you have this book with you, the assumption can be made that you like to drive, so Highway 94 is a "must-do" trip. Cross Interstate 40 outside St. Charles, go a mile, and turn into the **August A. Busch Memorial Wildlife Area**. This 7,000-acre preserve has nature trails, hunting areas, shooting ranges, and thirty-two lakes for fishing. It features a self-guided tour of native prairie, pine plantation, and farming practices that benefit wildlife. In the spring and fall, thousands of migrating birds can be seen at the shorebird and waterfowl preserve.

Missouri River State Trail, Missouri's part of the KATY Trail following the old MKT Railroad right-of-way, meanders through here, and on weekends large crowds of bikers and hikers wander along the 26 miles of trail from Highway 40 at Weldon Springs to Marthasville. If you have a bike on the roof, there is convenient parking all along the trail. There are plenty of places to get a meal or rent bikes if you didn't bring your own. There's even a bed-and-breakfast and a winery for a picnic lunch along the trail.

There's a spectacular view of the river beyond the outskirts of St. Louis on Interstate 70. There are so many good destinations along this route that you don't have to tell anyone that you are on it because you like to hug the corners and push the federally mandated speed limit to its max. This road will challenge the best Grand Prix wannabe with its collection of diamond-shaped signs warning of another set of sharp curves. But slow down and watch for wild turkey and deer. Enjoy the tidy farmhouses and pretty churches as you aim for towns like Augusta, Dutzow, and Hermann that wait along the route.

You will enjoy **Defiance's** little shops and taverns and be amazed to learn that this whole town was under water during the Great Flood of 1993. History buffs will want to take a 6-mile detour from Highway 94 down Highway F to the Daniel Boone home. You could also stop in for a visit to the **Sugar Creek Winery** at 125 Boone Lane, Defiance 63341, to taste

Trivia

Defiance is so named because the local townsfolk were so defiant in gaining a stop for their community when the railroad was being built through the area.

some of Missouri's wine. Call (636) 987–2400. Becky and Ken Miller will show you around.

Somehow you would imagine a log cabin—or a sod hut, maybe. This beautiful stone house with ivy clinging to its double chimneys, crisply painted shutters, and ample back porch is not what you'd expect at all. Built in 1803, **Daniel Boone's Home,** 1868 Highway F, Defiance 63341, is ruggedly elegant and comfortable. Add a VCR and a microwave, and you could move in tomorrow. Boone lived to a ripe old age. The naturalist John James Audubon described him as a "stout, hale, hearty man." He died here in 1820 at eighty-six.

Here are Daniel's powder horn and his long rifles, his writing desk, and the very bed where his long career on the American frontier ended. It's a small bedchamber; the four-poster bed looks as if it were just made up with fresh sheets and a clean white counterpane, ready for the man himself to come in from a hard day of hunting, settling the frontier, and making history. Daniel kept a coffin under the bed he had made for himself and periodically tried it out. Alas, he grew too big for it and had to give it away!

The kitchen is cozy, with low beams and a huge fireplace. Mrs. Boone's butter churn sits nearby, and you can almost see the family gathered here, waiting expectantly for that rich, yellow butter to spread on hearth-baked bread. Your tour guide will point out where the whole foundation of the house moved thanks to an earthquake. A chapel, summer kitchen, and spool house have been added on the grounds, and down the little valley are a number of historic structures that have been moved to the property. A small chapel done in blue and white still hosts weddings set to its 1860 organ music.

Tours are given daily during the winter from 9:00 A.M. to 4:00 P.M. Call Monday through Saturday and Sunday from noon to 4:00 P.M. Spring/summer hours are Monday through Saturday, 9:00 A.M. to 6:00 P.M., and Sunday noon to 6:00 P.M. Call (636) 798–2005 for more information.

Leaving Defiance, you'll enter the Missouri River Valley wine region. There are more wineries along Highway 94 than anywhere else in the state. You can visit **Montelle Winery** at Osage Ridge (201 Montelle Drive, Augusta 63332; 636–228–4464), **Augusta Winery** (636–228–4301) and Mount Pleasant Wine Company in Augusta, and Blumenhof Vineyards in Dutzow. All offer wine tasting and sales as well as great spots to enjoy a bottle of wine with a picnic lunch.

Just down the road apiece from Dan'l's house you'll find the little German wine-producing town of *Augusta.* A hundred and fifty years ago it was a self-sufficient town with a cooperage works, stores, and a German school. Before Prohibition, when Missouri was the second-largest wine-producing state in the nation, there were thirteen wineries located in Augusta's valley, beyond the bluffs above the southernmost bend of the river. Deep, well-drained soil and freedom from spring frosts were perfect for viticulture. This is recognized as America's first official wine district and the first in the New World to bear an official "Appellation Control" designation.

Augusta still deserves its reputation. *Mount Pleasant Wine Company,* 5634 High Street, Augusta 63332 (636–482–4419), at Interstate 44 at the Highway UU exit, 2 miles east of Cuba, was purchased in 1966 by Lucian and Eva Dressel (it's now owned by MPW, Inc.). A short twenty years later, the Dressels' 1986 Vintage Port took top port honors in the International Wine and Spirit Competition in London, England, making theirs the first Missouri winery since Prohibition to win an international gold medal, from a field of 1,175 wines and more than twenty countries.

Mount Pleasant's 1987 Jour de la Victoire Ice Wine also won a silver medal, the highest award given to an American ice wine. The *Cheese Wedge,* on-site at the winery, features products made in Missouri. You can buy cheese from Emma (that's a town), sausage from Washington, and mustard from Wolf Island, Missouri. There is cider and grape juice and fresh area fruits in season, along with the Missouri cheeses and sausage for a picnic in the grape-entwined patio. Hours are noon to 5:00 P.M. Mount Pleasant even delivers! Call (636) 482–4419 or (800) 467–WINE, or fax (636) 228–4126 for more information. Visit the Web

Missouri Vintners—1800s and Beyond

*W*ine making isn't new to the state. In the 1800s the wine business thrived here and the wines were internationally acclaimed. By the late-nineteenth century, the entire nation's wine manufacturing and distribution was centered in St. Louis, and Missouri was producing two million gallons a year. It was second only to California in wine production. Then Prohibition shut down the wineries, and the state's wine industry all but disappeared for more than four decades. Only one winery continued to operate during the 1920s: St. Stanislaus Winery, located at a seminary, made sacramental wine for religious orders.

Trivia

Mount Pleasant's sparkling wine Genesis was used to christen the aircraft carrier U.S.S. Harry Truman in 1996. At first the shipbuilders sent the bottles back because they wouldn't break, so the people at Mount Pleasant just rebottled the wine in cheaper, thinner bottles for the occasion.

site at www.mtpleasant wines.com or e-mail at mailto@mountpleasantwinery.com.

Gleaming copper and brass, the work of more than thirty potters and craftspeople, greet your eyes at **Americana Galleries,** corner of Walnut & Ferry Streets, Augusta 63332 (636–228–4494), a cluster of reconstructed early log buildings. Coppersmith Michael Bruckdorfer keeps random hours, but is usually open Tuesday through Saturday 10:00 A.M. to 5:00 P.M., Sunday noon to 5:00 P.M. The shop features turned-wood pieces, pottery, folk art, and brilliantly colored ornamental glass. Michael suggests lunch next door at **Augusta White Haus,** 5567 Walnut Street, Augusta 63332 (636–482–4048).

If you love fine furniture with an elegant, contemporary feel, you'd hardly expect to find it in the backcountry. But at **Nona Woodworks,** furniture maker Michael Bauermeister is full of surprises. He works with Missouri woods to create delicate, finely designed pieces that would grace the best of homes. "Rita's Desk," for example, is a lovely little fall-front desk of cherry wood. The angular top is a beautiful contrast to the curved and hard-carved legs.

Michael's shop is in an old-fashioned store building in the town of Nona, which isn't a town anymore. It's just Michael's house and shop and a few other buildings. Follow High Street west, which turns into

Mount Pleasant Wine Company

Augusta Bottom Road, 3 miles to the shop on the left side of the road. Shop hours are unpredictable because special orders and commissions keep the craftsman hopping. Call (636) 228–4663 to make sure your trip won't be for nothing.

Augusta is a town worth the visit. Click on www.augusta-missouri.com for the grand tour. There you will find a link to **Augusta Wood Ltd.** at 5558 Walnut, Augusta 63332, which was established in 1979. Works by Thomas Kinkade are on display—beautifully hand-carved furniture, some very expensive—as well as art by Jesse Barnes. You can reach them at (636) 228–4406 or (800) 748–7638. There are several B&Bs in Augusta. The most luxurious is the **H. S. Clay House** on 219 Public Street, Augusta 63332 (636–482–4004). Leigh and Alan Buehre give 100 percent to making guests feel like royalty, including a gourmet breakfast. They serve not just home-made cookies but smoked salmon and wine at 5:00 P.M., and a glass of port appears in your room with the turndown service. Visit the Web site for more about the Buehres and their beautiful home surrounded with 1,600 feet of deck at www.hsclayhouse.com. You can e-mail at hsclayhouse@msn. com or call toll-free, (636) 482–4004 or (888) 309–7334. Rooms range from $125 to $175.

A one-lane bridge followed by a ninety-degree turn leads you to **Dutzow.** (If you found Augusta charming, Dutzow is downright quaint.) This historic Dutch town, founded in 1832 by Baron Von Bock, was the first German settlement in the Missouri River Valley. In the mid-nineteenth century "Missouri's Rhineland" attracted immigrants who were inspired by enthusiastic accounts of natural beauty and bounty; among the most convincing was Gottfried Duden's *Report on a Journey to the Western States of North America,* published in 1829, which contributed to the settlement of these lovely little enclaves all up and down the Missouri River. The town offers several antiques shops and a pretty good sandwich at the **Dutzow Deli,** 8080 South Highway 94, Dutzow 63342, right off Highway 94 and right on the KATY Trail. Korine Haug, owner, can direct you to bike rentals. Hours are 9:00 A.M. to 5:00 P.M. Monday through Saturday, 9:00 A.M. until 10:00 P.M. on Friday, closed on Sundays. Call (636) 433–5118.

The severe floods of 1993 and 1995 were setbacks for KATY Trail State Park, which runs along the river for more than 200 miles. This long, skinny state park snakes along connecting towns from St. Louis to Sedalia. Completed portions are at each end, and work is continuing between them. The finely crushed gravel trail allows biking or hiking for 45 miles, from St. Charles west to Treloar. You cross bottomland forests filled with migratory birds, wetlands, fields of wildflowers, and dolomite bluffs. The small towns along the way welcome trail users. You can stop for wine tastings at Defiance and Marthasville and lunch at Augusta.

Blumenhof Vineyards and Winery, Dutzow 63342 (636–433–2245), takes its name from the Blumenberg family's ancestral farm in the Harz Mountains of Germany; *blumenhof* translates as "court of flowers." Enjoy the winery's Teutonic decor and the welcome invitation to stop and smell the flowers—along with the bouquet of the wine. Blumenhof produces wines from the finest American and European varietal grapes. There's a full range of wines, but dry table wines are a tour de force. (The Vidal Blanc won a gold medal in international competition.) Visit any day except Easter, Thanksgiving, Christmas, or New Year's, 10:30 A.M. to 5:30 P.M. Monday through Friday, Saturday from 10:00 A.M. to 5:30 P.M., and from 11:30 A.M. to 5:30 P.M. on Sunday.

Marthasville celebrates *Deutsch* Country Days every October—rain or shine—a German living-history festival on the Luxenhaus Farm, 3 miles northeast of town on Highway O. Everything from homemade jellies and apple butter to crafts and lace are there. There's a covered bridge that takes you to a time when life was simpler. The sweet aromas of sorghum and grilled *wurst* and *aptel nachtisch* (apple cake) fill the air. Crafters in nineteenth-century costumes make the weekend educational and fun. Watch a lantern being made in a tin shop or see gourd crafters at work. Drink ice-cold, homemade root beer while you watch gunsmithing and listen to period music, whistling steam engines, and the ring of the blacksmith's anvil. There is a gate donation, $12 for adults, $10 for seniors, and children ages six to sixteen, $6. There is no charge for children under six. For more information call (636) 433–5669, or visit the Web site at www.deutschcountrydays.org.

The *Concord Hill Bed and Breakfast,* 473 Concord Hill Road, Marthasville 63357 (636–932–4228), offers city-weary guests two large bedrooms and a huge loft that comfortably sleeps five adults. Add a hot tub and full kitchen; it's an ideal weekend retreat for groups of up to eleven. A full breakfast is provided, and anything from elegant candlelight dinners to simple box lunches can be prearranged; now *that's* a getaway. This nineteenth-century farmhouse is in the tiny agricultural town of Concord Hill, population forty; this is definitely off the beaten path! Rooms cost $80 for two guests. Call hosts James and Vicki Cunningham for more information. E-mail at chickenman@socket.net.

When you are ready for dinner, find *The Gables* at 101 West Highway 47, Marthasville 63357, and let owner and cook Linda Murphy fix you some real down-home food. You are especially lucky if you happen to be there on a Friday or Saturday night, when she's out back fixing her famous barbecued pork. Your nose will lead you to the building with the four gables. It is a "family tavern," as locals describe it, a very casual place with a full bar ("John the Bartender" handles orders here), where children are welcome. Hours are 11:00 A.M. to 1:30 A.M. Monday through Saturday and from 11:00 A.M. to 8:00 P.M. on Sunday. Call (636) 433–5048 for more information.

There is one more KATY stop at Marthasville. "Over the river and through the woods, to Grandmother's house we go. . . ." If you don't have a grandma in the country, visit *Gramma's House* (636–433–2675) at 1105 Highway D near Marthasville 63357; it's like going home. Enjoy a brisk game of horseshoes, look for a bluebird on the fence, or just skip stones in the creek. After sleeping like a stone in these peaceful surroundings, your "grandma"—that is, hostess—will fix you a hearty breakfast; best clean your plate. Weekend rates are $75 per couple; two lovely private cottages with real fireplaces are $115. Hosts Jim and Judy Jones are delighted with the cottages called the Smokehouse and the Playhouse. Both have fireplaces, but the Playhouse has a huge bathtub in front of the fireplace for a romantic bubblebath *à deux*. Gramma's House is popular with trail users; make this Gramma's a rest stop and stay on for the comfort and the ambience. Visit their Web site at www.grammashouse.com or e-mail at grammashouse@usmo.com.

Bluffs of the Mighty Mo

*H*ighway 94 winds over steep hills set with ponds and quiet, picturesque farms. Small and almost picture-postcard pretty buildings nestled in the trees are clearly visible in winter and half-hidden in summer; you'll have to look sharp. The highway follows the river through a series of tiny towns that give you a taste of Missouri past. Rhineland, Bluffton, Steedman, Mokane—each is as inviting as the last. Heads up: You may find a great little cafe here or a hidden mine of antiques.

Plan to stay awhile in *Columbia.* It's a great base camp for some far-flung exploring—that is, once you can tear yourself away from the town itself.

Columbia is home to the University of Missouri, which has a beautiful campus that houses a number of disciplines. If you have an interest in antiquities, don't miss the *Museum of Art and Archaeology,* boasting a collection from six continents and five millennia. The museum, in Pickard Hall at the corner of University Avenue and Ninth Street, is on

Future Anchors— Take Note!

University of Missouri, Columbia, was the first state university west of the Mississippi. The first school of journalism was founded and the first degree in journalism in the world was awarded at the University of Missouri, Columbia, in 1908.

the historic Francis Quadrangle. Built in 1894, it's on the National Register of Historic Places. You'll find artworks by Lyonel Feininger, Lakshmi, Francken the Younger, and many well-known classical and contemporary American artists. The museum is open 9:00 A.M. till 5:00 P.M. Tuesday through Friday and noon till 5:00 P.M. on weekends.

Archaeology has long been a strong field of study at the university, which offers B.A., M.A., and Ph.D. degrees as well as courses in museum studies. The museum's collections reflect almost a century of work by students and faculty in places as diverse as Africa, Egypt, South Asia, Greece, and the American Southwest. Pre-Columbian and Oceanic works round out the collection.

The museum is wheelchair accessible; there are tours for the visually impaired available without prior notice. Other guided tours can be arranged by calling (573) 882–3591 (at least two weeks in advance for groups).

The **Museum of Anthropology** reopened after extensive renovations and now has displays of Native America that are most interesting. Included in the displays are an Arctic fishing village and a pre-pioneer Midwest settlement—a one-room prairie cabin and a fur trader's canoe filled with beaver pelts and ropes of tobacco. Call (573) 882–3764) for more information.

While the museums are easy to find, a well-guarded secret on the university campus is **Bucks Ice Cream,** in Eckles Hall, at the corner of Rollins and College Streets, Columbia 65201, part of the food and nutrition service. Ice cream and frozen yogurt are made here daily, and it is wonderful stuff. Try their own special Tiger Stripe ice cream. (Just because the nutrition service makes this wonderfully sinful treat doesn't mean it isn't high in butterfat. It is. But what the heck, it is sooooo good.) Hours are noon to 5:00 P.M. Monday through Friday and on Saturday during warm weather (Bucks is closed between semesters). Call (573) 882–1088.

Downtown a pub and brewery has opened up. The **Flat Branch Pub and Brewery,** 115 South Fifth Street, Columbia 65201, needless to say, is very popular with students here. (Students love the homemade root beer and ginger ale.) You can tour the brewing area or have lunch in the pub. Call

(573) 499–0400. Hours are 11:00 A.M. to 1:00 P.M. Monday through Saturday, Sunday from 11:00 A.M. until midnight.

Columbia has an active and varied crafts community. *Bluestem Missouri Crafts* (573–442–0211) showcases the work of more than eighty Missouri artists and craftspeople. Whatever your particular weakness, from wrought iron to weaving, from folk-art whirligigs to fine jewelry, you'll find it at Bluestem (named after the native prairie grass; the shop is located at 13 South Ninth Street, Columbia 65201. Shop 10:00 A.M. until 6:00 P.M. Monday through Saturday, until 8:30 P.M. Thursday night, and noon until 5:00 P.M. on Sunday.

Gail Shen's Chinatown is a toy store that is art in itself. You have to look for Gail's place because it is upstairs and doesn't even have a window display. But inside the shop is a bright, magical place filled with art and toys. The studio is so very colorful and lively that one little five-year-old boy stopped on the threshold and said, "Oh, this looks like fun!"

Much of Gail's fine art is on the walls, too. She carries her own handmade postcards and greeting cards. It is a festive spot where children can touch things and shop for themselves. Many of the toys are priced from 10 cents to 50 cents. Gail even keeps a tax fund in a little jar for kids who buy four 25-cent items and don't realize a dollar won't cover it.

As the name of the studio implies, she has a Chinese theme with posters, joss paper, new year's creatures, and lithographs. There are hats and some clothing, too. The shop is in the center of downtown Columbia at 5 South Ninth Street, Suite 200 (upstairs), Columbia 65201. Hours are somewhat eccentric because of her other job in the theater department of the university, where she makes costumes. Stop by Wednesday through Friday from 3:00 to 6:00 P.M. and on Saturday from 10:00 A.M. until 6:00 P.M. She is there full-time in the summer. Call her at (573) 499–3940 after 6:30 P.M. as there's no phone in the shop.

Another source for handmade and unusual items is *Poppy* at 914 East Broadway, Columbia 65201. Whether you are looking for a gift or just browsing around, this is a place with personality, upbeat and colorful. Barbara McCormic and Mary Ebert work directly with the artisans who do what they do for a living—professionals—as you can tell from the high quality of their work. There is hand-blown glass, pieces shaped in clay or created from fiber, and a line of exquisite—and expensive— jewelry. Although there is some two-dimensional art, it is mostly a gallery of fine crafts. The shop is open seven days a week: Monday through Saturday from 10:00 A.M. until 6:00 P.M.; Thursday evening till

A Place to Call Home

*The **Devil's Icebox** is a unique sinkhole in Rock Bridge Memorial State Park near Columbia. It is the only habitat worldwide for a small flatworm called the pink planarian.*

8:00 P.M.; and Sunday from noon till 5:00 P.M. Call (573) 442–3223.

One more gustatory note—okay, two: truffles and chocolate pizza. You'll find these and too many other rich temptations to mention at the **Candy Factory,** 701 Cherry Street, Columbia 65201. These folks call themselves "your home-town candy makers," but the good news is that even if Columbia isn't your home town, they'll be glad to ship anything you want, nationwide. Use the special order number: (573) 443–8222. You can even buy sugar-free chocolates for those people on restricted diets who still need a treat. Prices seem moderate enough; a holiday gift basket ranges from $12 to $52. Summer hours are 10:00 A.M. to 6:00 P.M. weekdays and 1:00 to 5:30 P.M. on Saturday; winter hours are 9:30 A.M. to 6:00 P.M. weekdays, 10:00 A.M. to 5:30 P.M. on Saturday, and noon to 5:00 P.M. on Sunday.

Carol Leigh Brack-Kaiser is the talent behind two businesses: **Carol Leigh's Specialties** and Hillcreek Fiber Studio. Carol Leigh's Specialties was created to market products made by Carol's own hands: handspun yarns and fabrics colored with natural dyes, woven shawls, blankets and wall hangings. Hillcreek Fiber Studio is for teaching. It all began with a spinning class at the nearby university. Spinning led to weaving then to dyeing, which led to advanced studies in fiber arts. Carol began to take her work to living-history events and rendezvous where people appreciated the labor and old-world methods of her handmade textiles. Now she sits by her adjustable, triangular-shaped loom which she and her son Carl Spriggs patented and now manufacture at her home at 7001 Hillcreek Road, just outside Columbia. Today she has several classes in spinning special fibers, floor loom, and in the ancient methods of inkle and tablet weaving. She also conducts classes in Navajo-style weaving and a designer's yarn class. Standing over a simmering vat of wool dye, she produces vibrant colors from indigo; Osage orange (also called hedge apple), which gives vibrant yellows and golds; brazilwood for red, purple, plum, maroon, and burgundy; logwood for lavender and black; cochineal, a bug from Central and South America, for bright reds; madder root for orange-red, and other natural dyes. Carol Leigh asks that you call before you visit (573–874–2233). The shop is open Tuesday through Saturday from 9:00 A.M. to 5:00 P.M.

Trattoria Strata Nova at 21 North Ninth, Columbia 65201, is an elegant spot and a favorite with almost everyone you ask. The food is more northern Italian—not so much pasta, more Continental—almost French. Mike, Cheryl, and Rocky are proud of this place and well they should be. But don't bother trying to make reservations. It is strictly first-come, first-served. The restaurant is open Tuesday through Friday from 11:30 A.M. until 10:00 P.M. Call (573) 442–8992 for more information.

Formosa Restaurant is upstairs over 913 East Broadway, Columbia 65201 (573–449–3339), and serves seven styles of Chinese cooking. While this little spot is sort of hidden away, plenty of people know about it. Lunch is served from 11:00 A.M. until 2:00 P.M. Monday though Saturday, dinner is from 4:30 to 9:00 P.M. Monday through Thursday, and until 10:00 P.M. on Friday and Saturday nights. There is full bar service.

Missouri's answer to the Hard Rock Cafe—*The 63 Diner*—is just outside Columbia at 5801 North New Highway, 763 Columbia 65202 (573–443–2331). Bright black, white, and chrome decor, dozens of photos of rock 'n' roll favorites and old movie stars, waitresses in saddle shoes and circle skirts, and the end of that big red '59 Cadillac sticking out of the front wall make the place loaded with atmosphere. The food's every bit as good as you remember, too. Hours are 11:00 A.M. to 9:00 P.M. Tuesday through Saturday.

There are three nice bed and breakfasts in Columbia. The *Gathering Place* at 606 South College, Columbia 65201, is practically on the university campus. The 1905 residence was once a fraternity house and has four queen suites and one king suite with eighteenth- and nineteenth-century American antiques. All have private baths and three have Jacuzzis. There are cable television and data-port phones for the modern business traveler. Contact hosts Ross and Shirley Duff, or Jim and Kristin Steelman at (573) 815–0606 or (800) 731–6888. E-mail them at ross duff@aol.com. Fax (573) 817–1653. Rates are $85–$130.

Another place to bed down is the *University Avenue Bed and Breakfast* at 1315 University Avenue, Columbia 65201 (573– or 800–499–1920), affectionately known as "The U" around campus. It is in the historic (and somewhat eclectic) east campus neighborhood. Innkeepers make this a home-away-from-home for alumni. Rooms are $80 to $90.

The other B&B offers the more intimate charm of an English manor house. Built in 1930, the home has a cherry staircase inviting you up to your room and fountains and perennial gardens outside. *Missouri Manor* is at 1121 Ashland Road, Columbia 65201; Web site: www.missouri manor.com. It is also in walking distance to the campus. Hosts Lyria and

Ron Bartlett can be reached by calling (573) 499–4437 or faxing (573) 449–2971. Rates are $100 to $175. You can learn much more about the inn at www.missourimanor.com. When you see the pictures of this elegant inn, you will want to visit. In the mornings you will enjoy a sideboard breakfast of freshly baked pastries, fresh fruit, and cereal. An intimate library is for the use of guests. The suites are large and rich with light and color.

About 11 miles east of Columbia on Highway WW and then some gravel roads (County Road 246), *Patrick Nelson* makes eighteenth- and nineteenth-century reproductions and architectural pieces on his small farm. Using cherry, oak, poplar, walnut, hickory—traditional woods used in American furniture—Nelson can reproduce anything you can show him a picture of, including fireplace mantels and custom molding. He makes doors, bedroom and dining room sets, Windsor chairs, and greenwood country chairs. He can alter pieces to fit modern homes or oversized customers. Call ahead for directions to his shop, which is out back in a shed on the farm. There are usually a few pieces in progress to indicate the caliber of his skill, and you can show him what you have in mind and discuss the price. Call him at (573) 642–7776.

Rocheport is a good spot to sample the KATY Trail through Missouri's middle; it is among the longest of the nation's growing network of rail-trails and eventually will stretch 200 miles from Machens just north of St. Louis to Sedalia 90 miles east of Kansas City. The KATY Trail follows the old Missouri-Kansas-Texas Railroad bed that curves along the north bank of the Missouri River, and one of the most scenic parts of the trail rolls from Rocheport southeast to Jefferson City along a wooded band between the river and the cliffs—sheer limestone walls rising 100 feet above the Muddy Mo. The compacted rock pathway is easy riding even for thin racing tires; the canopy of oak and sycamore trees offers brilliant color in the fall, and the trail is flowered with dogwood and redbud in the spring. Summertime rides lead through kaleidoscopic colors of wildflowers and trumpet vine blossoms fluttering with hummingbirds.

Rocheport is an interesting hamlet; it is so historic that the whole town was placed on the National Register of Historic Places. It basks in the sun on the banks of the wide Missouri River and still has dirt streets, which is fine with the bicyclists who flock there to ride the KATY Trail. But there are outstanding antiques shops, such as *Richard Saunders Antiques* (where a fire burns in the fireplace on crisp fall days), and Whitehorse Antiques. *Flavors of the Heartland* is the place to stop to fill your picnic basket.

You can rent bikes from the *Trailside Cafe & Bike Rental* ($10 a day) and eat pasta at *Abigail's,* located in an old church. The town is small so it's easy to find things.

You might look for Judy Alexander's bears, which are sold from her charming Victorian bungalow, the 1894 *Alexander Cottage* at 301 Central, Rocheport 65279. She lovingly makes bears with names like Aunt Myrtle, Beulah, and Willard. But these are no ordinary bears. These elegant creatures are custom-made from dated fur coats and stoles. Judy will make a keepsake bear from your grandmother's old mink coat. Large 24-inch custom-made bears are $175, and she will dress them in vintage hats and clothing if you like. There are bears tucked in every corner of her house. Needless to say, she has a hard time selling them because she gets so attached to them. Bears are not the only reason to find the cottage, though. There are three rooms filled with American-made crafts and products—handmade soaps from Missouri, Burt's Bees Cosmetics from North Carolina, garden pieces from the South, candles from the East Coast, Hanna's Treasures (band boxes) from Iowa, and buckwheat hull pillows and dream pillows filled with aromatic herbs to help you sleep. Judy makes floral decorations and pillows from vintage fabrics for the shop, too. There are three rooms packed full of goodies with a nice variety of old and new items, including a room full of children's furniture and accessories. The cottage is open from 10:00 A.M. until 5:00 P.M. every day but Sunday, when the shop opens at 1:00 P.M. Call her at (573) 698–3409.

If it's not telling tales out of school, you may want to enroll for a term at the *School House Bed and Breakfast* at 504 Third Street, Rocheport 65279 (573–698–2022). Innkeepers John and Vicki Ott have restored this big foursquare edifice at Third and Clark Streets and made it more inviting than any school we've seen. The three-story school was built in 1914 and served as the area's cultural center for more than sixty years.

There are now nine guest rooms, each with its own style; there are even antique bathtubs, sinks, and toilets. The Bridal Suite contains a heart-shaped Jacuzzi. The garden courtyard invites relaxation, and the period reception room is available for meetings, business retreats, and intimate parties. Room rates are from $95 to $228 per night and include a hearty country breakfast. *Whitehorse Antiques,* with ten dealers, is on the lower level of the school.

The family-owned winery *Les Bourgeois Vineyards* (573–698–3401) welcomes visitors. It is located south of Rocheport on Highway BB, 1 mile north of Interstate 70. Admire a spectacular view of the Missouri

River and watch the barges float by as you sample Bordeaux-style wines—plus a generous basket of Missouri sausage, cheese, and fresh fruit. Wine garden hours are noon to sunset, Monday through Saturday; Sunday noon to 6:00 P.M. from March through November, but the winery and sales room are open every day of the year from 11:00 A.M. to 6:00 P.M. Now lunch is served daily except Wednesday, and ethnic or regional theme dinners are served from 5:30 to 8:30 P.M. on Friday and Saturday.

All this driving makes a body thirsty, but by now you've had enough wine; how about an old-fashioned cherry phosphate? Or maybe a thick, rich malt made with hand-dipped ice cream? Stop by tiny *Glasgow,* where you'll find *Henderson's,* at 523 First Street, Glasgow 65254, a fifth-generation drugstore on the main drag. They'll fix you the fantasy float of your dreams. Hours are Monday through Friday from 7:00 A.M. until 5:30 P.M., Saturday till 4:00 P.M. Call (660) 338–2125.

Glasgow's narrow, two-story city hall has a surprised expression; the round-topped windows look like raised eyebrows. But there's nothing too shocking in this historic little town unless you discover that the old bridge on Highway 240 is the world's first all-steel bridge, built in 1878. Eight hundred tons of steel were used in construction at a cost of $500,000; it costs more than that to salt the wintry streets of a small city today.

Near Fayette is the only spot in the entire Western Hemisphere—that's hemisphere, folks—where you'll find inland salt grass. *Moniteau Lick,* near the more familiar Boone's Lick, is the place. This area was once important for naturally occurring salt; there are more than eighty place-names in Missouri containing the word "salt" or "saline."

Glaciated Plains

Civil War buffs will discover the General Sterling Price Monument by the highway at *Keytesville.* This is the heart of Little Dixie, the part of the state with its roots firmly in the South. The original courthouse, circa 1834, was burned by Bushwackers—bands of Confederate renegades who spent their time burning farms and killing Union sympathizers—in 1864. George Todd and John Thralkill, with 130 men, surrounded a Union garrison of thirty-five men stationed in the fortified courthouse. When they surrendered, it was torched.

Sterling Price came to Missouri from his native Virginia in 1831. His father, mother, sisters, and brothers, who were all adults, came by ox wagon with their household goods. Slaves drove the livestock. He married and raised seven children at Val Verde, his family home. He became

Missouri's eleventh governor in 1853 and served two terms. But with the threat of war he felt compelled to cast his lot with the Confederacy, although he favored the Union. He became a Confederate General in April 1862 and participated in several battles for the state—at Lexington, Pea Ridge, Poison Springs, Helena, Wilsons Creek, and West Port—but was forced to retreat south.

At the close of the war, General Price went to Cordova, Mexico, where he was granted a tract of land by Emperor Maxmillian to establish a colony for ex-Confederate soldiers. That failed with the fall of Maxmillian's government. Price returned to Missouri in 1867 and died in St. Louis that year. The *General Sterling Price Museum* is at 303 West Bridge Street, Keytesville 65261, in the Masonic Lodge Building.

The magnificent, three-story *Hill Homestead,* also in Keytesville, is open for tours during the summer months. It was built by William Redding in 1832. He was killed there by Union soldiers.

Farther north you'll pass through a real Mickey Mouse town (*Marceline* is where Walt Disney grew up) on your way to Brookfield. Every Labor Day, hot-air balloon races are held nearby. There's a sustained "swooooosh" as the balloons lift off; it sounds like the sharp intake of the watching crowd's breath, but it's the hot breath of the craft themselves, rising in the morning air. More than fifty balloons join in the fun, filling the sky with crayon-box colors.

From here, a short jaunt north and west will take you to *Laclede* and the *General John J. Pershing Boyhood Home.* The rural gothic building is a National Historic Landmark and is as ramrod straight as the old man himself, softened with just a bit of gingerbread. The museum highlights Pershing's long career. Only 3 miles away is *Pershing State Park,* with the largest remaining wet prairie in Missouri, Late Woodsland Indian mounds, and the War Mothers Statue. Also, Locust Creek Covered Bridge State Historic Site is just north of Pershing's home.

You are now in what is known as the Glaciated Plains. A good example of the huge Laurentide ice-sheet movement is the Bairdstown Church Erratic, a huge, pink, lichen-covered granite boulder that stands 10 feet high, 20 feet wide, and 24 feet long and is estimated to weigh the same as a Boeing 747 (768,000 pounds). It sits in the middle of a pasture on the Dunlop family farm near Milan. Over the years these huge gifts from the north have been cut by pioneers for mill stones or converted to monuments. This one remains untouched. It came to the state when the glacier pushed its way from Canada 175,000 years ago. It is obviously a very strange visitor to this flatland.

Open farmland dominates Highway 5 North; the rolling hills recall the prairie that covered much of presettlement Missouri. East of Milan on Highway 6 discover busy *Kirksville* and environs. There's a lot happening in Kirksville, as always in a college town. This is the home of Truman University and the *Kirksville College of Osteopathic Medicine*—lots of lively young things running around here, having fun, eating out, and just generally being college kids.

Is your family doctor an M.D. or a D.O.? If he is a Doctor of Osteopathy (D.O.), his profession got its start right here in Kirksville when Andrew Taylor Still established the first school of the osteopathic profession in 1892, in a one-room schoolhouse. The college has grown; today there are fifteen buildings (including two hospitals) on a fifty-acre campus, and the student body numbers more than 500. Former United States Surgeon General C. Everett Koop himself delivered the 1988 commencement address.

Visit the *Andrew Taylor Still National Osteopathic Museum* at 311 South Fourth Street, Kirksville 63501, weekdays from 10:00 A.M. to 4:00 P.M., noon to 4:00 P.M. Saturday. It's a three-building complex that includes the log cabin birthplace of Dr. Still, the tiny white clapboard cabin that served as the school, and the museum itself, with its impressive collection of osteopathic paraphernalia. Admission is free.

Buildings of many architectural styles, from Romanesque and Renaissance Revival to Italianate and Victorian, from Art Deco and Art Nouveau to Beaux Arts and Prairie, strut their stuff on the walking tour of Old Towne Kirksville. Begin the grand tour at Old Towne Park (Elson and Washington Streets) and follow the signs, or pick up a map at any of the businesses marked with a red flag. It's only 1½ miles by foot—but well over one hundred years if you're traveling in time.

When the nightlife gets too much for you in hoppin' Kirksville, head out of town to *Thousand Hills State Park.* This part of Missouri was sculpted by glaciers; rich, glacial soil is the norm, not the exception, and the streams and rivers that cut through this deep soil formed the "thousand hills."

The park straddles the Grand Divide. Like the Continental Divide, this geologic landform is an area where high ground determines the direction of surface water drainage. It always seems as if you should feel the difference as you cross, but you don't. This mini-mountain ridge runs along Highway 63 from the Iowa-Missouri border to just south of Moberly; western streams and rivers flow into the Missouri River, eastern waters into the Mississippi.

Much of the park is remnant prairie—look for big bluestem, rattlesnake master, blazing star, and Indian grass, which are maintained by periodic burning. Because of the cooler climate here, you'll find plants not found in other parts of the state, such as the lovely interrupted fern in the deep ravines in the park. There is a natural grove of large-toothed aspen, a tree common to northern states but quite rare in Missouri. In Thousand Hills State Park you can find our grand-champion aspen.

If prehistory interests you more than natural history, don't miss the petroglyphs near camping area no. 3. Archaeologists believe these crosses, thunderbirds, sunbursts, and arrows were scratched into the native sandstone by peoples who inhabited the site between A.D. 1000 and 1600. They may have been reminders of the order of the ceremonial rituals passed along by the Middle Mississippi culture, which were in use for a long period of time. Many glyphs appear to have been carved by hunters of the Late Woodland culture between A.D. 400 and 900. The site is listed on the National Register of Historic Places; it's nice to know this list contains more than the usual antebellum mansions and federal-style courthouses we seem to expect.

Take the highway south to **Ethel**—that is, if you love hand-thrown pottery. This little town is the home of **Clay Images,** 23067 State Highway 149, Ethel 63539 (660–486–3471). Jim and Melissa Hogenson are well-known artists who work in clay; you may have seen their whimsies—dragons and wizards—at Renaissance festivals around the country. Don't miss this little gold mine (all right, clay mine). Visit the Web site at www.clayimages.com or e-mail at clayimages@cvalley.net.

There is a bed-and-breakfast in Ethel, too. The **Recess Inn** at 203 East Main, Ethel 63539, is a beautifully renovated 1910 brick schoolhouse. Innkeeper Nancy Morford will cook up a delicious country breakfast served grandma style, with plenty of everything. This three-story home has a chapel on the third floor as well as four rooms with private baths—

Where to Winter If You're a Canada Goose

Swan Lake National Wildlife **Refuge** is the wintering grounds for one of the largest concentrations of Canada geese in North America. This 10,670-acre refuge also attracts more than one hundred bald eagles each winter. The main entrance is 1 mile south of Sumner on County Road RA. Photography and bird-watching are permitted, and there is a ¾-mile habitat trail and observation tower.

featuring not only antique tubs for bubble baths but showers as well. You can reach the inn by e-mail at recessinn@cvalley.net or you can visit online at www.bbonline-com/mo/recessinn. Rooms start at $65. Call (660) 486–3328 or (800) 628–5003 for reservations.

It seems that everyone in this town of barely a hundred people must own a little business of some kind. Start at the Recess Inn and head down Main Street to the **Ethel General Store** at 205 East Main Street, Ethel 63539 (660–486–3350). It has an old-fashioned soda fountain where you can enjoy a chocolate soda with David and Tori Young while you rest up for the rest of the block. Next stop is **The Emporium** at 211 West Main Street, Ethel 63539. Browse among the gifts and primitive antiques by appointment. Call the Recess Inn (660–486–3328) or Hunter's Inn (660–486–3403). Next stop on Main is the **Buttercup Quilt Shop** at 120 East Main Ethel 63539. Ursula Gordon has filled this shop with hand-crafted quilts and collectibles. Call (660) 486–3335. That wasn't too strenuous now, was it? Want to venture out farther? Search out **White Oak Farms and Gift House** at 22593 State Highway 149, Ethel 63539, and leaf through the herbs and everlastings that Dean and Barbara Rauer lovingly put together. Call (660) 486–3266.

Oh yes, and there is another B&B in town, too. **Hunters' Inn** at 120 Ralph Street, Ethel 63539, is remarkable in that it is a Montgomery Ward home brought to Ethel on a train and carried by oxcart up the hill where it was assembled and now commands a view of the town. It looks like a hunting lodge, hence the name, and for $60 a night (shared bath) includes a large hunter's breakfast. You can also rent the whole inn for $185 a night. Owners Ralph and Sandy Clark and Donald and Linda Souther invite you to visit their Web site at www.bbonline.com or call the inn at (660) 486–3403.

Macon is known all over the state for good antiques shopping. The prices are very reasonable and the shops are full. Start at the largest, **Carrousel Antiques,** at 125 Vine Street, Macon 63552 (660–385–4284). Ruth Norton will show you around the thirty-five booths in the mall. Hours are 10:00 A.M. until 5:00 P.M. seven days a week.

There are three B&Bs in Macon, too, so if you shop till you drop, you can choose where to drop.

One of them is **St. Agnes Hall** at 502 Jackson Street, Macon 63552. This is just what it sounds like, a former girls school—from 1884 to 1895—turned bed-and-breakfast. This stately 1846 three-story home is filled with period furnishings and is surrounded with gardens and a park for strolling about. Hosts Carol and Scott Phillips fix a full breakfast for guests and invite you to relax and enjoy the nearby golf course and antiques shops in town. For reservations call (660) 385–2774, fax (660) 385–4436, or e-mail at stagneshall@hotmail.com. Rates are $68 to $98.

Tiny **Ten Mile** just north of Macon doesn't even show on the map; it's an Amish community near Ethel. Watch for little yard signs; many of these places have tiny shops on the farmstead where baked goods, yard goods, homemade candy, and baskets or quilts are sold.

If you can, find Founder's Cemetery on the north edge of Paris. It is listed in Ripley's Believe It or Not *because it is the home of possibly the only tombstone in the world to list three wives of one husband.*

As long as you are searching out cemeteries, find the Walnut Grove Cemetery and take a good look at the caretaker's building. Its architecture is Little Dixie Victorian, and it was constructed around 1870. The round turret originally enclosed a water tower for water storage.

Moberly, at the junction of Highways 24/63, has a beautiful bed-and-breakfast at 516 West Urbandale Drive, Moberly 65270. The **Terrill House** is an elegant circa-1860 home. The rooms have private baths (although not in the rooms) with turn-of-the-century-style tubs that also provide a shower as well as a soak. The floor-to-ceiling windows allow a view of the more than three acres of countryside on the outskirts of town. Rooms are $65 with a full breakfast. Proprietors Chuck Davis and Dot Maasen welcome guests to this home they have worked so hard to restore. Call (800) 215–5422 (PIN 9175) or (660) 263–1944. You may also tour the house for $5.00, which includes a dessert and beverage ($10 from December to January 15).

Chuck and Dot will give you a map outlining the way to all the farms in the Amish countryside, which begins at the end of Urbandale Drive and goes all the way to the town of Clark. (Chuck will direct you to one farm in particular and ask you to bring him a jar of Honeydew Jelly, to which he claims to be addicted.) There are a couple of eating places recommended by the couple: **C.C. Sawyer's** at 104 West Wightman Street in Moberly 65270 has great steaks (660–263–7744), while **Jeffrey's,** a restaurant that has been around forever at 107 West Williams in Moberly 65270, is known generally for its good food. Call (660) 263–3005.

Take the grand tour through **Paris** (no, not the long way around; this is Paris, Missouri). Tiny **Florida** is the closest town to the **Mark Twain Birthplace State Historic Site** (573–565–3449) and Mark Twain State Park, which offers camping, swimming, and river recreation. The two-room cabin where Samuel Clemens came into the world reminds you of something; it could have come straight from one of his books. A bit of Twain was Tom Sawyer and Huck Finn (you remember Huck, that red-haired scamp who lived life to the hilt, devil-take-the-hindmost). If you've read *The Adventures of Huckleberry Finn*, this won't come as a big surprise.

What is a surprise is that the two-room cabin is totally enclosed in an ultramodern museum, which houses first editions of Clemens's works, including the handwritten version of *Tom Sawyer* done for British publication. Sit in the public reading room to conduct personal research—or just to get in touch with the old wag. For example, Twain once wrote, "Recently someone in Missouri has sent me a picture of the house I was born in. Heretofore I always stated that it was a palace but I shall be more guarded now." There is an admission charge.

On the second full weekend of August each year, the U. S. Army Corps of Engineers, the Missouri Department of Natural Resources, and the Friends of Florida sponsor the **Salt River Folklife Festival** in the tiny town of Florida.

Although this is not Madison County, 5 miles west of Paris and 3 miles south on County Route C, you'll find a different kind of nostalgic symbol, the **Union Covered Bridge.** It is the only Burr-arch covered bridge left in the state. Named for the Union Church, which once stood nearby, this 125-foot-long, 17½-foot-wide bridge was built in 1871.

You can almost hear the clatter of horses' hooves and the rumble of wagon wheels through the old wooden tunnel. (You'll have to use your imagination; the recently restored bridge is open to foot traffic only—it's blocked to vehicles.) A set of interpretive displays at the unmanned site fills you in on covered-bridge history in Missouri. Call the Mark Twain Birthplace at (573) 565–3449 for information and directions to the bridge.

After a picnic at the covered bridge, continue west on Highway 24 to Highway 151. (Pay attention, now.) Go south to Highway M. After a few miles you will come to Highway Y. A drive south on Y will take you through another Amish community. There are no retail shops along the route except Sam's Store, which has no sign out front—you have to ask for directions—but there are signs in the yards offering a variety of handmade goods. The signs advertise homemade candy, quilts, and furniture. Fresh garden produce, eggs, and honey are also sold. You can get off the highway and take many small buggy roads to explore the community. Small schools, like the one named Plain View, dot the landscape, and buggies leave dust trails on the roads. This is Middle America in its simplest form.

There are some pretty exotic destinations around here, aren't there? Milan, Paris—and now **Mexico,** south of "gay Paree." Mexico is called

"Little Dixie," because of its strong Southern sympathies during the Civil War; now you can visit the Little Dixie Wildlife Area nearby.

In **Mexico** is the **Graceland House Museum,** at 501 South Muldrow, Mexico 65265, a stately antebellum mansion housing the Audrain County Historical Society. It is located in the eleven-acre Robert S. Green Park, which has a playground, picnic area, and gracious lawn. It is one of the oldest homes in the county, built in 1857. This Greek Revival home is listed in the National Register of Historical Places. You can experience the lifestyle of the era with wedding dresses, an extensive doll collection, china, silver, and antique furniture as well as antique tools. Hours are from 1:00 to 4:00 P.M. Tuesday through Saturday and from 2:00 to 5:00 P.M. Sunday. Admission is $2.00 for adults and 50 cents for children.

> ## Ancient Trees
>
> *If you are interested in antique trees, look at the bicentennial tree at 710 Cleveland. This oak tree is more than 300 years old. There is a California redwood tree at 406 West Monroe that was brought by covered wagon from California in 1832.*

American Saddlebred Horse Museum is also at 501 South Muldrow. Here is a fine art exhibit including works by artists George Ford Morris, Gladys Brown, and B. Beaumont, and Saddlebred primitives by Audrain McDonough from the 1920s. Many famous horses are featured in the photographs and paintings. Hours and admission are the same as Graceland.

The **Audrain Country School,** also part of this complex, was constructed in 1903 and is furnished with authentic items used in country schools—slate blackboards, desks, games, and other memorabilia saved from rural schools in the county. An outhouse behind the school adds to the authenticity of the setting. Call (573) 581–3910 for information on all three places.

Notice all the red-brick buildings in the Mexico/Vandalia area? The land is underlaid with a type of refractory clay that makes great bricks; there are still four brick plants in Audrain County.

A 14-mile jog back east from Mexico will take you to **Centralia.** Don't miss it if you enjoy "kinder, gentler" countryside. **Chance Gardens** includes a turn-of-the-century mansion, home of the late A. Bishop Chance. Built in 1904, its onion-domed turret, gracious porticoes, and ornate woodwork invite visitors with an eye for elegance. A gift to the public from the A. B. Chance Company (the town's largest industry), it's been Centralia's showplace for years.

The gardens that surround the home say something about the kind of luxury money can't buy. It takes time to plan those masses of color that bloom continuously through the seasons and lead the eye from one brilliant display to another—time to plan and time to maintain. That's a luxury most of us don't have.

While you are in there, you will want to visit the **Centralia Historical Society Museum** at 319 East Sneed Street, Centralia 65240, in a house built in 1904 and dedicated to preserving and exhibiting artifacts that document the history of the area. In the fall the museum is host to a quilt show, and hundreds have been showcased here. Hours are from 2:00 to 4:00 P.M. Wednesday and Sunday, May through November. Call (573) 682–5711.

Tiny **Clark,** a hoot and a holler from Centralia, is the birthplace of General Omar Bradley. There's an active Amish community in the Clark area; watch for those horses and buggies. Some sport bumper stickers, much easier to read at this speed than on the interstates. I'M NOT DEAF, I'M IGNORING YOU and I MAY BE SLOW, BUT I'M AHEAD OF YOU seem to be local favorites. You'll want to slow down yourself to admire the clean, white homes and commodious barns of the Amish.

Missouri's Monarchy

Winston Churchill journeyed to **Fulton** to address Westminster College in 1946 just after he had been defeated for reelection as England's Prime Minister. Churchill delivered the most famous speech of his life, the "Iron Curtain" speech. "From Stettin in the Baltic to Trieste in the Adriatic, an iron curtain has descended across the Continent. Behind that line lie all the capitals of the ancient states of Central and Eastern Europe...."

The invitation to speak at Westminister College had a handwritten note at the bottom in a familiar scrawl: "This is a wonderful school in my home state. Hope you can do it. I'll introduce you. Best regards, Harry Truman." The president and his respected friend arrived in Fulton on March 5, 1946. The cold war is over now and the iron curtain lowered, but the ties between the college, the town, and Great Britain remain unbroken. In the 1960s Westminster President R.L.D. Davidson wanted to honor those ties. The resulting plan was bold and perfect—if not as well-publicized as the move of the London Bridge to Arizona. The college acquired the centuries-old Church of St. Mary the Virgin, Aldermanbury, England, and dismantled it stone by stone. The edifice was shipped across the Atlantic and cross-country to Fulton, where it was reconstructed on the Westminster campus (Harry Truman himself turned the first spade of earth in

1964), and rededicated in 1969. It now houses the ***Winston Churchill Memorial and Library*** (573–592–5369 or –6648), currently the only center in the United States dedicated to the study of the man and his works. Churchill's original oil paintings (the very public man had a private side, and enjoyed relaxing with his paints), letters, manuscripts, personal family mementos, and other memorabilia are on display, in addition to the fire-scarred communion plate rescued from the ruins of the church after World War II.

Callaway County in effect seceded from both North and South and stood independent briefly as the Kingdom of Callaway, when federal troops deposed Governor Jackson and established a provisional government in Jefferson City during the Civil War.

The church itself is deeply historical; built in twelfth-century London, it was redesigned in 1677 by Sir Christopher Wren, one of the finest architects of the period. Damage caused by German bombs seemed to signal its end until Westminster College stepped in to rescue the building. It is open from 10:00 A.M. to 4:30 P.M. seven days a week.

The Berlin Wall fell in 1989 and a piece of it, marked with angry graffiti of the past, was made into a sculpture by Churchill's granddaughter, Edwina Sandys. She cut out simple but powerful shapes of a man and a woman as openings in the wall and called it *Breakthrough.* That piece now stands on campus. In 1992 Mikhail Gorbachev spoke at Westminister, further symbolizing the end of the Cold War.

There is a memorial of a different kind in the same town: the ***George Washington Carver Memorial*** at 909 Westminster Avenue, Fulton 6251 (573–642–5551) honors the Diamond, Missouri, native and presents information about one of our greatest humanitarians and scientists. The memorial includes a study of black history in Missouri as well. It is open on weekends, and there is a small admission charge.

The ***Auto World Museum*** at 1920 North Bluff (Business 54 North) in Fulton 65251 has rare cars (among them the shiny black 1931 Marmon, a sixteen-cylinder car gangsters made infamous), vintage fire trucks (including a 1922 Ahrens Fox Pumper), tractors, and buggies. It is the dream-come-true of Bill Backer and his wife, Marge. Bill has been collecting and restoring old cars for forty-four years. When the local K-Mart left town, Bill had the opportunity to grab 37,000 square feet of work space. When he moved in he thought he would open a museum for a month or so to show off his cars. It became so popular that he decided to divide the area and use the front as a museum and the back as a workroom. The rare cars were a hit—cars like a Stanley Steamer, a DeLorean, and a 1986 Pulse (not old, but only sixty of these motorcycles-become-cars were made). They are right there with the Edsel and Studebaker as unique collectibles. He also has an 1875 Haynes, which is the only one in the United States in private hands (there is one in the Smithsonian in Washington, D.C.). If you want to see a great collection of more than one hundred vehicles, from horseless carriages to solar cars, this is the place.

There is also a gift shop with local artisans contributing military memo-

Biscuits and Gravy—the Ultimate Test

I have been writing since 1985, and as I read my notes and journals, it seems that most of my memories revolve around food. So it doesn't surprise me that I gain weight with each book I write. I have photos to remind me of the Eiffel Tower, but when someone asks, "Best meal of your life?" my memory of sweetbreads in champagne sauce take me back to Paris, the world's most beautiful city.

And so it is with Missouri. I remember strolling along Washington's Front Street and watching the river amble by, hearing the trains approaching along the track that parallels the river, but if someone asks, "Best biscuits and gravy?" I remember a little diner in town. The waitress heard me say I had never had biscuits and gravy. So she gave me no breakfast option. I would have biscuits and gravy. They were wonderful: soft flaky biscuits covered with thick, sausage-filled gravy. Since that fateful day I have ordered B&G at hundreds of restaurants, and it has never been the same. Hockey pucks covered with Elmer's glue—bland, dry, tasteless attempts at a meal fit for the gods. It is my ultimate test of an eating establishment that claims to serve breakfast.

Fried chicken—now there's another test. The best pan-fried chicken in the state is at Stroud's in Kansas City. Served family style on big platters with green beans and mashed potatoes covered with pan gravy, it is an all-you-can-eat-and-take-the-rest-home heaven. Oh my, is it any wonder you have to get there before they open to line up for a seat?

When I wrote about Arkansas, it was fried catfish and hamburgers (in honor of President William Jefferson Clinton) I searched out, but none of the hamburgers matched the tiny burgers at Hayes Hamburgers in suburban Kansas City.

In Kansas it was fried chicken and muffins (it seems that most of the B&Bs in Kansas make delightful muffins that are soft and warm and huge) that drew my attention. And while Missouri is famous for its steak and barbecue, there is a cold, smoked-trout dish at the Blue Heron in Osage Beach that has lingered in my memory for years.

Say what you will about scenic highways, back-road museums, and shopping, what is really important is the answer to the age-old question: "Where should we eat?"

rabilia, railroad collectibles, fine china and crystal, and a little bit of flea market. In addition there's a large display of Kennedy memorabilia. The museum is open daily from 10:00 A.M. to 4:00 P.M. Monday through Saturday, Sunday 12:30 to 4:00 P.M. Call (573) 642–2080.

The **Loganberry Inn,** a turn-of-the-century Victorian home, offers guests B&B accommodations at 310 West Seventh Street, Fulton 65251, only a block from Westminster College. This inviting 1899 Victorian home welcomed Margaret Thatcher in 1996. Hosts Carl and Cathy McGeorge bake fresh cookies for your arrival and serve a gourmet breakfast on fine china each morning. It is walking distance from the Churchill Memorial Museum and the Rare Car Museum downtown. Rooms (and a suite) are $85 to $135 ($95 to $160 on weekends). Call (573) 642–9229 or (888) 866–6661 for more information. Visit their Web site at www.loganberryinn.com.

Fulton was also the home of Henry Bellamann, author of *King's Row.* Set in Fulton, the novel was made into a movie in the 1940s starring none other than Missourian Bob Cummings and a prepresidential Ronald Reagan. The chamber of commerce displays memorabilia from the movie and offers a walking tour of the *King's Row* setting.

Thence hie thyself back east along Interstate 70 to **Graham Cave State Park** (314–564–3476) near **Danville.** (Oops, this royalty stuff gets to you!) Graham Cave is a huge arch of sandstone that dwarfs its human visitors. This rainbow-shaped cave is shallow, so the tour is a self-guided one. Spelunkers, don't let that put you off. Although this is not a deep-earth cave with spectacular formations, artifacts were found here dating from the area's earliest human habitation, some 10,000 years ago. Before the Native Americans formed themselves into tribes, Graham Cave was an important gathering place. Spear-type flints, made before the bow was invented, were found here, along with other signs of human use. The dig itself is fenced to prevent finds from being removed, but you can admire these fine examples of the earliest Show-Me State inhabitants in the small museum in the park office. Take the Danville/Montgomery City exit off the interstate and follow Outer Road TT 2 miles west; it dead-ends at the park, so you can't go wrong. Check in at the park office to pick up a map to the cave.

PLACES TO STAY IN NORTHEAST MISSOURI

HANNIBAL
Days Inn of Hannibal, 123 Huckleberry Drive, 63401; (573) 221–9988

Best Western Hotel Clemons, 401 North Third Street, 63401; (573) 248–1150

COLUMBIA
Best Western Columbia Inn, 3100 Interstate 70 Drive S.E., 65201; (573) 474–6161

Holiday Inn, 2200 Interstate 70 Drive S.W., 65203; (573) 445–8531

CLARKSVILLE
Clarksville Motel, Highway 79, 63336; (573) 242–3324

LOUISIANA
River's Edge Motel, 201 Mansion Street, 63353; (573) 754–4522

ST. CHARLES
Red Roof Inn, I-70 and Zumbehl Road, 63303; (636) 947–7770

Days Inn, Noah's Ark, 1500 South Fifth Street, 63303; (636) 946–1000

MOBERLY
Ramada Inn, Junction of Highways 63/24, 65270; (660) 263–6540

MARCELINE
Lamplighter Motel, 101 West Ira, 64658; (660) 376–3517

KIRKSVILLE
Days Inn, Highway 63 South, 63501 (660) 665–8244

Super 8 Motel, 1101 Country Club Drive, 63501; (660) 665–8826

Best Western Shamrock Inn, Highways 6/63 South, 63501; (660) 665–8352

MACON
Super 8 Motel, 1420 N. Rutherford Street, 63552; (660) 385–5788

Best Western Inn, 28933 Sunset Drive, 63552; (660) 385–2125

MEXICO
Villager Lodge, 1010 Liberty, 65265; (573) 581–1440 or (800) 528–1234

FULTON
Budget Host Westwood Motel, 422 Gaylord Drive, 65251; (573) 642–5991

KINGDOM CITY
Super 8 Motel, Interstate 70 and Highway 54, 65262; (573) 642–2888

PERRY
Junction Inn, Junction of Highway 19 and 154, 63462; (573) 565–2665

KEARNEY
Super 8 Motel, 210 Platte Clay Way, 64060; (816) 628–6800

ST. JOSEPH
Best Western, Junction of Interstate 29 and Highway 169, 64501; (816) 232–2345

ALBANY
Eastwood Motel, Highway 136 East, 64402; 64402; (660) 726–5208

BETHANY
Family Budget Inn, Exit 93, Highway 1351, 64824; (660) 425–7015

MARYVILLE
Comfort Inn, 2817 South Main, 64468; (660) 562–2002 or (800) 528–1234

Selected Chambers of Commerce

Kirksville, (816) 665–3766

Kearney, (816) 628–4229

Marceline, (816) 376–3092

Paris, (816) 327–4450

Plattsburg, (816) 539–2649

CAMERON
Days Inn, 501 Northland
Drive, 64429;
(816) 632-6623

PLACES TO EAT IN NORTHEAST MISSOURI

HANNIBAL
Lula Belle's, 111 Bird,
63401; (573) 221-6662

MARTHASVILLE
Loretta's Place, P.O. Box
162, 63357; (314) 433-5775
(in town and in sight of the
KATY Trail)

COLUMBIA
Booches Billiard Hall,
110 South Ninth Street,
65201; (573) 874-9519

T.P.' s Bar & Grill,
119 Seventh Street,
65201; (573) 449-0132

Shakespeare's Pizza,
Ninth and Elm Streets,
65201; (573) 449-2454

KIRKSVILLE
Rosie's Northtown Cafe,
2606 N. Baltimore,
63501; (660) 665-8881

KINGDOM CITY
Iron Skillet, Interstate 70
and Highway 54,
65262; (573) 642-8684

LOUISIANA
Beldanes Restaurant,
Highway 54/79,
63353; (573) 754-6869

KEARNEY
Outlaw Barbecue,
129 East Washington,
64060; (816) 628-6500

MARYVILLE
A&G Restaurant,
Business 71,
64468; (660) 582-4421

CAMERON
The Cactus Grill,
923 Walnut, 64429;
(816) 632-6110

LAWSON
Catrick, 410 N. Penn,
64062; (816) 296-4170

Indexes

Entries for bed-and-breakfasts and inns appear in the special index
beginning on page 253.

A

Abigail's, 229
Acapulco Restaurant, 165
Adam-Ondi-Ahman Shrine, 175
Akers, Tom, 67
Alba, 80
Albrecht-Kemper Art Museum, 196
Alexander Cottage, 229
Alley Spring, 68
Alley Spring Mill, 69
Altenberg, 45
Amenistar Casino St. Charles, 208
American Bounty, The, 19
American Bowman, 192
American Kennel Club Museum of
   the Dog, 12
American Saddlebred Horse Museum, 237
Americana Antique, Art, and
   Curio Shop, 24
Americana Galleries, 220
Anderson House State Historic Site, 128
Andrew Taylor Still National
   Osteopathic Museum, 232
Angel Lady, 123
Angie's Beanie Babies, 184
Anna's Bake Shop, 174
Annapolis, 38
Annie Gunn's, 15
Antique Tulip, 182
Antiqueland, 122
Antonio's Pizza, 114
Anvil, The, 43
Arcadia Valley, 37
Arri's Pizza, 134
Arrow Rock, 129
Arthur Bryant Barbecue, 103
Ash Grove, 63
Assumption Abbey, 75
Attic Treasures, 18
Audrain Country School, 237
August A. Busch Memorial
   Wildlife Area, 217
Augusta, 219
Augusta White Haus, 220
Augusta Winery, 218
Augusta Wood Ltd., 221
Aurora, 64
Auto World museum, 239

Ava, 75
Avalon, 193
Avondale, 165
Avondale Furniture and Antiques, 165
Ayers Pottery, 213

B

B&B's Lawnside Bar-B-Que, 103
Bagnell Dam, 148
Bankhead Chocolates, 210
Barn Swallow, 27
Barnett, 150
Bass Pro Shops Outdoor World, 60
B-Bax Consignment Shoppe, 117
"Becky Thatcher" House, 212
Benton Street Cafe, 66
Berger, 20
Bert & Ernie's, 200
Beryl White's Studio and Gallery, 134
Best of Kansas City, 118
Bethel, 216
Beverly Hills Antiques Mall, 194
Bias Vineyards & Winery, 20
Big Bay Campgrounds, 84
Big Oak Tree State Park, 52
Big Piney River National Scenic
   Trail Rides, 66
Big Spring, 74
Big Spring Lodge, 73
Bingham-Waggoner Estate, 121
Birk's Gasthous, 22
Bixby, 37
Black Archives of Mid-America, 107
Black Madonna of Czestochowa
   Shrine and Grottos, 15
Blue Bayou, 49
Blue Owl Restaurant and Bakery, 34
Blueberry Hill, 8
Bluebird Cafe, 115
Bluestem Missouri Crafts, 225
Blumenhof Vineyards and Winery, 222
Bolduc House Museum, 42
Bollinger Mill, 47
Bonne Terre, 35
Bonne Terre Mines, 36
Bonnotts Mill, 23
Boonville, 131
Bootheel region, 52

Bothwell State Park, 136
Bourbon, 30
Bowling Green, 210
Branson, 86
Branson Scenic Railway, 89
Bratcher Cooperage, 168
Brick House Cafe and Pub, 202
Bristle Ridge Winery, 143
Bromley's, 147
Brookfield, 213
Broussard's Cajun Restaurant, 48
Brunke's Supply, 180
Bucks Ice Cream, 224
Buffalo Creek Vineyards and Winery, 154
Burfordville, 47
Burfordville Covered Bridge, 47
Burgers' Smokehouse, 134
Burroughs Audubon Society Library, 138
Buttercup Quilt Shop, 234
Bynum Winery, 141

C

C.C. Sawyer's, 235
Cafe Allegro, 113
Cafe Cedar, 188
Cafe Periwinkle, 140
Cafe Petit Four, 139
California, 134
Camdenton, 155
Candlestick Inn, 88
Candy Factory, 226
Candyman's Mule Barn, 200
Cape Girardeau, 47
Carl's Gun Shop, 158
Carmen's Cafe, 112
Carol Leigh's Specialties, 226
Carroll's Antiques, 27
Carrousel Antiques, 234
Carter's Gallery, 143
Carthage, 77
Casa de Fajita, 112
Cascone's Grill, 109
Cassville, 83
Cathedral Church of the Prince of Peace, 92
Cattlener's Steak House, 187
Caveman BBQ, 67
Central Dairy, 133
Central Park Gallery, 113
Centralia, 237
Centralia Historical Society Museum, 238
Cezanne's Garden, 188
Chance Gardens, 237

Char's on the Riverfront, 19
Charlie Gitto's, 10
Cheep Antiques River Market
    Emporium, 110
Cheese Wedge, 219
Chesterfield, 15
Chicken and Blues, 139
Chillicothe, 171
Church of St. Luke, the Beloved
    Physician, 182
City Market, 108
Civil War Museum, 78
Clark, 238
Clarksville, 211
Classic Cub, 116
Clay Images, 233
Claybrook Mansion, 187
Clem's Cafe, 187
Clifford Wirick Centennial House, 211
Clinton, 157
Clinton's, 120
Club 60, 77
Clyde's General Store, 203
Colby's, 160
Coldwater Ranch, 70
Collections Old and New, 20
Colleen's Cottage, 180
Colonial Rug and Broom Shop, 174
Columbia, 223
Commerce, 50
Conception Abbey, 199
Concordia, 144
Contemporary Gallerie, 142
Cooky's, 158
Corbin Mill Place, 168
Corbin Mill Restaurant, 168
Country Club Plaza, 103
Country Cupboard
    Restaurant, 175
Courthouse Exchange, 119
Creative Candles, 112
Cross Country Trail Rides, 70
Crown Candy Kitchen, 7
Cuivre River State Park, 210
Cunetto's House of Pasta, 10
Curiosity Corner, 200
Custard's Last Stand, 139

D

Daniel Boone State Park, 30
Daniel Boone's Home, 218
Danville, 241

Darcy Ann's Restaurant and Pub, 170
Dawt Mill, 74
Defiance, 217
Der Essen Platz, 144
Devil's Icebox, 226
Devil's Kitchen Trail, 84
Die Brok Pann Bakery, 170
Dillard, 40
Dillard Mill State Historic Site, 40
Dogwood Canyon Nature Park, 95
Doll Museum, 196
Dorothea B. Hoover Historical Museum, 80
Downhome Oak and Spice, 174
Dutch Bakery and Bulk Food Store, 135
Dutch Country Store, 150
Dutzow, 221
Dutzow Deli, 221
Dwell's Coach Stop, 159

E

Ed Gilliam's Shop, 203
Edgerton, 201
1858 Patee House, 196
El Dorado Springs, 158
Elephant Rocks State Park, 40
Elijah McLean's Restaurant, 19
Ella's Reflexology, 175
Elvis Museum, 209
Eminence, 68
Emporium, The, 234
Enchanted Frog Antiques, 179
End of the Trail Native American Arts
    and Crafts, 193
Englewood Theater, 119
English Landing, 188
Eolia, 210
Ethel, 233
Ethel General Store, 234
Eureka, 15
Eureka Antique Mall, 15
Evergreen Restaurant, 129
Ewe's in the Country, 159
Excelsior, 150
Excelsior Fabric, 150
Excelsior Springs, 176
Excelsior Springs Fine Art Gallery, 182

F

Fannie's, 190
Faucett, 195
Fayette, 230
Fest Hall, The, 216

Finders Keepers, 168
Firehouse Gallery & Antiques, 15
Five Mile Corner Antique Mall, 199
Flavors of the Heartland, 228
Fleming Park, 138
Float Stream Cafe, 73
Florida, 235
Florissant, 13
Formosa Restaurant, 227
Fort Davidson State Historic Site, 37
Fort Leonard Wood, 67
Fort Osage, 124
Francine's Pastry Parlor, 171
Fresh Ayers, 213
Frisco Railroad Museum, 59
Fulton, 238

G

G&S General Store, 126
Gables, The, 222
Gail Shen's Chinatown, 225
Galloway, 64
Garden Goddess, 189
Garozza's Ristorante, 110
Gary R. Lucy Gallery, 17
Gates and Sons Bar-B-Que, 103
Gates of Peace Jewish Cemetery, 212
Gateway Arch, 3
Gateway Riverboat Cruises, 5
Gem Theater Cultural and
    Performing Arts Center, 107
General John J. Pershing Boyhood
    Home, 231
General Sterling Price Museum, 231
General Sween's Museum of
    Civil War History, 64
Genghis Khan Mongolian Barbecue, 114
George Washington Carver Memorial, 239
George Washington Carver National
    Monument, 81
Ginerich Dutch Pantry and Bakery, 174
Glasgow, 230
Glenn House, The, 48
Glore Psychiatric Museum, 196
Golden City, 158
Golden Pioneer Museum, 94
Golden Prairie, 159
Good Ole Days Country Store, 37
Goody's General Store, 23
Gorilla Burger, 153
Gower, 201
Gower Good Times Hall, 201

INDEX

Graceland House Museum, 237
Graham Cave State Park, 241
Grand Divide, 232
Grand Gulf State Park, 74
Grand River Historical Society
   Museum, 171
Graniteville, 40
Gravois Mills, 153
Gray/Campbell Farmstead, 61
Greenview, 155
Greenwood, 140
Greenwood Antiques and Country
   Tea Room, 140
Gruhlkes, 21

H

H&M Country Store, 174
Ha Ha Tonka State Park, 155
Hall of Waters, 176
Hamilton, 176
Hammon Glass, 213
Hammons Pantry, 158
Handel House, 146
Hannibal, 212
Hard Luck Diner, 87
Hardware Cafe, 168
Harling's Upstairs, 114
Harlow's, 171
Harmer's Cafe, 201
Harrisonville, 157
Harry S Truman's Birthplace, 158
Hayes Hamburgers, 166
Heaton-Bowman-Smith and
   Sidenfaden Funeral Museum, 197
Heinrichshaus Vineyards and Winery, 29
Henderson's 230
Henry County Museum, 157
Hermann, 21
Hermann Visitors' Information
   Center, 21
Hermannhoff Winery Festhalle, 22
Hess Pottery, 85
Hidden Log Cabin Museum, 72
Highlandville, 92
Hill Homestead, 231
Historic Liberty Jail, 169
Hodge Park, 166
Hogwild BBQ, 64
Home Embellishments, 189
Honeyshuck, 210
Hot Tamale Brown's Cajun express, 114
Hungry Mule Cafe, 200

Hunter-Dawson Home and
   Historic Site, 53

I

Ice House Antiques, 15
Independence, 118
Inge's Lounge, 118
International Bowling Museum, 5
Iron Mountain Railway, 46
It's a Hoot, 174
It's a Small World Christmas Haus, 34

J

J&S Enterprises, 147
J.C. Penney Memorial Library and
   Museum, 176
Jackie's Country Store, 72
Jackson, 45
Jaegers Subsurface Paintball, 167
Jail Marshall's Home and Museum, 120
Jak's Pizza, 146
Jamesport, 173
Japanese Stroll Garden, 61
Jefferson City, 133
Jeffrey's, 235
Jeremiah's, 49
Jerre Anne Cafeteria and Bakery, 198
Jesse James Bank Museum
   Historic Site, 169
Jesse James Cafe, 209
Jesse James Farm Historic Site, 185
Jesse James Museum, 196
Jesse James Wax Museum, 32
Joe D's Winebar, 117
Johnson Shut-ins, 38
Jolly Mill, 82
Joplin, 80

K

Kansas City, 101
Kansas City Jazz Museum, 105
Kansas City Museum, 113
Karen's Kandies, 66
Kate's Attic Antiques and Mini Mall, 212
KATY Trail, 217, 221
Katzen Jammer Gifts and Antiques, 146
Kearney, 185
Kehde's Barbecue, 135
Kelly's, 119
Kelly's Bakery, 200
Keytesville, 230
Kimmswick, 33

Kimmswick Bone Bed, 33
Kimmswick Korner
    Gift Shoppe, 35
Kimmswick Pottery, 35
King Jack Park, 83
Kirksville, 232
Kirksville College of Osteopathic
    Medicine, 232
Kmetz Home Bakery, 42
Knob Noster, 143
Kobe House Bakery, 124

L

La Posada Grocery, 112
Laclede, 231
Lake Jacomo, 138
Lake of the Ozarks, 148
Lake Springs, 28
Lamar, 158
Lambert's Cafe, 50
Lander, 62
Lathrop, 200
Laumeier Sculpture Park, 9
Laura Ingalls Wilder–Rose Wilder Lane
    Museum and Home, 76
Laurie, 154
Le Fou Frog, 110
Leasburg, 30
Lebanon, 65
Lee's Summit, 139
Lehman's, 149
Leila's Hair Museum, 123
Les Bourgeois Vineyards, 229
Lesterville, 38
Levee, 115
Lewis and Clark State Park, 196
Lexington, 126
Liberty, 168
Liberty Quilt Shoppe, 168
Lillie's Cupboard, 35
Linen & Lace, 18
Little Jake's, 103
Lock and Dam No. 25, 210
Log Cabin Pottery, 14
Log House Museum, 128
Lone Jack, 140
Long Creek Herb Farm, 94
Louisiana, 211
Louisiana Historical
    Museum, 212
Lyceum Repertory Theatre, 130
Lydia's, 112

M

Ma & Pa's Bakin' Place, 128
Ma & Pa's Riverview Antiques Mall, 126
Macon, 234
Maggie's Attic, 186
Magic House, 11
Maine Streete Mall, 96
Malmaison, 16
Mama Toscano's, 11
Mansfield, 76
Maple Street Cafe, 146
Marceline, 231
Margaret Harwell Art Museum, 51
Maries Hollow Herb Farm and Antiques, 27
Marigold's, 173
Mark Twain Birthplace State
    Historic Site, 235
Mark Twain National Forest, 40
Mark Twain State Park, 235
Martha Lafite Thompson Nature
    Sanctuary, 169
Marthasville, 222
Martin city, 124
Mary's Tiques and Treasures, 179
Maryville, 199
Mastodon State Park, 33
Maxwell's Woodcarving, 146
McClay House, 135
McCormick Distilling Company, 191
Meramec State Park Lodge, 32
Mercer, 172
Mexico, 237
Mill Inn Restaurant, 183
Milo's Bocce Garden, 11
Mina Sauk Falls, 39
Mingo National Wildlife Refuge, 51
Miniature Museum of Greater
    St. Louis, The, 12
Miss Aimee B's Tea Room, 208
Missouri Bluffs Boutique and
    Gallery, 193
Missouri Highland Farms, 134
Missouri River State Trail, 217
Missouri State Fair, 136
Missouri Town 1855, 138
Missouri's Stonehenge, 28
Mistiques, 127
Moberly, 235
Molly's, 49
Moniteau Lick, 230
Montelle Winery, 218
Mother-in-Law House, 208

INDEX

Mound City, 199
Mount Pleasant Wine Company, 219
Mountain Grove, 77
Mrs. Clemens Antique Mall, 215
Mt. Olivet Cemetery, 187
Museum at the Old Courthouse, 29
Museum of Anthropology, 224
Museum of Art and Archaeology, 223
Museum of Western Expansion, 4
Mutual Musicians' Foundation, 105
Myers, Jim, 141

N

Nancy Ballhagen's Puzzles, 65
Napoleon, 126
National Frontiers Trails Center, 121
Nature's Own Emu Products, 195
Negro League Baseball Museum, 106
Nelson, Patrick, 228
Nevada, 162
New Haven, 20
New Franklin, 136
New Madrid, 52
New Madrid Historical Museum, 53
Nichols Pottery Shop and Studio, 165
Noel, 81
Nona Woodworks, 220
Nonie Lani's Tattoo Art Studio, 90
Norborne, 171
North Kansas City, 163
Not Just Cut and Dried, 18

O

Old Bank Museum, 179
Old Brick House, 42
Old Cathedral Museum, 5
Old Cooper County Jail and
    Hanging Barn, 131
Old Hoof and Horn Steakhouse, 197
Old House, 35
Old Mill Stitchery, 168
Old Miner's Inn, The, 80
Old Post Office, 112
Old St. Ferdinand's Shrine, 13
Old St. Vincent's Church, 47
Old Stagecoach Inn Museum, 67
Old Trail House, 155
Olde English Garden Shoppe, 179
Oliver House, 46
Omega Pottery Shop, 85
Onondaga Cave, 30
Orr Gallery and Studio, 152

Osage Beach, 151
Osceola, 159
Osceola Cheese Shop, 159
Owensville, 14
Ozark, 96
Ozark Hills Senior Citizens
    Craft Shop, 154
Ozark Mountain Country
    Reservation Service, 11
Ozark National Scenic
    Riverways, 69
Ozark Trail, 39
Ozarks, The, 148

P

Paradise, 203
Paradise Playhouse, 178
Paris, 235
Parkville, 188
Parkville Coffee & Fudge, 189
Party Odyssey Costumes
    and More, 147
Peace-'n'-Plenty Country Cafe, 151
Peddler's Wagon, 189
Peola Valley Pottery, 38
Perryville, 45
Pershing State Park, 231
Peter Street Leaf and Bean, 14
Peters Market, 129
Phillips Museum, 212
Phoenix, The, 115
Pierce City, 82
Pilot Knob, 37
Pirtle's Weston Vineyards Winery, 191
Planters' Seed and Spice Co., 109
Platte City, 190
Plattsburg, 200
Pleasant Valley Quilts, 149
Pony Express Museum, 196
Pop's General Store, 207
Poplar Bluff, 51
Poppy, 225
Potted Steer Restaurant, 152
Potter's Obsession, 124
Powell Gardens, 137
"Praying Hands," 83
President Casino on the
    Admiral, The, 8
Puxico, 51

Q

Quackers Bar and Grill, 199

R

Rainey House, 27
Ray County Museum, 170
Ray's Lunch, 178
Real Hatfield Smokehouse, 81
Reeds Spring, 85
Republic, 64
Rheinland Restaurant, 119
Rib, The, 83
Richard Saunders Antiques, 228
Richard's Puzzles, 65
Richland, 67
Richmond, 170
Ridgedale, 92
Riley's Irish Pub and Grill, 127
River Ridge Winery, 49
River's Edge Resort, 72
River's Edge Restaurant, 23
Riverside Country Club, 172
Roaring River State Park, 84
Rocheport, 228
Rockcliffe Mansion, 214
Rolla, 28
Rolling Hills Store, 175
Rosebud, 14
Roubidoux Row, 196
Rozart Pottery, 180

S

Sainte Genevieve Winery, 45
Salt River Folklife Festival, 236
Sara's Ice Cream and Antiques, 42
School of the Ozarks, 90
Schulte's Baker Deli & Coffee Shoppe, 14
Scimeca's, 111
Sedalia, 135
Shady Oak Market, 150
Sheffler Rock Shop and Geode Mine, 215
Shepherd of the Hills Fish Hatchery, 92
Shepherd of the Hills Inspiration Tower, 86
Sherwood Quilts and Crafts, 175
Shoal Creek, 166
Shrine of Mary Mother of the Church, 154
Shrine of St. Patrick, 215
Sikeston, 50
Silver Dollar City, 86
63 Diner, The, 227
Slice of Pie, 29
Smithville, 202
Smithville Lake, 202
Smoke House Market, 15
Sneathen Enterprises, 48

Snow Creek Ski Area, 194
Soulard, 11
Spease Antiques, 200
Spiva Center for the Arts, 81
Spring Lake Lodge and Antiques, 153
Springfield, 57
Springfield Art Museum, 61
Squaw Creek National Wildlife Refuge, 198
St. John's Episcopal Church, 210
St. Agnes Hall, 234
St. Albans, 16
St. Ambrose Church, 11
St. Charles, 207
St. Ferdinand's Shrine, Old, 13
St. James, 29
St. James Winery, 29
St. Joseph, 196
St. Joseph Museum, 197
St. Louis, 3
St. Louis Cardinals Hall of Fame, 5
St. Louis Cathedral, 7
St. Louis Mercantile Library
    Association, 7
St. Mary of the Barrens Church, 45
St. Mary's Episcopal Church, 111
St. Patrick, 215
Stanton, 32
Ste. Genevieve, 41
Ste. Genevieve Museum, 42
Steamboat *Arabia* Museum, 109
Stephenson's Old Apple Farm
    Restaurant, 122
Stockton, 158
Stone Canyon Pizza, 189
Stone Hill Wine Company, 90
Stone Hill Winery, 22
Stover, 154
Strother's, 139
Stroud's, 104
Sugar Creek, 124
Sugar Creek Winery, 217
Sullivan, 31
Sun Ray Cafe, 115
Swan Lake National Wildlife Refuge, 233
Sweet Things, 45

T

Table Rock Lake, 96
Table Rock State Park, 86
Teatro Ristorante, 62
Ted Drewes Frozen Custard, 7
Ten Mile, 235

Thespian Hall, 132
Thousand Hills State Park, 232
Three Dog Bakery, 116
Tightwad, 157
Tipton, 135
Tiques & Stuff, 200
Top of the Rock golf course, 92
Total-e-Clips, 187
Touring Cyclist, 209
Tower Grove House, 3
Towosahgy State Historic Site, 52
Toys and Miniatures Museum, 116
Trailhead Brewing Company, 208
Trailside Cafe and Bike Rental, 229
Trattoria Strata Nova, 226
Trenton, 171
Tric's Family Restaurant, 45
Tropical Mexican Restaurant and
    Cantina, 178
Troutdale Ranch, 153
Truman Presidential Library, 118
Trunk Shop, 160

U

U.S. Army Engineer Museum, 67
Union, 14
Union Covered Bridge, 236
Union Italian Market, 14
Union Station, 3
Unity Village, 140
University of Missouri, 223

V

Vaile Mansion, 121
Van Buren, 72
Velvet Pumpkin Antiques, 128
Versailles, 147
Vichy, 28
Vichy Wye Restaurant, 28
Victorian Era Powers Museum, 78
Victorian Garden Tea Room, 60
Victorian Peddler Antiques Shop
    and Tea Room, 127
Vienna, 24
Vienna Flea Market, 27
Vineyards, The, 192
Vintage 1847 Restaurant, 22

W

Wabash Barbecue, 182
Wacky Wagon's Lady Bug, 180
Wallach House Antiques, 15
Warrensburg, 141
Washington, 17
Watkins Woolen Mill State Historic Site, 184
Waverly, 128
Waynesville, 66
Weavers' Market, 150
Webb City, 83
Webster Groves, 14
Westminster College, 238
Weston, 190
Weston Bend State Park, 193
Weston Cafe, 193
Weston Museum, 191
Westphalia, 23
Westphalia Inn, 24
Wheel Inn, 135
Whistle Stop Cafe, 46
White Oak Farms, 234
Whitehorse Antiques, 229
Wild Canid Survival and Research
    Center, 13
Wild Flower Inn, 31
Winery of the Little Hills, 208
Winston, 176
Winston Churchill Memorial and
    Library, 239
Winston Station Antiques, 176
With a French Accent, 168
Woodhenge, 202
Woodland Carvings, 63
World Craft and Thrift Shop, 147
Wright City, 209

Y

Yellow Valley Forge, 38

Z

Zanoni, 74
Zinnia, 10

Bed-and-Breakfasts and Inns

Note: All accommodations listed are bed-and-breakfast establishments except as noted.

Barn Again, 97
Basswood Country Inn Resort, 190
Bellevue, 49
Benner House, 192
Bethel German Colony, 216
Big Cedar Lodge, 92
Birk's Gasthaus, 22
Boone's Lick Trail Inn, 207
Borgman's, 130
Bucks and Spurs Scenic River Guest
    Ranch, 76
Buhlig Hospitality Inn, 187

Camel Crossing, 142
Caverly Farm Orchard B&B, 14
Cedarcroft Farm, 141
Chateau on the Lake, 92
Cliff House, 157
Concord Hill, 222
Country Colonial, 175
Creole House, 43

Dauphine Hotel, 23
Dear's Rest, 96
Depot, The, 36
Down to Earth Lifestyles, 189

Eastlake Inn, 9
Elms Hotel, 180

Ferrigno's Winery and B&B, 31
Friendship House, 76

Garth Woodside Mansion, 213
Gathering Place, 227
Georgetown, 136
Gramma's House, 223
Grand Avenue, 79
Gray's Country Home, 152

Hael Cottage, 45
Harding House, 198
Hilty Inn, 147
Home Place, The, 66
H.S. Clay House, 221
Huber's Ferry, 24
Hugh Montgomery House, 198–99
Hunters' Inn, 234
Hyde Mansion, 172

Inn on Crescent Lake, 183
Inn St. Gemme Beauvais, 44

James Inn, and Day Spa, 169
Jefferson Inn, 133

Klein House, 51

Le Belle Maison, 200
Leggett House, 78
Loganberry Inn, 241
Louisiana Guest House, 212

Mansion Hill, 35
Marigold Inn, 173
Meramec Farm Cabins and Trail
    Riding Vacations, 30
Miner Indulgence B&B, 29
Miss Nellie's, 131
Missouri Manor, 227
Mockville Land & Cattle
    Company, 172
Montagues, 22
Morgan Street Repose, 132
Mrs. G's, 144

Oak Tree Inn, 175
Old Blue House, 71
Ozark Mountain Country Reservation
    Service, 11

Parkcliff Cabins, 87

Rachel's, 38
Recess Inn, 233
Rivercene, 132
Roaring River Inn, 87
Rock Eddy Bluff Farm, 26
Rosecliff on the River Lodge, 73

School House, 229
Schwegmann House, 20
Serendipity, 120
Shakespeare Chateau, 197
Smokey Hollow Lake, 97
Southern Hotel, 43
St. Agnes Hall, 234
Staats Waterford Estate, 16

INDEX

Steiger Haus, 44
Steiger Haus Downtown, 45

Temerity Woods, 28
Terrill House B&B, 235
Trisha's Bed and Breakfast and
    Tea Room and Craft Shop, 46

University Avenue, 227

Victorian, The, 127
Victorian Veranda, The, 36
Virginia Rose, 62

Walnut Street, 60
Washington House Inn, 18
Wenom Drake House, 35
Western Way, 188
White Rose, 79
Wild Flower Inn, 31
Wilderness Lodge, 38
Woodstock Inn, 122

Zanoni Mill Inn, 75

About the Author

Patti DeLano is a travel writer and photographer who has lived in the Ozarks of Missouri and vacationed across the border in Arkansas for more than twenty years. She has also written *Arkansas Off the Beaten Path* and *Kansas Off the Beaten Path* for The Globe Pequot Press.

About the Editor

Editor Jeanie Ransom is a freelance writer living in Missouri. In addition to her work in advertising and public relations, she has written about food, travel, and interior design, and has been an editor and columnist for *Innsider,* a national country-inn travel magazine.